SUPERMAN: LOIS AND CLARK

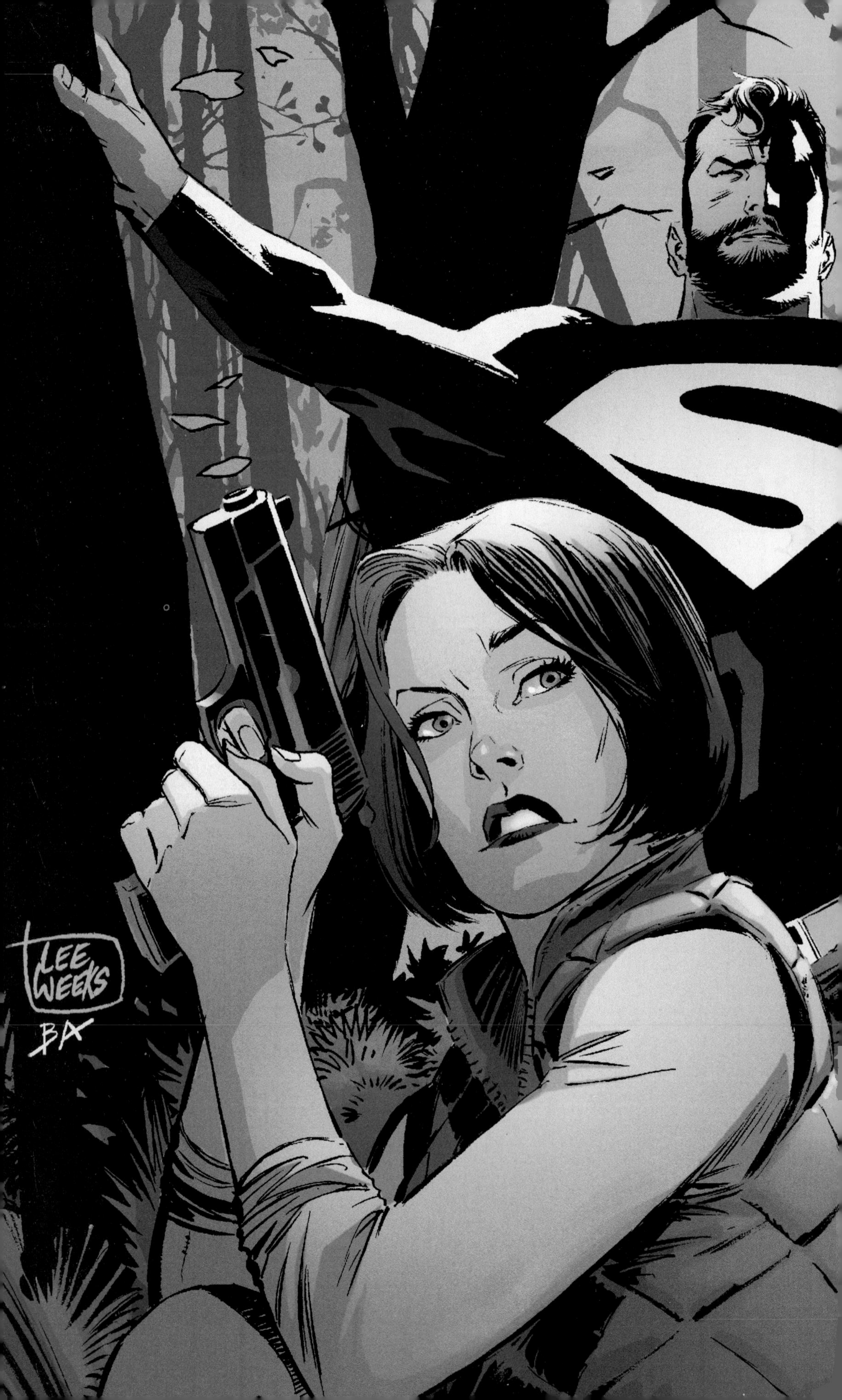
LEE WEEKS
BA

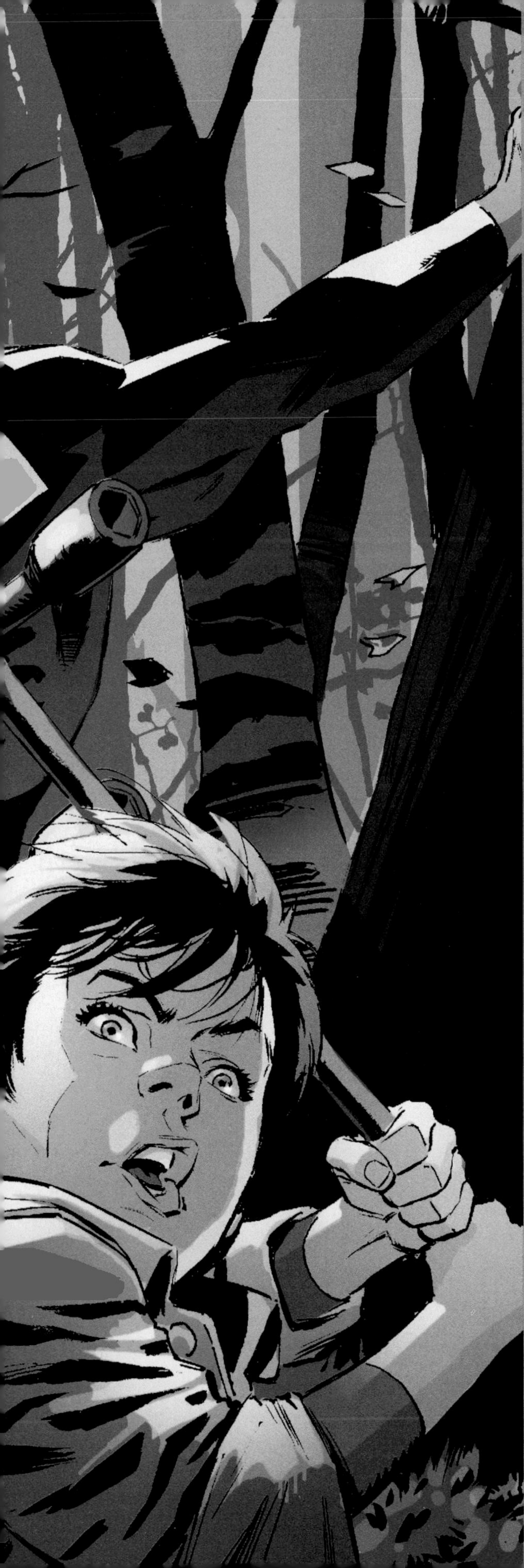

SUPERMAN: LOIS AND CLARK

WRITTEN BY
DAN JURGENS

PENCILS BY
NEIL EDWARDS
MARCO SANTUCCI
STEPHEN SEGOVIA
LEE WEEKS

INKS BY
SERGIO CARIELLO
NEIL EDWARDS
SCOTT HANNA
JAY LEISTEN
ART THIBERT
LEE WEEKS

COLOR BY
BRAD ANDERSON
JEROMY COX

LETTERS BY
A LARGER WORLD STUDIOS'
JOSHUA COZINE
& TROY PETERI

COLLECTION COVER ART BY
BRAD ANDERSON
LEE WEEKS

SUPERMAN CREATED BY
JERRY SIEGEL
& JOE SHUSTER
BY SPECIAL ARRANGEMENT
WITH THE JERRY SIEGEL FAMILY

EDDIE BERGANZA Editor – Original Series
ANDREW MARINO Assistant Editor – Original Series
JEB WOODARD Group Editor – Collected Editions
PAUL SANTOS Editor – Collected Edition
STEVE COOK Design Director – Books
DAMIAN RYLAND Publication Design

BOB HARRAS Senior VP – Editor-in-Chief, DC Comics

DIANE NELSON President
DAN DIDIO and JIM LEE Co-Publishers
GEOFF JOHNS Chief Creative Officer
AMIT DESAI Senior VP – Marketing & Global Franchise Management
NAIRI GARDINER Senior VP – Finance
SAM ADES VP – Digital Marketing
BOBBIE CHASE VP – Talent Development
MARK CHIARELLO Senior VP – Art, Design & Collected Editions
JOHN CUNNINGHAM VP – Content Strategy
ANNE DEPIES VP – Strategy Planning & Reporting
DON FALLETTI VP – Manufacturing Operations
LAWRENCE GANEM VP – Editorial Administration & Talent Relations
ALISON GILL Senior VP – Manufacturing & Operations
HANK KANALZ Senior VP – Editorial Strategy & Administration
JAY KOGAN VP – Legal Affairs
DEREK MADDALENA Senior VP – Sales & Business Development
JACK MAHAN VP – Business Affairs
DAN MIRON VP – Sales Planning & Trade Development
NICK NAPOLITANO VP – Manufacturing Administration
CAROL ROEDER VP – Marketing
EDDIE SCANNELL VP – Mass Account & Digital Sales
COURTNEY SIMMONS Senior VP – Publicity & Communications
JIM (SKI) SOKOLOWSKI VP – Comic Book Specialty & Newsstand Sales
SANDY YI Senior VP – Global Franchise Management

SUPERMAN: LOIS AND CLARK

Published by DC Comics. Compilation and all new material Copyright © 2016 DC Comics. All Rights Reserved.

Originally published in single magazine form in SUPERMAN: LOIS AND CLARK 1-8. Copyright © 2015, 2016 DC Comics.
All Rights Reserved. All characters, their distinctive likenesses and related elements featured in this publication are
trademarks of DC Comics. The stories, characters and incidents featured in this publication are entirely fictional.
DC Comics does not read or accept unsolicited submissions of ideas, stories or artwork.

DC Comics, 2900 West Alameda Ave., Burbank, CA 91505
Printed by RR Donnelley, Owensville, MO, USA. 7/29/16. First Printing.
ISBN: 978-1-4012-6249-5

Library of Congress Cataloging-in-Publication Data is available.

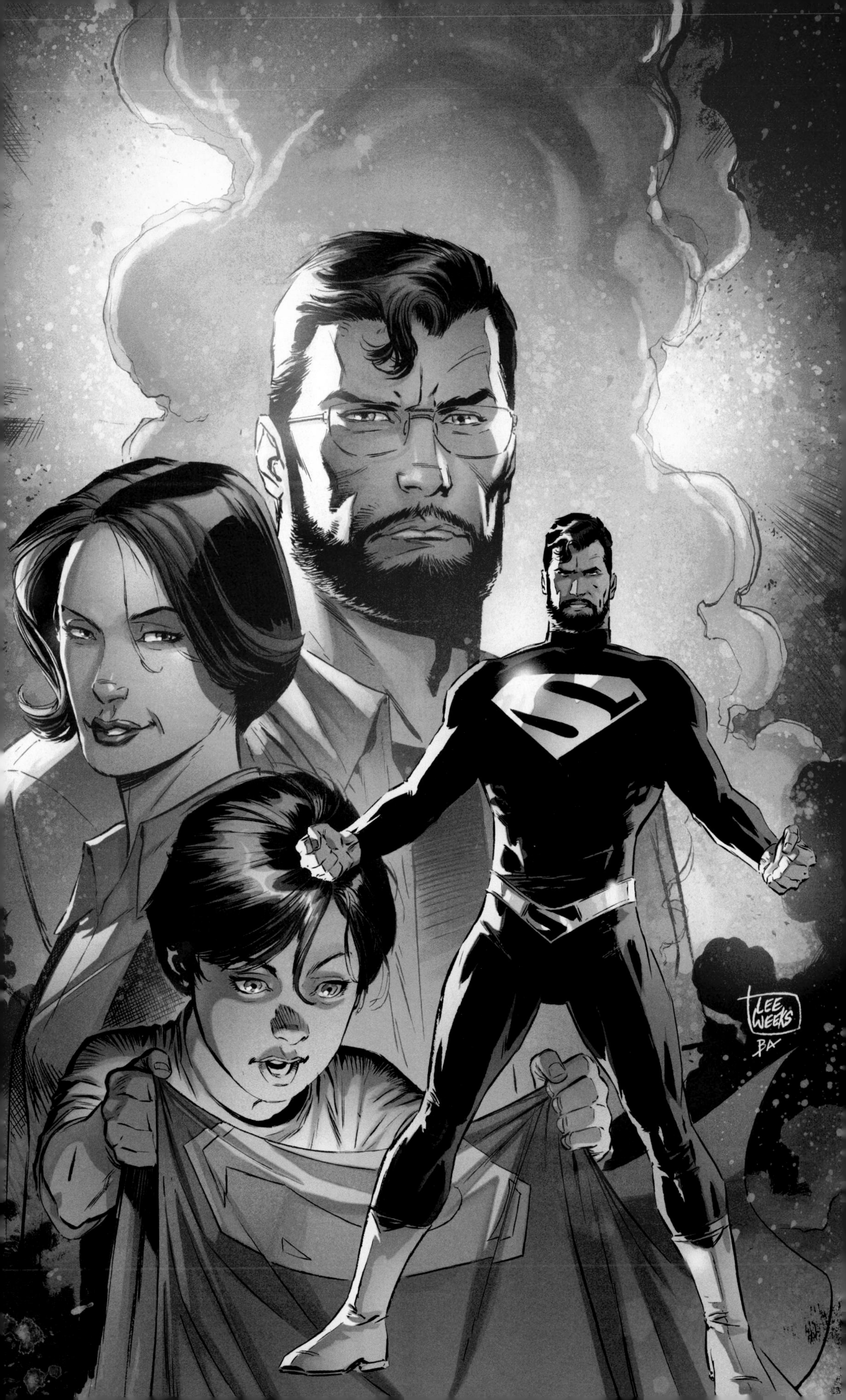
LEE WEEKS
BA

ARRIVAL: PART I

DAN JURGENS writer LEE WEEKS penciller SCOTT HANNA inker BRAD ANDERSON colorist A LARGER WORLD STUDIOS' JOSHUA COZINE & TROY PETERI letterers
LEE WEEKS BRAD ANDERSON cover artists

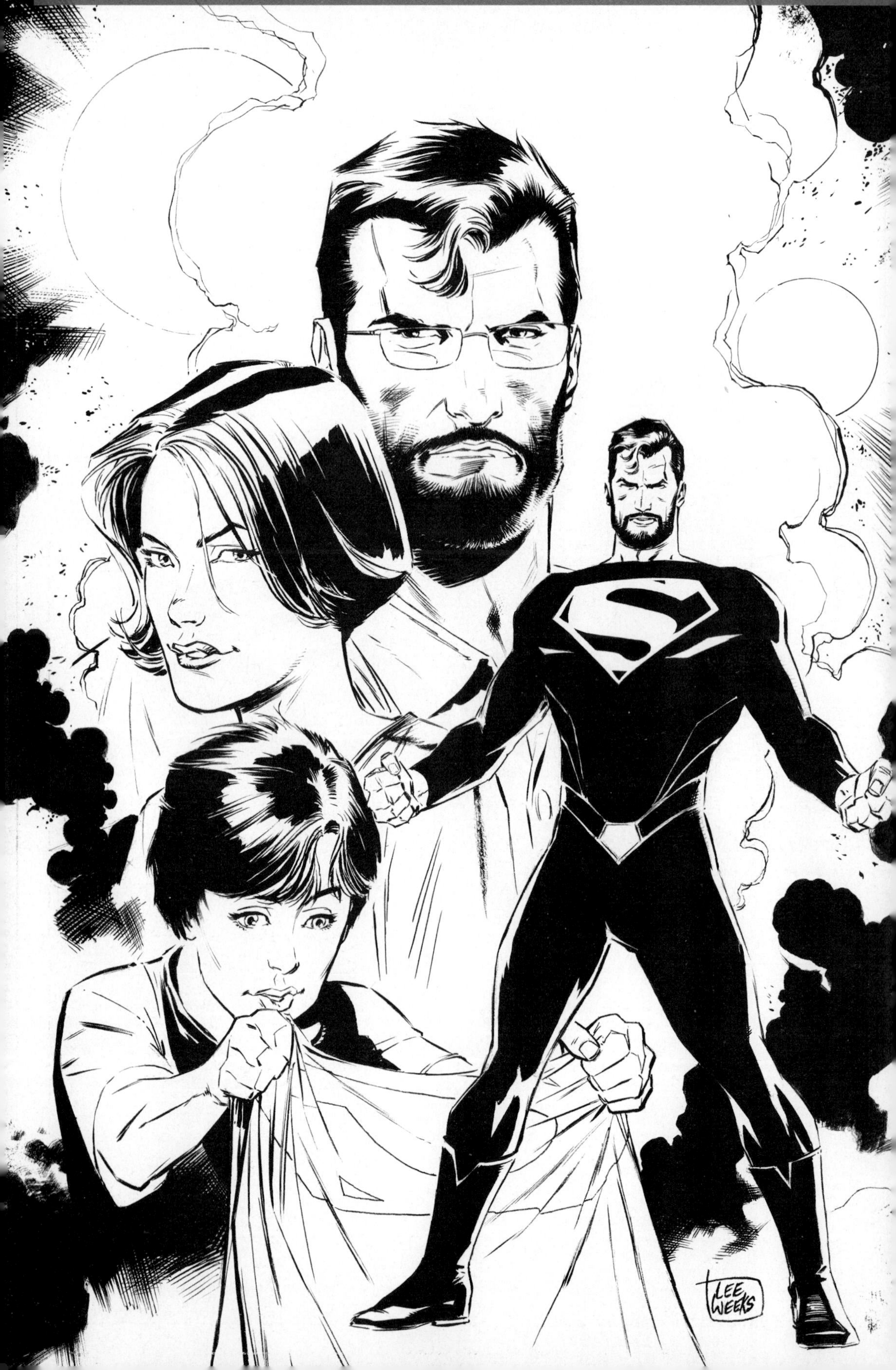
LEE WEEKS

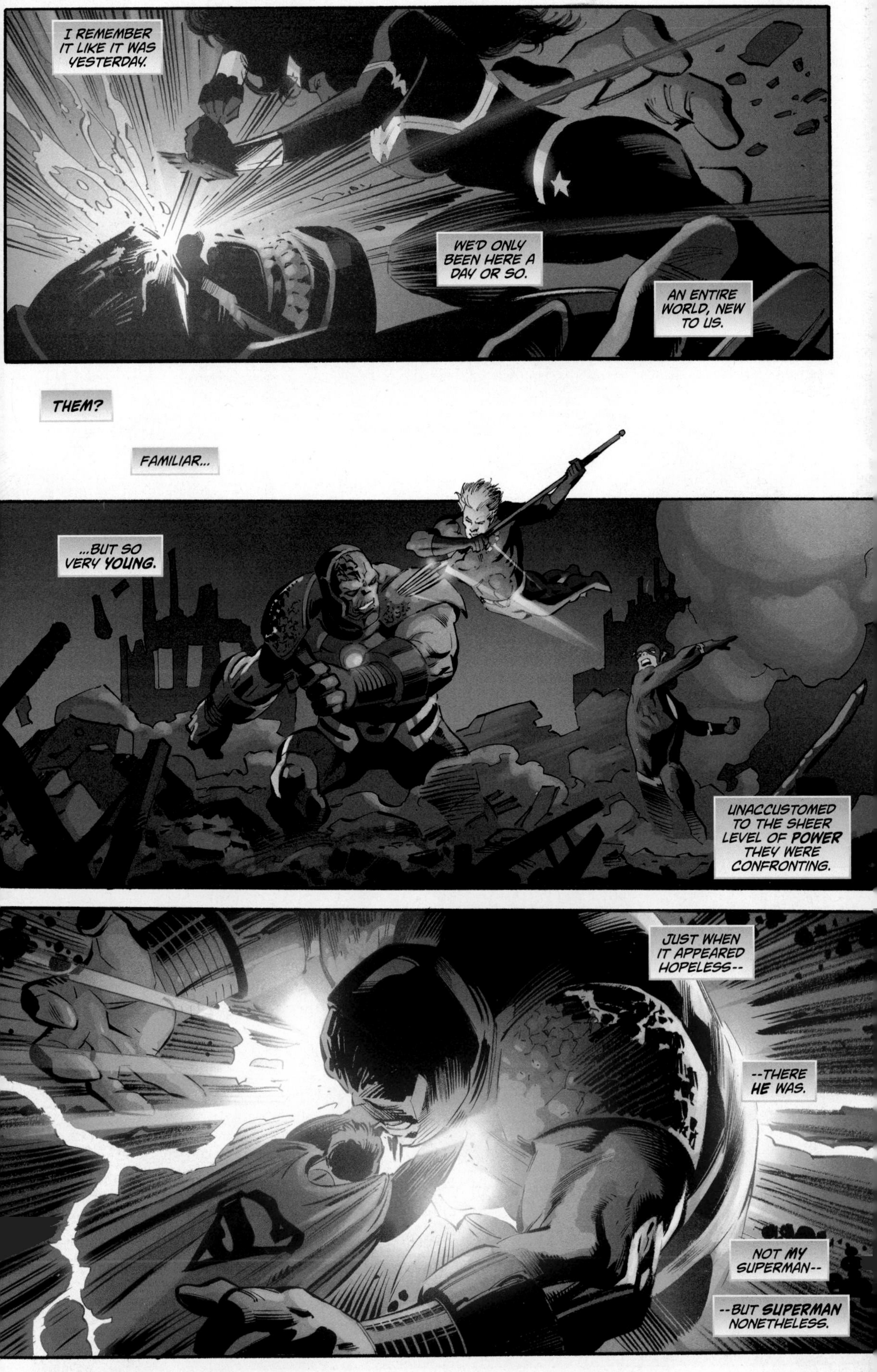
I REMEMBER IT LIKE IT WAS YESTERDAY.
WE'D ONLY BEEN HERE A DAY OR SO.
AN ENTIRE WORLD, NEW TO US.
THEM?
FAMILIAR...
...BUT SO VERY YOUNG.
UNACCUSTOMED TO THE SHEER LEVEL OF POWER THEY WERE CONFRONTING.
JUST WHEN IT APPEARED HOPELESS--
--THERE HE WAS.
NOT MY SUPERMAN--
--BUT SUPERMAN NONETHELESS.

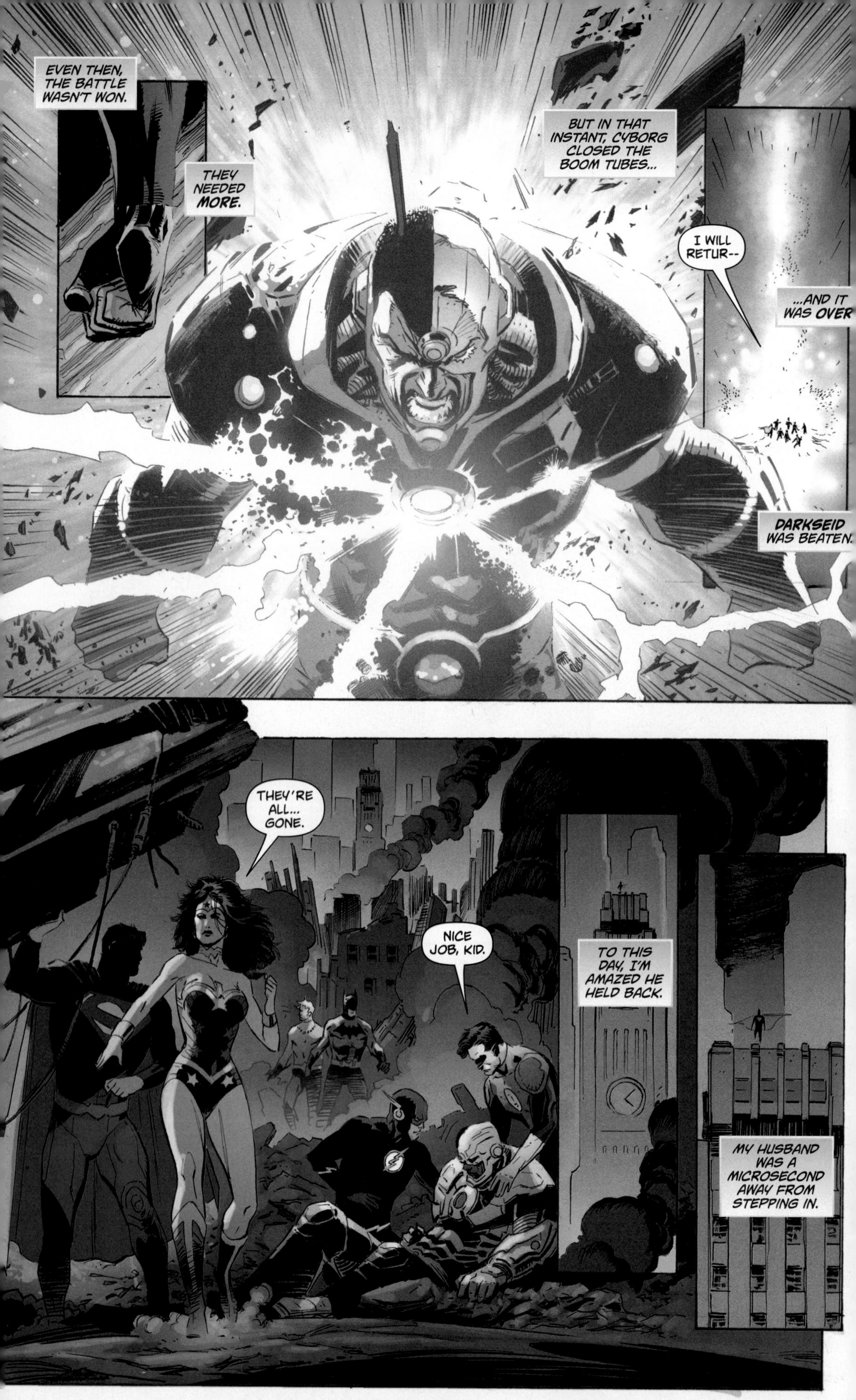
EVEN THEN, THE BATTLE WASN'T WON.
THEY NEEDED MORE.
BUT IN THAT INSTANT, CYBORG CLOSED THE BOOM TUBES...
I WILL RETUR--
...AND IT WAS OVER
DARKSEID WAS BEATEN.
THEY'RE ALL... GONE.
NICE JOB, KID.
TO THIS DAY, I'M AMAZED HE HELD BACK.
MY HUSBAND WAS A MICROSECOND AWAY FROM STEPPING IN.

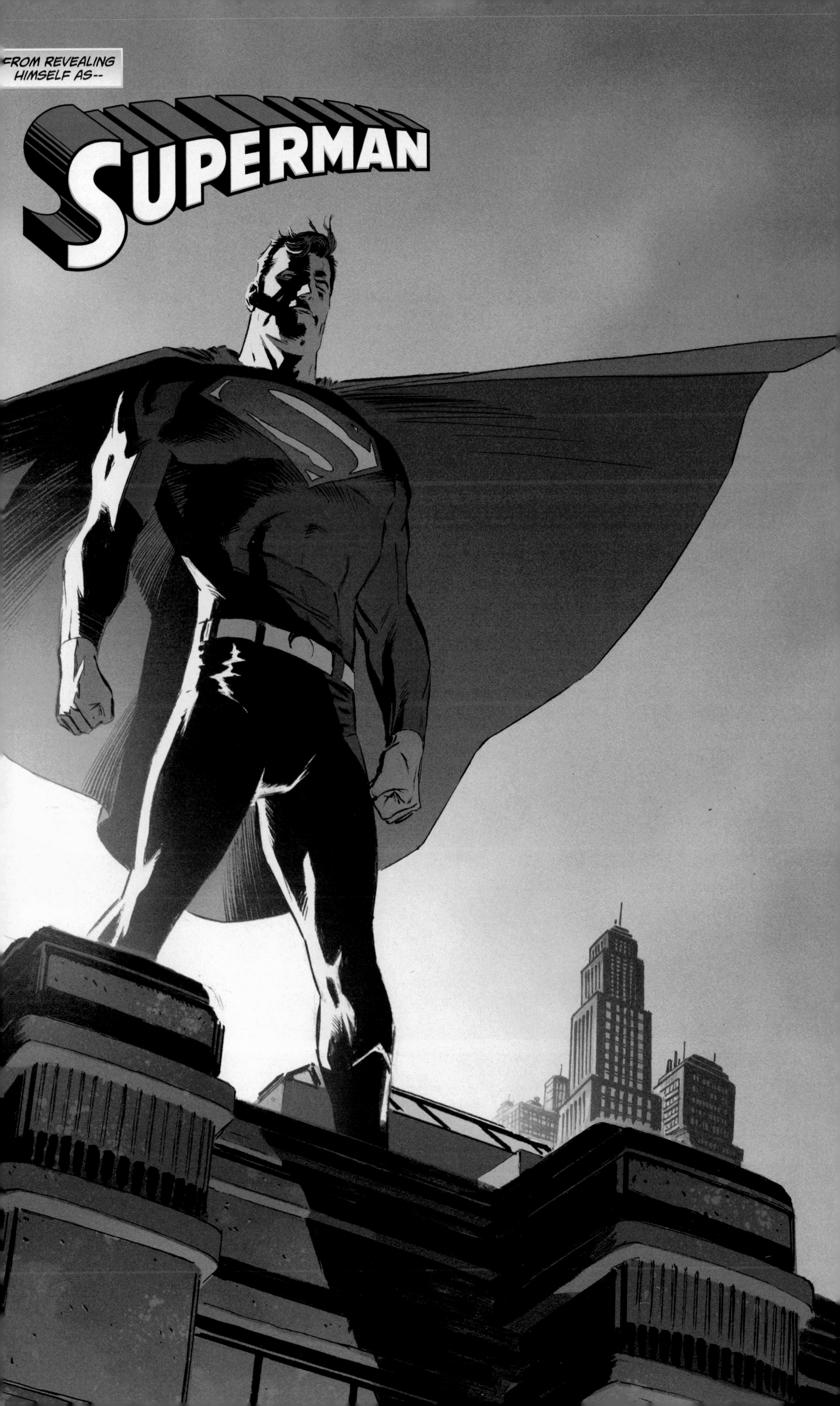
FROM REVEALING HIMSELF AS--
SUPERMAN

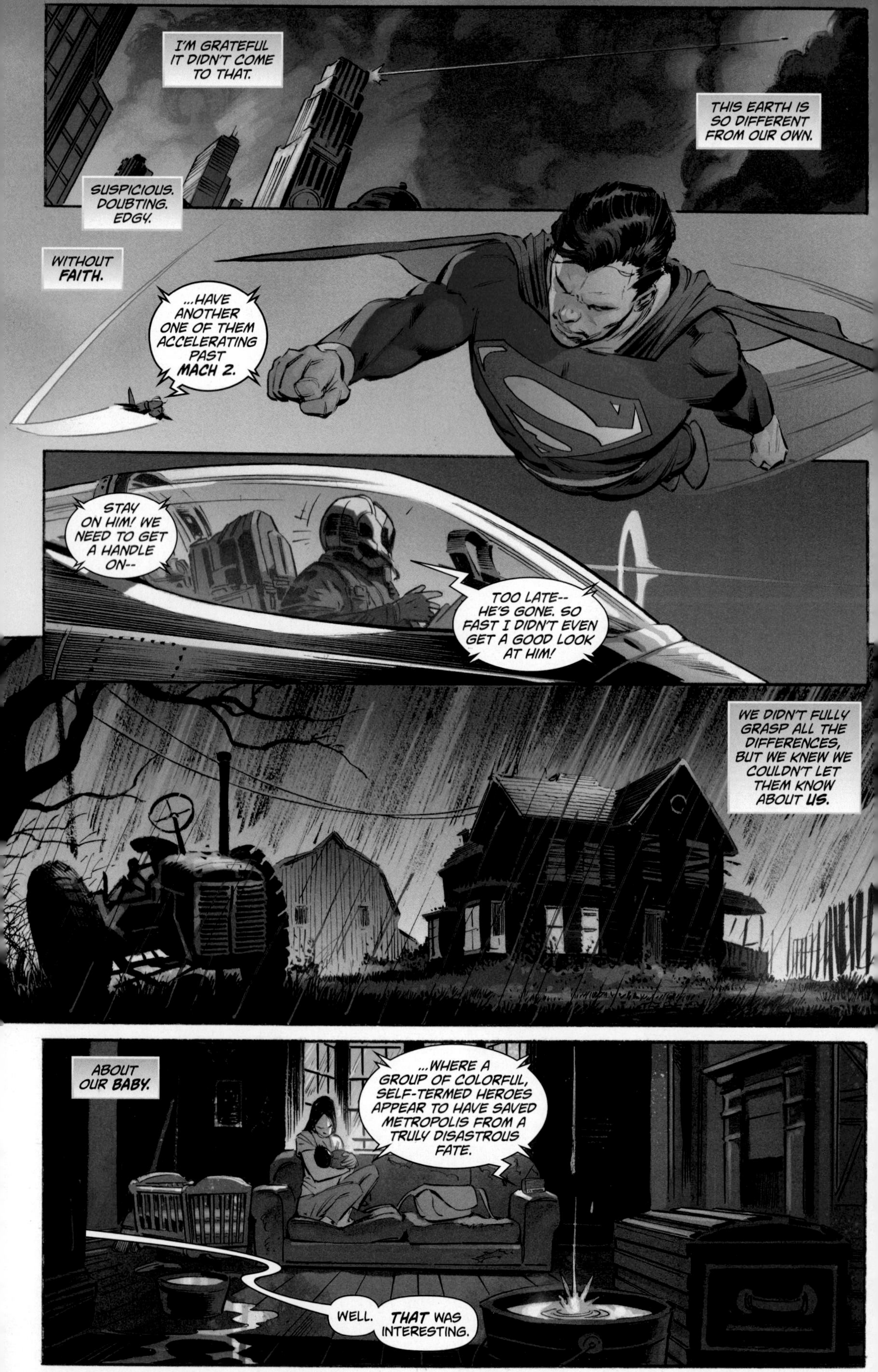
I'M GRATEFUL IT DIDN'T COME TO THAT.
THIS EARTH IS SO DIFFERENT FROM OUR OWN.
SUSPICIOUS. DOUBTING. EDGY.
WITHOUT FAITH.
...HAVE ANOTHER ONE OF THEM ACCELERATING PAST MACH 2.
STAY ON HIM! WE NEED TO GET A HANDLE ON--
TOO LATE-- HE'S GONE. SO FAST I DIDN'T EVEN GET A GOOD LOOK AT HIM!
WE DIDN'T FULLY GRASP ALL THE DIFFERENCES, BUT WE KNEW WE COULDN'T LET THEM KNOW ABOUT US.
ABOUT OUR BABY.
...WHERE A GROUP OF COLORFUL, SELF-TERMED HEROES APPEAR TO HAVE SAVED METROPOLIS FROM A TRULY DISASTROUS FATE.
WELL. THAT WAS INTERESTING.

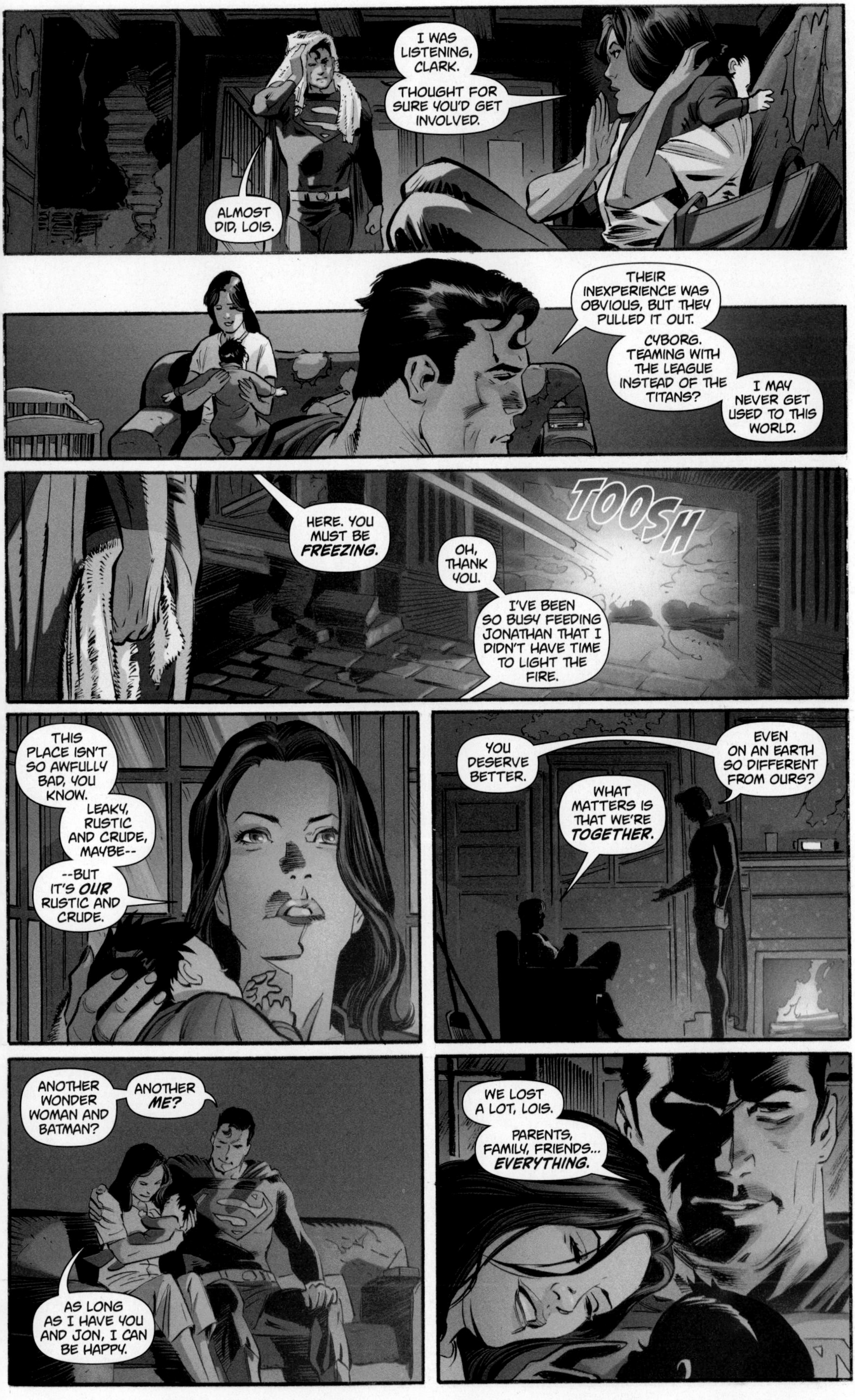

I WAS LISTENING, CLARK.
THOUGHT FOR SURE YOU'D GET INVOLVED.
ALMOST DID, LOIS.
THEIR INEXPERIENCE WAS OBVIOUS, BUT THEY PULLED IT OUT.
CYBORG. TEAMING WITH THE LEAGUE INSTEAD OF THE TITANS?
I MAY NEVER GET USED TO THIS WORLD.
HERE. YOU MUST BE FREEZING.
TOOSH
OH, THANK YOU.
I'VE BEEN SO BUSY FEEDING JONATHAN THAT I DIDN'T HAVE TIME TO LIGHT THE FIRE.
THIS PLACE ISN'T SO AWFULLY BAD, YOU KNOW.
LEAKY, RUSTIC AND CRUDE, MAYBE--
--BUT IT'S OUR RUSTIC AND CRUDE.
YOU DESERVE BETTER.
EVEN ON AN EARTH SO DIFFERENT FROM OURS?
WHAT MATTERS IS THAT WE'RE TOGETHER.
ANOTHER WONDER WOMAN AND BATMAN?
ANOTHER ME?
AS LONG AS I HAVE YOU AND JON, I CAN BE HAPPY.
WE LOST A LOT, LOIS.
PARENTS, FAMILY, FRIENDS... EVERYTHING.

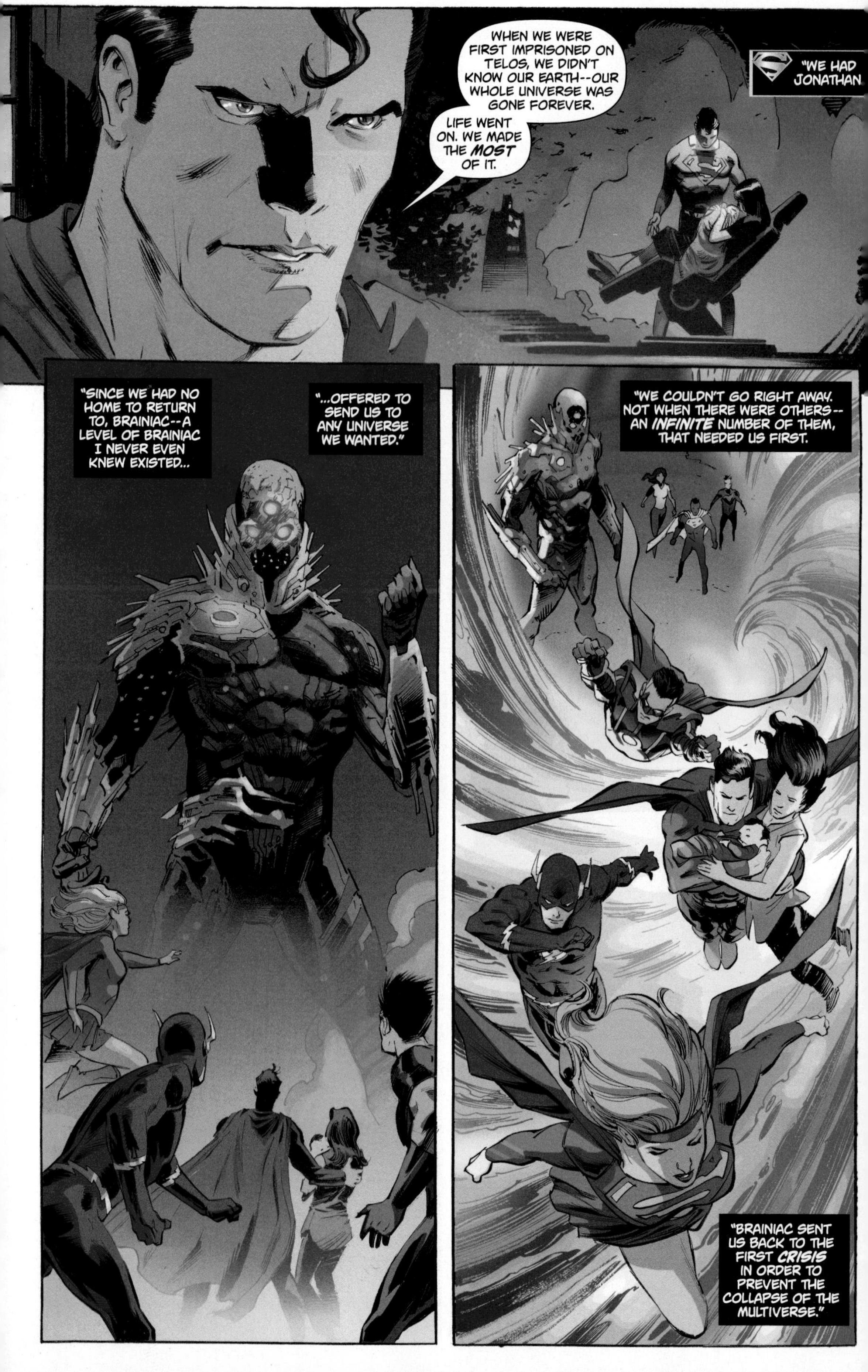

WHEN WE WERE FIRST IMPRISONED ON TELOS, WE DIDN'T KNOW OUR EARTH--OUR WHOLE UNIVERSE WAS GONE FOREVER.
LIFE WENT ON. WE MADE THE *MOST* OF IT.
"WE HAD JONATHAN.
"SINCE WE HAD NO HOME TO RETURN TO, BRAINIAC--A LEVEL OF BRAINIAC I NEVER EVEN KNEW EXISTED...
"...OFFERED TO SEND US TO ANY UNIVERSE WE WANTED."
"WE COULDN'T GO RIGHT AWAY. NOT WHEN THERE WERE OTHERS--AN *INFINITE* NUMBER OF THEM, THAT NEEDED US FIRST.
"BRAINIAC SENT US BACK TO THE FIRST *CRISIS* IN ORDER TO PREVENT THE COLLAPSE OF THE MULTIVERSE."

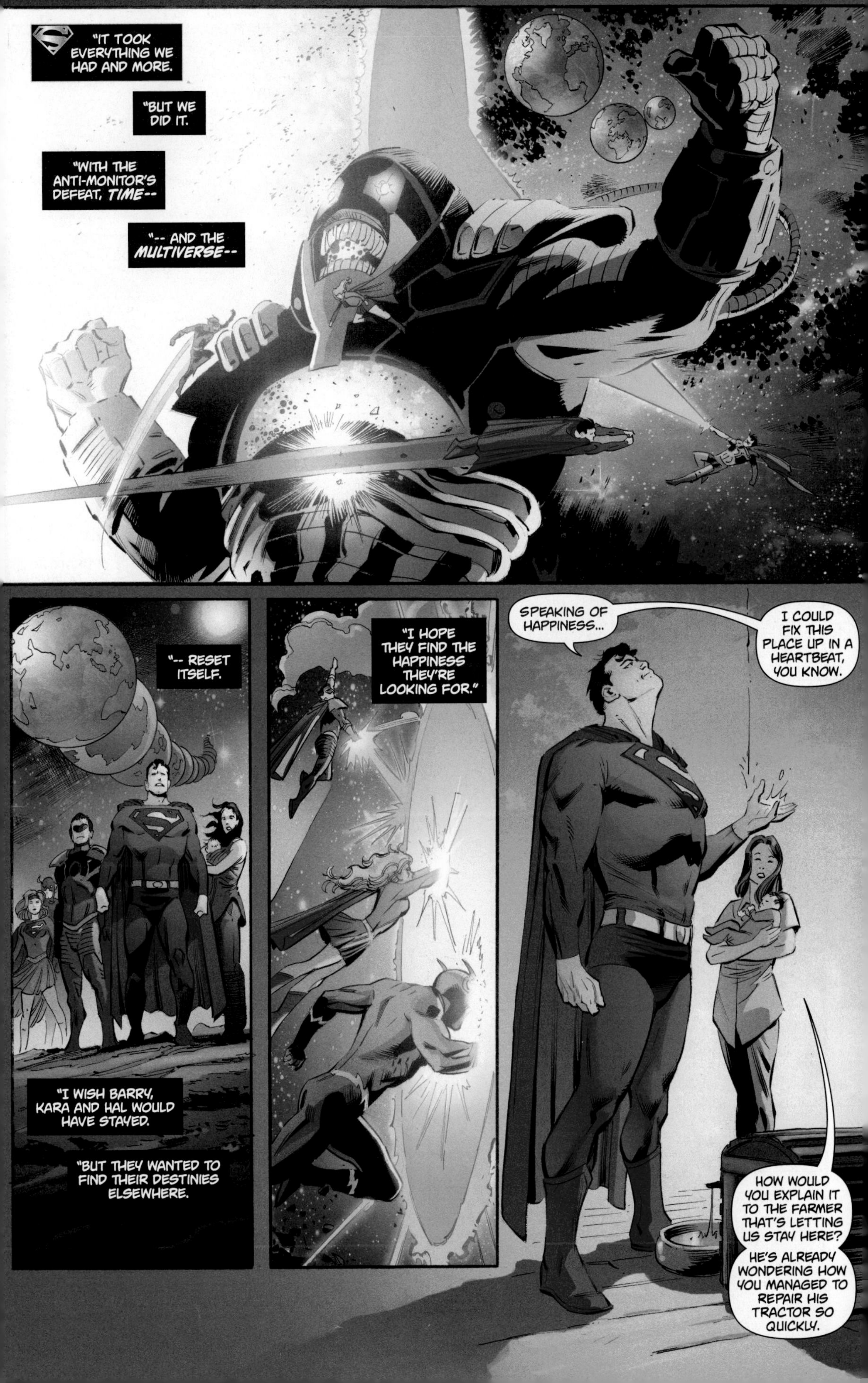
"IT TOOK EVERYTHING WE HAD AND MORE.
"BUT WE DID IT.
"WITH THE ANTI-MONITOR'S DEFEAT, TIME--
"-- AND THE MULTIVERSE--
"-- RESET ITSELF.
"I WISH BARRY, KARA AND HAL WOULD HAVE STAYED.
"BUT THEY WANTED TO FIND THEIR DESTINIES ELSEWHERE.
"I HOPE THEY FIND THE HAPPINESS THEY'RE LOOKING FOR."
SPEAKING OF HAPPINESS...
I COULD FIX THIS PLACE UP IN A HEARTBEAT, YOU KNOW.
HOW WOULD YOU EXPLAIN IT TO THE FARMER THAT'S LETTING US STAY HERE?
HE'S ALREADY WONDERING HOW YOU MANAGED TO REPAIR HIS TRACTOR SO QUICKLY.

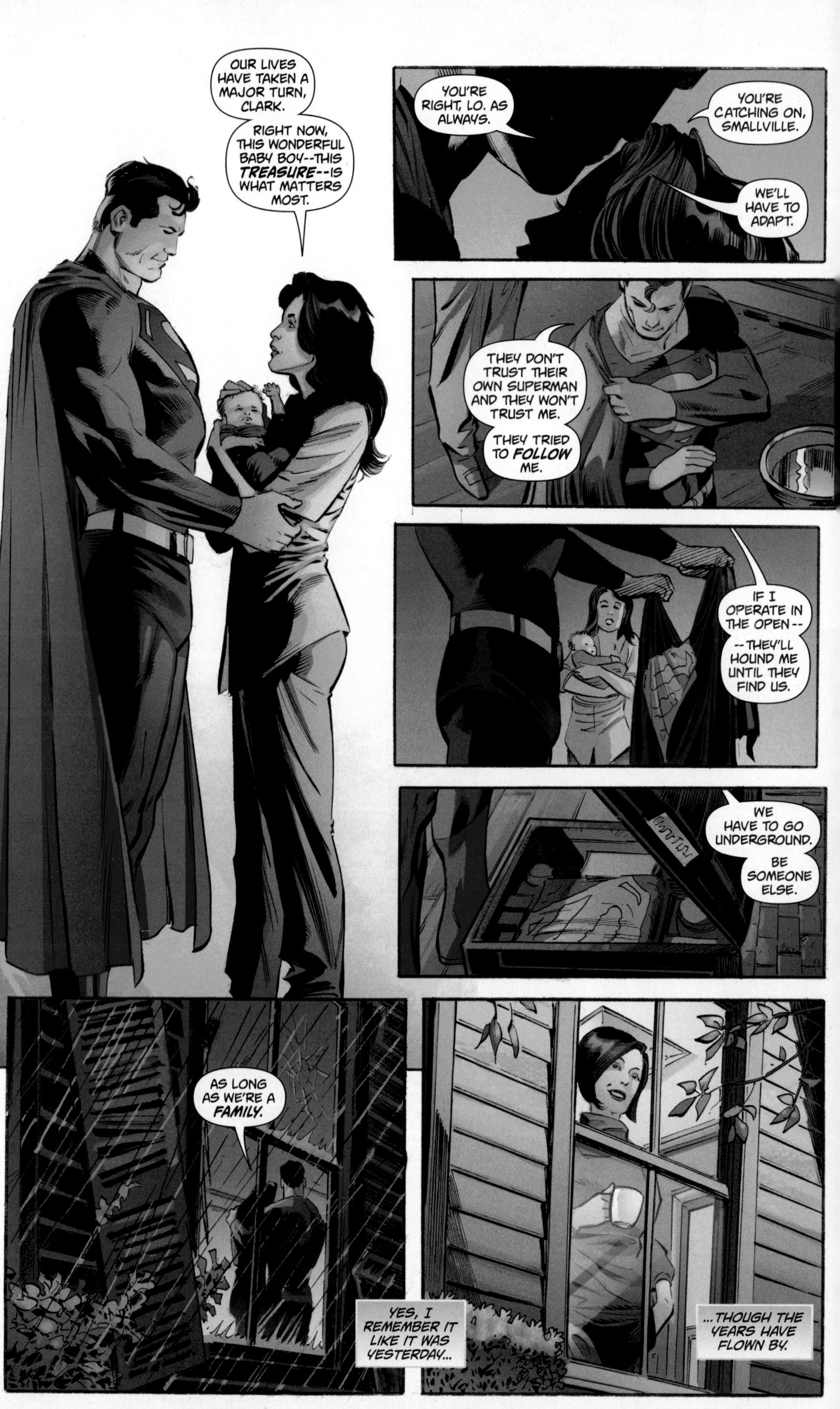
OUR LIVES HAVE TAKEN A MAJOR TURN, CLARK.
RIGHT NOW, THIS WONDERFUL BABY BOY--THIS TREASURE--IS WHAT MATTERS MOST.
YOU'RE RIGHT, LO. AS ALWAYS.
YOU'RE CATCHING ON, SMALLVILLE.
WE'LL HAVE TO ADAPT.
THEY DON'T TRUST THEIR OWN SUPERMAN AND THEY WON'T TRUST ME.
THEY TRIED TO FOLLOW ME.
IF I OPERATE IN THE OPEN--
--THEY'LL HOUND ME UNTIL THEY FIND US.
WE HAVE TO GO UNDERGROUND.
BE SOMEONE ELSE.
AS LONG AS WE'RE A FAMILY.
YES, I REMEMBER IT LIKE IT WAS YESTERDAY...
...THOUGH THE YEARS HAVE FLOWN BY.

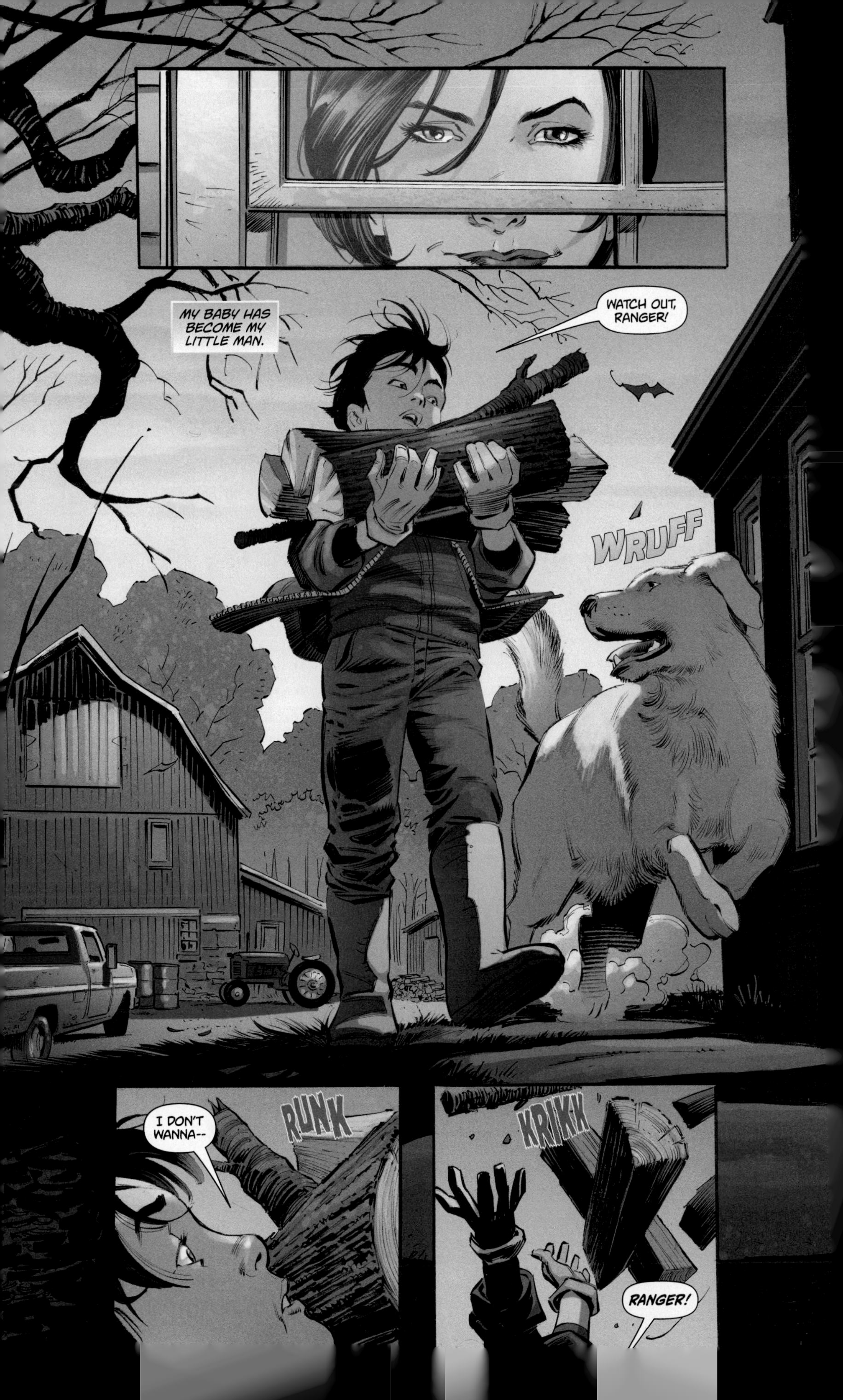
MY BABY HAS BECOME MY LITTLE MAN.
WATCH OUT, RANGER!
WRUFF
I DON'T WANNA--
RUNK
KRIKK
RANGER!

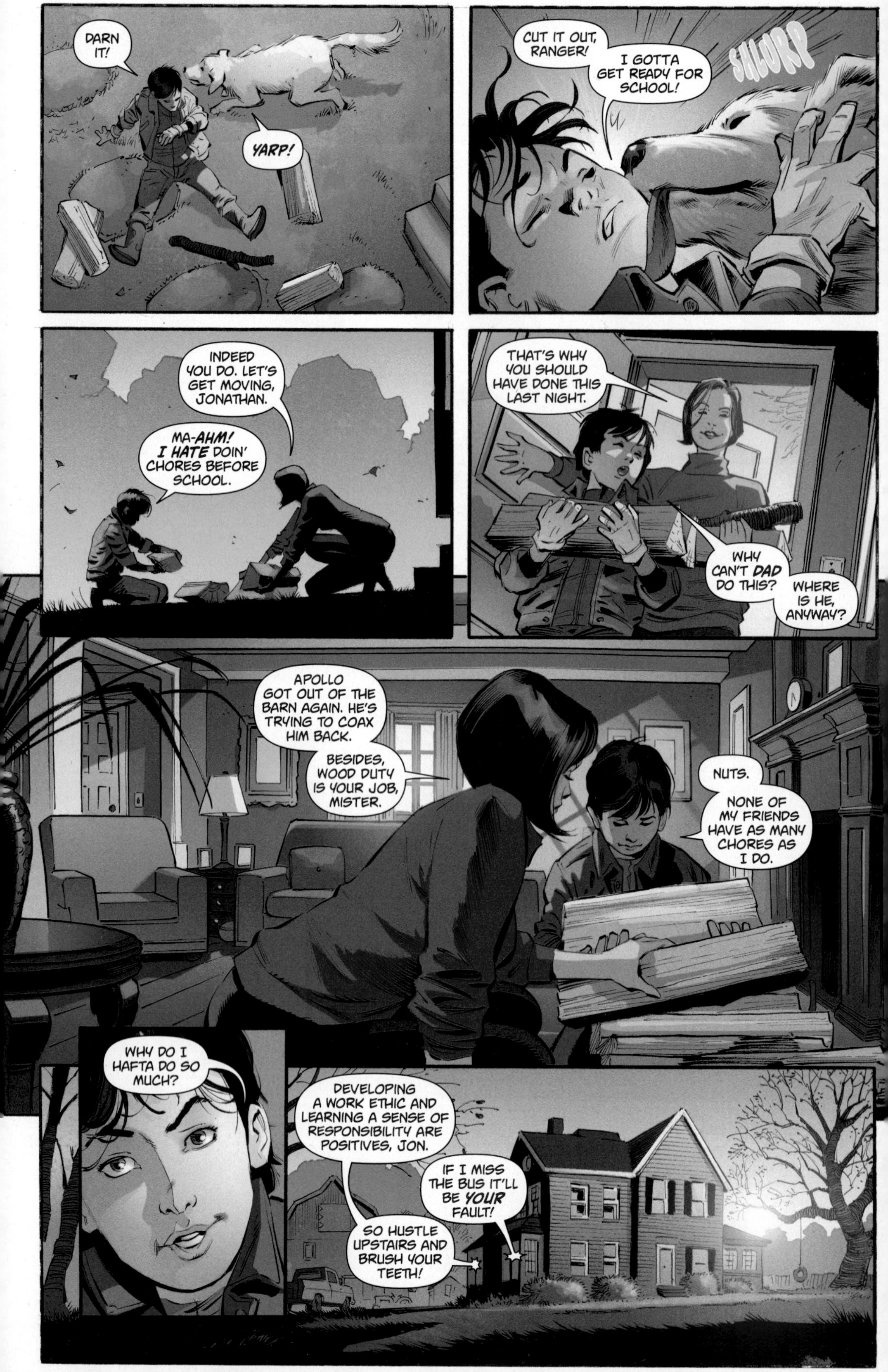
DARN IT!
YARP!
CUT IT OUT, RANGER!
I GOTTA GET READY FOR SCHOOL!
SHLORP
INDEED YOU DO. LET'S GET MOVING, JONATHAN.
MA-AHM! I HATE DOIN' CHORES BEFORE SCHOOL.
THAT'S WHY YOU SHOULD HAVE DONE THIS LAST NIGHT.
WHY CAN'T DAD DO THIS?
WHERE IS HE, ANYWAY?
APOLLO GOT OUT OF THE BARN AGAIN. HE'S TRYING TO COAX HIM BACK.
BESIDES, WOOD DUTY IS YOUR JOB, MISTER.
NUTS.
NONE OF MY FRIENDS HAVE AS MANY CHORES AS I DO.
WHY DO I HAFTA DO SO MUCH?
DEVELOPING A WORK ETHIC AND LEARNING A SENSE OF RESPONSIBILITY ARE POSITIVES, JON.
IF I MISS THE BUS IT'LL BE YOUR FAULT!
SO HUSTLE UPSTAIRS AND BRUSH YOUR TEETH!

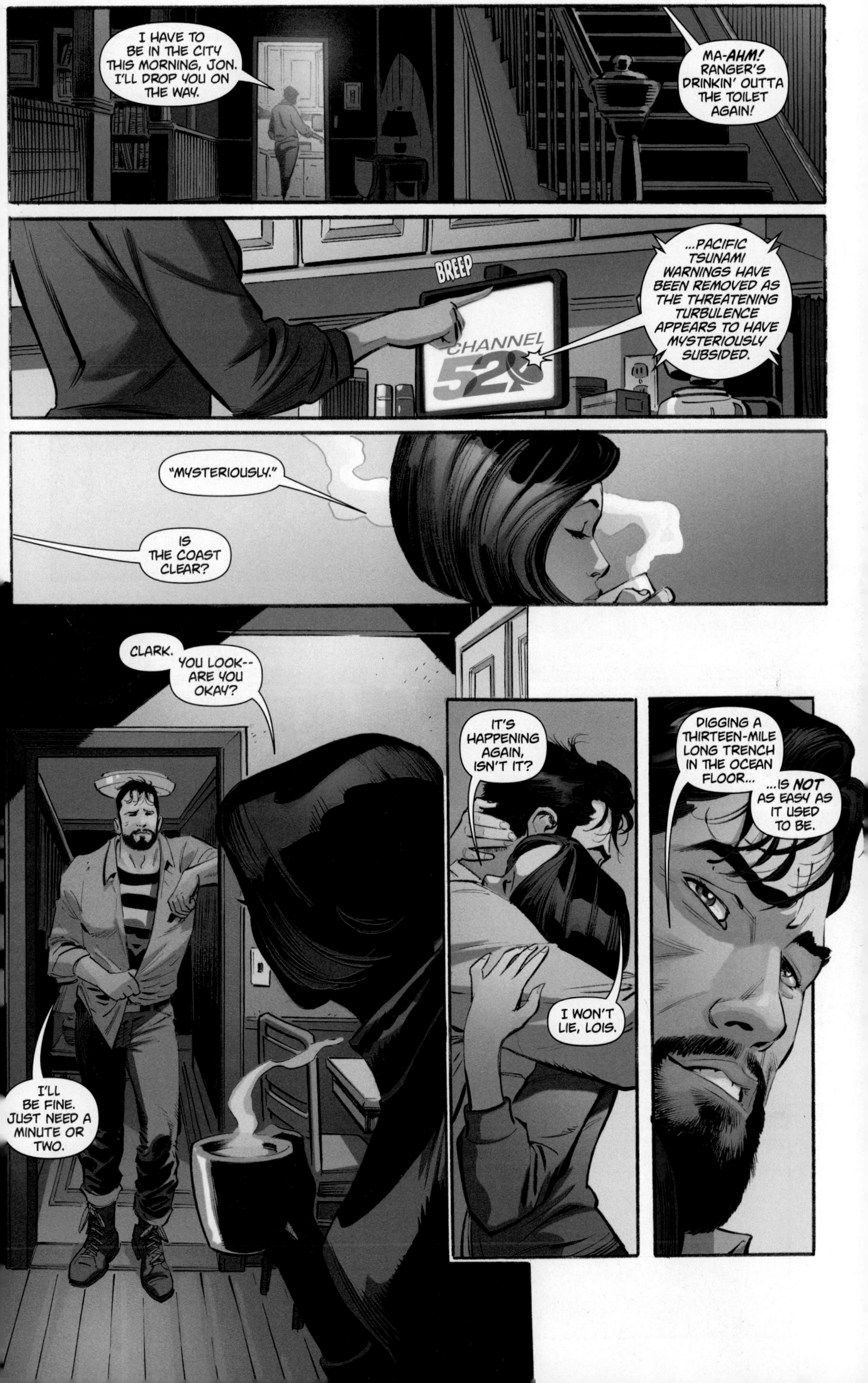
I HAVE TO BE IN THE CITY THIS MORNING, JON. I'LL DROP YOU ON THE WAY.
MA-AHM! RANGER'S DRINKIN' OUTTA THE TOILET AGAIN!
BREEP
...PACIFIC TSUNAMI WARNINGS HAVE BEEN REMOVED AS THE THREATENING TURBULENCE APPEARS TO HAVE MYSTERIOUSLY SUBSIDED.
CHANNEL 52
"MYSTERIOUSLY."
IS THE COAST CLEAR?
CLARK.
YOU LOOK-- ARE YOU OKAY?
I'LL BE FINE. JUST NEED A MINUTE OR TWO.
IT'S HAPPENING AGAIN, ISN'T IT?
I WON'T LIE, LOIS.
DIGGING A THIRTEEN-MILE LONG TRENCH IN THE OCEAN FLOOR...
...IS NOT AS EASY AS IT USED TO BE.

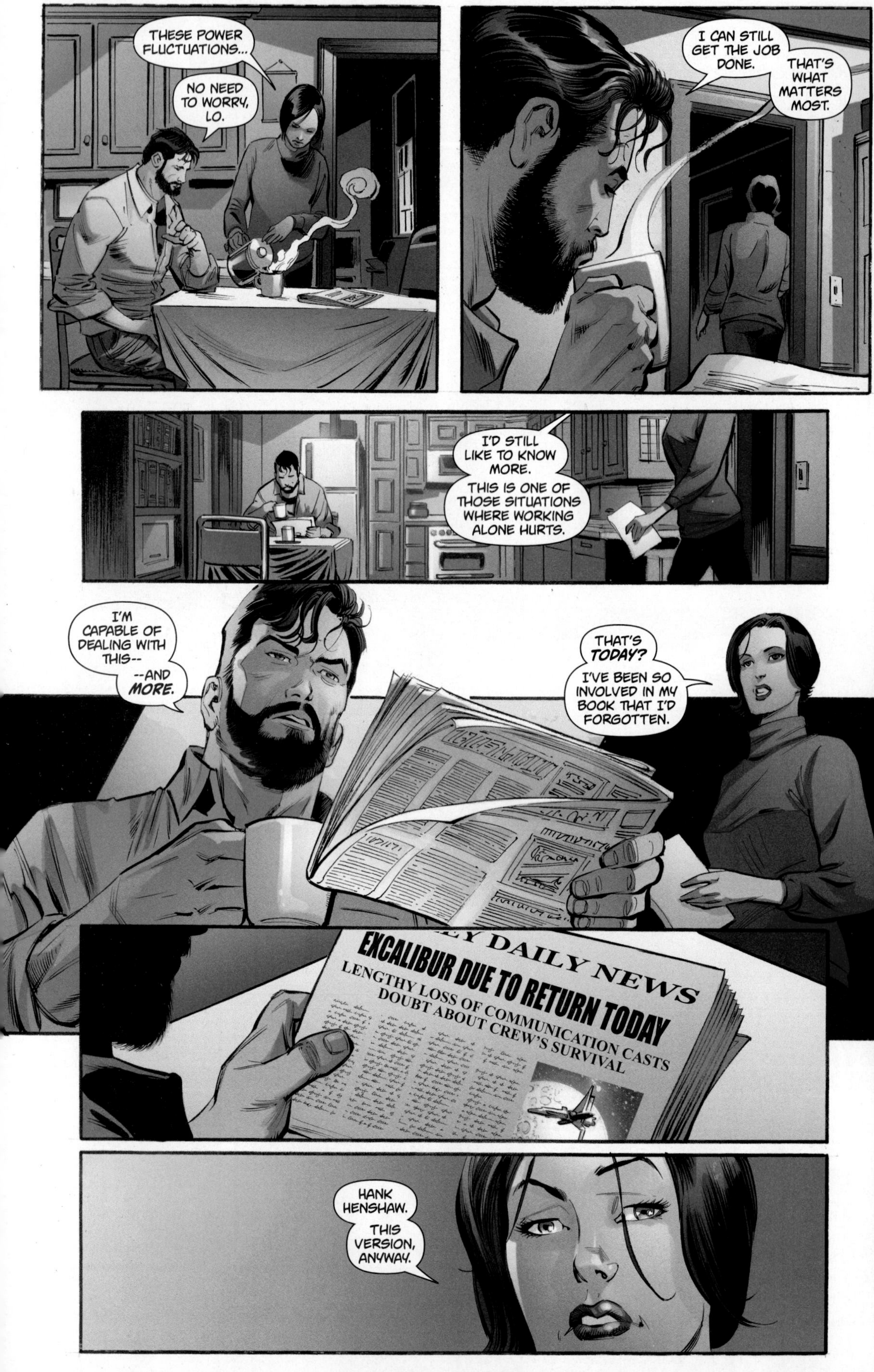
THESE POWER FLUCTUATIONS...
NO NEED TO WORRY, LO.
I CAN STILL GET THE JOB DONE.
THAT'S WHAT MATTERS MOST.
I'D STILL LIKE TO KNOW MORE.
THIS IS ONE OF THOSE SITUATIONS WHERE WORKING ALONE HURTS.
I'M CAPABLE OF DEALING WITH THIS--
--AND MORE.
THAT'S TODAY?
I'VE BEEN SO INVOLVED IN MY BOOK THAT I'D FORGOTTEN.
EY DAILY NEWS
EXCALIBUR DUE TO RETURN TODAY
LENGTHY LOSS OF COMMUNICATION CASTS DOUBT ABOUT CREW'S SURVIVAL
HANK HENSHAW.
THIS VERSION, ANYWAY.

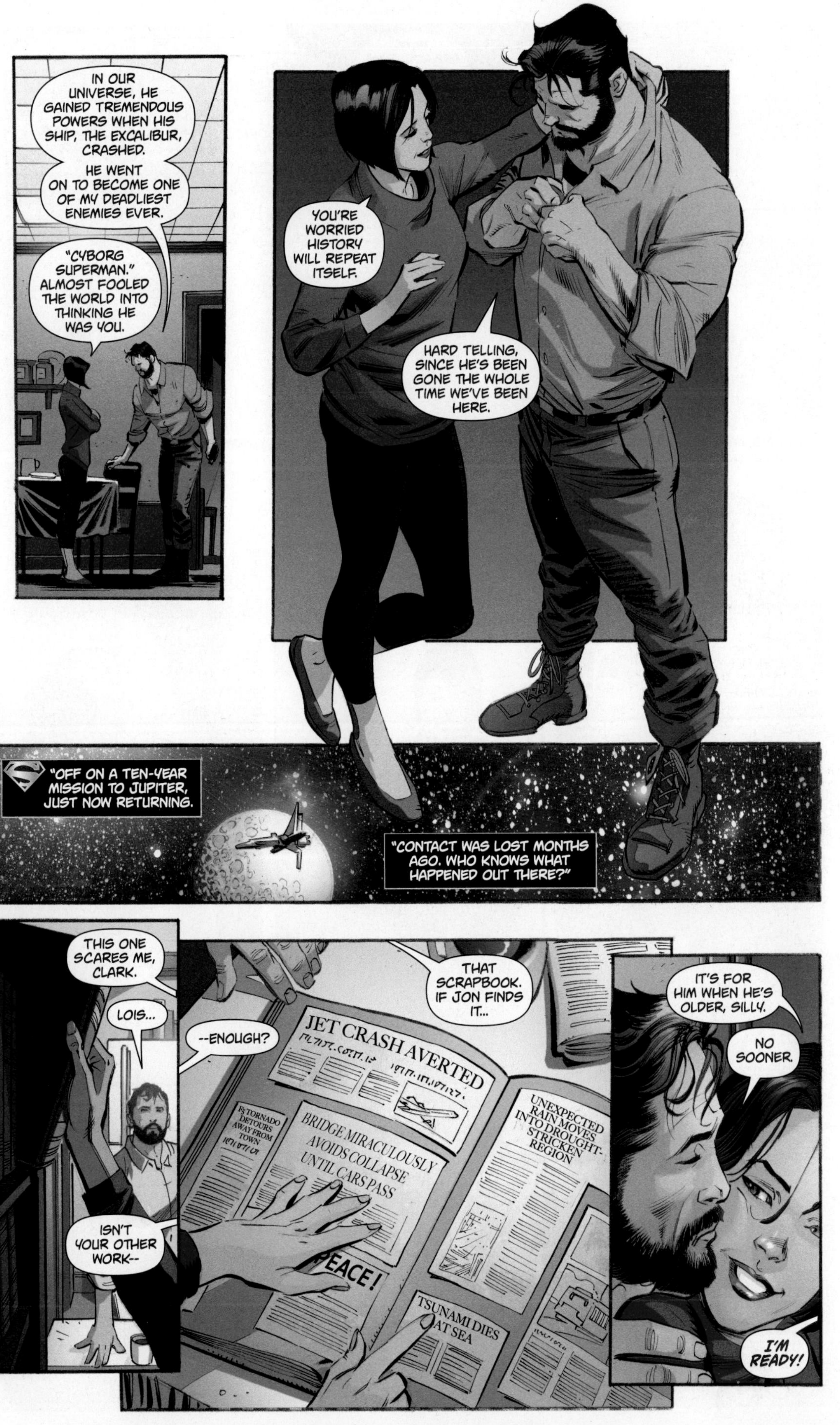

IN OUR UNIVERSE, HE GAINED TREMENDOUS POWERS WHEN HIS SHIP, THE EXCALIBUR, CRASHED.
HE WENT ON TO BECOME ONE OF MY DEADLIEST ENEMIES EVER.
"CYBORG SUPERMAN." ALMOST FOOLED THE WORLD INTO THINKING HE WAS YOU.
YOU'RE WORRIED HISTORY WILL REPEAT ITSELF.
HARD TELLING, SINCE HE'S BEEN GONE THE WHOLE TIME WE'VE BEEN HERE.
"OFF ON A TEN-YEAR MISSION TO JUPITER, JUST NOW RETURNING.
"CONTACT WAS LOST MONTHS AGO. WHO KNOWS WHAT HAPPENED OUT THERE?"
THIS ONE SCARES ME, CLARK.
LOIS...
ISN'T YOUR OTHER WORK--
--ENOUGH?
THAT SCRAPBOOK. IF JON FINDS IT...
JET CRASH AVERTED
TORNADO DETOURS AWAY FROM TOWN
BRIDGE MIRACULOUSLY AVOIDS COLLAPSE UNTIL CARS PASS
UNEXPECTED RAIN MOVES INTO DROUGHT-STRICKEN REGION
PEACE!
TSUNAMI DIES AT SEA
IT'S FOR HIM WHEN HE'S OLDER, SILLY.
NO SOONER.
I'M READY!

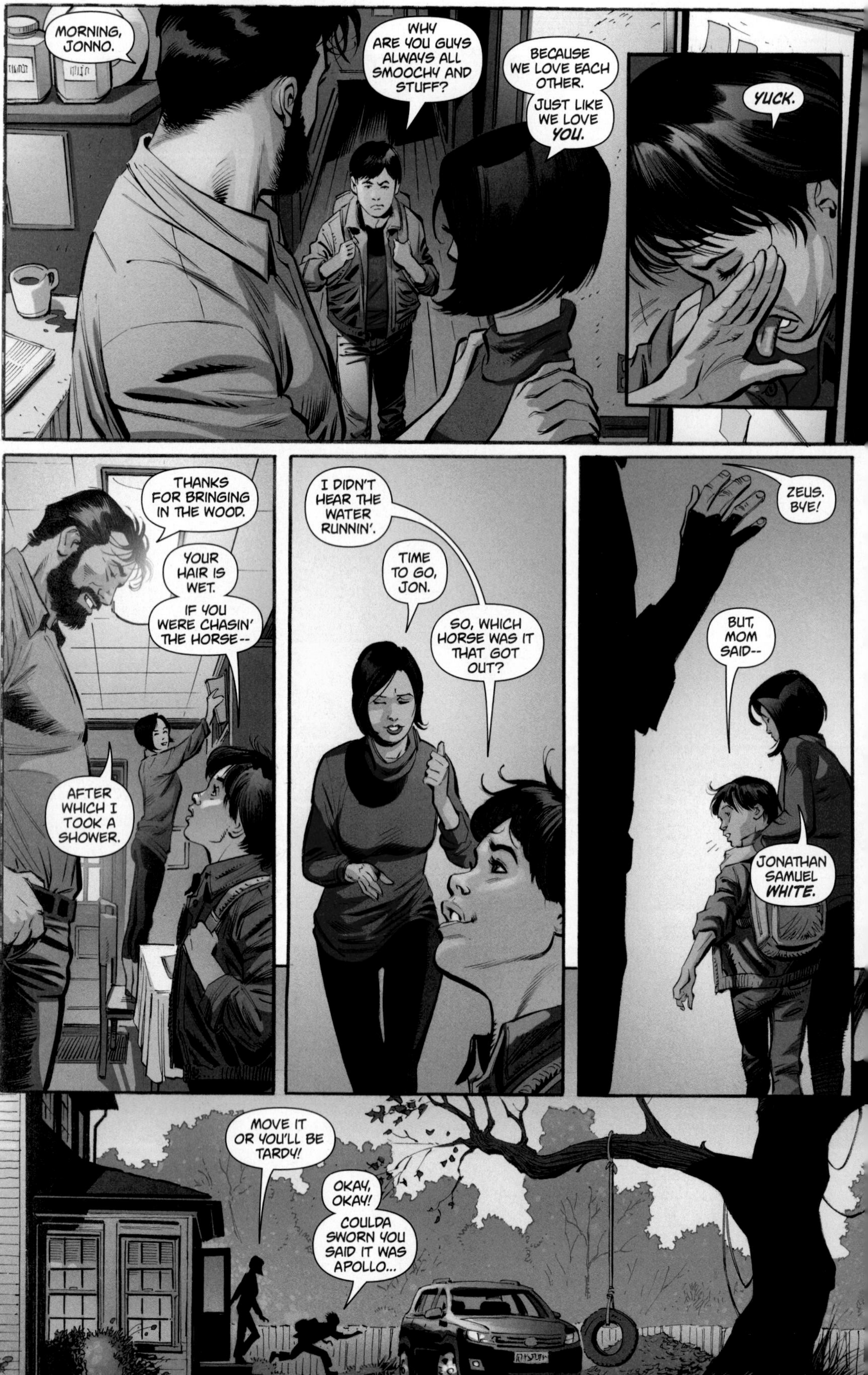
MORNING, JONNO.
WHY ARE YOU GUYS ALWAYS ALL SMOOCHY AND STUFF?
BECAUSE WE LOVE EACH OTHER.
JUST LIKE WE LOVE YOU.
YUCK.
THANKS FOR BRINGING IN THE WOOD.
YOUR HAIR IS WET.
IF YOU WERE CHASIN' THE HORSE--
AFTER WHICH I TOOK A SHOWER.
I DIDN'T HEAR THE WATER RUNNIN'.
TIME TO GO, JON.
SO, WHICH HORSE WAS IT THAT GOT OUT?
ZEUS. BYE!
BUT, MOM SAID--
JONATHAN SAMUEL WHITE.
MOVE IT OR YOU'LL BE TARDY!
OKAY, OKAY!
COULDA SWORN YOU SAID IT WAS APOLLO...

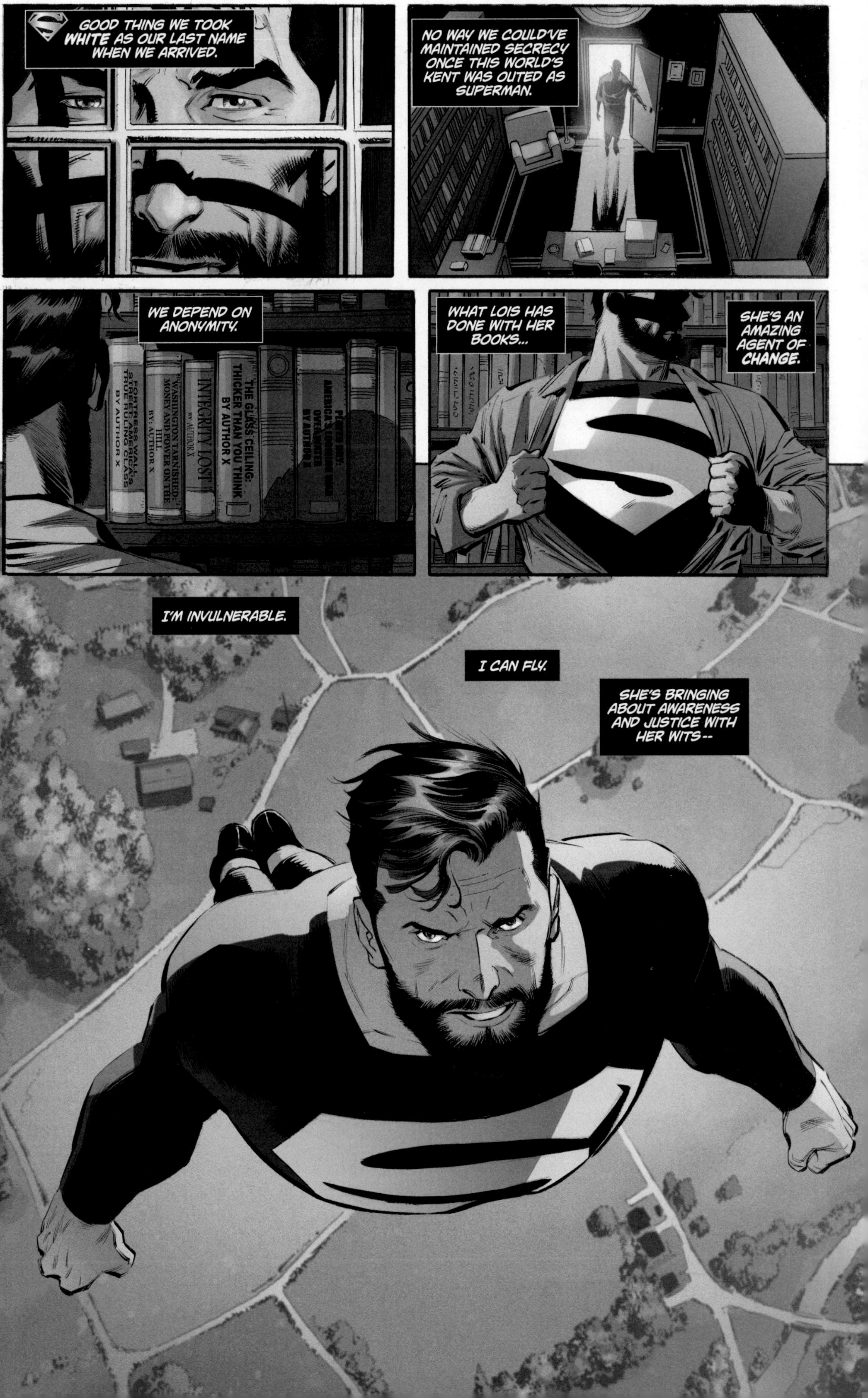
GOOD THING WE TOOK WHITE AS OUR LAST NAME WHEN WE ARRIVED.
NO WAY WE COULD'VE MAINTAINED SECRECY ONCE THIS WORLD'S KENT WAS OUTED AS SUPERMAN.
WE DEPEND ON ANONYMITY.
"WASHINGTON TARNISHED:" MONEY AND POWER ON THE HILL BY: AUTHOR X
INTEGRITY LOST BY AUTHOR X
THE GLASS CEILING: THICKER THAN YOU THINK BY AUTHOR X
WHAT LOIS HAS DONE WITH HER BOOKS...
SHE'S AN AMAZING AGENT OF CHANGE.
I'M INVULNERABLE.
I CAN FLY.
SHE'S BRINGING ABOUT AWARENESS AND JUSTICE WITH HER WITS--

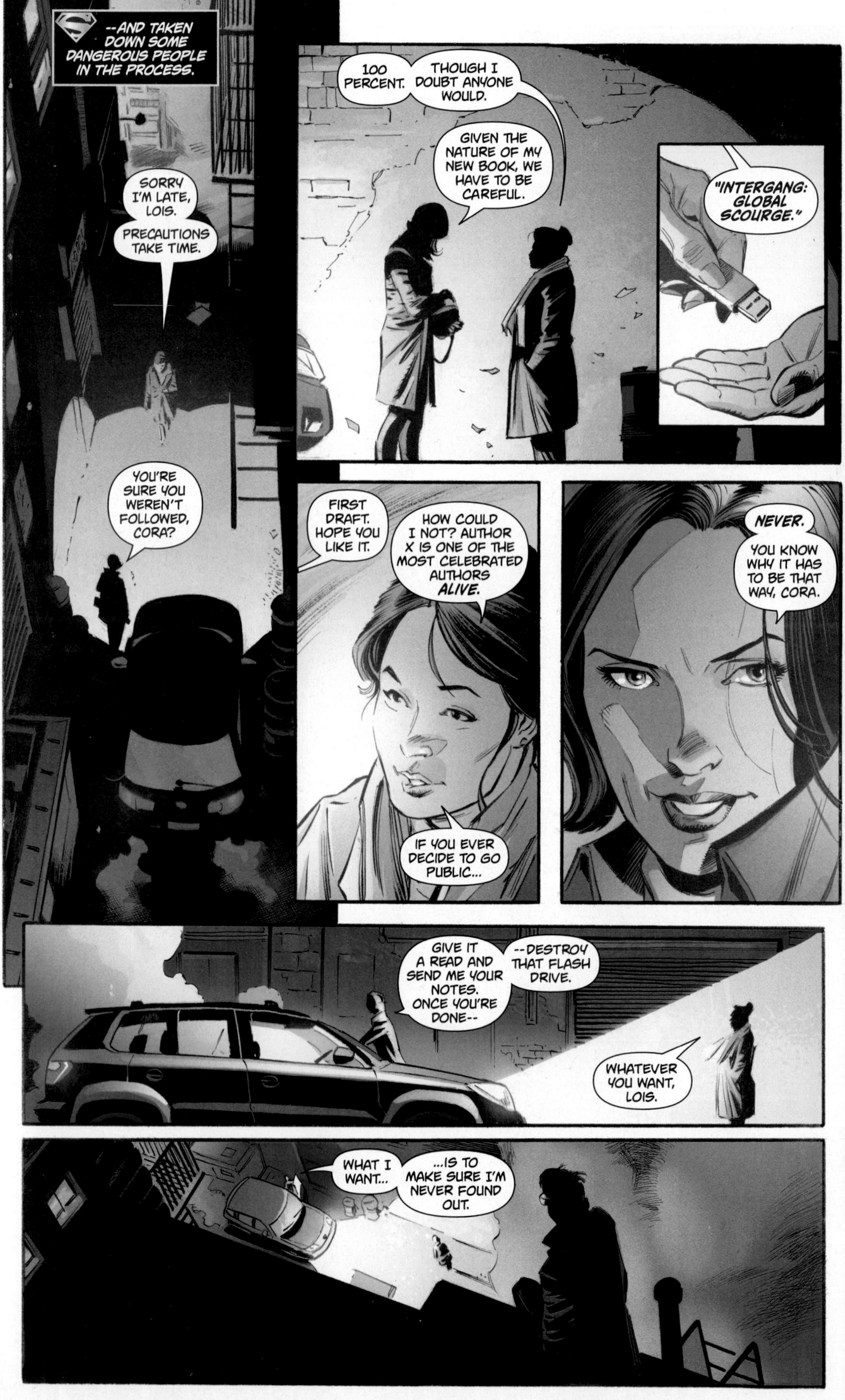
--AND TAKEN DOWN SOME DANGEROUS PEOPLE IN THE PROCESS.
SORRY I'M LATE, LOIS.
PRECAUTIONS TAKE TIME.
YOU'RE SURE YOU WEREN'T FOLLOWED, CORA?
100 PERCENT.
THOUGH I DOUBT ANYONE WOULD.
GIVEN THE NATURE OF MY NEW BOOK, WE HAVE TO BE CAREFUL.
"INTERGANG: GLOBAL SCOURGE."
FIRST DRAFT. HOPE YOU LIKE IT.
HOW COULD I NOT? AUTHOR X IS ONE OF THE MOST CELEBRATED AUTHORS ALIVE.
IF YOU EVER DECIDE TO GO PUBLIC...
NEVER.
YOU KNOW WHY IT HAS TO BE THAT WAY, CORA.
GIVE IT A READ AND SEND ME YOUR NOTES. ONCE YOU'RE DONE--
--DESTROY THAT FLASH DRIVE.
WHATEVER YOU WANT, LOIS.
WHAT I WANT...
...IS TO MAKE SURE I'M NEVER FOUND OUT.

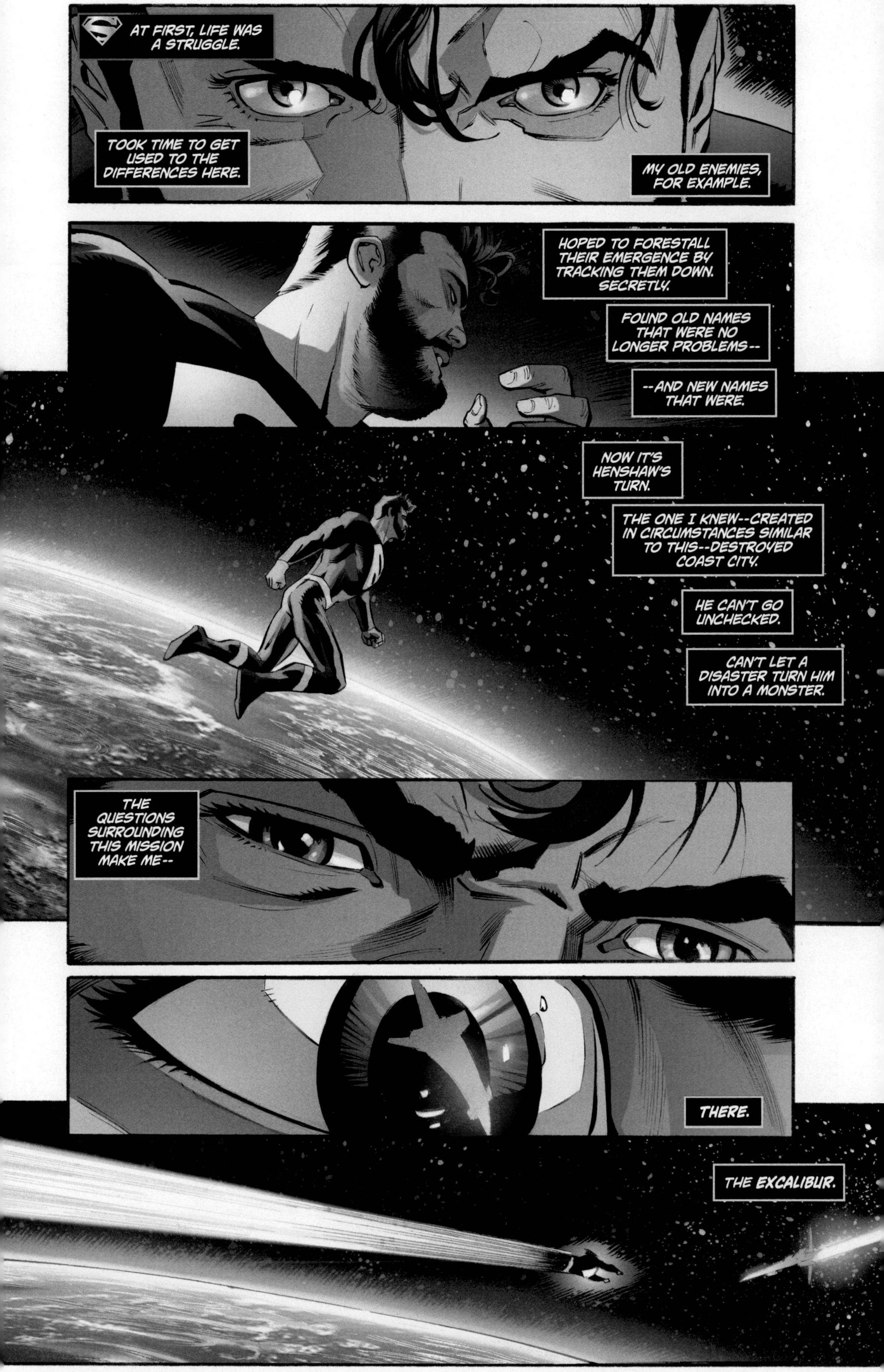
AT FIRST, LIFE WAS A STRUGGLE.
TOOK TIME TO GET USED TO THE DIFFERENCES HERE.
MY OLD ENEMIES, FOR EXAMPLE.
HOPED TO FORESTALL THEIR EMERGENCE BY TRACKING THEM DOWN. SECRETLY.
FOUND OLD NAMES THAT WERE NO LONGER PROBLEMS--
--AND NEW NAMES THAT WERE.
NOW IT'S HENSHAW'S TURN.
THE ONE I KNEW--CREATED IN CIRCUMSTANCES SIMILAR TO THIS--DESTROYED COAST CITY.
HE CAN'T GO UNCHECKED.
CAN'T LET A DISASTER TURN HIM INTO A MONSTER.
THE QUESTIONS SURROUNDING THIS MISSION MAKE ME--
THERE.
THE EXCALIBUR.

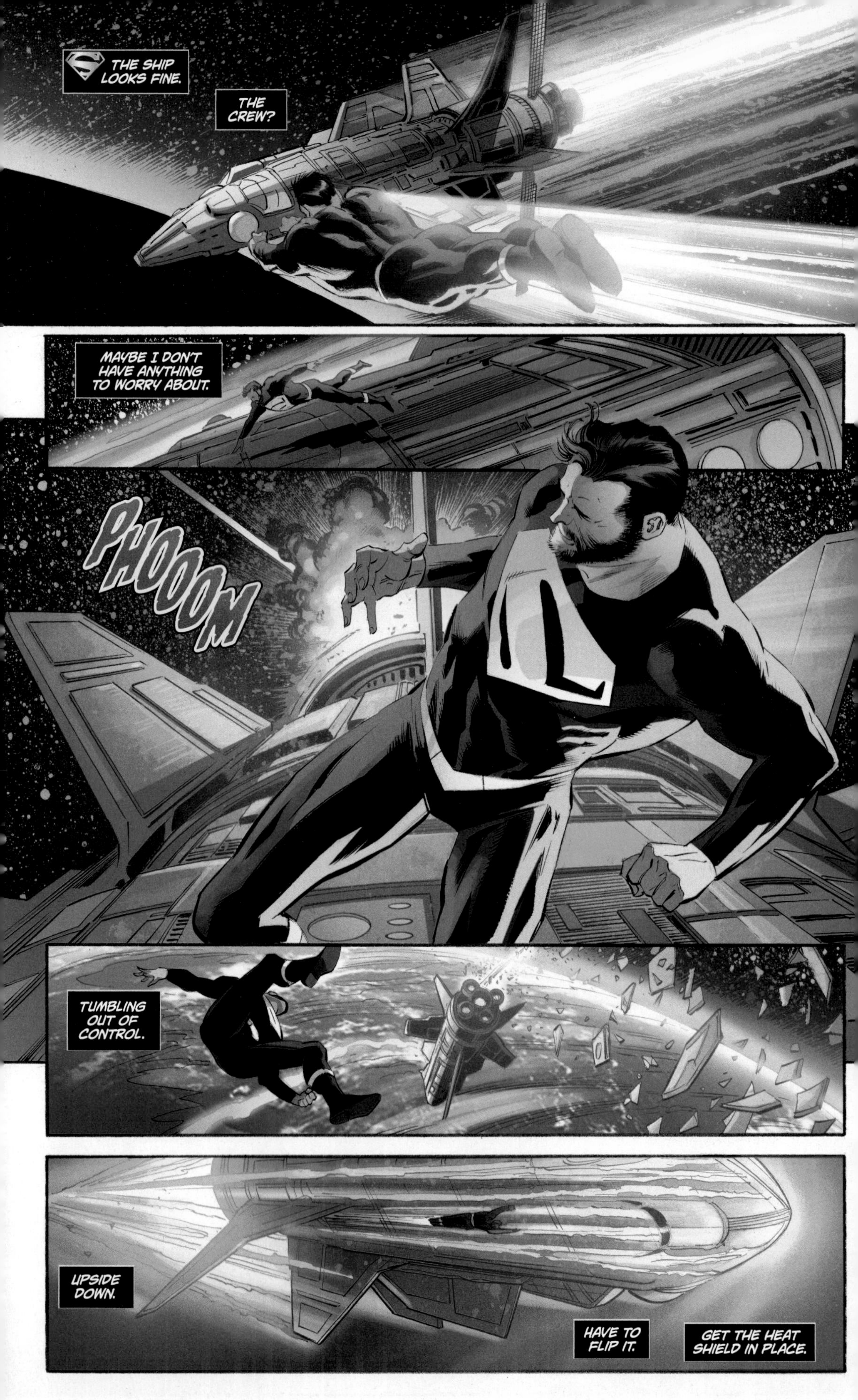
THE SHIP LOOKS FINE.
THE CREW?
MAYBE I DON'T HAVE ANYTHING TO WORRY ABOUT.
PHOOOM
TUMBLING OUT OF CONTROL.
UPSIDE DOWN.
HAVE TO FLIP IT.
GET THE HEAT SHIELD IN PLACE.

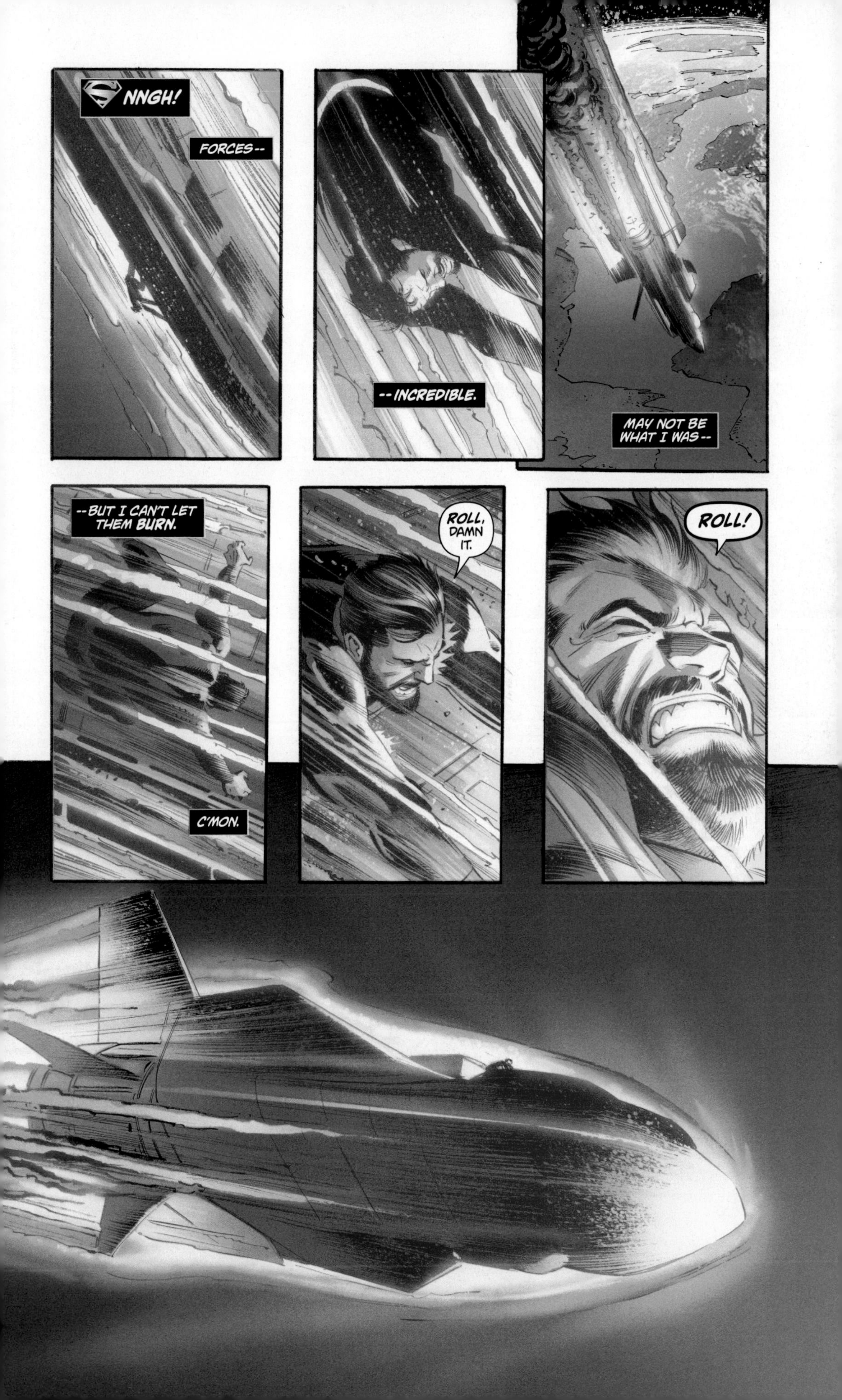
NNGH!
FORCES--
--INCREDIBLE.
MAY NOT BE WHAT I WAS--
--BUT I CAN'T LET THEM BURN.
C'MON.
ROLL, DAMN IT.
ROLL!

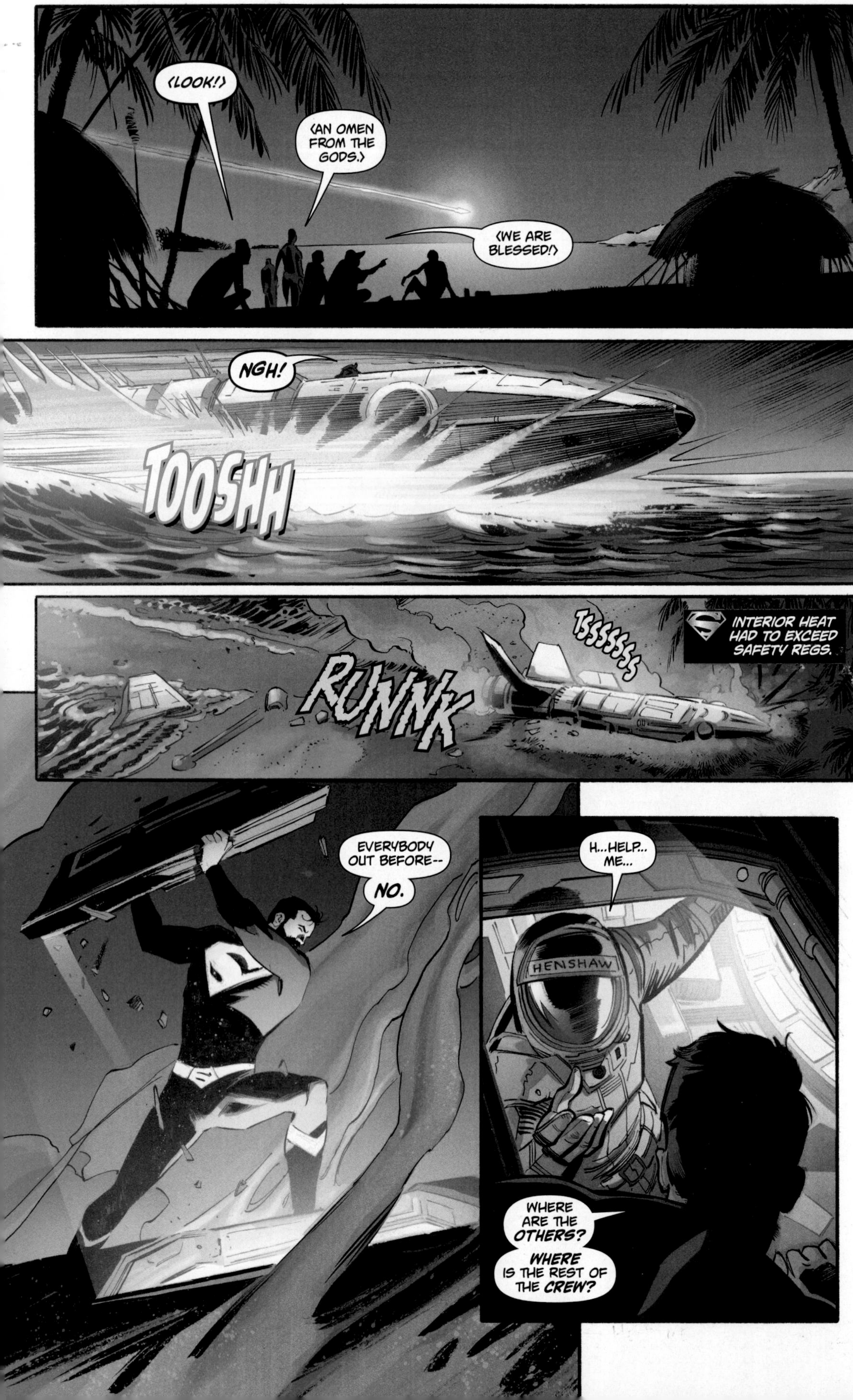
‹LOOK!›
‹AN OMEN FROM THE GODS.›
‹WE ARE BLESSED!›
NGH!
TOOSHH
TSSSSSSS
INTERIOR HEAT HAD TO EXCEED SAFETY REGS.
RUNNK
EVERYBODY OUT BEFORE--
NO.
H...HELP... ME...
HENSHAW
WHERE ARE THE OTHERS?
WHERE IS THE REST OF THE CREW?

CALIFORNIA.

LANCASTER ELEMENTARY SCHOOL

JASON PAID $42 FOR HOT DOGS, $12 FOR BUNS...

...$18.37 FOR SODA AND $11.59 ON PLASTIC PLATES AND TABLEWARE.

HOW MUCH CHANGE WILL HE GET BACK IF HE PAYS WITH A $100 BILL?

LET'S SEE...

JON?

MR. WHITE?

PSST.

JON.

WAKE UP, DOOFUS!

...AIRLINE PILOT REPORTS SEEING A MAN TRYING TO SAVE THE EXCALIBUR...

WN BREAKING NEWS

JONATHAN!

UM... HE SHOULDN'T BUY PLASTIC BECAUSE IT ISN'T SUSTAINABLE?

WRONG ANSWER.

SLAMM

IF YOU WON'T LISTEN TO ME, PERHAPS YOU'LL LISTEN TO PRINCIPAL SIMMONS!

UM... $16.05?

$16.04! THAT'S IT!

AW, NUTS.

AaBbCcDdEeFf GgHhIiJ

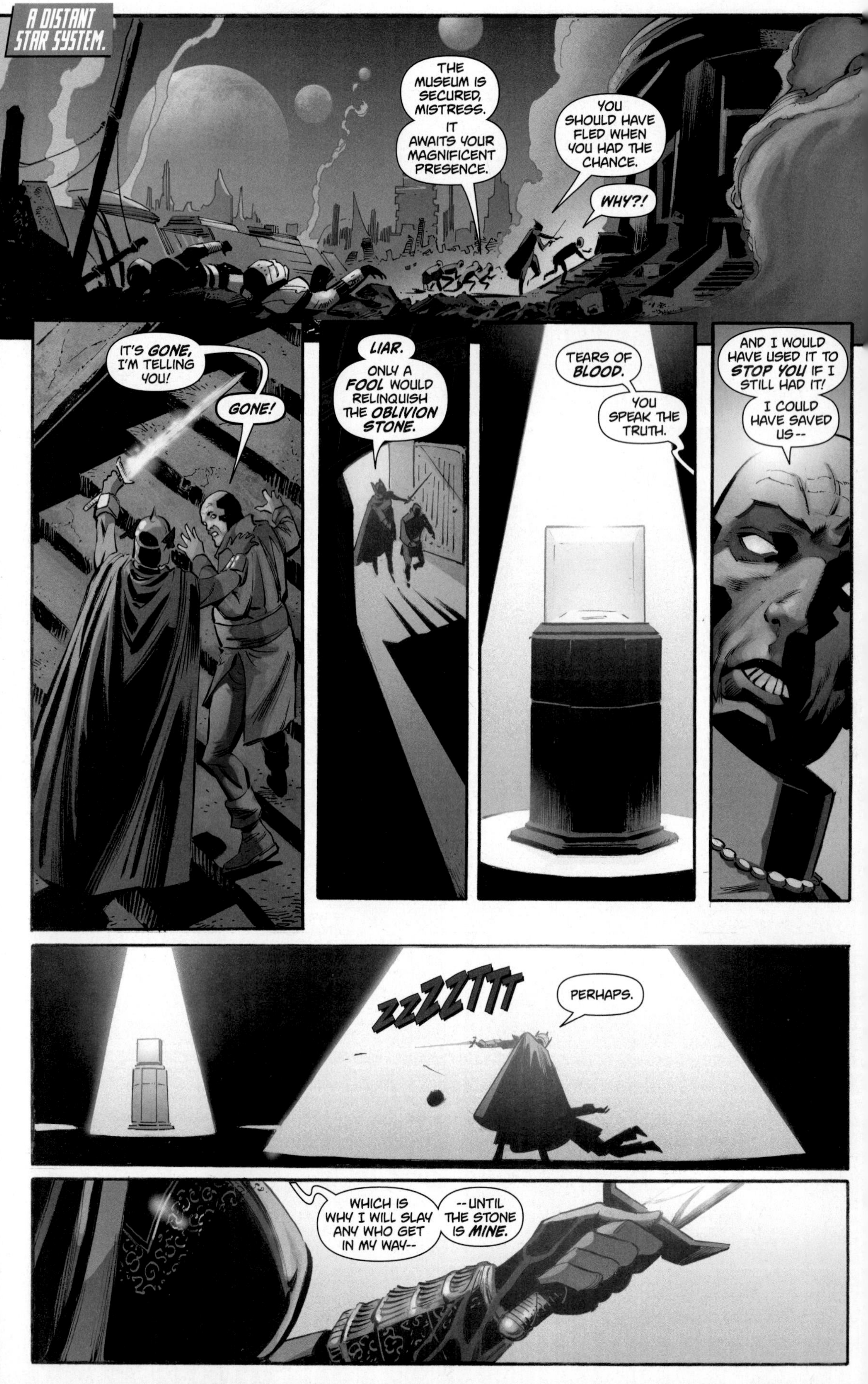
A DISTANT STAR SYSTEM.
THE MUSEUM IS SECURED, MISTRESS.
IT AWAITS YOUR MAGNIFICENT PRESENCE.
YOU SHOULD HAVE FLED WHEN YOU HAD THE CHANCE.
WHY?!
IT'S GONE, I'M TELLING YOU!
GONE!
LIAR.
ONLY A FOOL WOULD RELINQUISH THE OBLIVION STONE.
TEARS OF BLOOD.
YOU SPEAK THE TRUTH.
AND I WOULD HAVE USED IT TO STOP YOU IF I STILL HAD IT!
I COULD HAVE SAVED US--
ZZZZTTTT
PERHAPS.
WHICH IS WHY I WILL SLAY ANY WHO GET IN MY WAY--
--UNTIL THE STONE IS MINE.

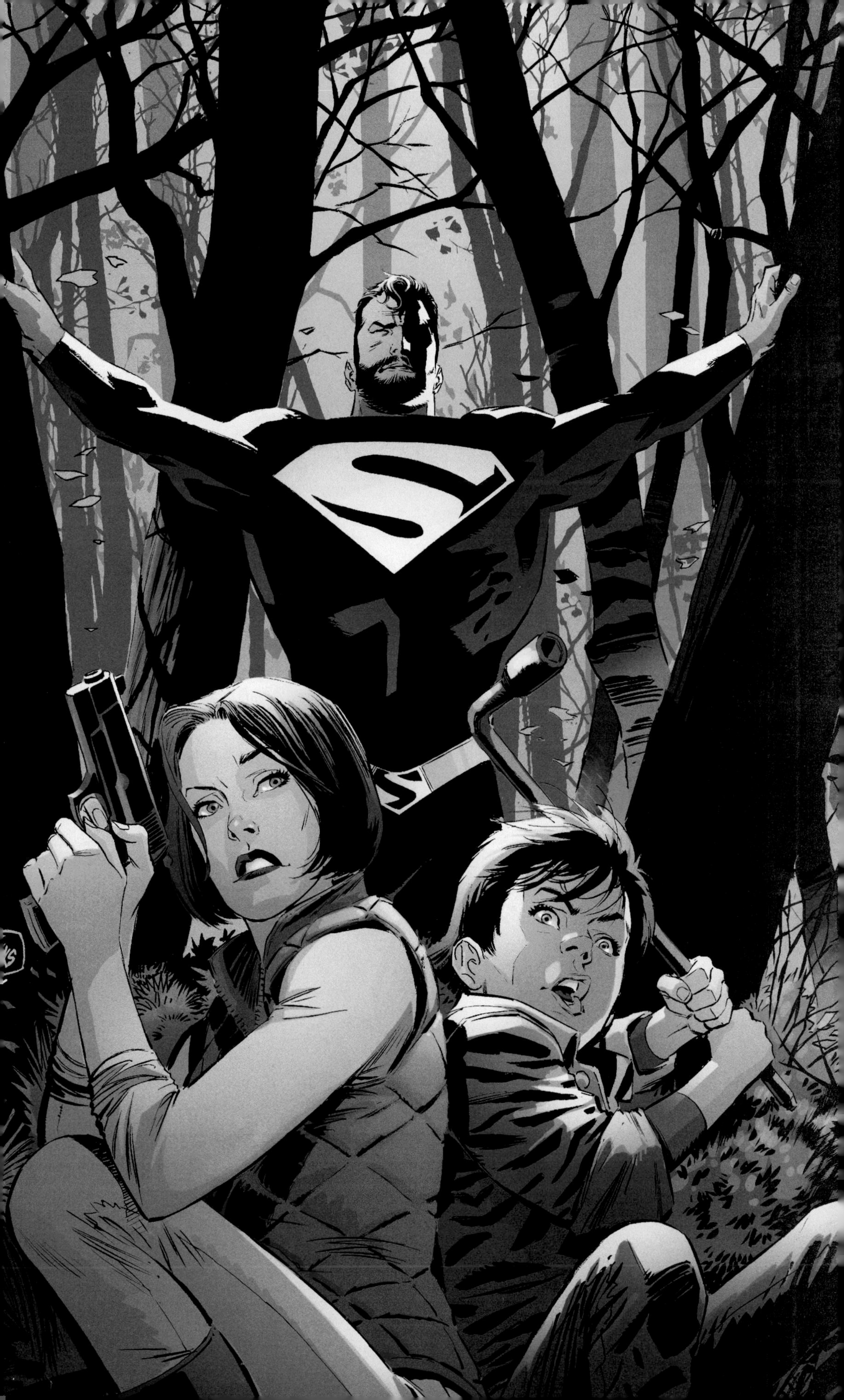

ARRIVAL: PART II

DAN JURGENS writer **LEE WEEKS** penciller **SCOTT HANNA** inker **BRAD ANDERSON** colorist **A LARGER WORLD STUDIOS** letterer **LEE WEEKS BRAD ANDERSON** cover artists

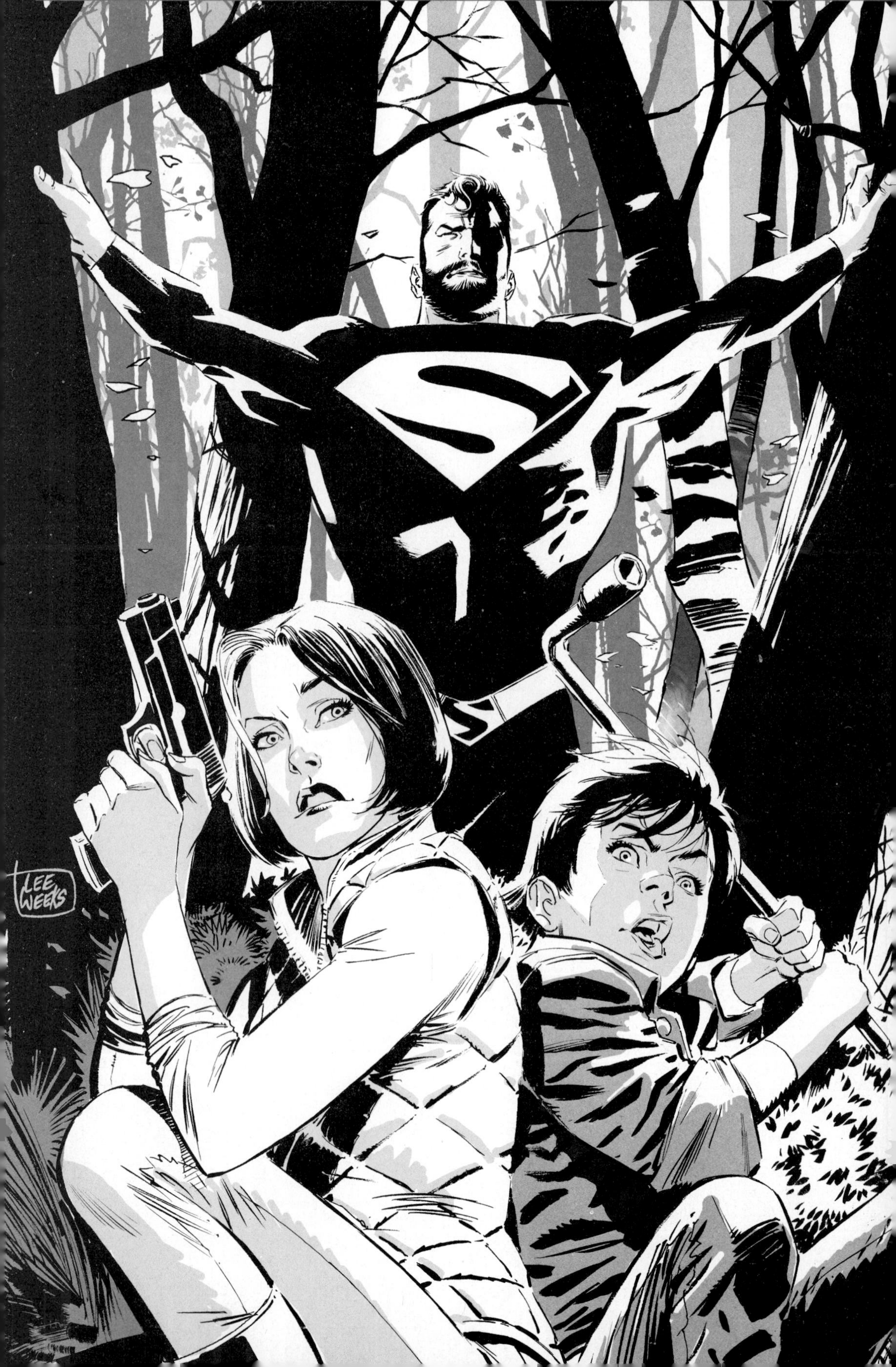
LEE WEEKS

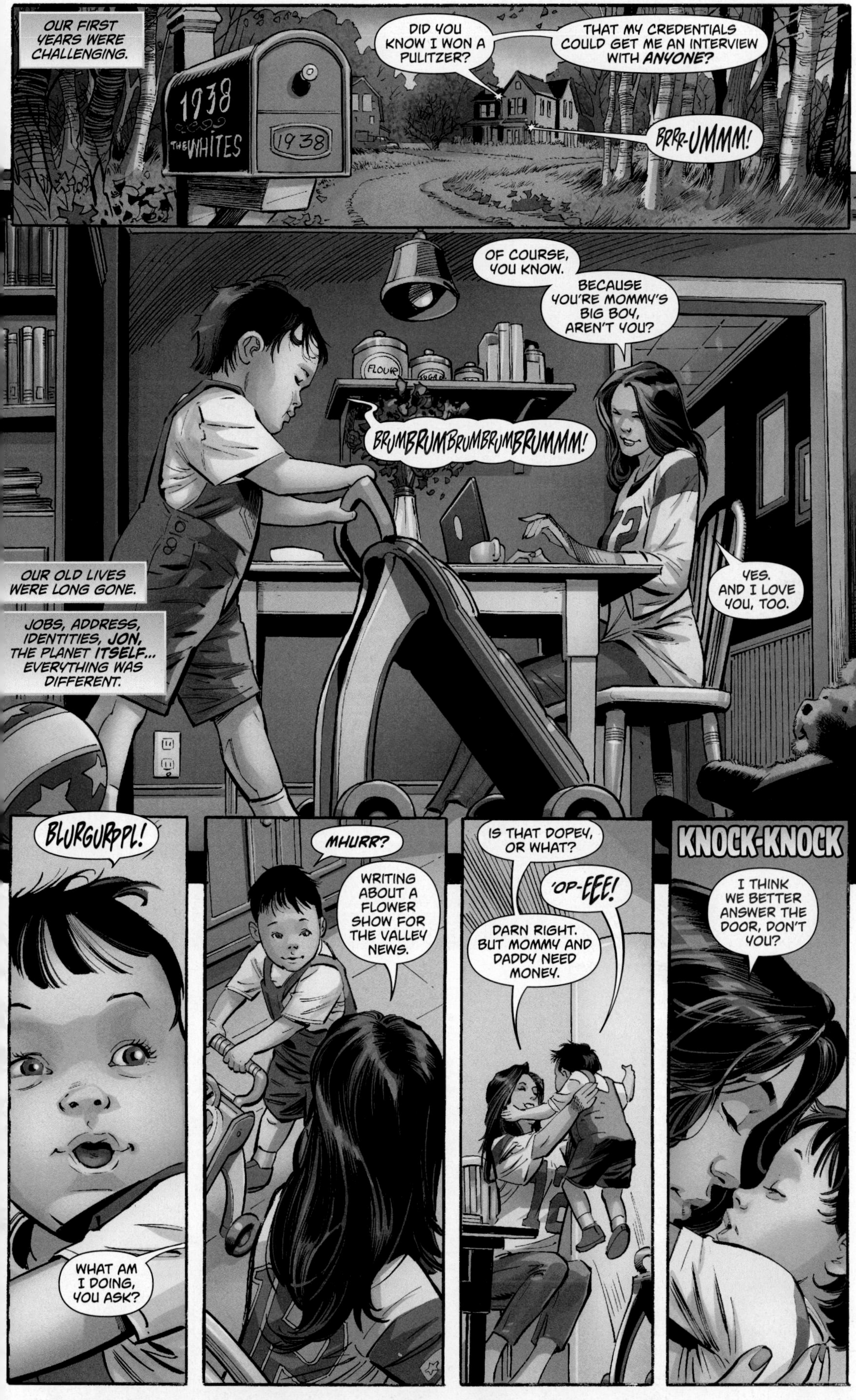
OUR FIRST YEARS WERE CHALLENGING.
1938
THE WHITES
1938
DID YOU KNOW I WON A PULITZER?
THAT MY CREDENTIALS COULD GET ME AN INTERVIEW WITH ANYONE?
BRRR-UMMM!
OF COURSE, YOU KNOW.
BECAUSE YOU'RE MOMMY'S BIG BOY, AREN'T YOU?
FLOUR
SUGAR
BRUMBRUMBRUMBRUMBRUMMM!
OUR OLD LIVES WERE LONG GONE.
JOBS, ADDRESS, IDENTITIES, JON, THE PLANET ITSELF... EVERYTHING WAS DIFFERENT.
YES. AND I LOVE YOU, TOO.
BLURGURPPL!
WHAT AM I DOING, YOU ASK?
MHURR?
WRITING ABOUT A FLOWER SHOW FOR THE VALLEY NEWS.
IS THAT DOPEY, OR WHAT?
'OP-EEE!
DARN RIGHT. BUT MOMMY AND DADDY NEED MONEY.
KNOCK-KNOCK
I THINK WE BETTER ANSWER THE DOOR, DON'T YOU?

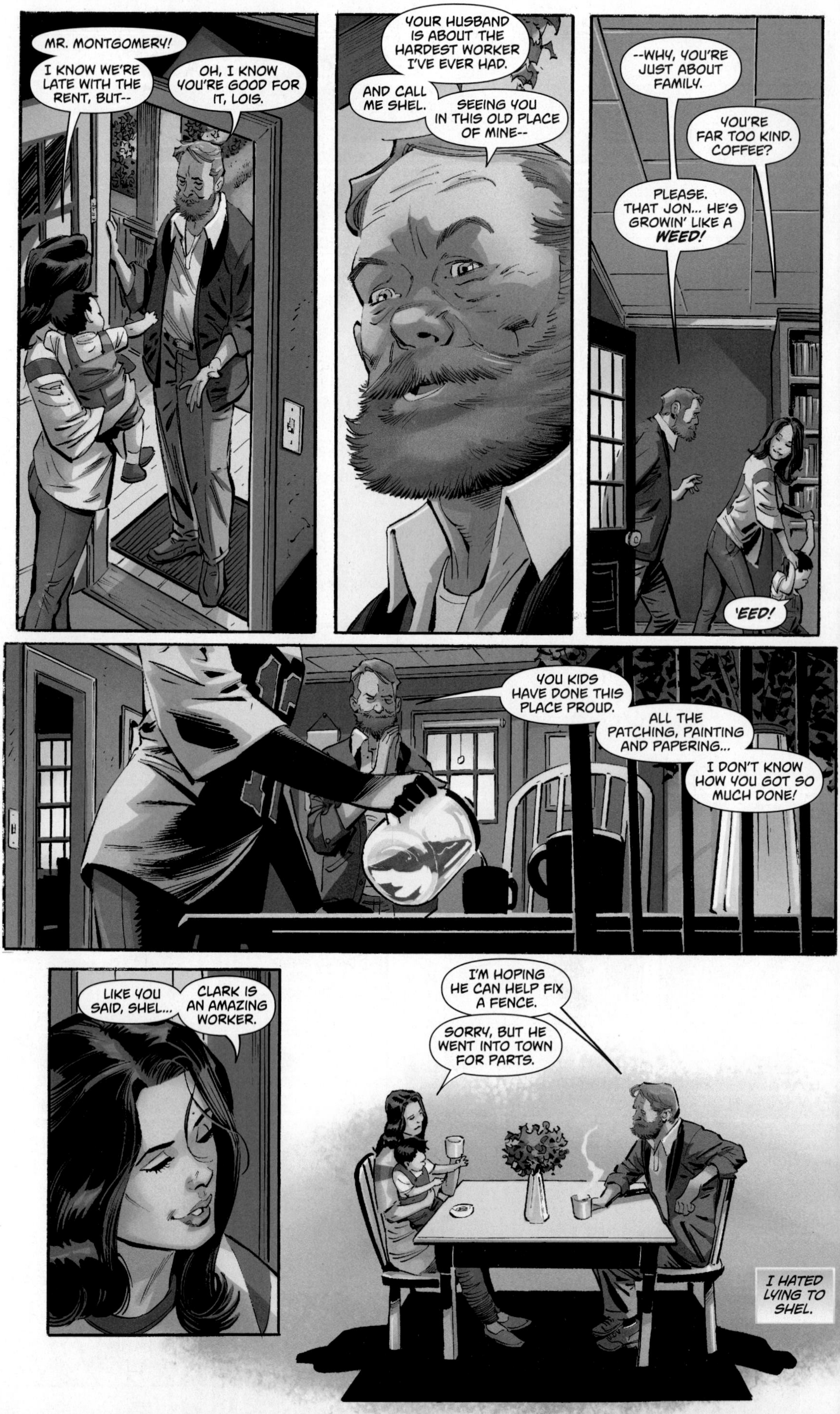

MR. MONTGOMERY!
I KNOW WE'RE LATE WITH THE RENT, BUT--
OH, I KNOW YOU'RE GOOD FOR IT, LOIS.
YOUR HUSBAND IS ABOUT THE HARDEST WORKER I'VE EVER HAD.
AND CALL ME SHEL.
SEEING YOU IN THIS OLD PLACE OF MINE--
--WHY, YOU'RE JUST ABOUT FAMILY.
YOU'RE FAR TOO KIND. COFFEE?
PLEASE. THAT JON... HE'S GROWIN' LIKE A WEED!
'EED!
YOU KIDS HAVE DONE THIS PLACE PROUD.
ALL THE PATCHING, PAINTING AND PAPERING...
I DON'T KNOW HOW YOU GOT SO MUCH DONE!
LIKE YOU SAID, SHEL...
CLARK IS AN AMAZING WORKER.
I'M HOPING HE CAN HELP FIX A FENCE.
SORRY, BUT HE WENT INTO TOWN FOR PARTS.
I HATED LYING TO SHEL.

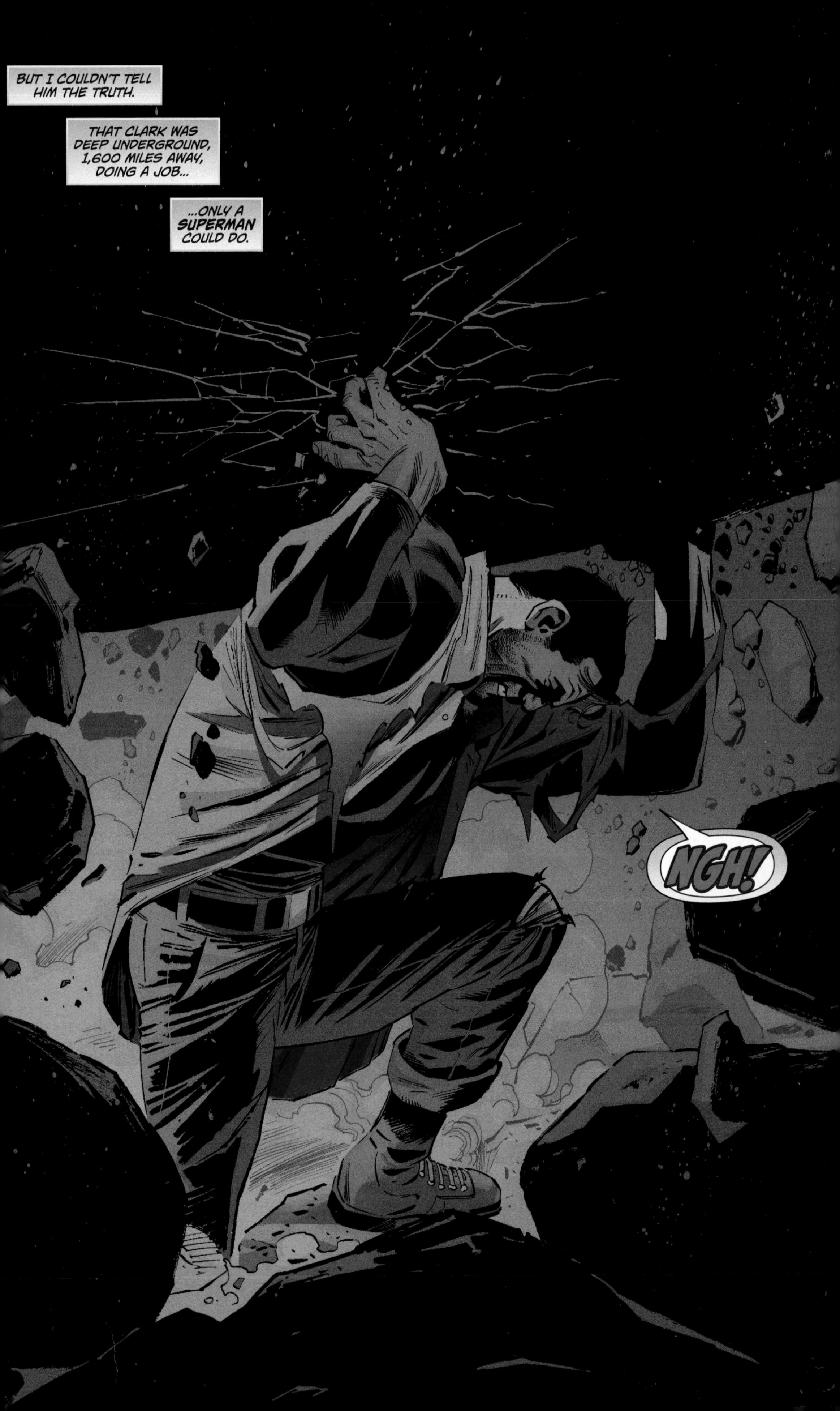
BUT I COULDN'T TELL HIM THE TRUTH.
THAT CLARK WAS DEEP UNDERGROUND, 1,600 MILES AWAY, DOING A JOB...
...ONLY A SUPERMAN COULD DO.
NGH!

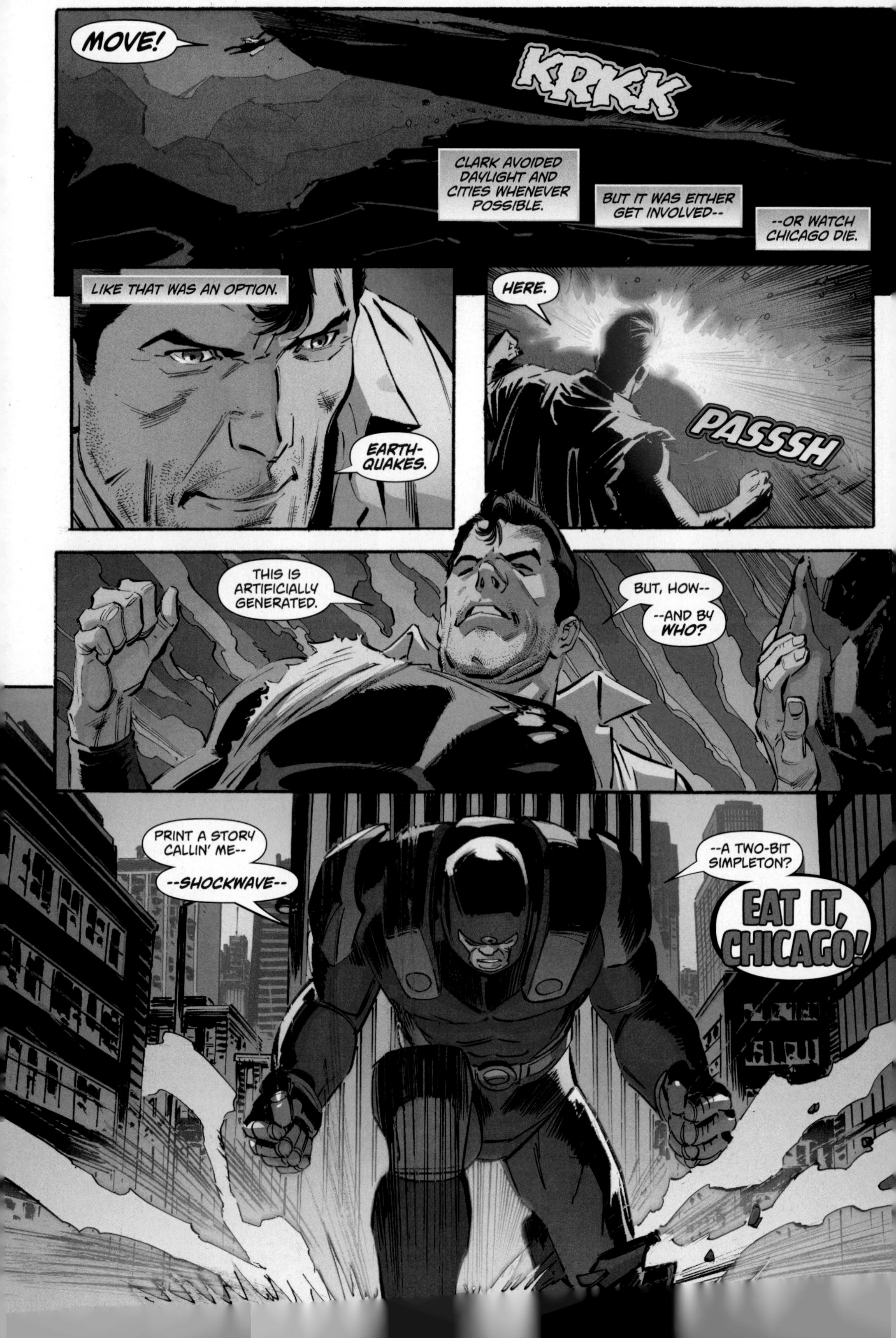
MOVE!
KRKK
CLARK AVOIDED DAYLIGHT AND CITIES WHENEVER POSSIBLE.
BUT IT WAS EITHER GET INVOLVED--
--OR WATCH CHICAGO DIE.
LIKE THAT WAS AN OPTION.
EARTH-QUAKES.
HERE.
PASSSH
THIS IS ARTIFICIALLY GENERATED.
BUT, HOW--
--AND BY WHO?
PRINT A STORY CALLIN' ME--
--SHOCKWAVE--
--A TWO-BIT SIMPLETON?
EAT IT, CHICAGO!

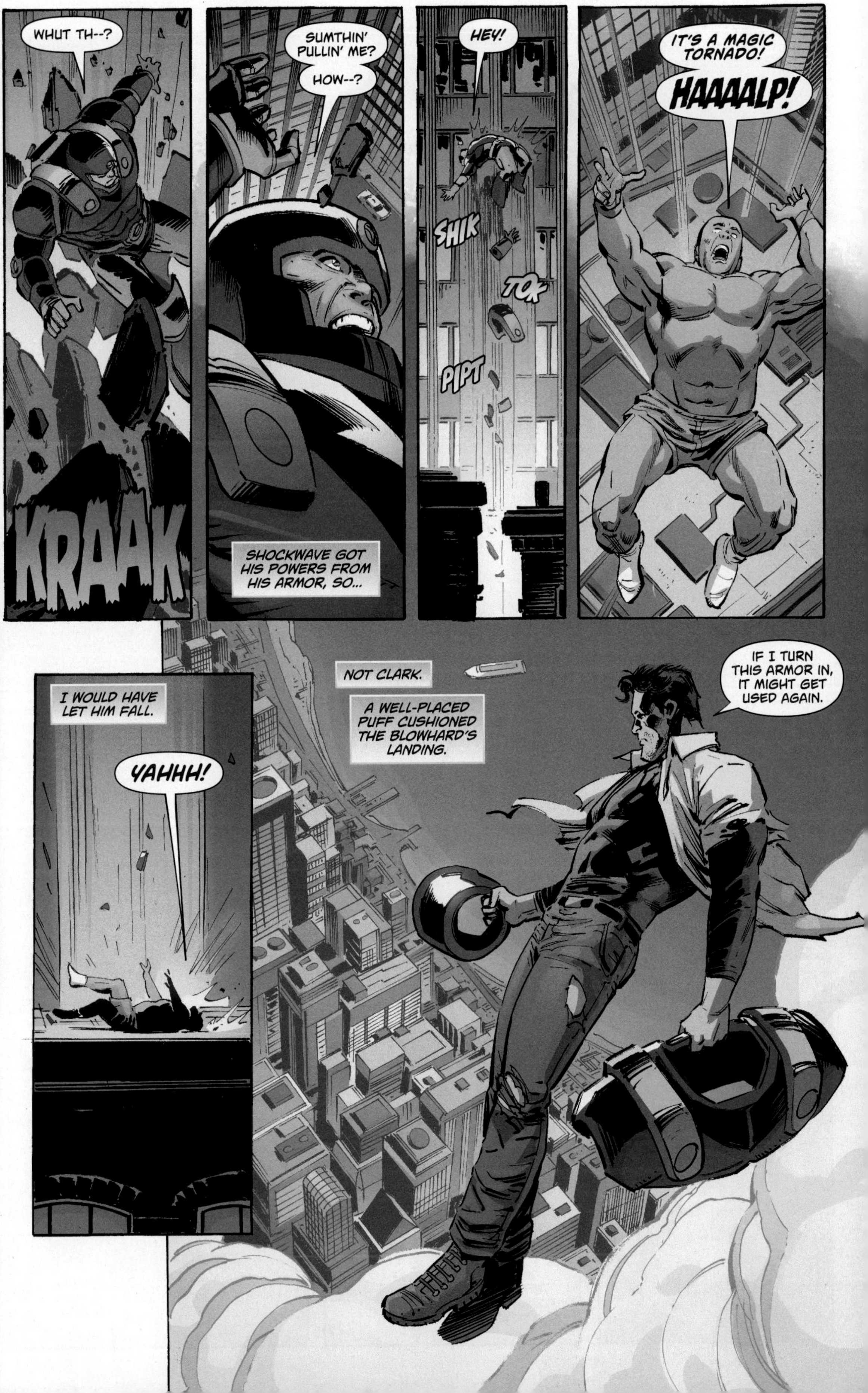
WHUT TH--?
KRAAK
SUMTHIN' PULLIN' ME?
HOW--?
SHOCKWAVE GOT HIS POWERS FROM HIS ARMOR, SO...
HEY!
SHIK
TOK
PIPT
IT'S A MAGIC TORNADO!
HAAAALP!
I WOULD HAVE LET HIM FALL.
YAHHH!
NOT CLARK.
A WELL-PLACED PUFF CUSHIONED THE BLOWHARD'S LANDING.
IF I TURN THIS ARMOR IN, IT MIGHT GET USED AGAIN.

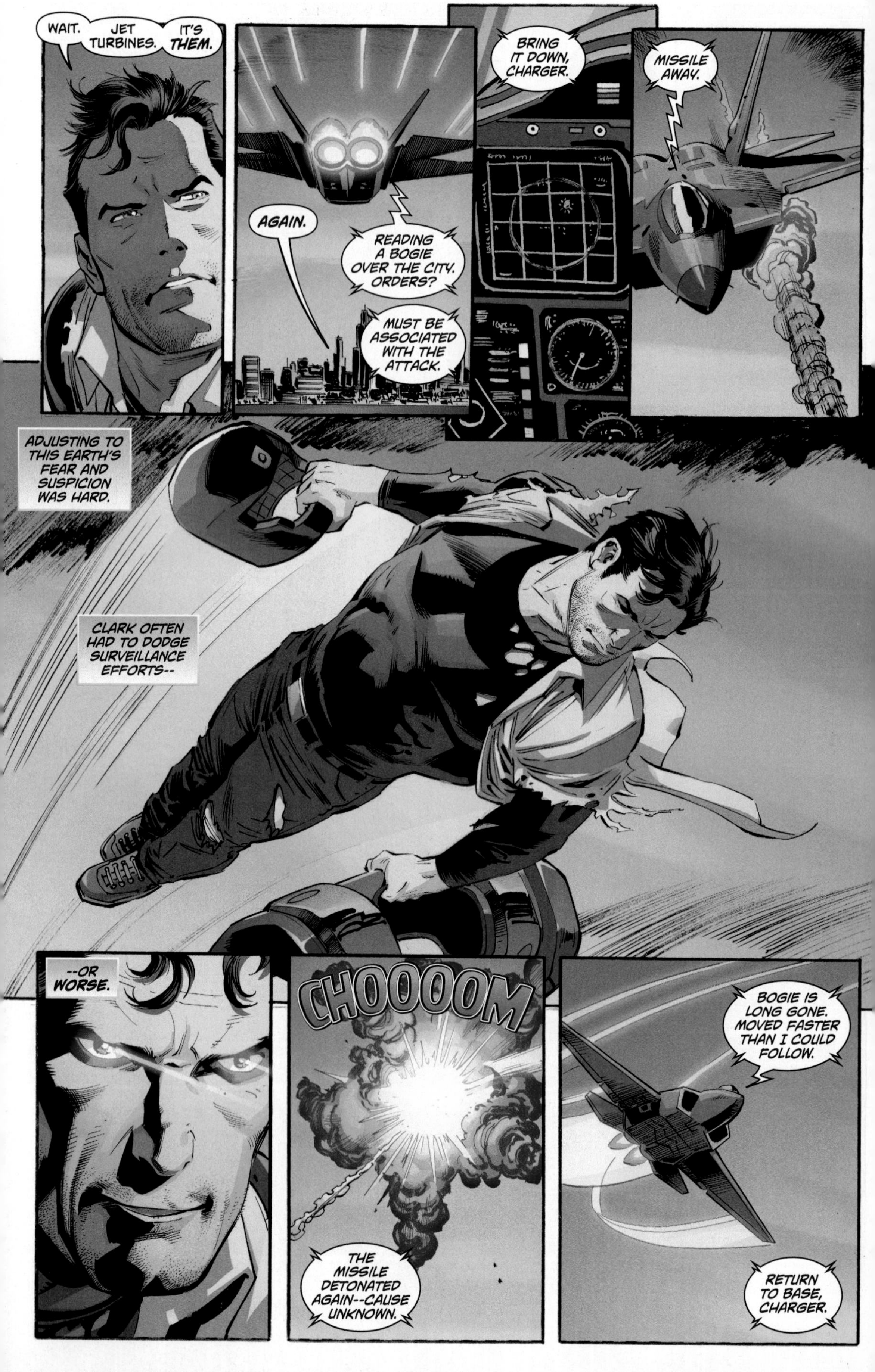
WAIT.
JET TURBINES.
IT'S THEM.
AGAIN.
READING A BOGIE OVER THE CITY. ORDERS?
MUST BE ASSOCIATED WITH THE ATTACK.
BRING IT DOWN, CHARGER.
MISSILE AWAY.
ADJUSTING TO THIS EARTH'S FEAR AND SUSPICION WAS HARD.
CLARK OFTEN HAD TO DODGE SURVEILLANCE EFFORTS--
--OR WORSE.
CHOOOOM
THE MISSILE DETONATED AGAIN--CAUSE UNKNOWN.
BOGIE IS LONG GONE. MOVED FASTER THAN I COULD FOLLOW.
RETURN TO BASE, CHARGER.

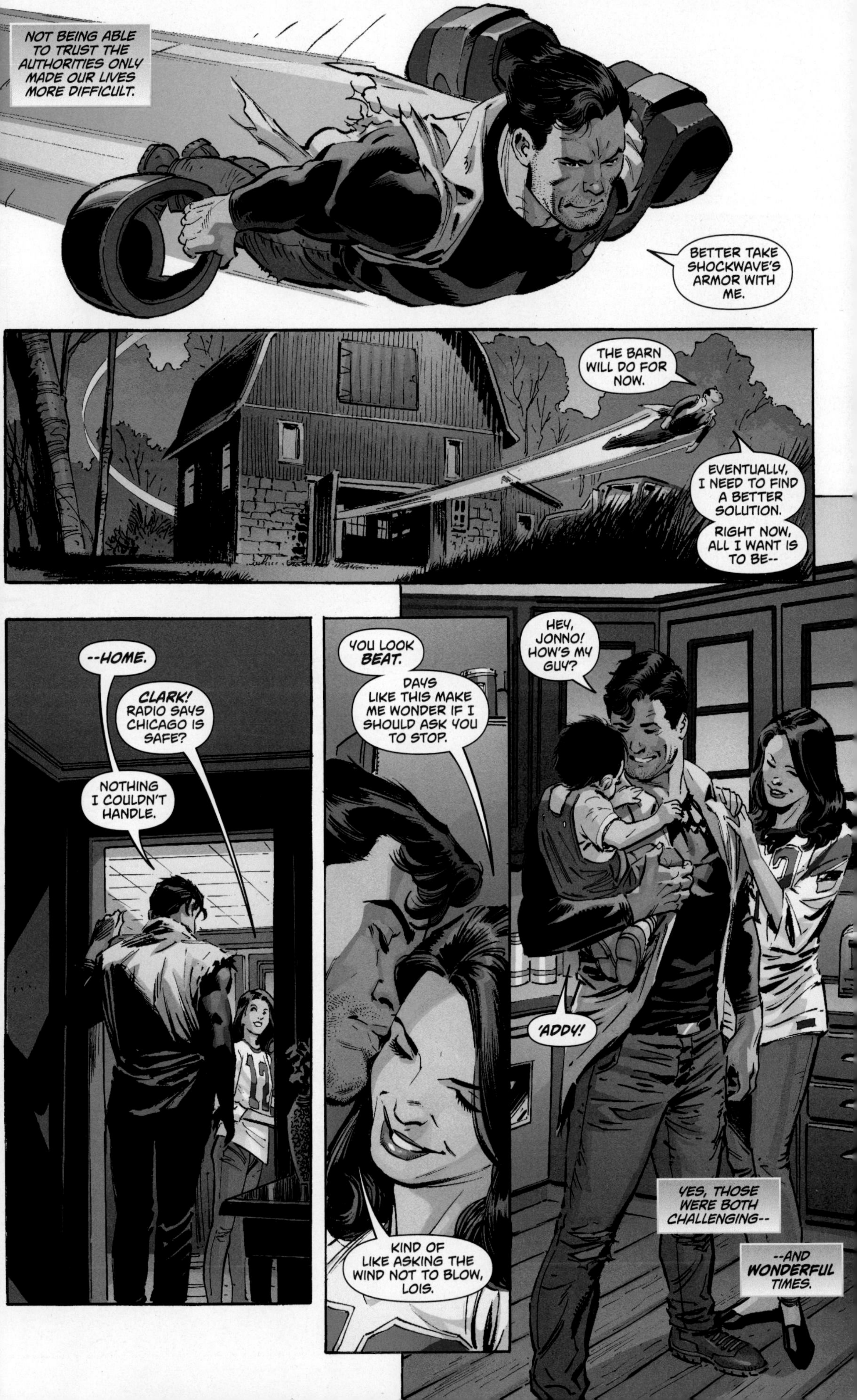
NOT BEING ABLE TO TRUST THE AUTHORITIES ONLY MADE OUR LIVES MORE DIFFICULT.
BETTER TAKE SHOCKWAVE'S ARMOR WITH ME.
THE BARN WILL DO FOR NOW.
EVENTUALLY, I NEED TO FIND A BETTER SOLUTION.
RIGHT NOW, ALL I WANT IS TO BE--
--HOME.
CLARK! RADIO SAYS CHICAGO IS SAFE?
NOTHING I COULDN'T HANDLE.
YOU LOOK BEAT.
DAYS LIKE THIS MAKE ME WONDER IF I SHOULD ASK YOU TO STOP.
KIND OF LIKE ASKING THE WIND NOT TO BLOW, LOIS.
HEY, JONNO! HOW'S MY GUY?
'ADDY!
YES, THOSE WERE BOTH CHALLENGING--
--AND WONDERFUL TIMES.

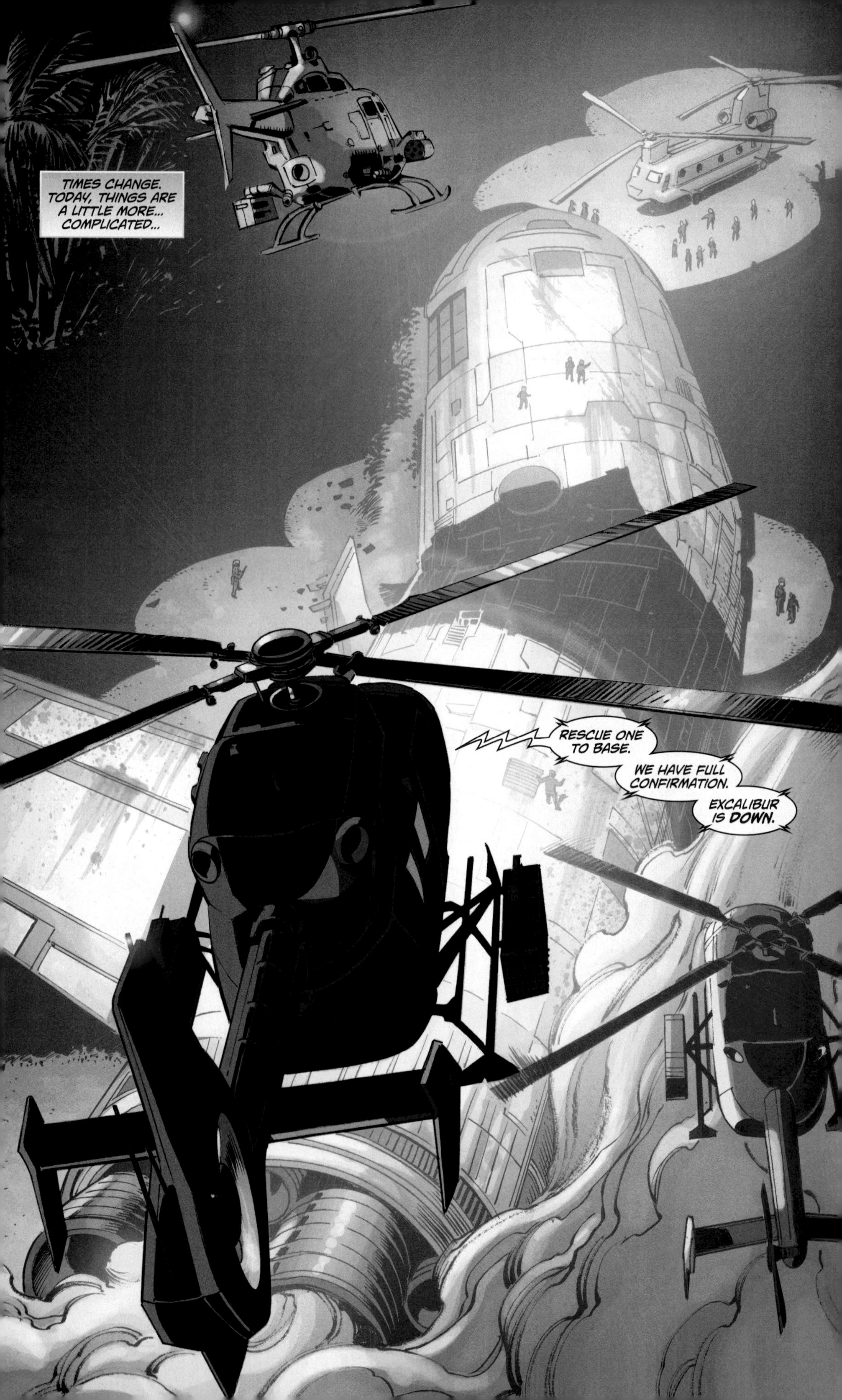
TIMES CHANGE. TODAY, THINGS ARE A LITTLE MORE... COMPLICATED...
RESCUE ONE TO BASE.
WE HAVE FULL CONFIRMATION.
EXCALIBUR IS DOWN.

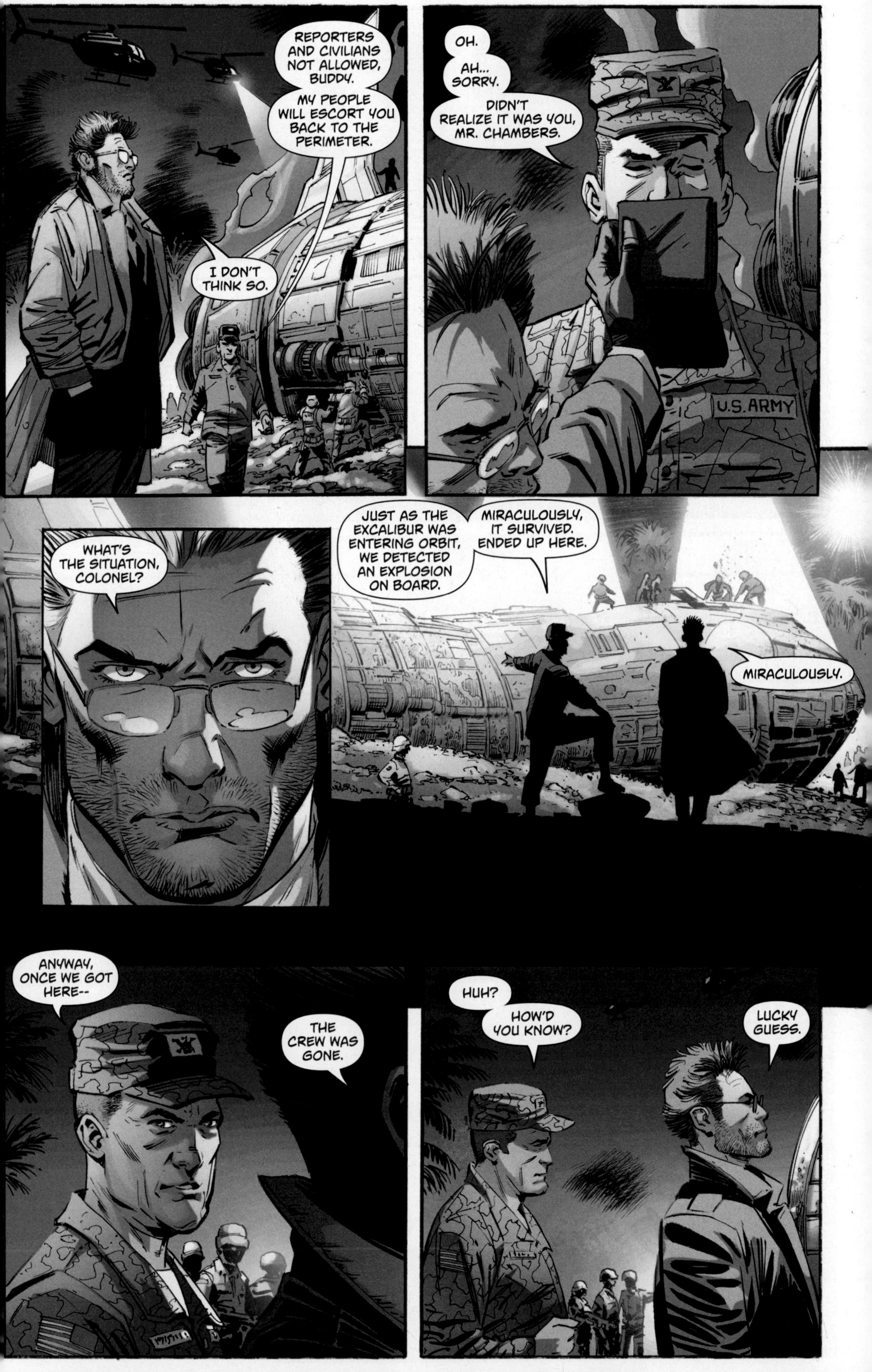
REPORTERS AND CIVILIANS NOT ALLOWED, BUDDY.
MY PEOPLE WILL ESCORT YOU BACK TO THE PERIMETER.
I DON'T THINK SO.
OH.
AH... SORRY.
DIDN'T REALIZE IT WAS YOU, MR. CHAMBERS.
U.S. ARMY
WHAT'S THE SITUATION, COLONEL?
JUST AS THE EXCALIBUR WAS ENTERING ORBIT, WE DETECTED AN EXPLOSION ON BOARD.
MIRACULOUSLY, IT SURVIVED. ENDED UP HERE.
MIRACULOUSLY.
ANYWAY, ONCE WE GOT HERE--
THE CREW WAS GONE.
HUH?
HOW'D YOU KNOW?
LUCKY GUESS.

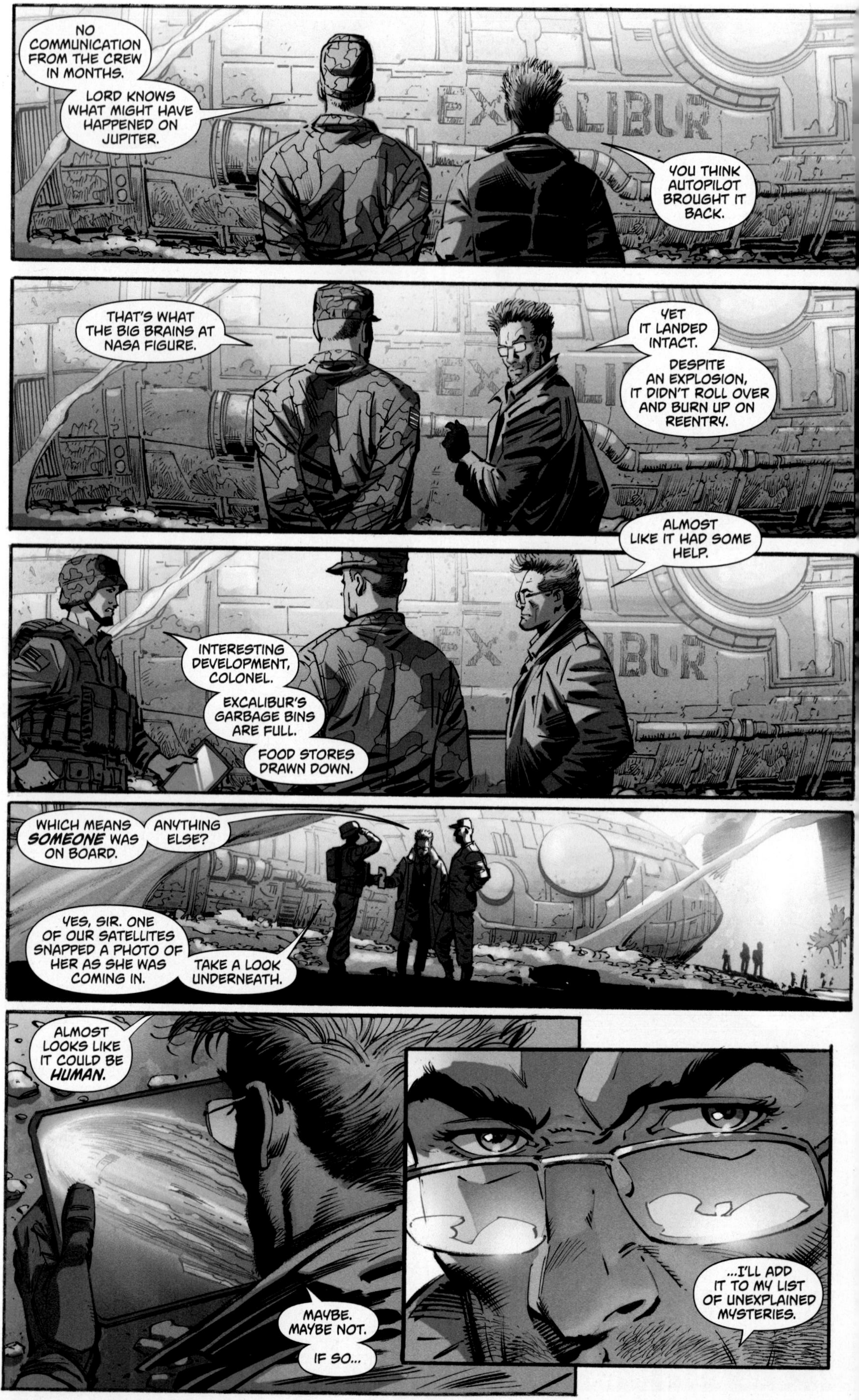
NO COMMUNICATION FROM THE CREW IN MONTHS.
LORD KNOWS WHAT MIGHT HAVE HAPPENED ON JUPITER.
EXCALIBUR
YOU THINK AUTOPILOT BROUGHT IT BACK.
THAT'S WHAT THE BIG BRAINS AT NASA FIGURE.
YET IT LANDED INTACT.
DESPITE AN EXPLOSION, IT DIDN'T ROLL OVER AND BURN UP ON REENTRY.
ALMOST LIKE IT HAD SOME HELP.
INTERESTING DEVELOPMENT, COLONEL.
EXCALIBUR'S GARBAGE BINS ARE FULL.
FOOD STORES DRAWN DOWN.
WHICH MEANS *SOMEONE* WAS ON BOARD.
ANYTHING ELSE?
YES, SIR. ONE OF OUR SATELLITES SNAPPED A PHOTO OF HER AS SHE WAS COMING IN.
TAKE A LOOK UNDERNEATH.
ALMOST LOOKS LIKE IT COULD BE *HUMAN*.
MAYBE. MAYBE NOT.
IF SO...
...I'LL ADD IT TO MY LIST OF UNEXPLAINED MYSTERIES.

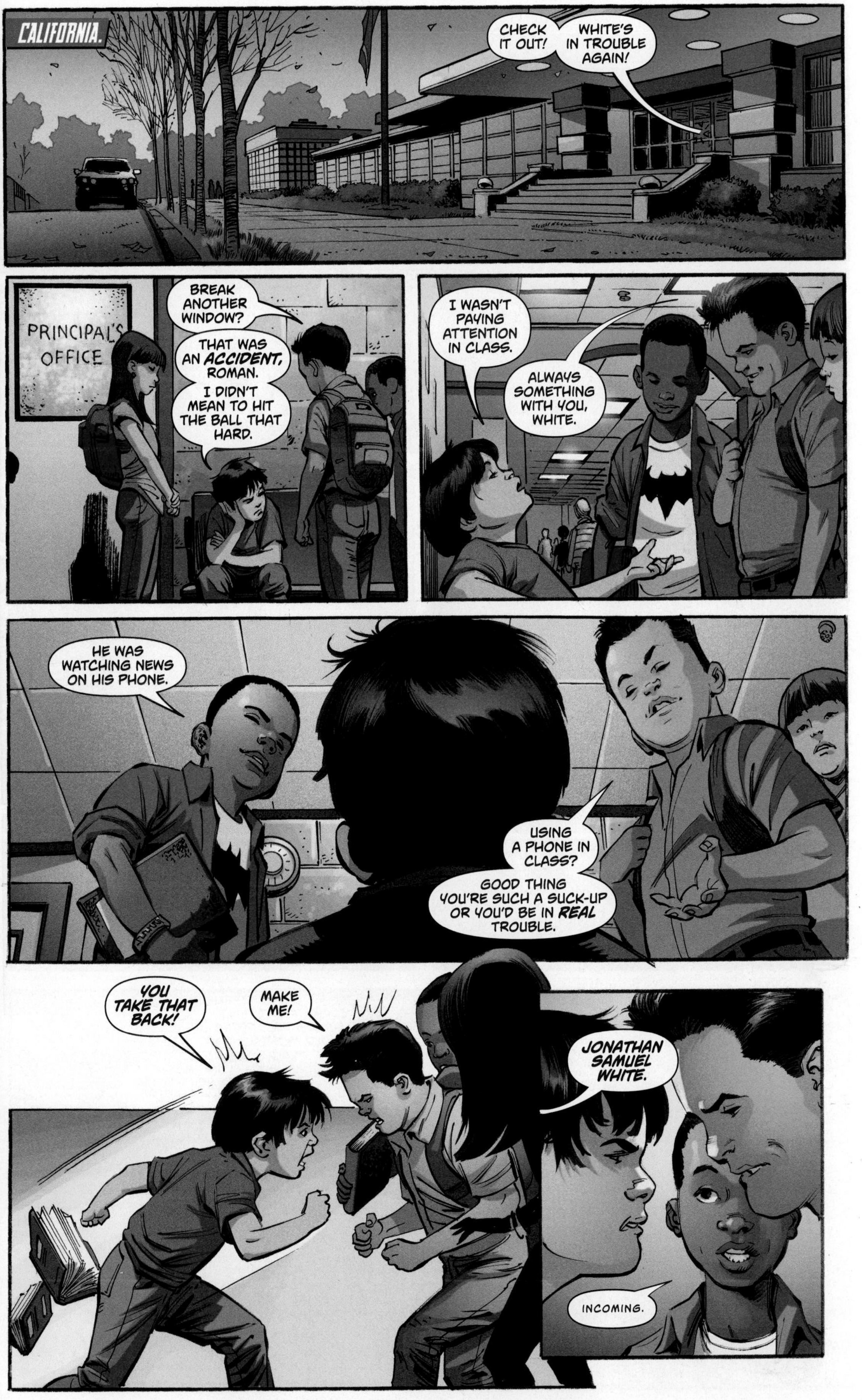
CALIFORNIA.
CHECK IT OUT!
WHITE'S IN TROUBLE AGAIN!
PRINCIPAL'S OFFICE
BREAK ANOTHER WINDOW?
THAT WAS AN *ACCIDENT,* ROMAN.
I DIDN'T MEAN TO HIT THE BALL THAT HARD.
I WASN'T PAYING ATTENTION IN CLASS.
ALWAYS SOMETHING WITH YOU, WHITE.
HE WAS WATCHING NEWS ON HIS PHONE.
USING A PHONE IN CLASS?
GOOD THING YOU'RE SUCH A SUCK-UP OR YOU'D BE IN *REAL* TROUBLE.
YOU TAKE THAT BACK!
MAKE ME!
JONATHAN SAMUEL WHITE.
INCOMING.

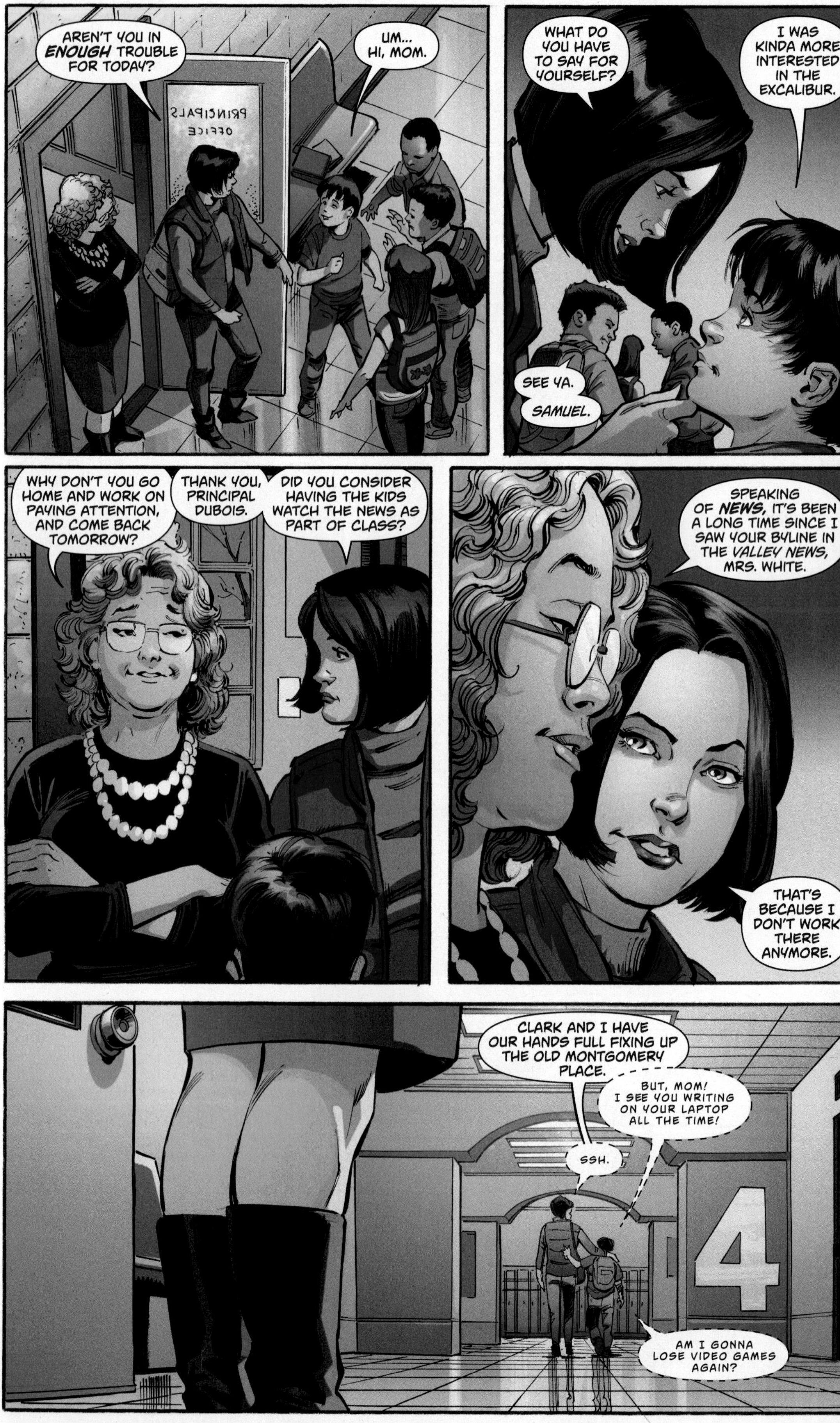
AREN'T YOU IN ENOUGH TROUBLE FOR TODAY?
PRINCIPALS OFFICE
UM... HI, MOM.
WHAT DO YOU HAVE TO SAY FOR YOURSELF?
I WAS KINDA MORE INTERESTED IN THE EXCALIBUR.
SEE YA.
SAMUEL.
WHY DON'T YOU GO HOME AND WORK ON PAYING ATTENTION, AND COME BACK TOMORROW?
THANK YOU, PRINCIPAL DUBOIS.
DID YOU CONSIDER HAVING THE KIDS WATCH THE NEWS AS PART OF CLASS?
SPEAKING OF NEWS, IT'S BEEN A LONG TIME SINCE I SAW YOUR BYLINE IN THE VALLEY NEWS, MRS. WHITE.
THAT'S BECAUSE I DON'T WORK THERE ANYMORE.
CLARK AND I HAVE OUR HANDS FULL FIXING UP THE OLD MONTGOMERY PLACE.
BUT, MOM! I SEE YOU WRITING ON YOUR LAPTOP ALL THE TIME!
SSH.
4
AM I GONNA LOSE VIDEO GAMES AGAIN?

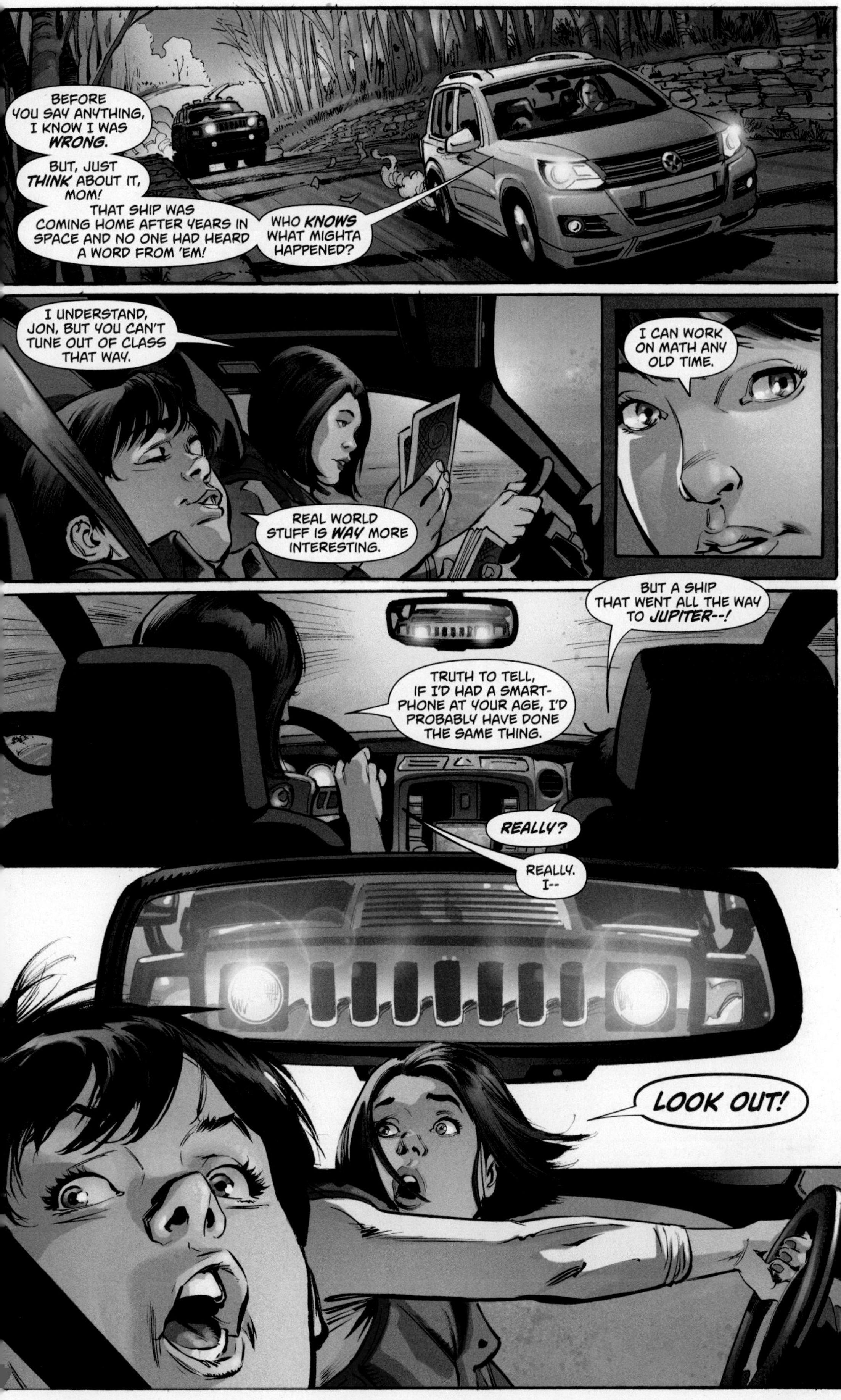
BEFORE YOU SAY ANYTHING, I KNOW I WAS WRONG.
BUT, JUST THINK ABOUT IT, MOM!
THAT SHIP WAS COMING HOME AFTER YEARS IN SPACE AND NO ONE HAD HEARD A WORD FROM 'EM!
WHO KNOWS WHAT MIGHTA HAPPENED?
I UNDERSTAND, JON, BUT YOU CAN'T TUNE OUT OF CLASS THAT WAY.
REAL WORLD STUFF IS WAY MORE INTERESTING.
I CAN WORK ON MATH ANY OLD TIME.
BUT A SHIP THAT WENT ALL THE WAY TO JUPITER--!
TRUTH TO TELL, IF I'D HAD A SMART-PHONE AT YOUR AGE, I'D PROBABLY HAVE DONE THE SAME THING.
REALLY?
REALLY. I--
LOOK OUT!

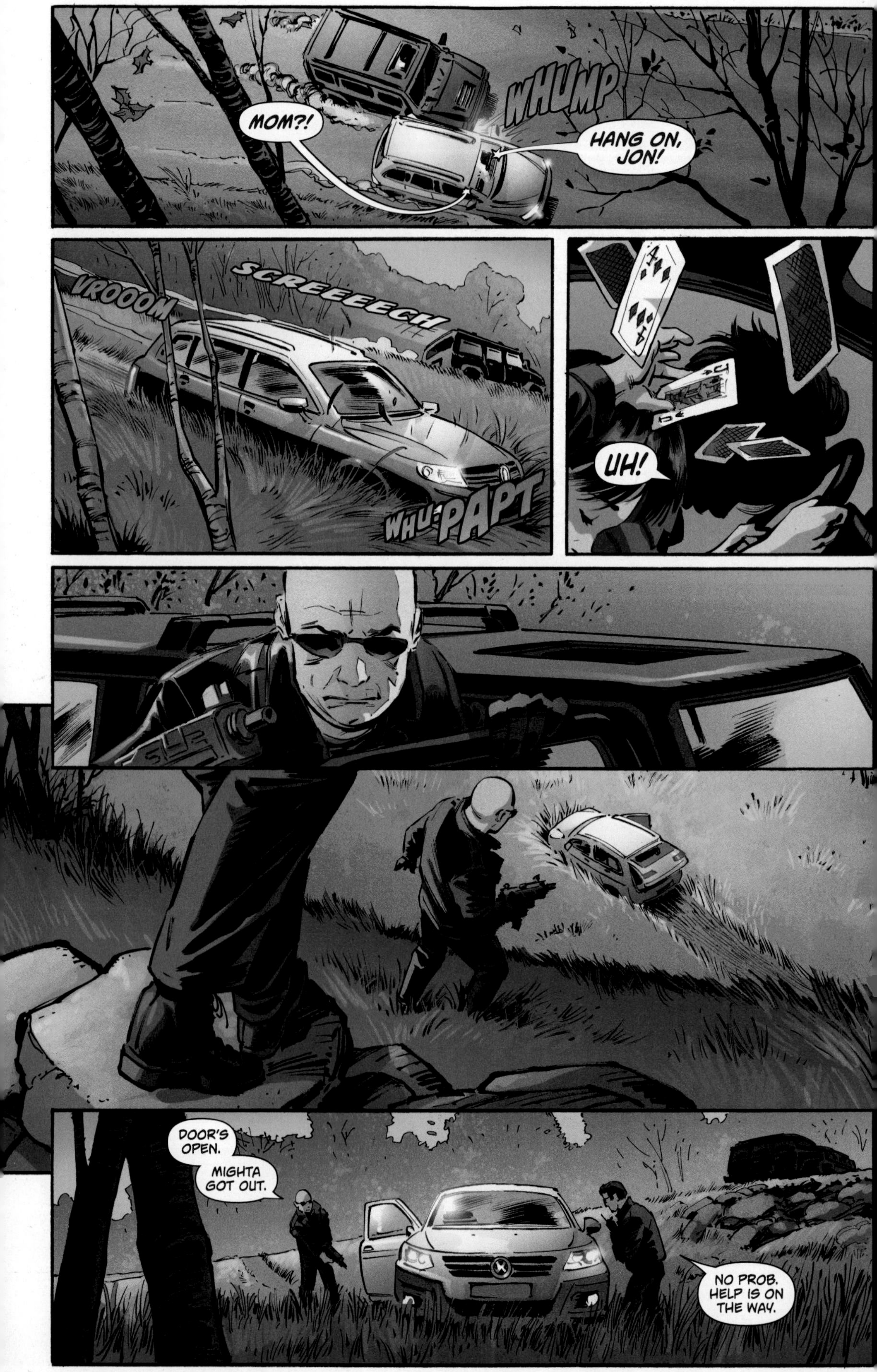
WHUMP
MOM?!
HANG ON, JON!
VROOOM
SCREEEEECH
WHU-PAPT
UH!
DOOR'S OPEN.
MIGHTA GOT OUT.
NO PROB. HELP IS ON THE WAY.

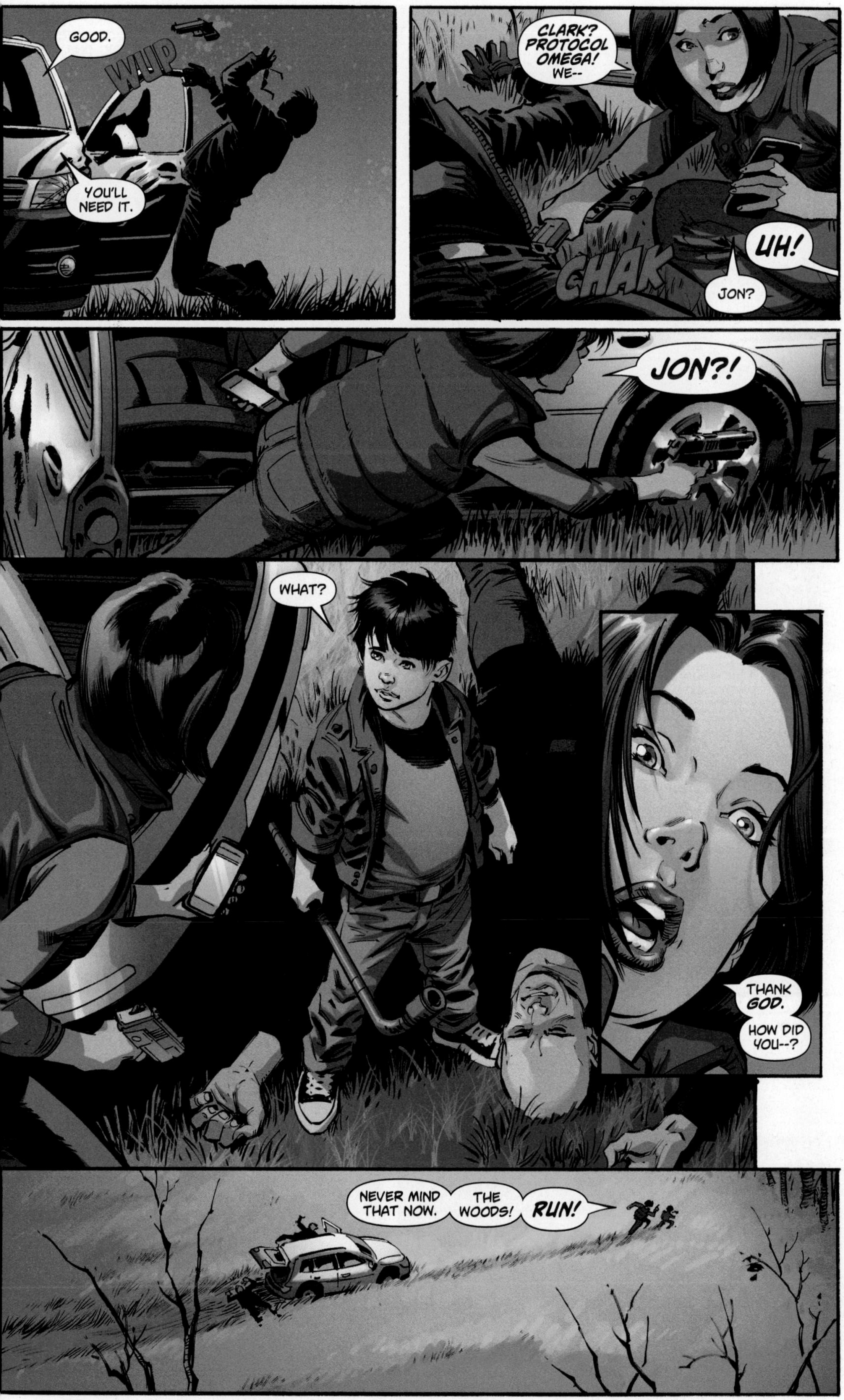
GOOD.
WUP
YOU'LL NEED IT.
CLARK? PROTOCOL OMEGA! WE--
CHAK
UH!
JON?
JON?!
WHAT?
THANK GOD.
HOW DID YOU--?
NEVER MIND THAT NOW.
THE WOODS!
RUN!

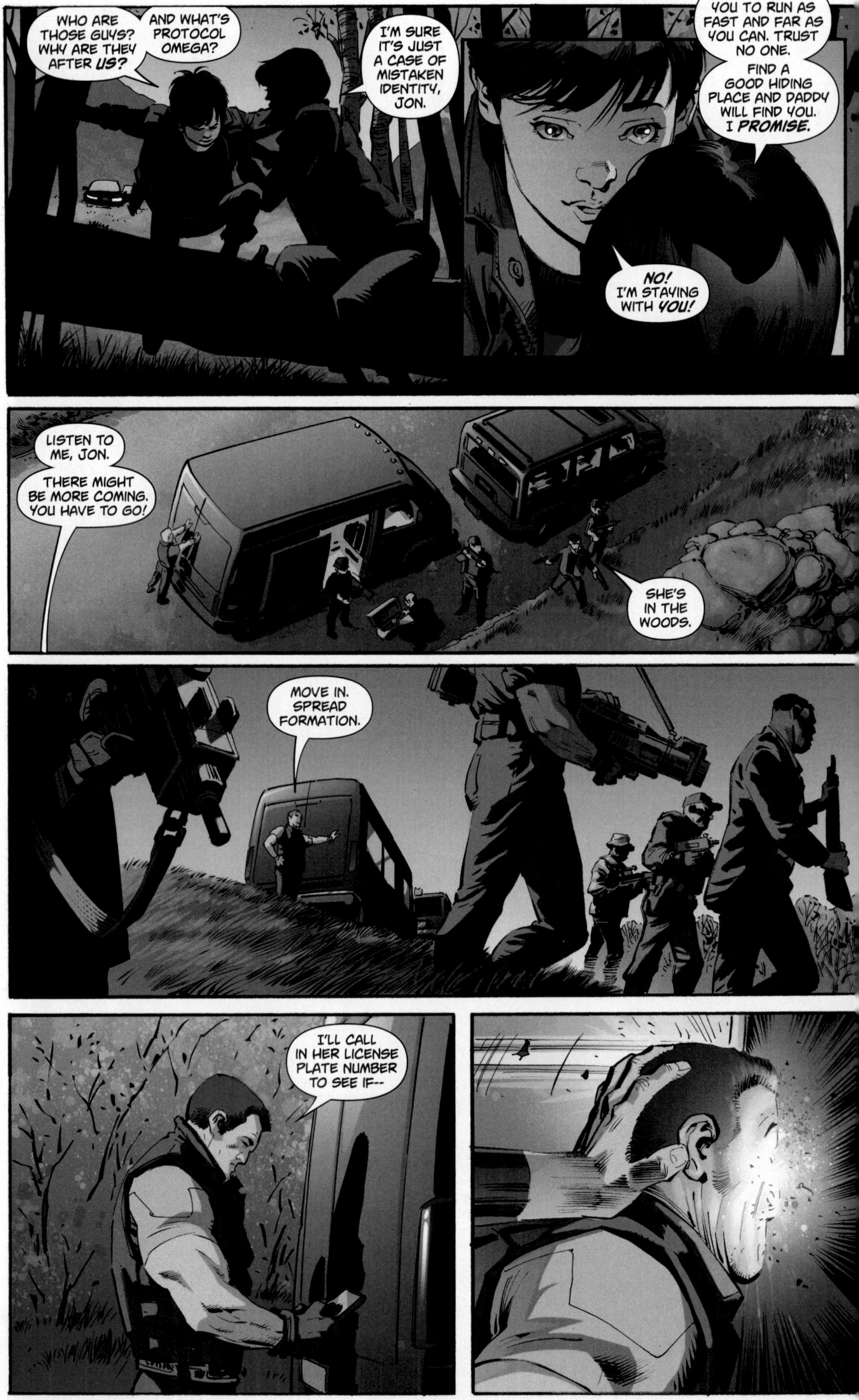

WHO ARE THOSE GUYS? WHY ARE THEY AFTER *US?*
AND WHAT'S PROTOCOL OMEGA?
I'M SURE IT'S JUST A CASE OF MISTAKEN IDENTITY, JON.
NOW, I WANT YOU TO RUN AS FAST AND FAR AS YOU CAN. TRUST NO ONE.
FIND A GOOD HIDING PLACE AND DADDY WILL FIND YOU. I *PROMISE.*
NO! I'M STAYING WITH *YOU!*
LISTEN TO ME, JON.
THERE MIGHT BE MORE COMING. YOU HAVE TO GO!
SHE'S IN THE WOODS.
MOVE IN. SPREAD FORMATION.
I'LL CALL IN HER LICENSE PLATE NUMBER TO SEE IF--

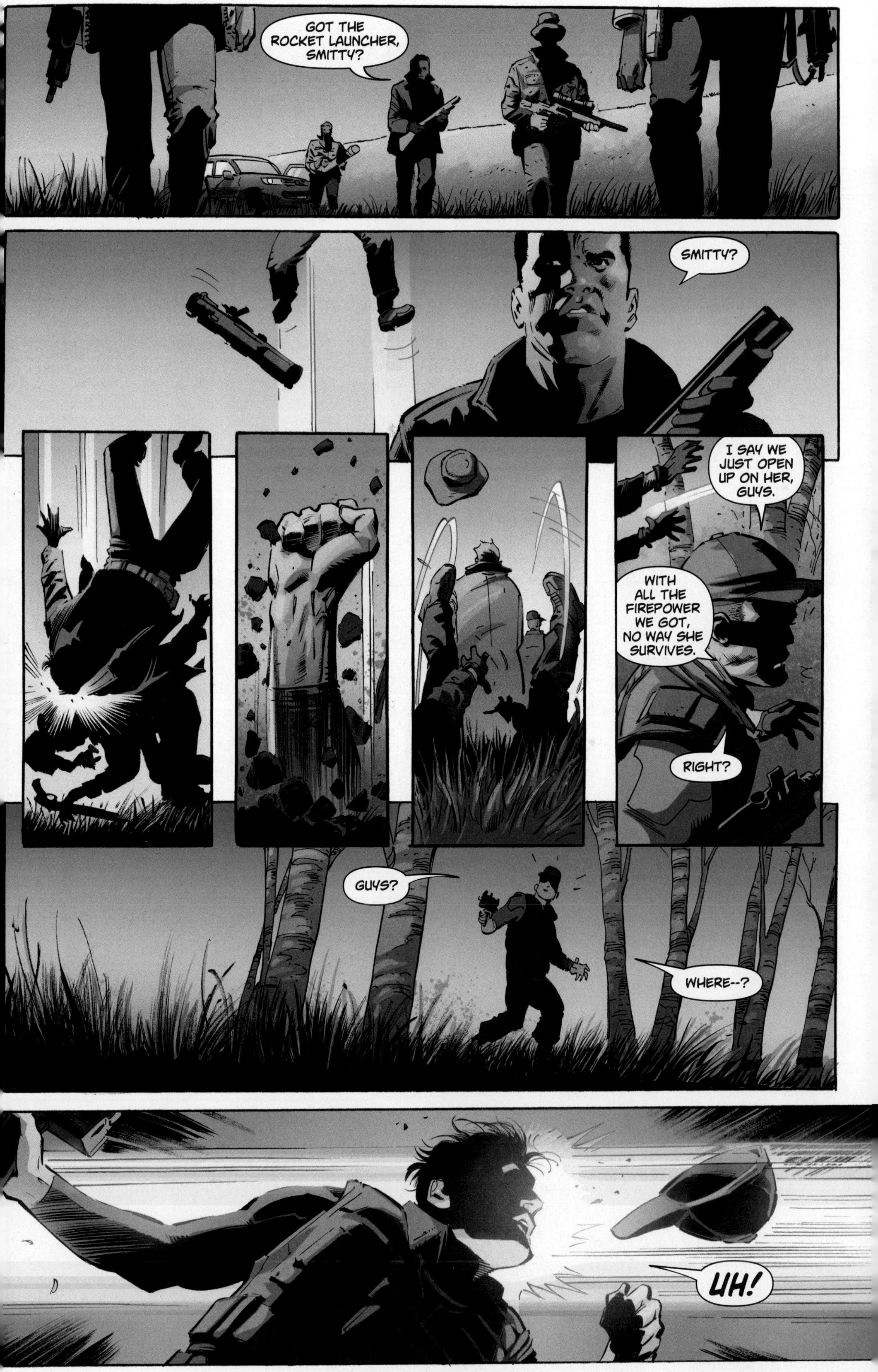
GOT THE ROCKET LAUNCHER, SMITTY?
SMITTY?
I SAY WE JUST OPEN UP ON HER, GUYS.
WITH ALL THE FIREPOWER WE GOT, NO WAY SHE SURVIVES.
RIGHT?
GUYS?
WHERE--?
UH!

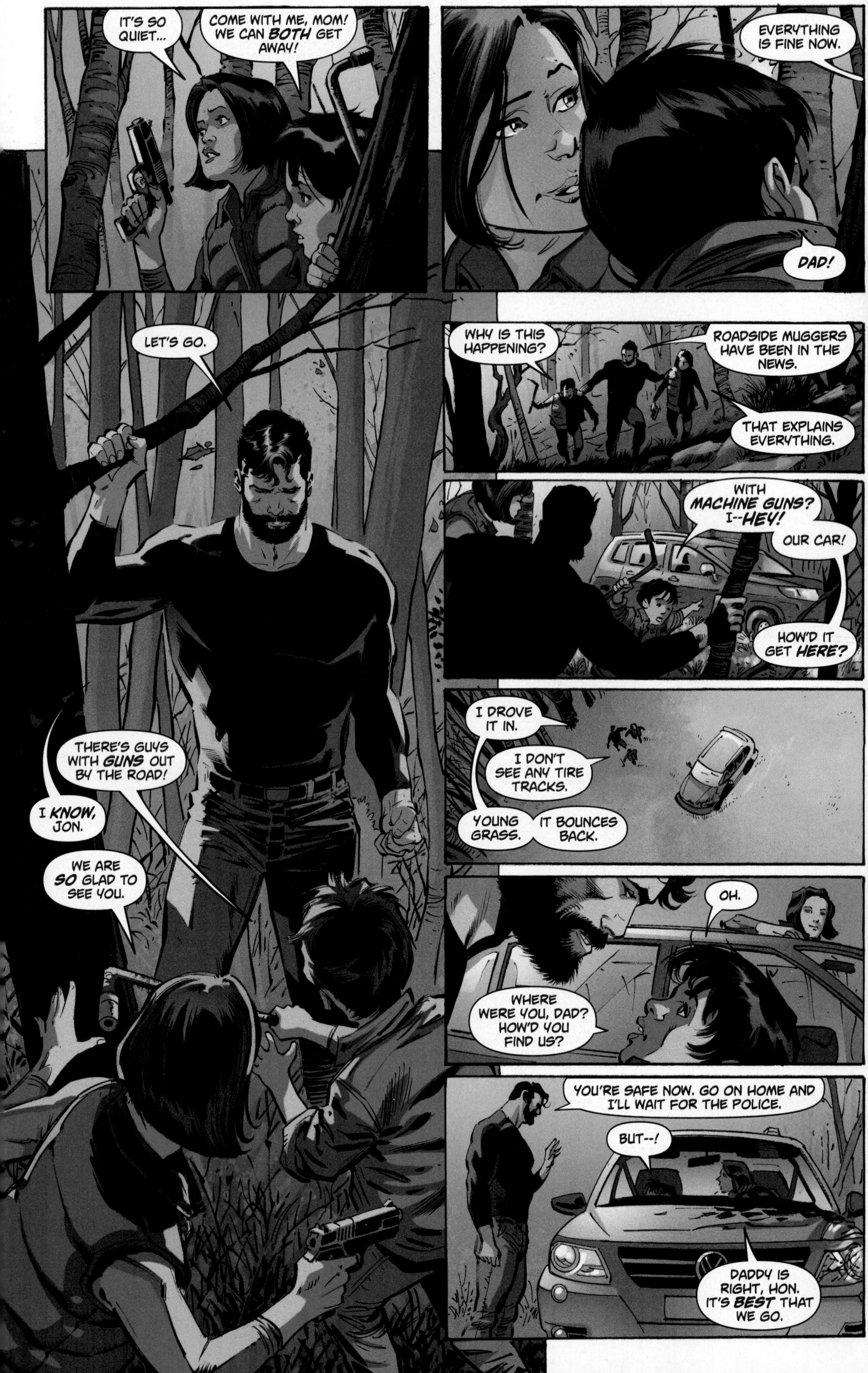
IT'S SO QUIET...
COME WITH ME, MOM! WE CAN BOTH GET AWAY!
EVERYTHING IS FINE NOW.
DAD!
LET'S GO.
THERE'S GUYS WITH GUNS OUT BY THE ROAD!
I KNOW, JON.
WE ARE SO GLAD TO SEE YOU.
WHY IS THIS HAPPENING?
ROADSIDE MUGGERS HAVE BEEN IN THE NEWS.
THAT EXPLAINS EVERYTHING.
WITH MACHINE GUNS? I--HEY!
OUR CAR!
HOW'D IT GET HERE?
I DROVE IT IN.
I DON'T SEE ANY TIRE TRACKS.
YOUNG GRASS.
IT BOUNCES BACK.
OH.
WHERE WERE YOU, DAD? HOW'D YOU FIND US?
YOU'RE SAFE NOW. GO ON HOME AND I'LL WAIT FOR THE POLICE.
BUT--!
DADDY IS RIGHT, HON. IT'S BEST THAT WE GO.

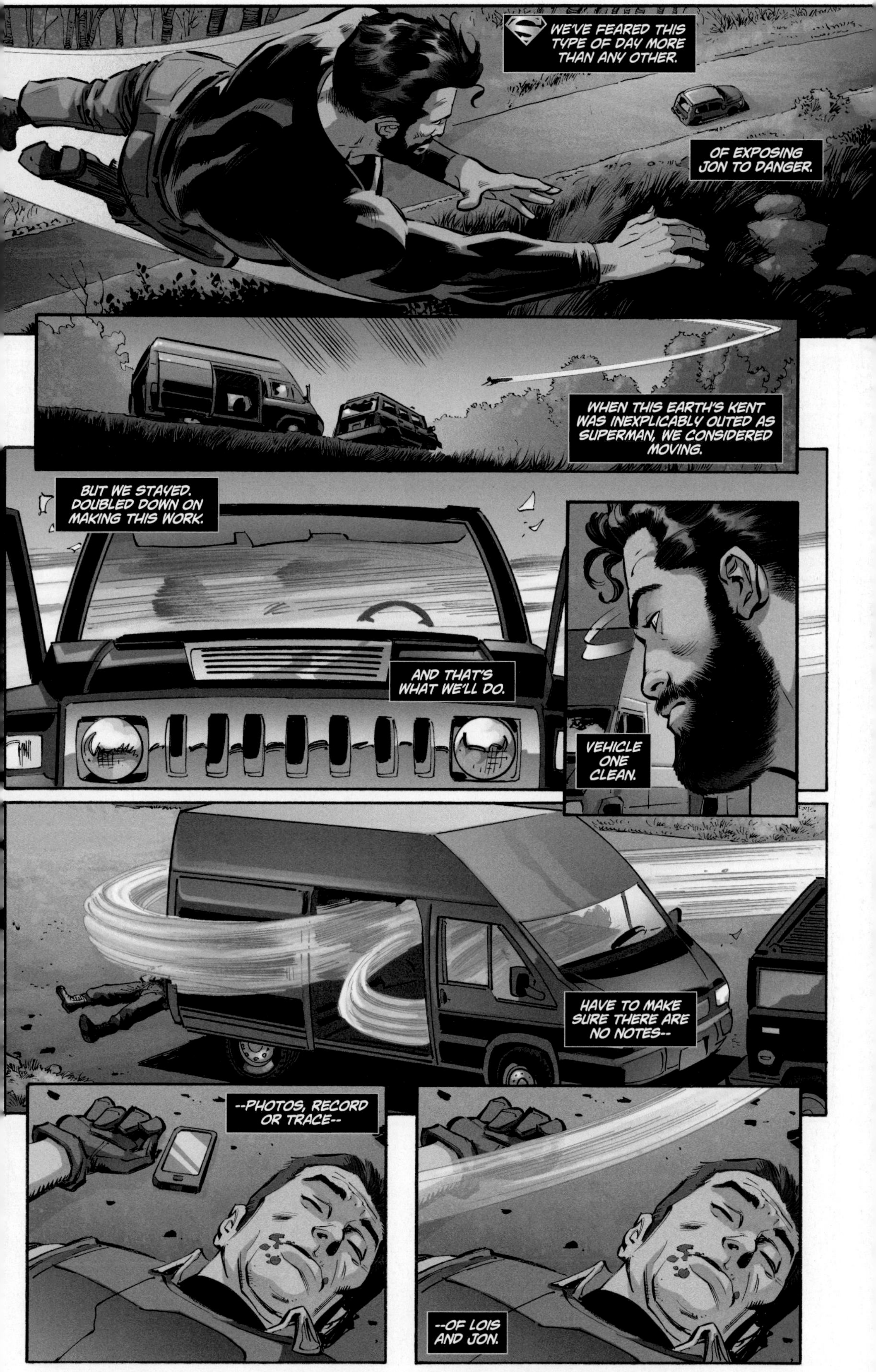
WE'VE FEARED THIS TYPE OF DAY MORE THAN ANY OTHER.
OF EXPOSING JON TO DANGER.
WHEN THIS EARTH'S KENT WAS INEXPLICABLY OUTED AS SUPERMAN, WE CONSIDERED MOVING.
BUT WE STAYED. DOUBLED DOWN ON MAKING THIS WORK.
AND THAT'S WHAT WE'LL DO.
VEHICLE ONE CLEAN.
HAVE TO MAKE SURE THERE ARE NO NOTES--
--PHOTOS, RECORD OR TRACE--
--OF LOIS AND JON.

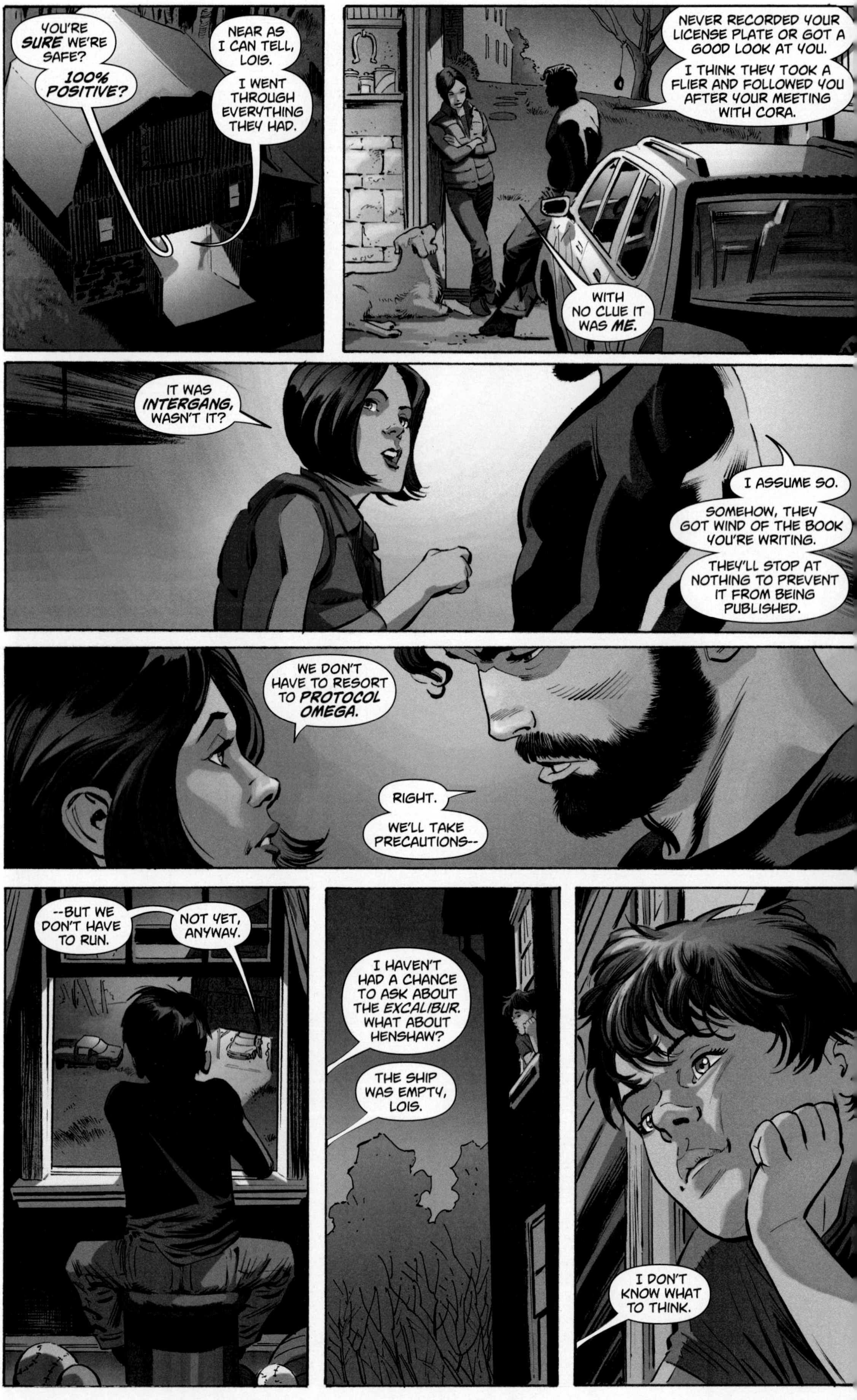

YOU'RE SURE WE'RE SAFE? 100% POSITIVE?
NEAR AS I CAN TELL, LOIS.
I WENT THROUGH EVERYTHING THEY HAD.
NEVER RECORDED YOUR LICENSE PLATE OR GOT A GOOD LOOK AT YOU.
I THINK THEY TOOK A FLIER AND FOLLOWED YOU AFTER YOUR MEETING WITH CORA.
WITH NO CLUE IT WAS ME.
IT WAS INTERGANG, WASN'T IT?
I ASSUME SO.
SOMEHOW, THEY GOT WIND OF THE BOOK YOU'RE WRITING.
THEY'LL STOP AT NOTHING TO PREVENT IT FROM BEING PUBLISHED.
WE DON'T HAVE TO RESORT TO PROTOCOL OMEGA.
RIGHT.
WE'LL TAKE PRECAUTIONS--
--BUT WE DON'T HAVE TO RUN.
NOT YET, ANYWAY.
I HAVEN'T HAD A CHANCE TO ASK ABOUT THE EXCALIBUR. WHAT ABOUT HENSHAW?
THE SHIP WAS EMPTY, LOIS.
I DON'T KNOW WHAT TO THINK.

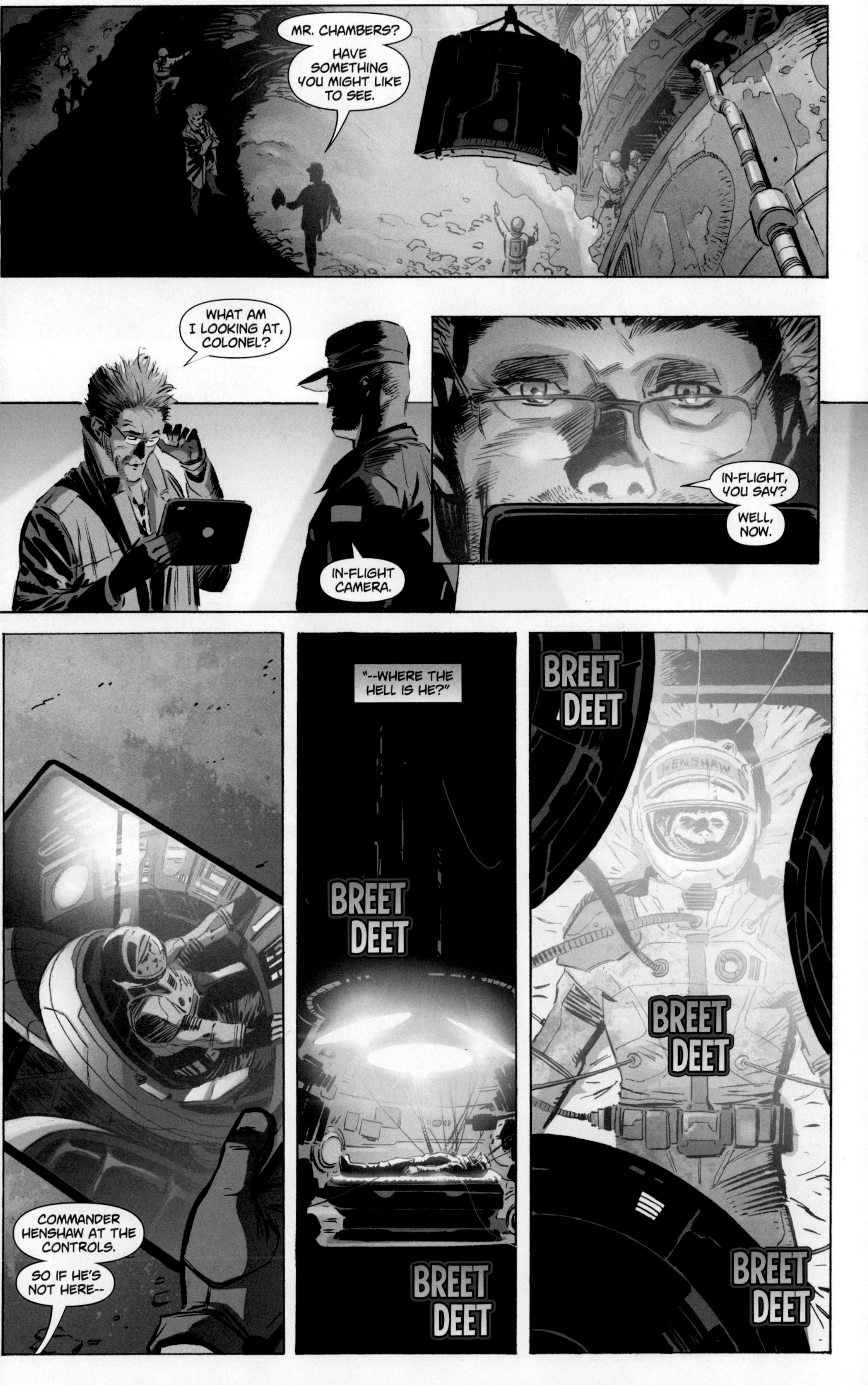
MR. CHAMBERS?
HAVE SOMETHING YOU MIGHT LIKE TO SEE.
WHAT AM I LOOKING AT, COLONEL?
IN-FLIGHT CAMERA.
IN-FLIGHT, YOU SAY?
WELL, NOW.
COMMANDER HENSHAW AT THE CONTROLS.
SO IF HE'S NOT HERE--
"--WHERE THE HELL IS HE?"
BREET DEET
BREET DEET
BREET DEET
HENSHAW
BREET DEET
BREET DEET

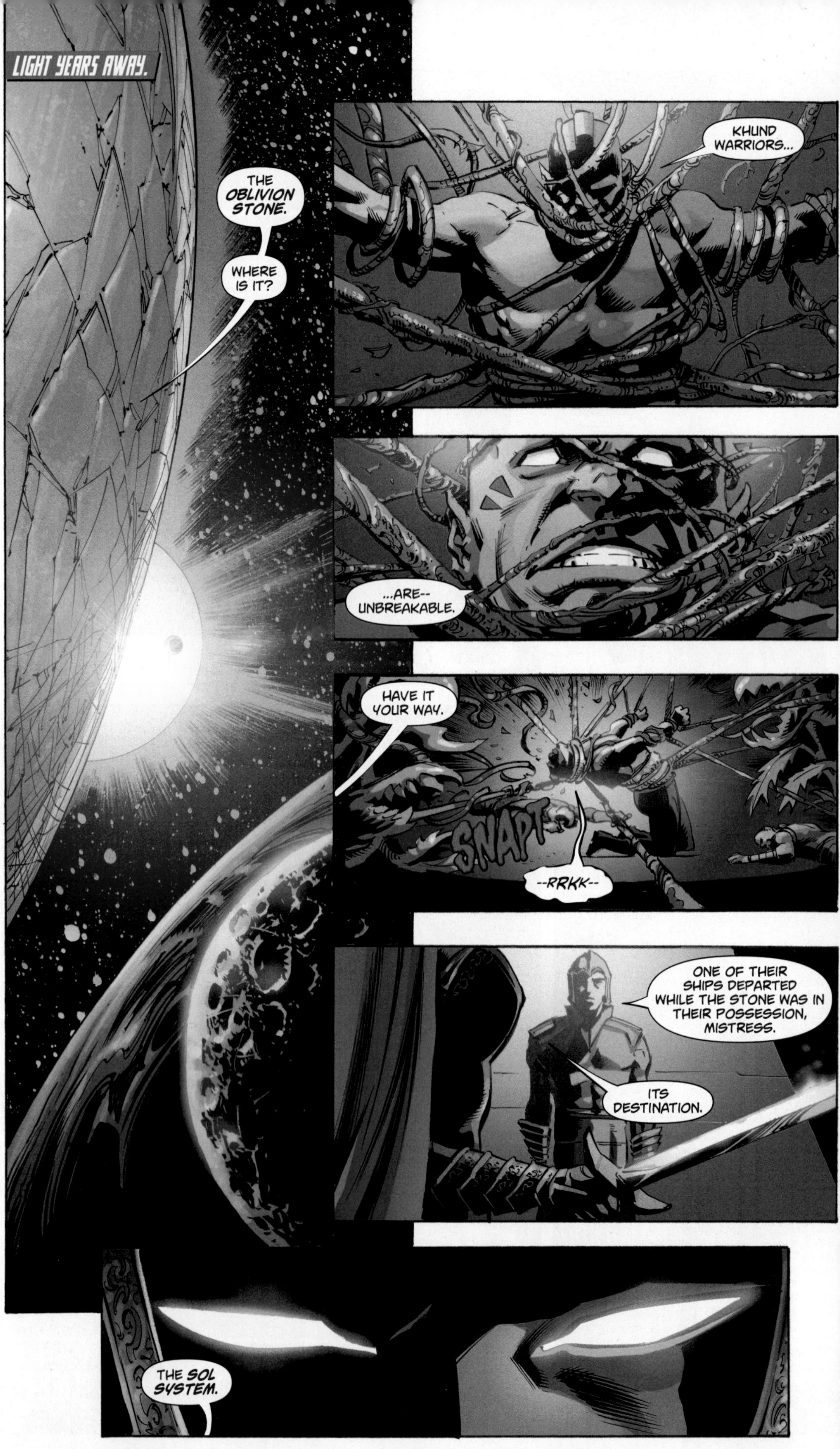
LIGHT YEARS AWAY.
THE OBLIVION STONE.
WHERE IS IT?
KHUND WARRIORS...
...ARE-- UNBREAKABLE.
HAVE IT YOUR WAY.
SNAP
--RRKK--
ONE OF THEIR SHIPS DEPARTED WHILE THE STONE WAS IN THEIR POSSESSION, MISTRESS.
ITS DESTINATION.
THE SOL SYSTEM.

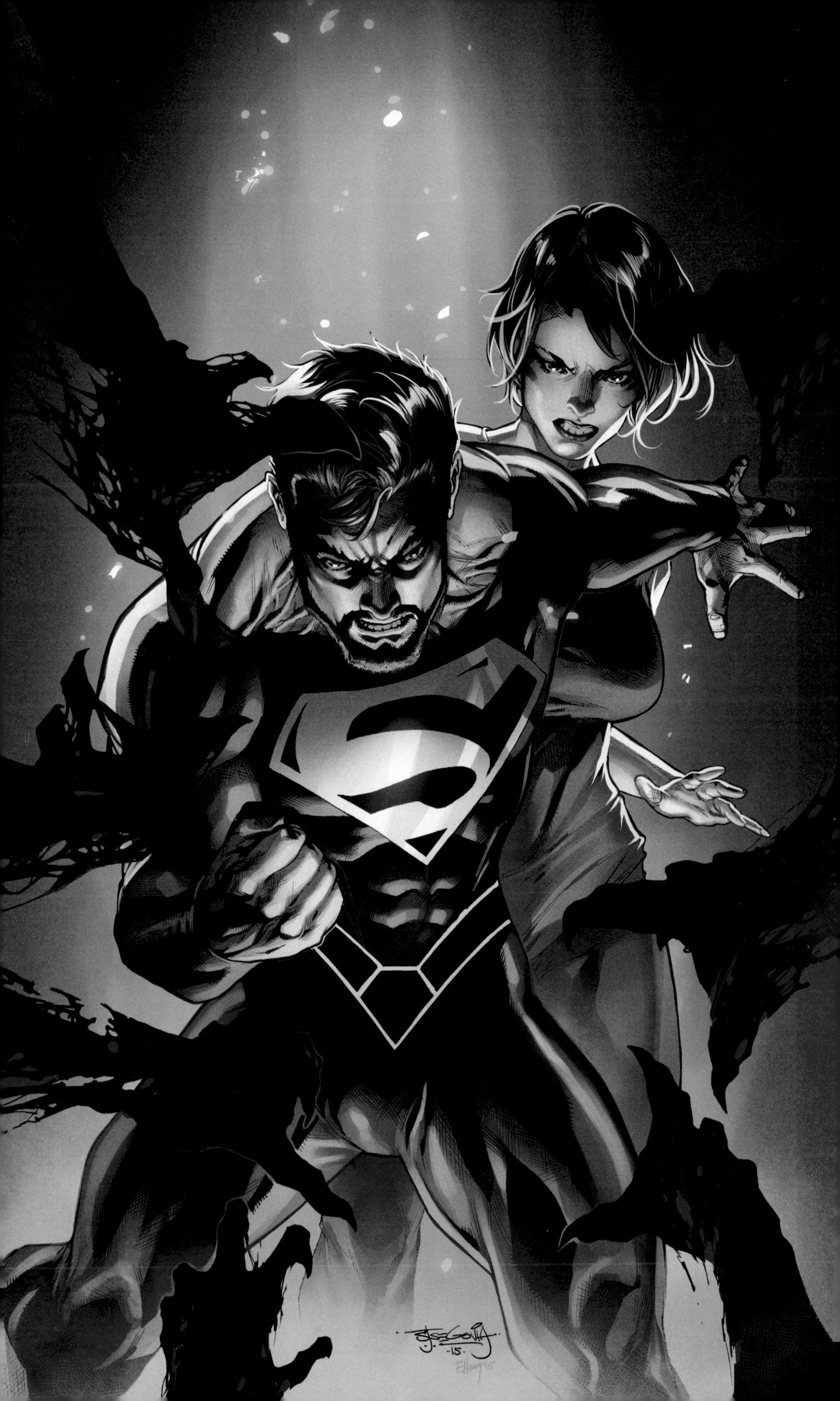

ARRIVAL: PART III

DAN JURGENS writer **LEE WEEKS** penciller **SCOTT HANNA SERGIO CARIELLO LEE WEEKS** inkers **BRAD ANDERSON** colorist **A LARGER WORLD STUDIOS** letterer
STEPHEN SEGOVIA ELLERY SANTOS cover artists

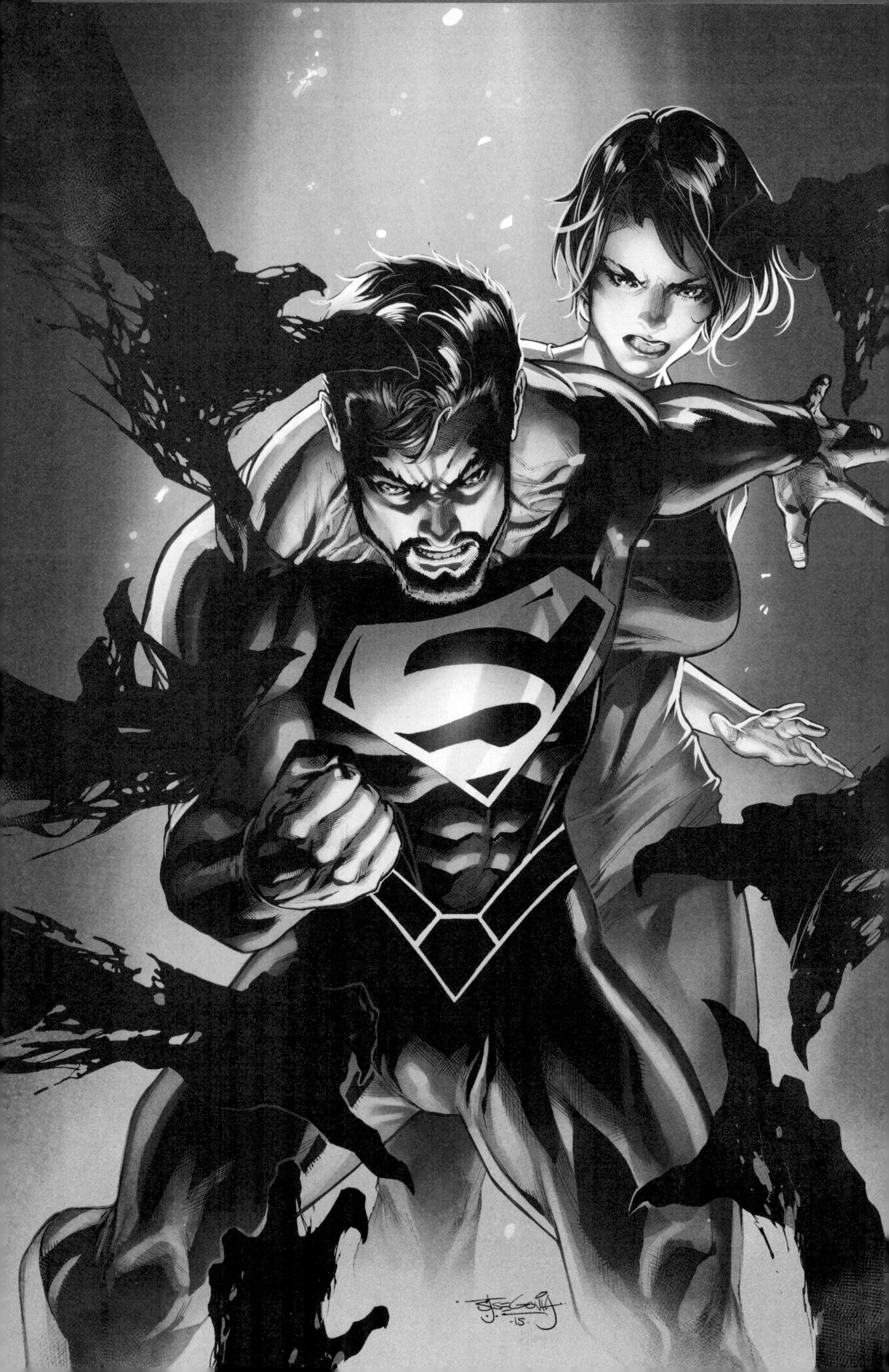

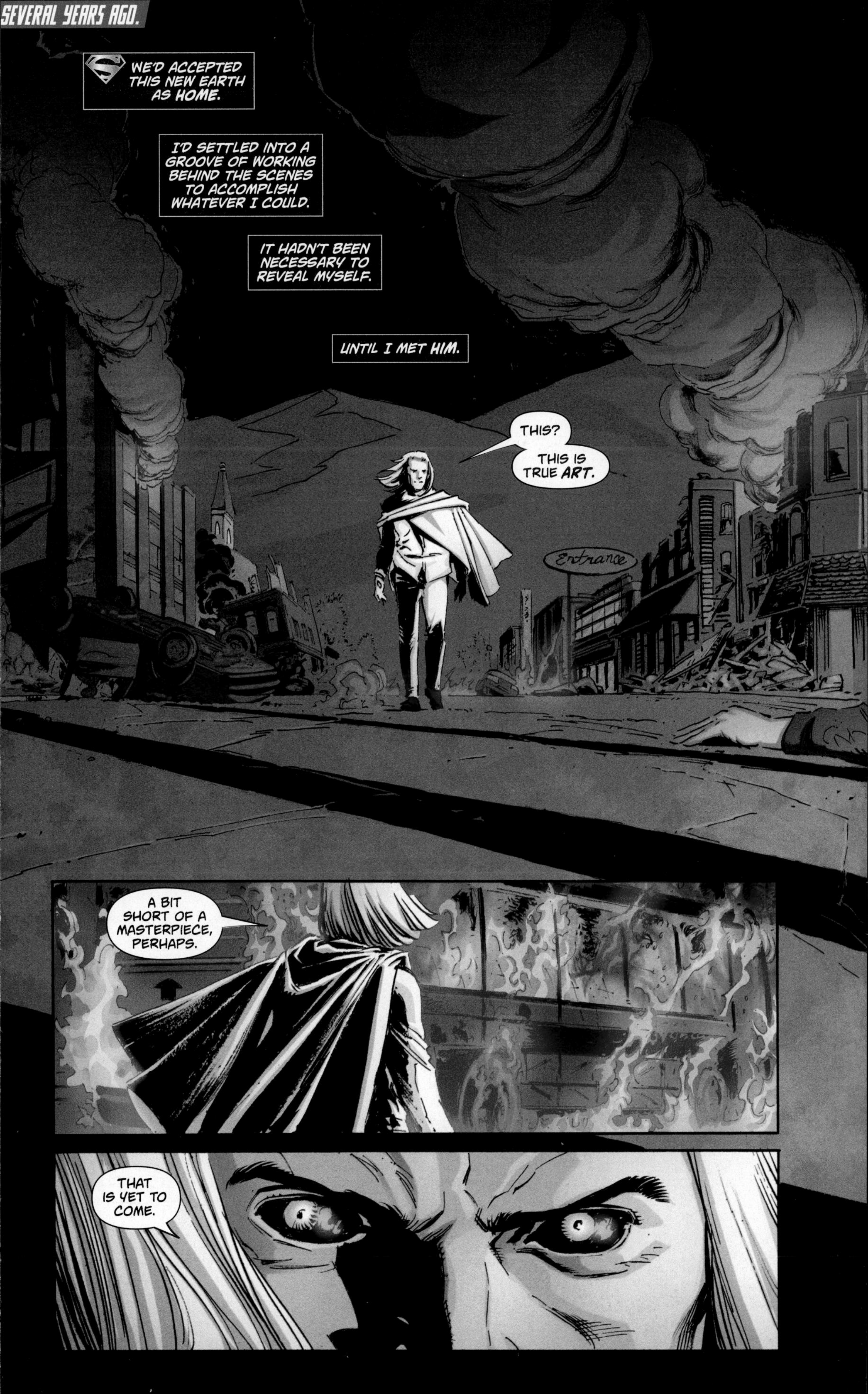
SEVERAL YEARS AGO.
WE'D ACCEPTED THIS NEW EARTH AS HOME.
I'D SETTLED INTO A GROOVE OF WORKING BEHIND THE SCENES TO ACCOMPLISH WHATEVER I COULD.
IT HADN'T BEEN NECESSARY TO REVEAL MYSELF.
UNTIL I MET HIM.
THIS?
THIS IS TRUE ART.
Entrance
A BIT SHORT OF A MASTERPIECE, PERHAPS.
THAT IS YET TO COME.

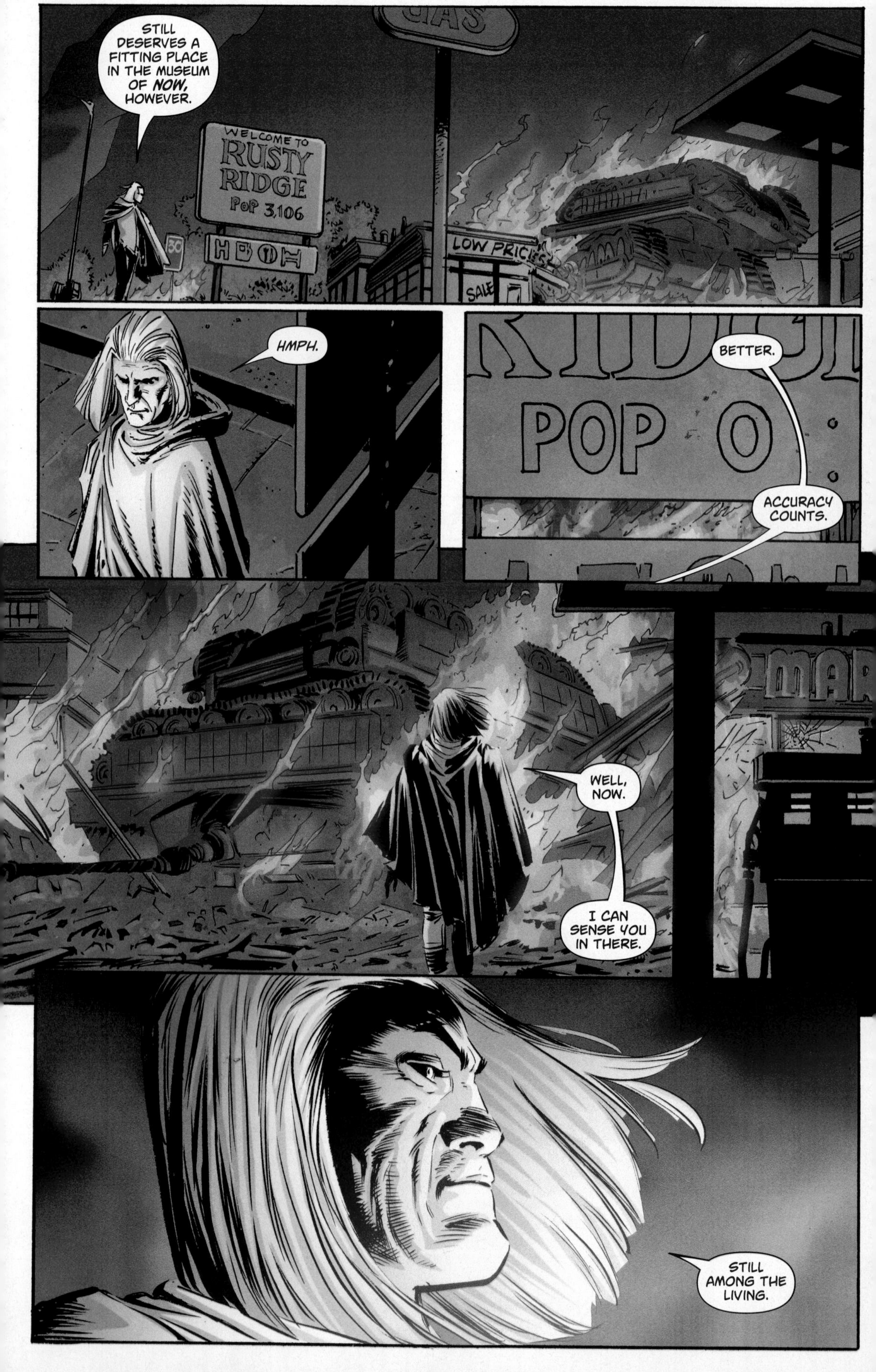

STILL DESERVES A FITTING PLACE IN THE MUSEUM OF *NOW,* HOWEVER.
WELCOME TO RUSTY RIDGE POP 3,106
LOW PRICES
SALE
HMPH.
POP 0
BETTER.
ACCURACY COUNTS.
WELL, NOW.
I CAN SENSE YOU IN THERE.
STILL AMONG THE LIVING.

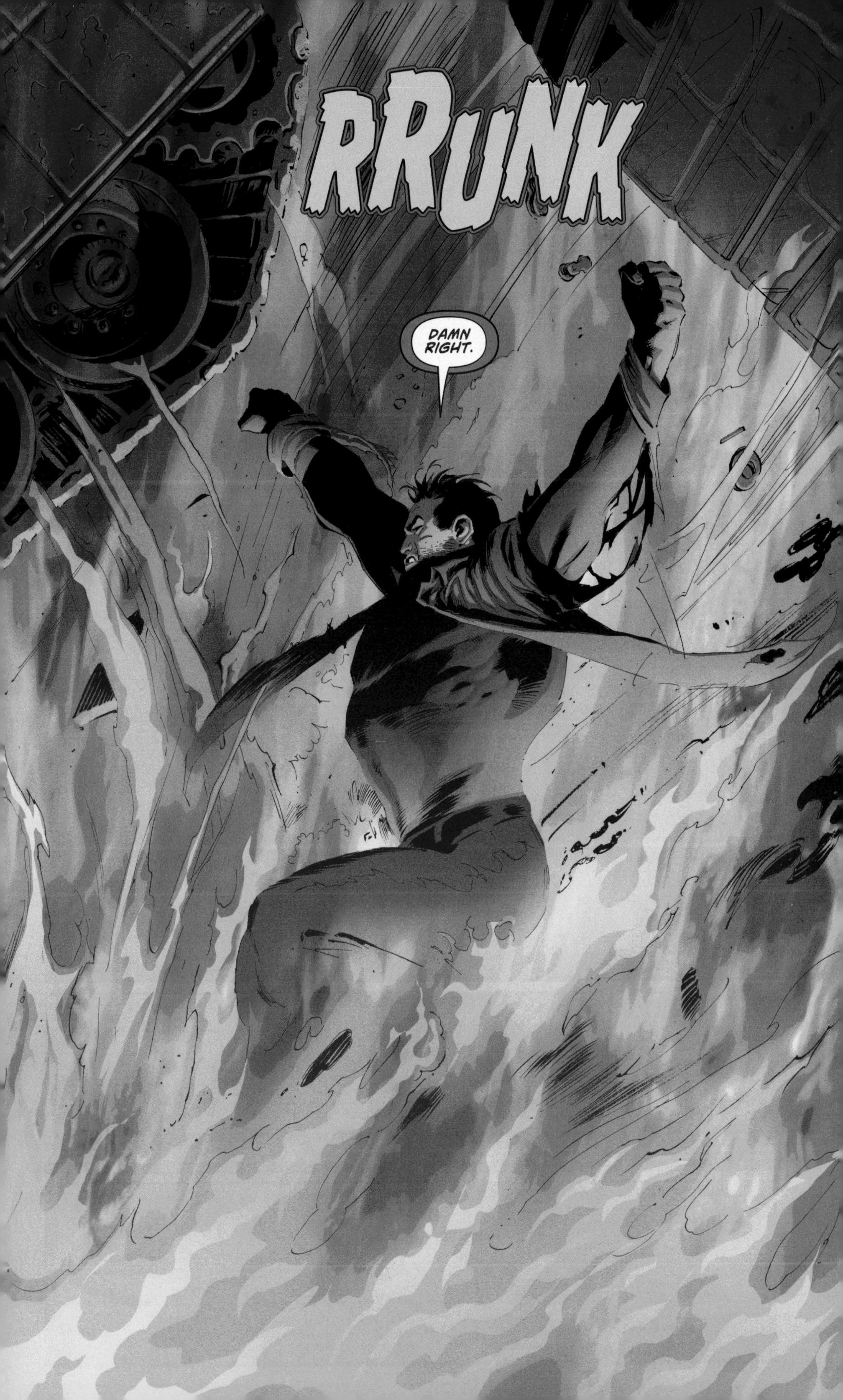
RRUNK
DAMN RIGHT.

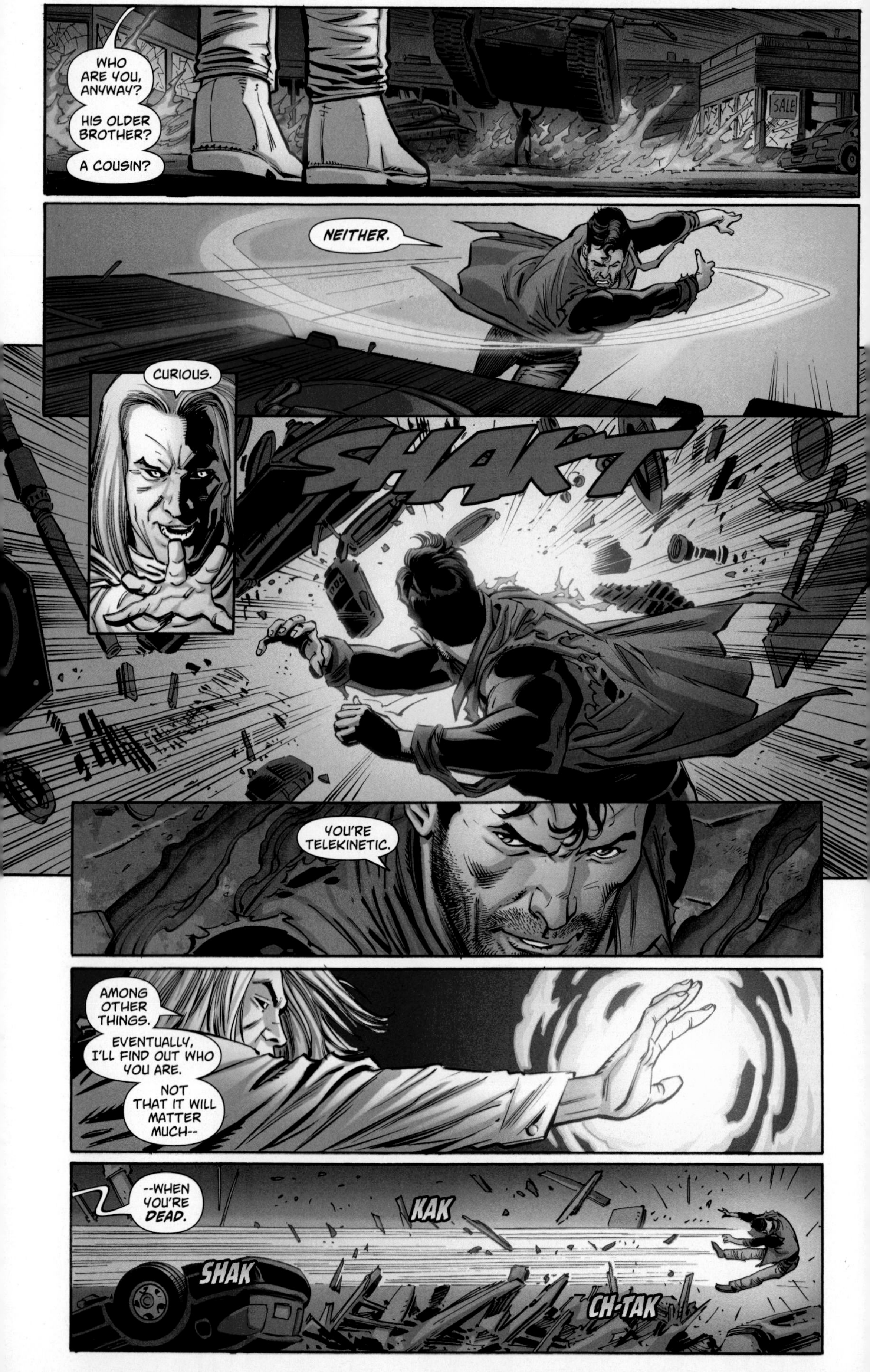
WHO ARE YOU, ANYWAY?
HIS OLDER BROTHER?
A COUSIN?
SALE
NEITHER.
CURIOUS.
SHAKT
YOU'RE TELEKINETIC.
AMONG OTHER THINGS.
EVENTUALLY, I'LL FIND OUT WHO YOU ARE.
NOT THAT IT WILL MATTER MUCH--
--WHEN YOU'RE DEAD.
KAK
SHAK
CH-TAK

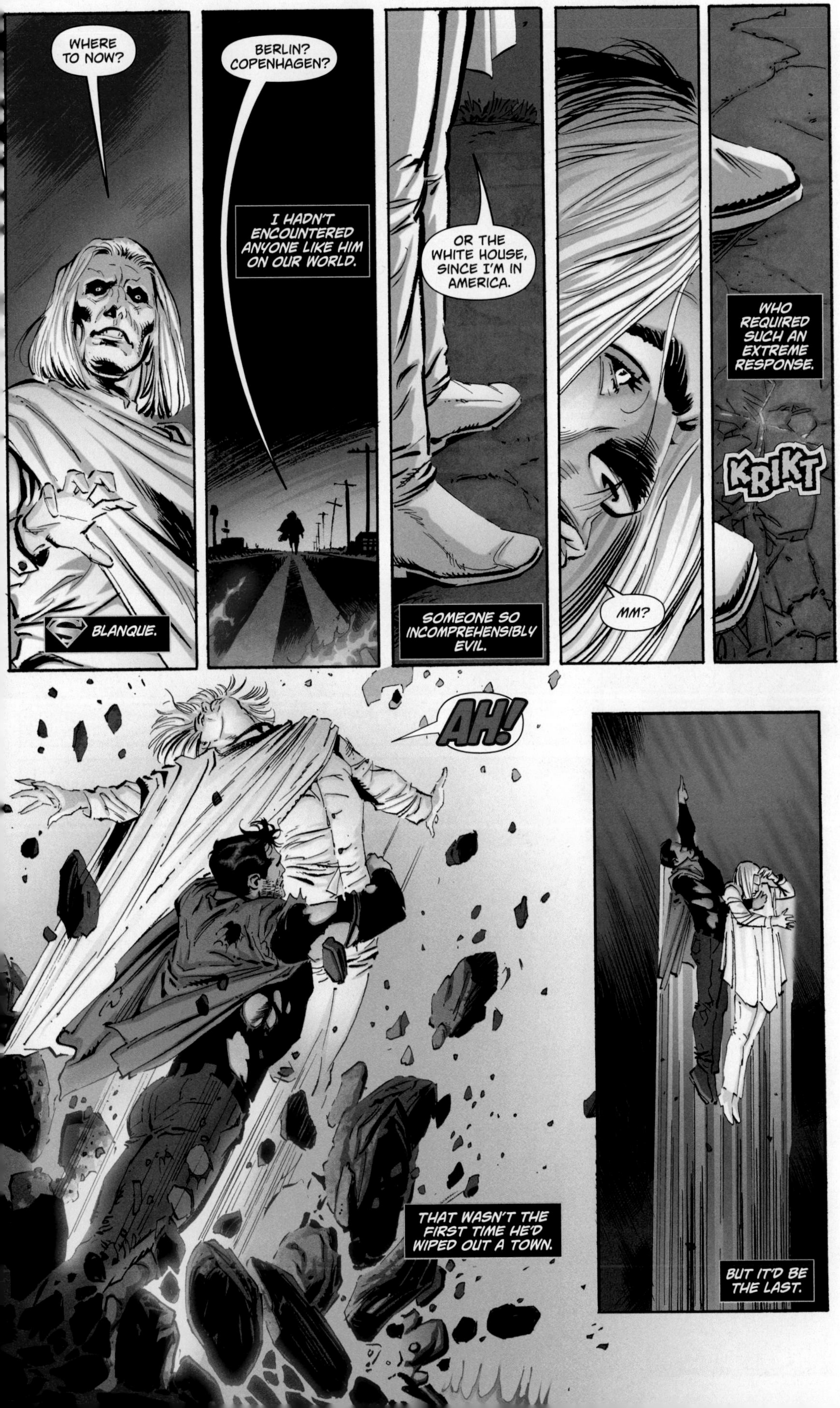
WHERE TO NOW?
BLANQUE.
BERLIN? COPENHAGEN?
I HADN'T ENCOUNTERED ANYONE LIKE HIM ON OUR WORLD.
OR THE WHITE HOUSE, SINCE I'M IN AMERICA.
SOMEONE SO INCOMPREHENSIBLY EVIL.
MM?
WHO REQUIRED SUCH AN EXTREME RESPONSE.
KRIKT
AH!
THAT WASN'T THE FIRST TIME HE'D WIPED OUT A TOWN.
BUT IT'D BE THE LAST.

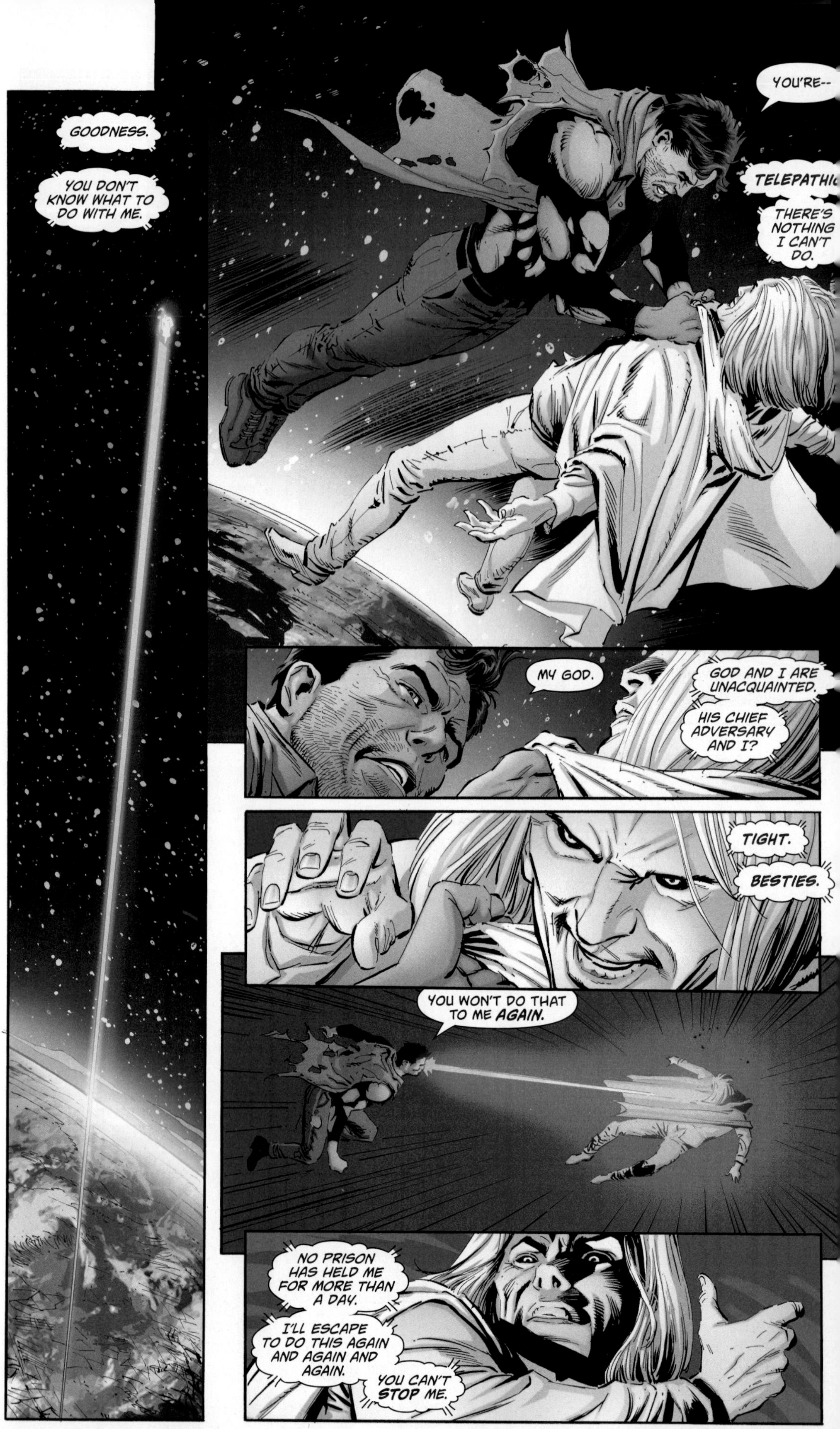
GOODNESS.
YOU DON'T KNOW WHAT TO DO WITH ME.
YOU'RE--
TELEPATHIC
THERE'S NOTHING I CAN'T DO.
MY GOD.
GOD AND I ARE UNACQUAINTED.
HIS CHIEF ADVERSARY AND I?
TIGHT.
BESTIES.
YOU WON'T DO THAT TO ME AGAIN.
NO PRISON HAS HELD ME FOR MORE THAN A DAY.
I'LL ESCAPE TO DO THIS AGAIN AND AGAIN AND AGAIN.
YOU CAN'T STOP ME.

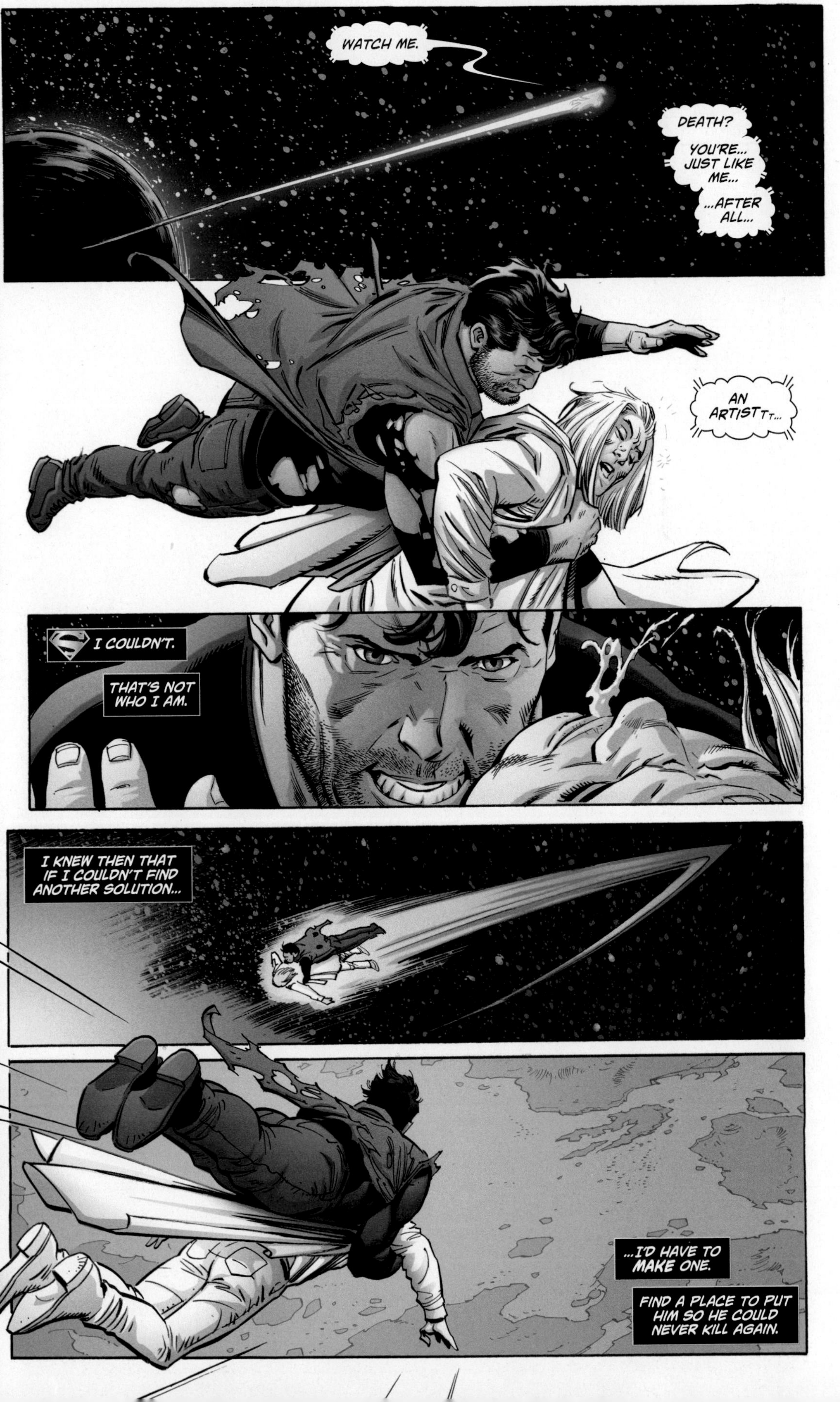
WATCH ME.
DEATH?
YOU'RE... JUST LIKE ME...
...AFTER ALL...
AN ARTISTTT...
I COULDN'T.
THAT'S NOT WHO I AM.
I KNEW THEN THAT IF I COULDN'T FIND ANOTHER SOLUTION...
...I'D HAVE TO MAKE ONE.
FIND A PLACE TO PUT HIM SO HE COULD NEVER KILL AGAIN.

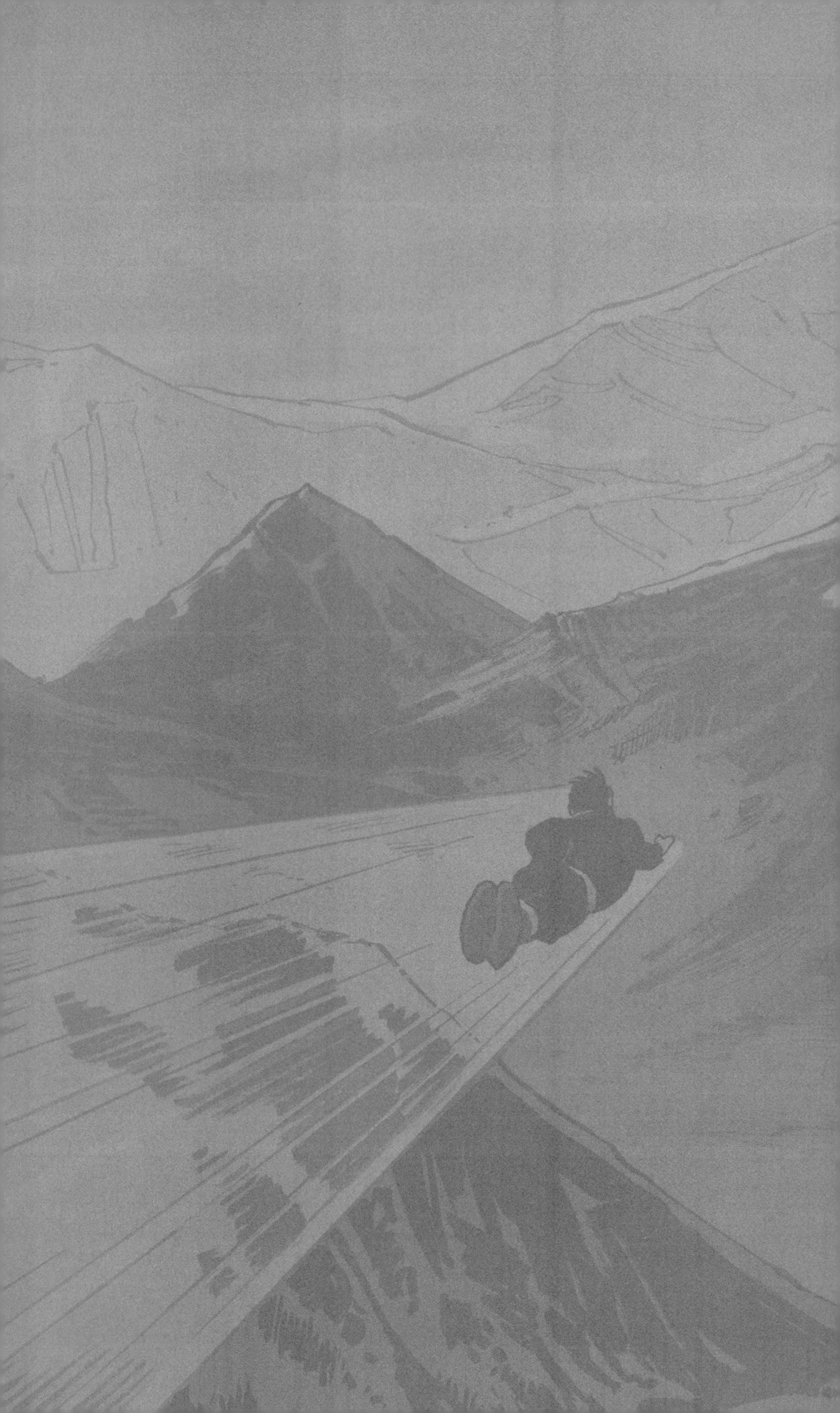

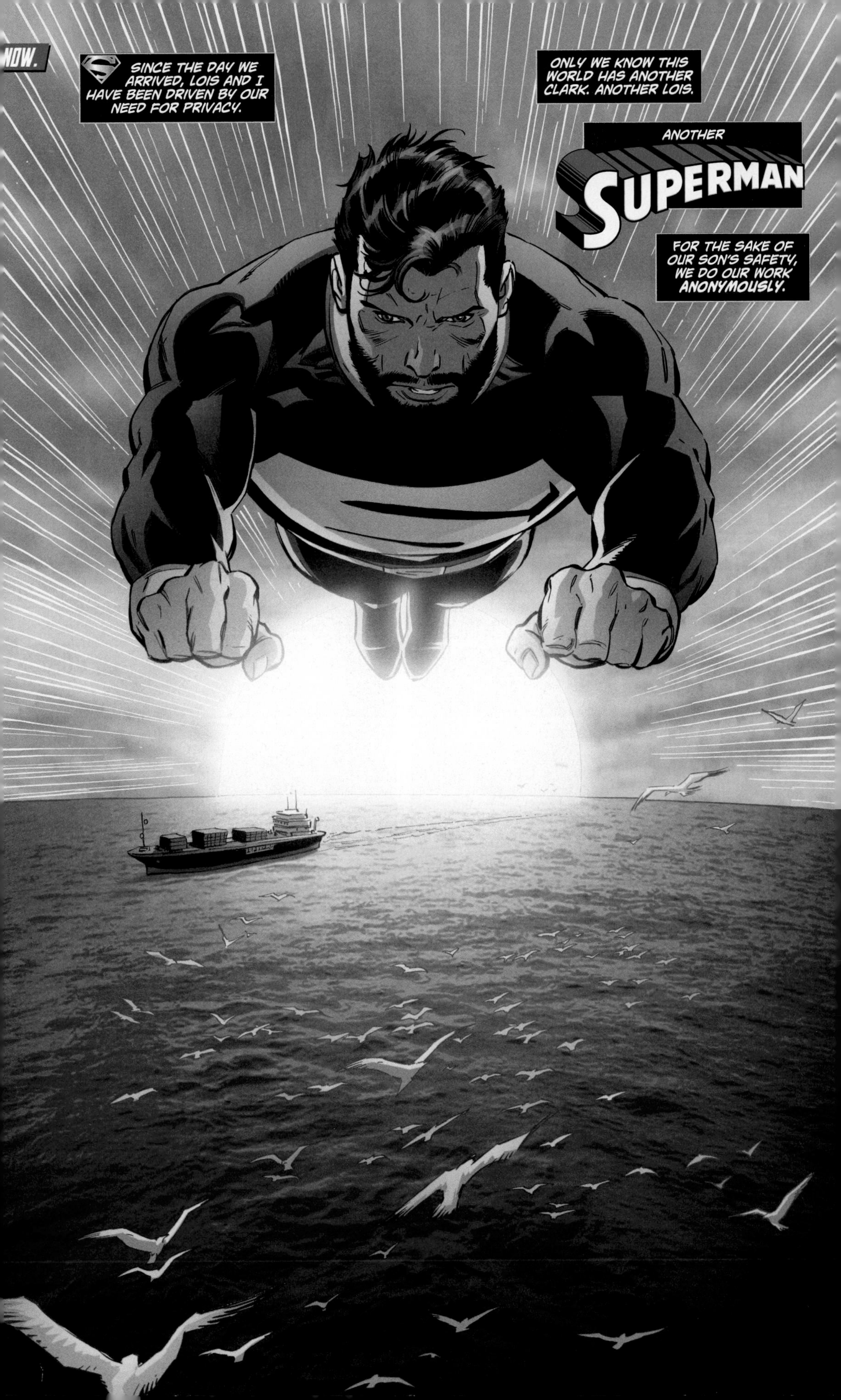
NOW.
SINCE THE DAY WE ARRIVED, LOIS AND I HAVE BEEN DRIVEN BY OUR NEED FOR PRIVACY.
ONLY WE KNOW THIS WORLD HAS ANOTHER CLARK. ANOTHER LOIS.
ANOTHER
SUPERMAN
FOR THE SAKE OF OUR SON'S SAFETY, WE DO OUR WORK ANONYMOUSLY.

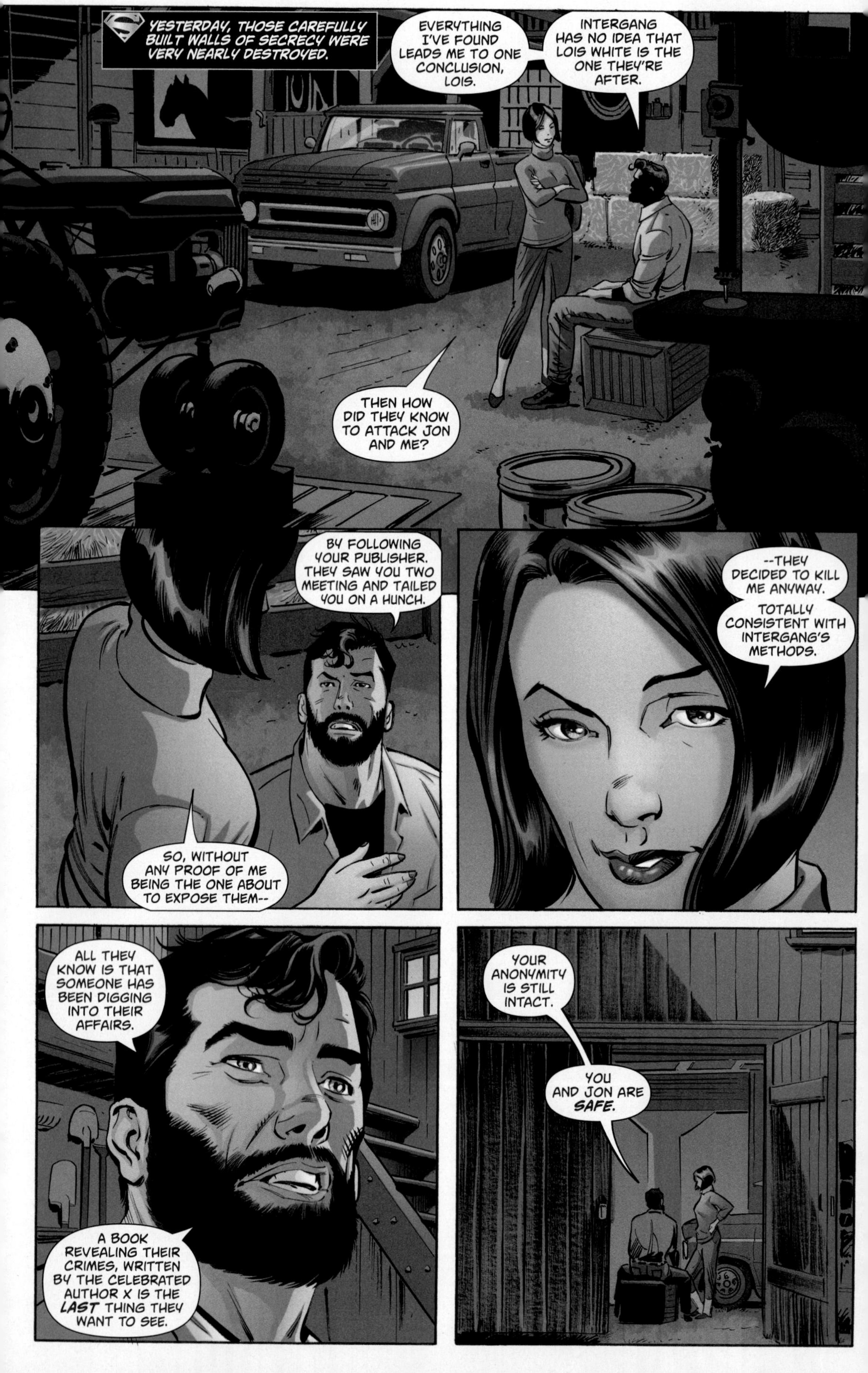
YESTERDAY, THOSE CAREFULLY BUILT WALLS OF SECRECY WERE VERY NEARLY DESTROYED.
EVERYTHING I'VE FOUND LEADS ME TO ONE CONCLUSION, LOIS.
INTERGANG HAS NO IDEA THAT LOIS WHITE IS THE ONE THEY'RE AFTER.
THEN HOW DID THEY KNOW TO ATTACK JON AND ME?
BY FOLLOWING YOUR PUBLISHER. THEY SAW YOU TWO MEETING AND TAILED YOU ON A HUNCH.
SO, WITHOUT ANY PROOF OF ME BEING THE ONE ABOUT TO EXPOSE THEM--
--THEY DECIDED TO KILL ME ANYWAY.
TOTALLY CONSISTENT WITH INTERGANG'S METHODS.
ALL THEY KNOW IS THAT SOMEONE HAS BEEN DIGGING INTO THEIR AFFAIRS.
A BOOK REVEALING THEIR CRIMES, WRITTEN BY THE CELEBRATED AUTHOR X IS THE *LAST* THING THEY WANT TO SEE.
YOUR ANONYMITY IS STILL INTACT.
YOU AND JON ARE ***SAFE***.

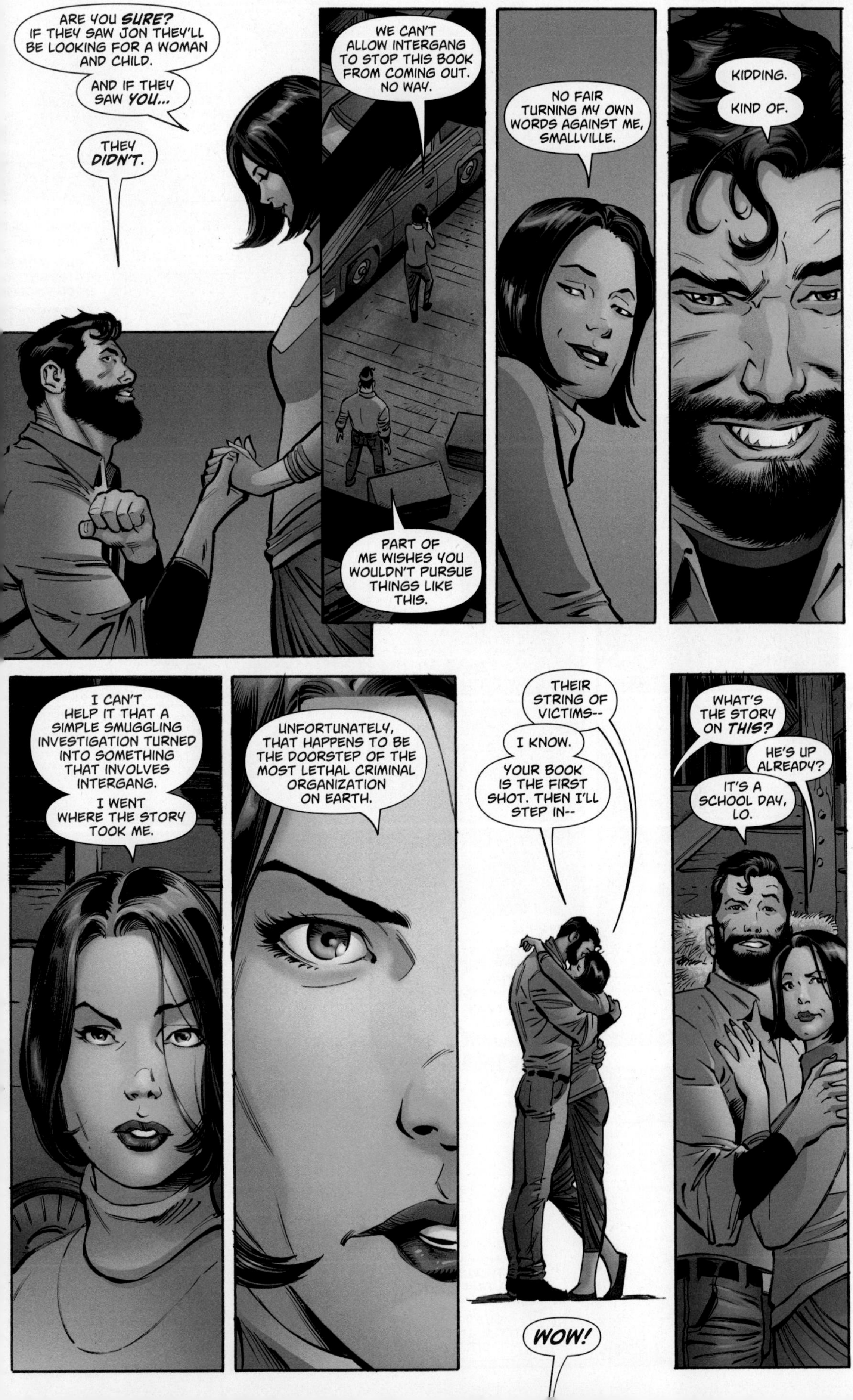
ARE YOU SURE? IF THEY SAW JON THEY'LL BE LOOKING FOR A WOMAN AND CHILD.
AND IF THEY SAW YOU...
THEY DIDN'T.
WE CAN'T ALLOW INTERGANG TO STOP THIS BOOK FROM COMING OUT. NO WAY.
PART OF ME WISHES YOU WOULDN'T PURSUE THINGS LIKE THIS.
NO FAIR TURNING MY OWN WORDS AGAINST ME, SMALLVILLE.
KIDDING.
KIND OF.
I CAN'T HELP IT THAT A SIMPLE SMUGGLING INVESTIGATION TURNED INTO SOMETHING THAT INVOLVES INTERGANG.
I WENT WHERE THE STORY TOOK ME.
UNFORTUNATELY, THAT HAPPENS TO BE THE DOORSTEP OF THE MOST LETHAL CRIMINAL ORGANIZATION ON EARTH.
THEIR STRING OF VICTIMS--
I KNOW.
YOUR BOOK IS THE FIRST SHOT. THEN I'LL STEP IN--
WOW!
WHAT'S THE STORY ON THIS?
HE'S UP ALREADY?
IT'S A SCHOOL DAY, LO.

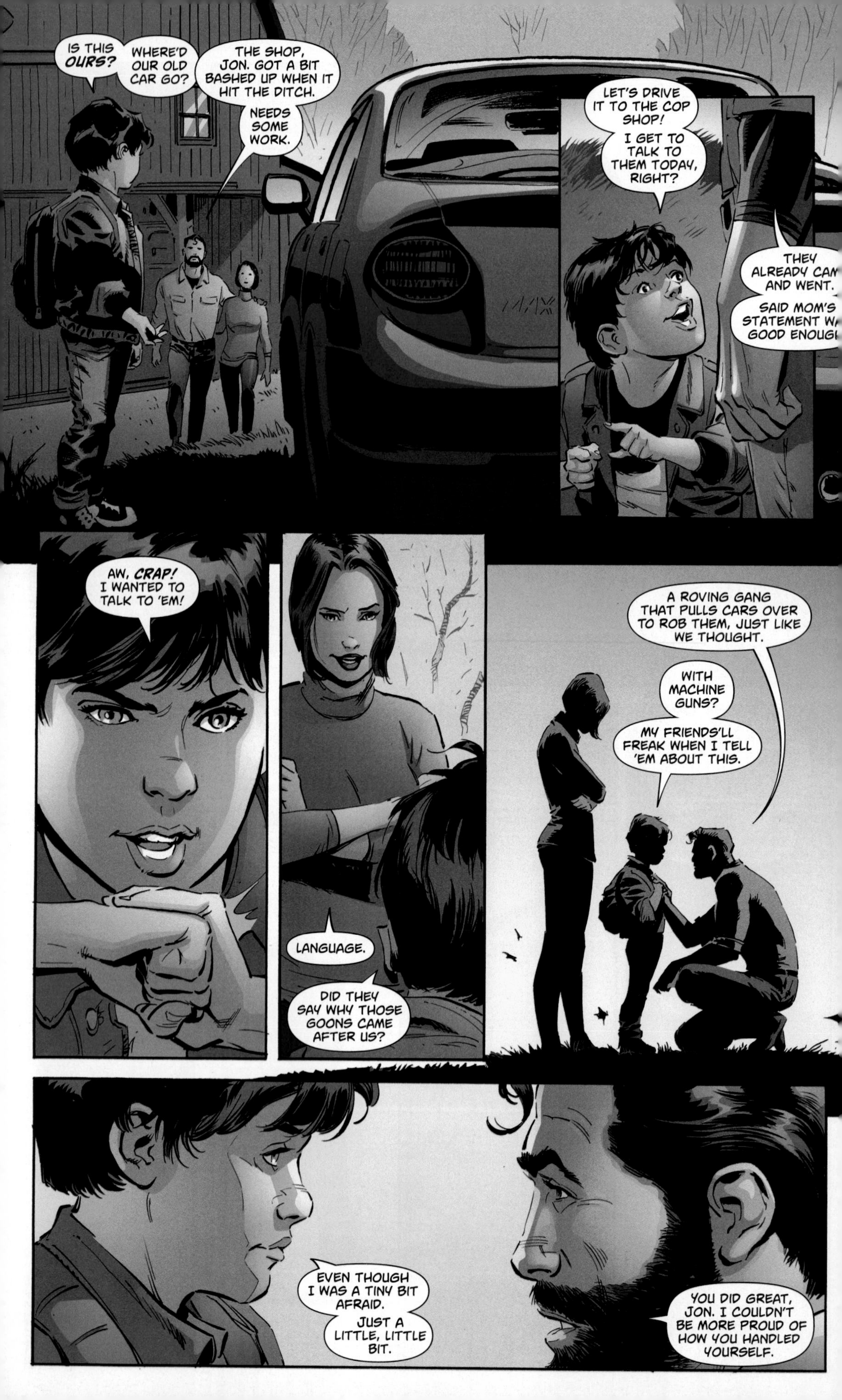
IS THIS *OURS?*
WHERE'D OUR OLD CAR GO?
THE SHOP, JON. GOT A BIT BASHED UP WHEN IT HIT THE DITCH.
NEEDS SOME WORK.
LET'S DRIVE IT TO THE COP SHOP!
I GET TO TALK TO THEM TODAY, RIGHT?
THEY ALREADY CAM AND WENT.
SAID MOM'S STATEMENT W GOOD ENOUG
AW, *CRAP!* I WANTED TO TALK TO 'EM!
LANGUAGE.
DID THEY SAY WHY THOSE GOONS CAME AFTER US?
A ROVING GANG THAT PULLS CARS OVER TO ROB THEM, JUST LIKE WE THOUGHT.
WITH MACHINE GUNS?
MY FRIENDS'LL FREAK WHEN I TELL 'EM ABOUT THIS.
EVEN THOUGH I WAS A TINY BIT AFRAID.
JUST A LITTLE, LITTLE BIT.
YOU DID GREAT, JON. I COULDN'T BE MORE PROUD OF HOW YOU HANDLED YOURSELF.

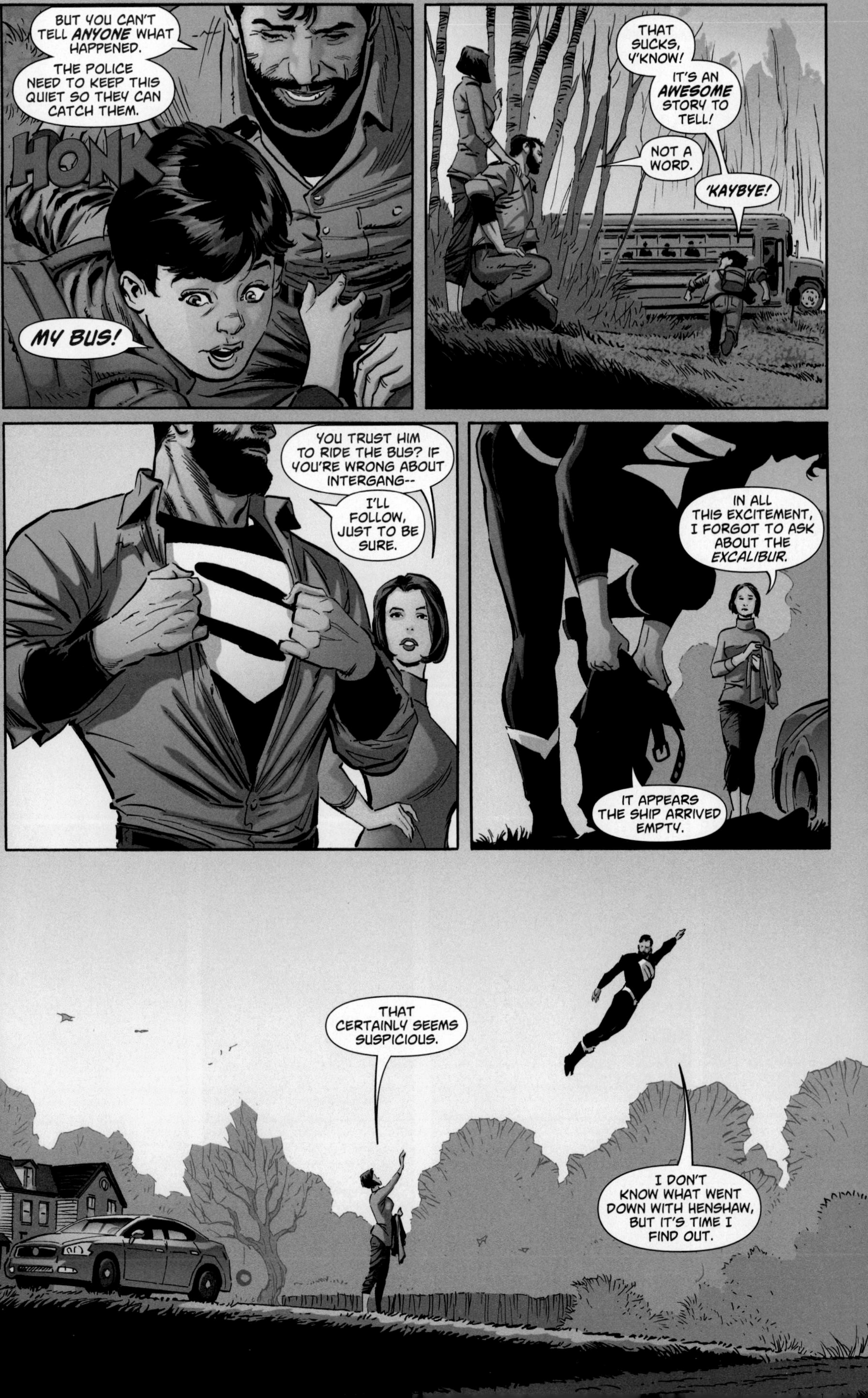
BUT YOU CAN'T TELL ANYONE WHAT HAPPENED.
THE POLICE NEED TO KEEP THIS QUIET SO THEY CAN CATCH THEM.
HONK
MY BUS!
THAT SUCKS, Y'KNOW!
IT'S AN AWESOME STORY TO TELL!
NOT A WORD.
'KAYBYE!
YOU TRUST HIM TO RIDE THE BUS? IF YOU'RE WRONG ABOUT INTERGANG--
I'LL FOLLOW, JUST TO BE SURE.
IN ALL THIS EXCITEMENT, I FORGOT TO ASK ABOUT THE EXCALIBUR.
IT APPEARS THE SHIP ARRIVED EMPTY.
THAT CERTAINLY SEEMS SUSPICIOUS.
I DON'T KNOW WHAT WENT DOWN WITH HENSHAW, BUT IT'S TIME I FIND OUT.

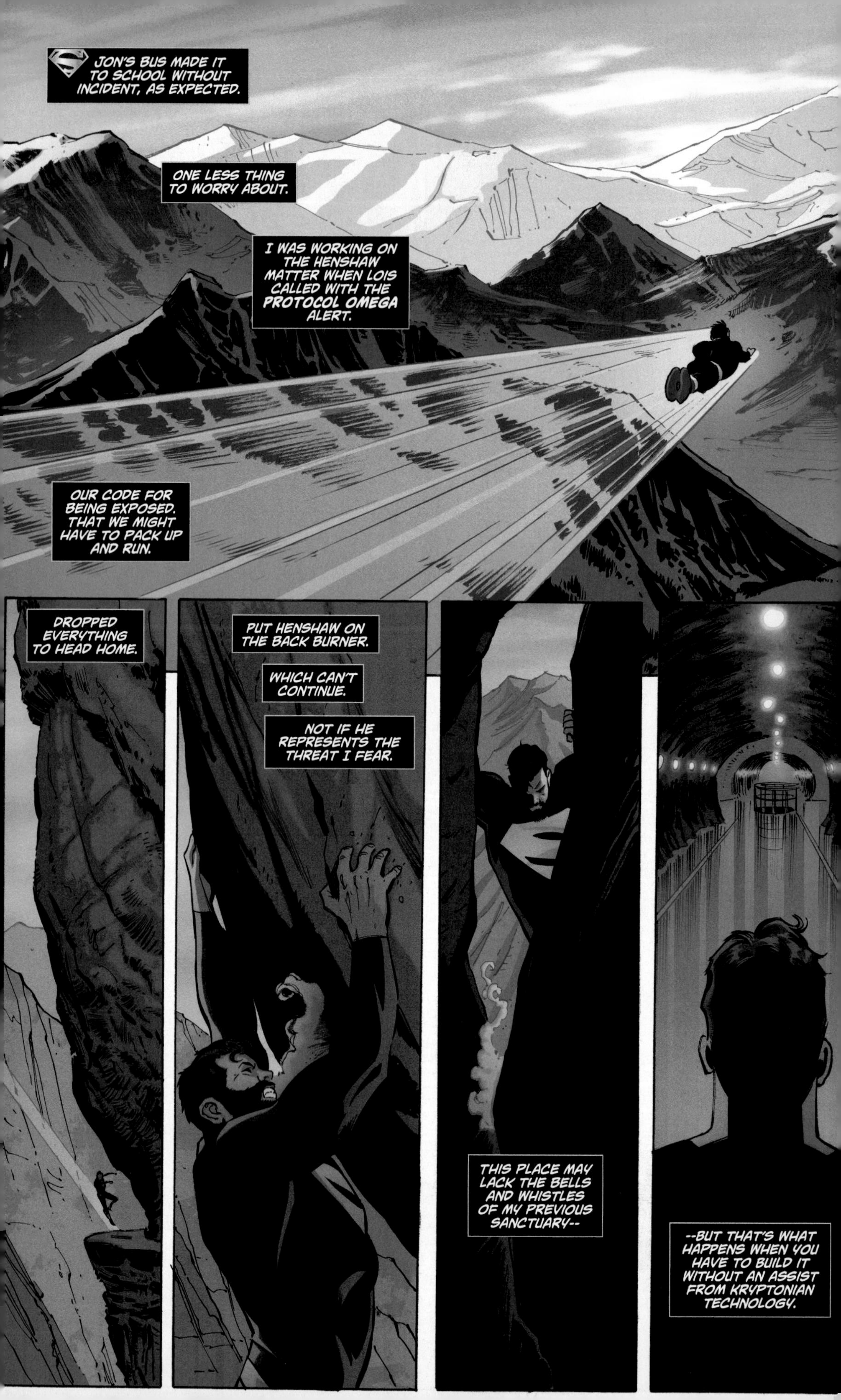
JON'S BUS MADE IT TO SCHOOL WITHOUT INCIDENT, AS EXPECTED.
ONE LESS THING TO WORRY ABOUT.
I WAS WORKING ON THE HENSHAW MATTER WHEN LOIS CALLED WITH THE PROTOCOL OMEGA ALERT.
OUR CODE FOR BEING EXPOSED. THAT WE MIGHT HAVE TO PACK UP AND RUN.
DROPPED EVERYTHING TO HEAD HOME.
PUT HENSHAW ON THE BACK BURNER.
WHICH CAN'T CONTINUE.
NOT IF HE REPRESENTS THE THREAT I FEAR.
THIS PLACE MAY LACK THE BELLS AND WHISTLES OF MY PREVIOUS SANCTUARY--
--BUT THAT'S WHAT HAPPENS WHEN YOU HAVE TO BUILD IT WITHOUT AN ASSIST FROM KRYPTONIAN TECHNOLOGY.

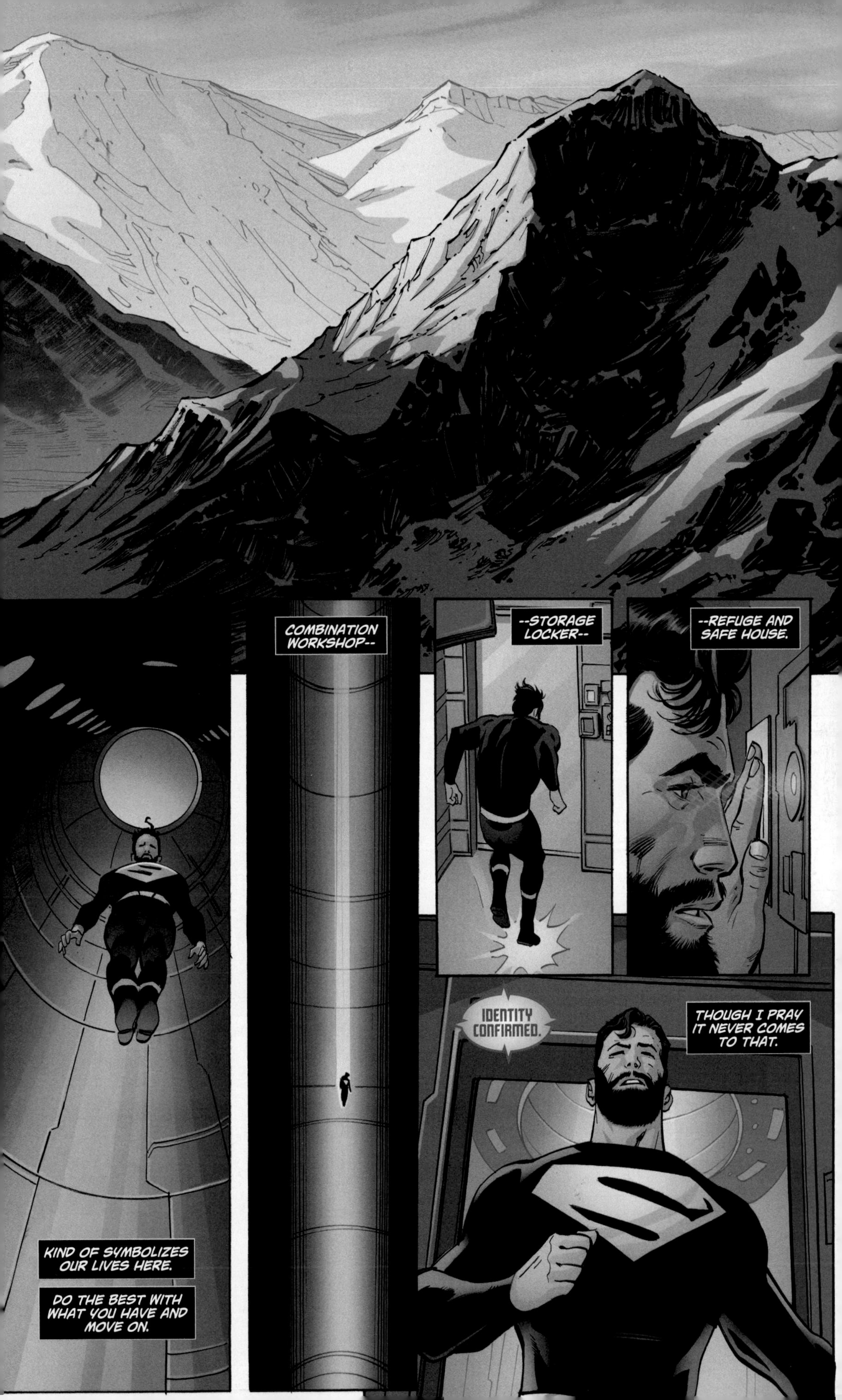
COMBINATION WORKSHOP--
--STORAGE LOCKER--
--REFUGE AND SAFE HOUSE.
KIND OF SYMBOLIZES OUR LIVES HERE.
DO THE BEST WITH WHAT YOU HAVE AND MOVE ON.
IDENTITY CONFIRMED.
THOUGH I PRAY IT NEVER COMES TO THAT.

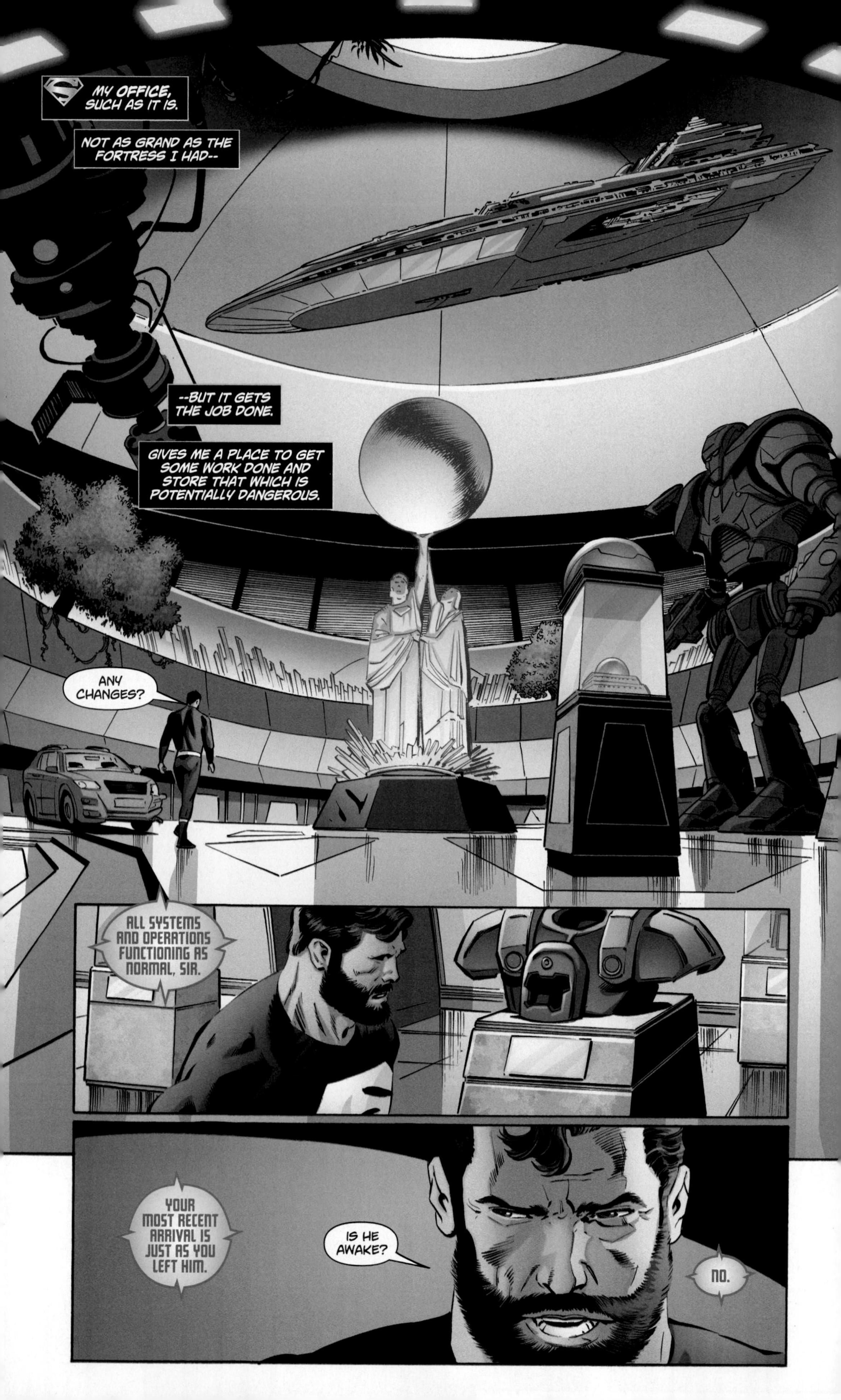
MY OFFICE, SUCH AS IT IS.
NOT AS GRAND AS THE FORTRESS I HAD--
--BUT IT GETS THE JOB DONE.
GIVES ME A PLACE TO GET SOME WORK DONE AND STORE THAT WHICH IS POTENTIALLY DANGEROUS.
ANY CHANGES?
ALL SYSTEMS AND OPERATIONS FUNCTIONING AS NORMAL, SIR.
YOUR MOST RECENT ARRIVAL IS JUST AS YOU LEFT HIM.
IS HE AWAKE?
NO.

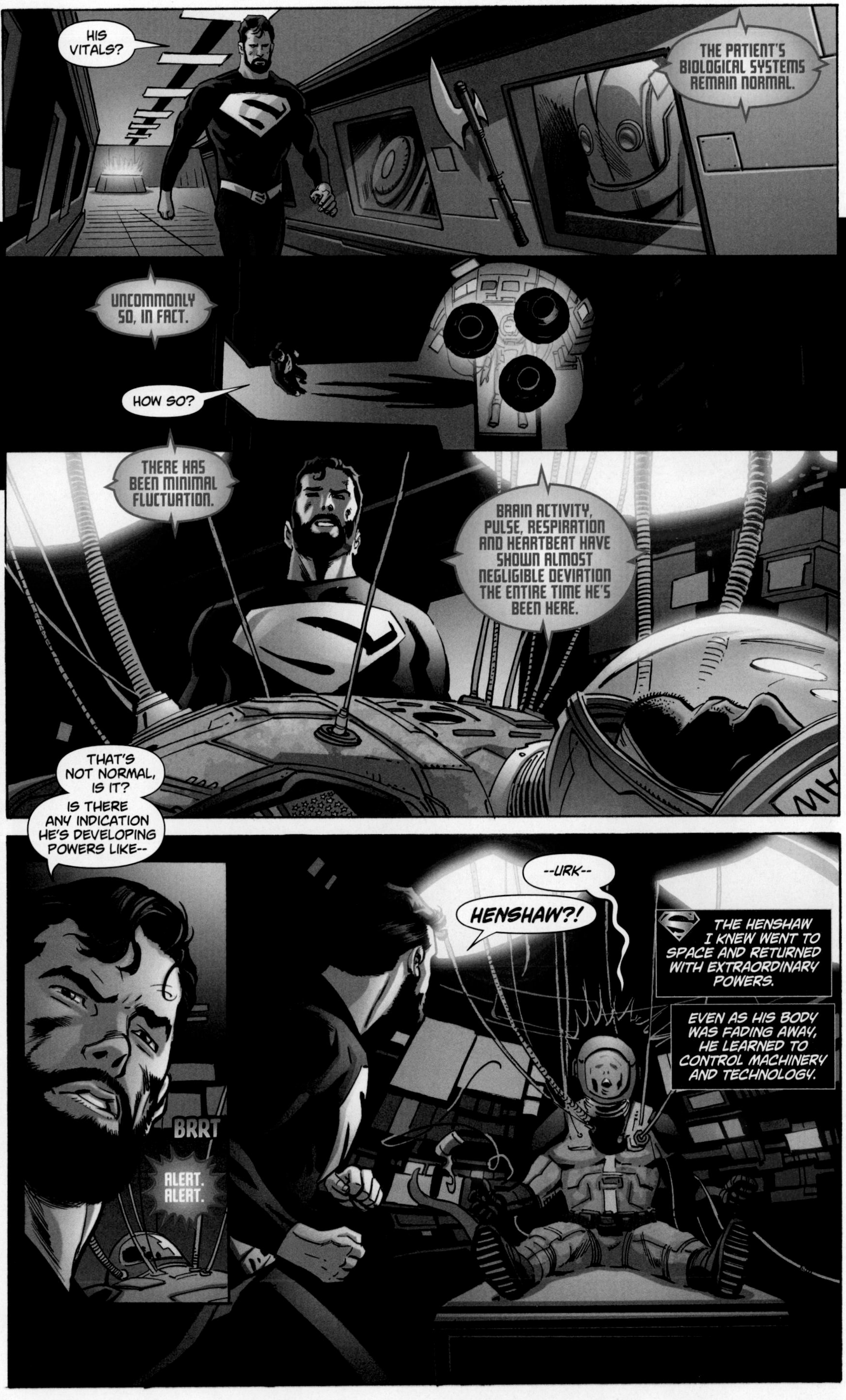
HIS VITALS?
THE PATIENT'S BIOLOGICAL SYSTEMS REMAIN NORMAL.
UNCOMMONLY SO, IN FACT.
HOW SO?
THERE HAS BEEN MINIMAL FLUCTUATION.
BRAIN ACTIVITY, PULSE, RESPIRATION AND HEARTBEAT HAVE SHOWN ALMOST NEGLIGIBLE DEVIATION THE ENTIRE TIME HE'S BEEN HERE.
THAT'S NOT NORMAL, IS IT?
IS THERE ANY INDICATION HE'S DEVELOPING POWERS LIKE--
BRRT
ALERT. ALERT.
--URK--
HENSHAW?!
THE HENSHAW I KNEW WENT TO SPACE AND RETURNED WITH EXTRAORDINARY POWERS.
EVEN AS HIS BODY WAS FADING AWAY, HE LEARNED TO CONTROL MACHINERY AND TECHNOLOGY.

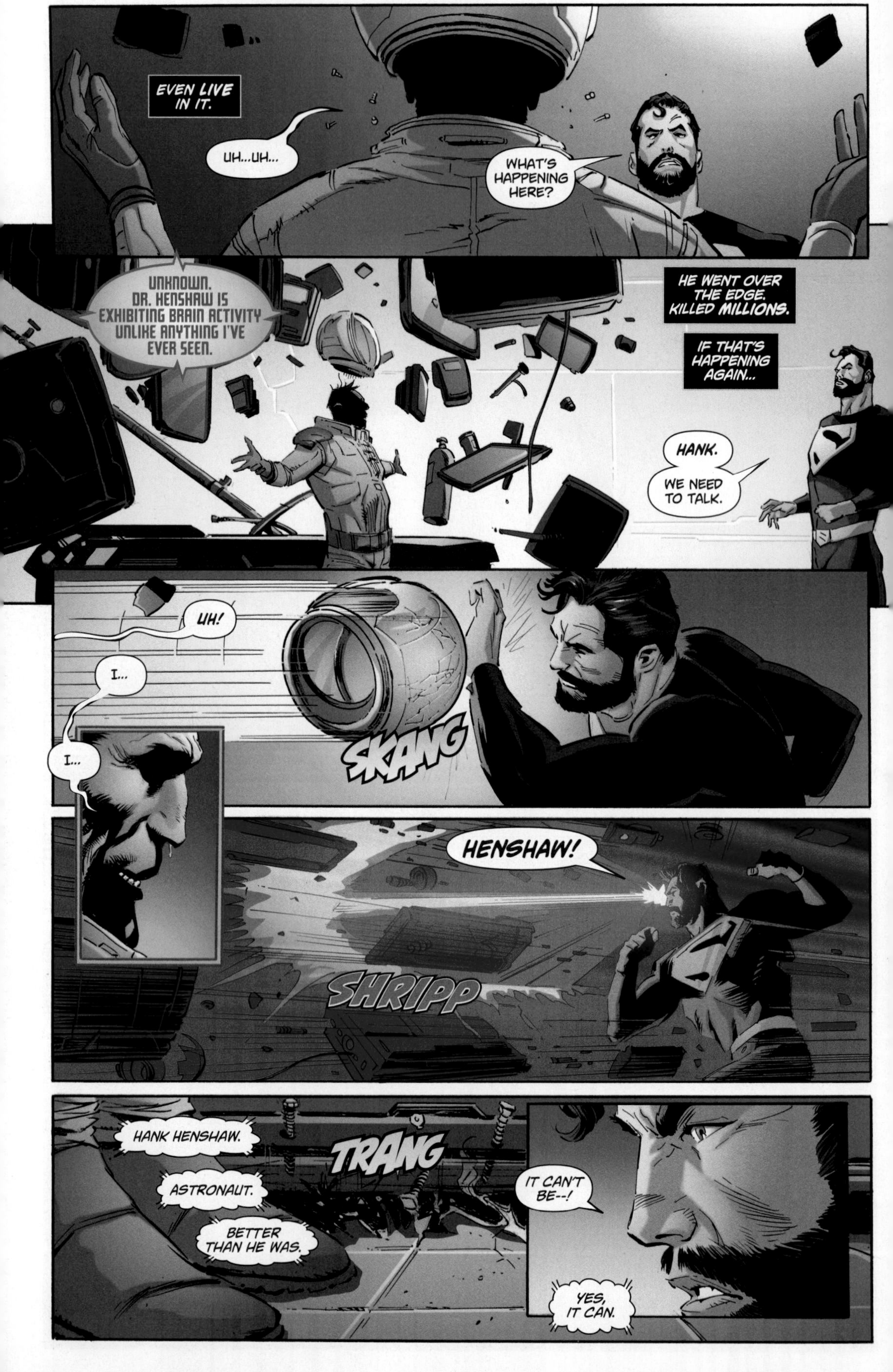

EVEN LIVE IN IT.
UH...UH...
WHAT'S HAPPENING HERE?
UNKNOWN. DR. HENSHAW IS EXHIBITING BRAIN ACTIVITY UNLIKE ANYTHING I'VE EVER SEEN.
HE WENT OVER THE EDGE. KILLED MILLIONS.
IF THAT'S HAPPENING AGAIN...
HANK.
WE NEED TO TALK.
UH!
I...
I...
SKANG
HENSHAW!
SHRIPP
HANK HENSHAW.
ASTRONAUT.
BETTER THAN HE WAS.
TRANG
IT CAN'T BE--!
YES, IT CAN.

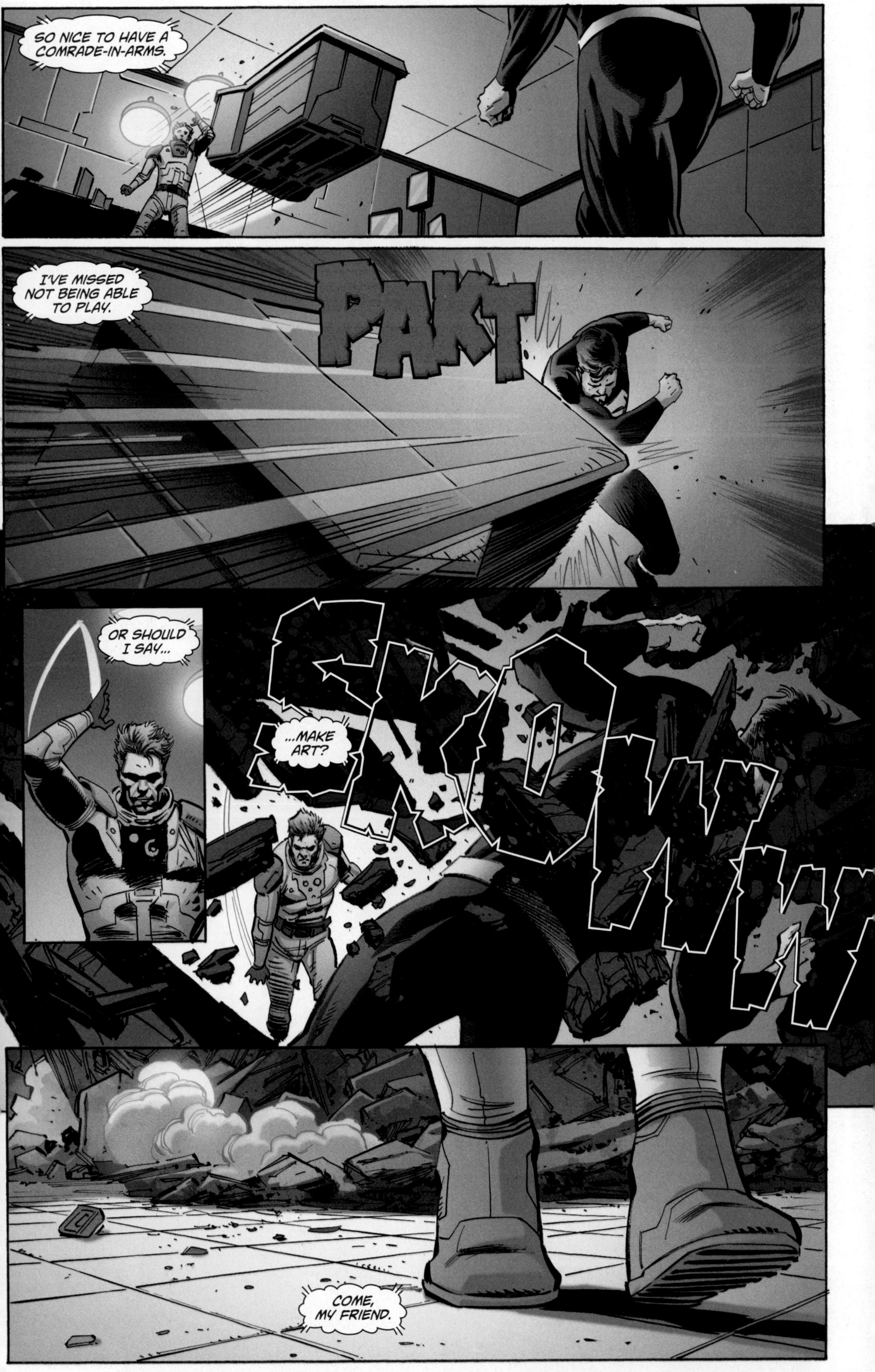
SO NICE TO HAVE A COMRADE-IN-ARMS.
I'VE MISSED NOT BEING ABLE TO PLAY.
PAKT
OR SHOULD I SAY...
...MAKE ART?
SKOWW
COME, MY FRIEND.

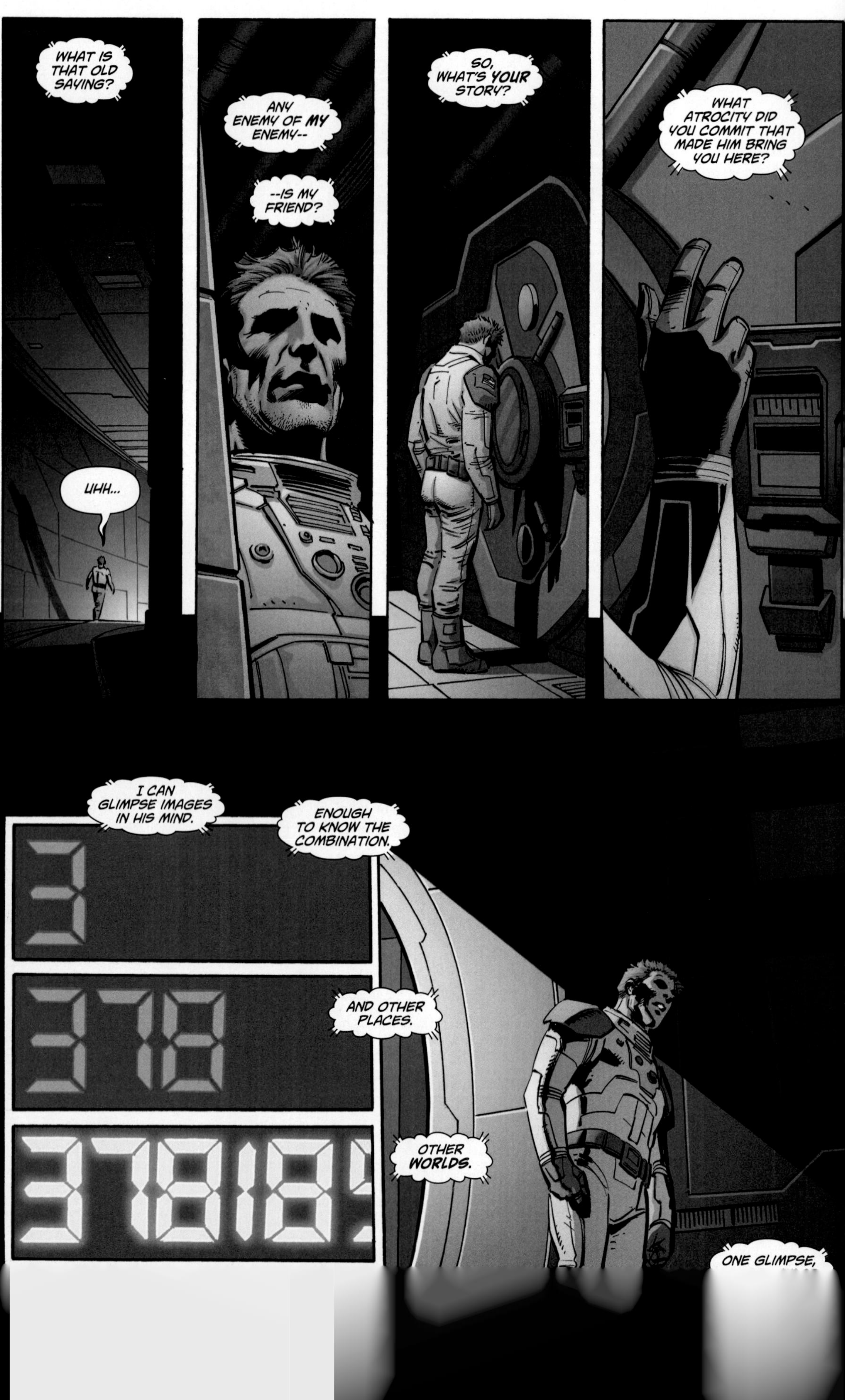

WHAT IS THAT OLD SAYING?
UHH...
ANY ENEMY OF MY ENEMY--
--IS MY FRIEND?
SO, WHAT'S YOUR STORY?
WHAT ATROCITY DID YOU COMMIT THAT MADE HIM BRING YOU HERE?
I CAN GLIMPSE IMAGES IN HIS MIND.
ENOUGH TO KNOW THE COMBINATION.
AND OTHER PLACES.
OTHER WORLDS.
ONE GLIMPSE,

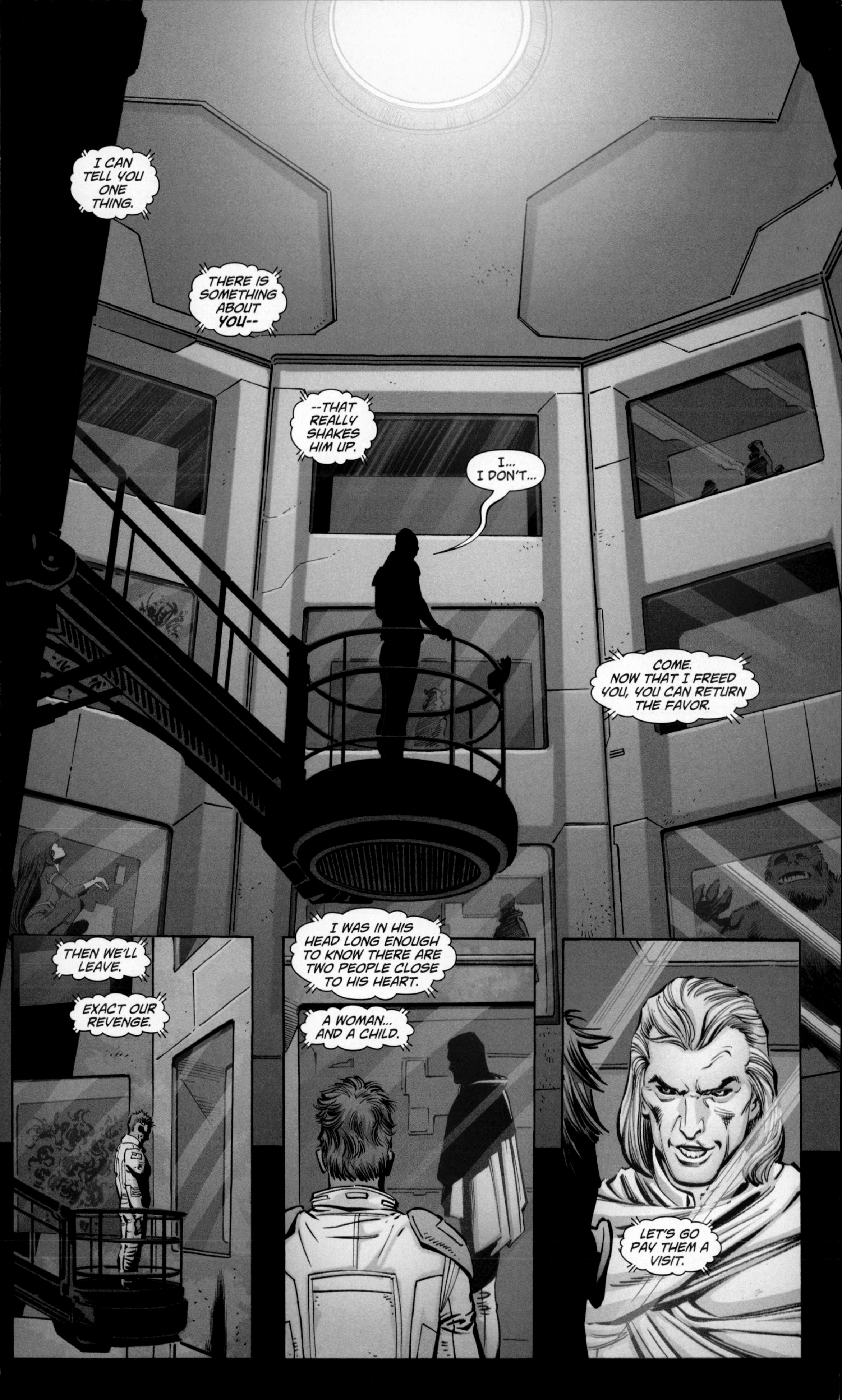
I CAN TELL YOU ONE THING.
THERE IS SOMETHING ABOUT YOU--
--THAT REALLY SHAKES HIM UP.
I... I DON'T...
COME. NOW THAT I FREED YOU, YOU CAN RETURN THE FAVOR.
THEN WE'LL LEAVE.
EXACT OUR REVENGE.
I WAS IN HIS HEAD LONG ENOUGH TO KNOW THERE ARE TWO PEOPLE CLOSE TO HIS HEART.
A WOMAN... AND A CHILD.
LET'S GO PAY THEM A VISIT.

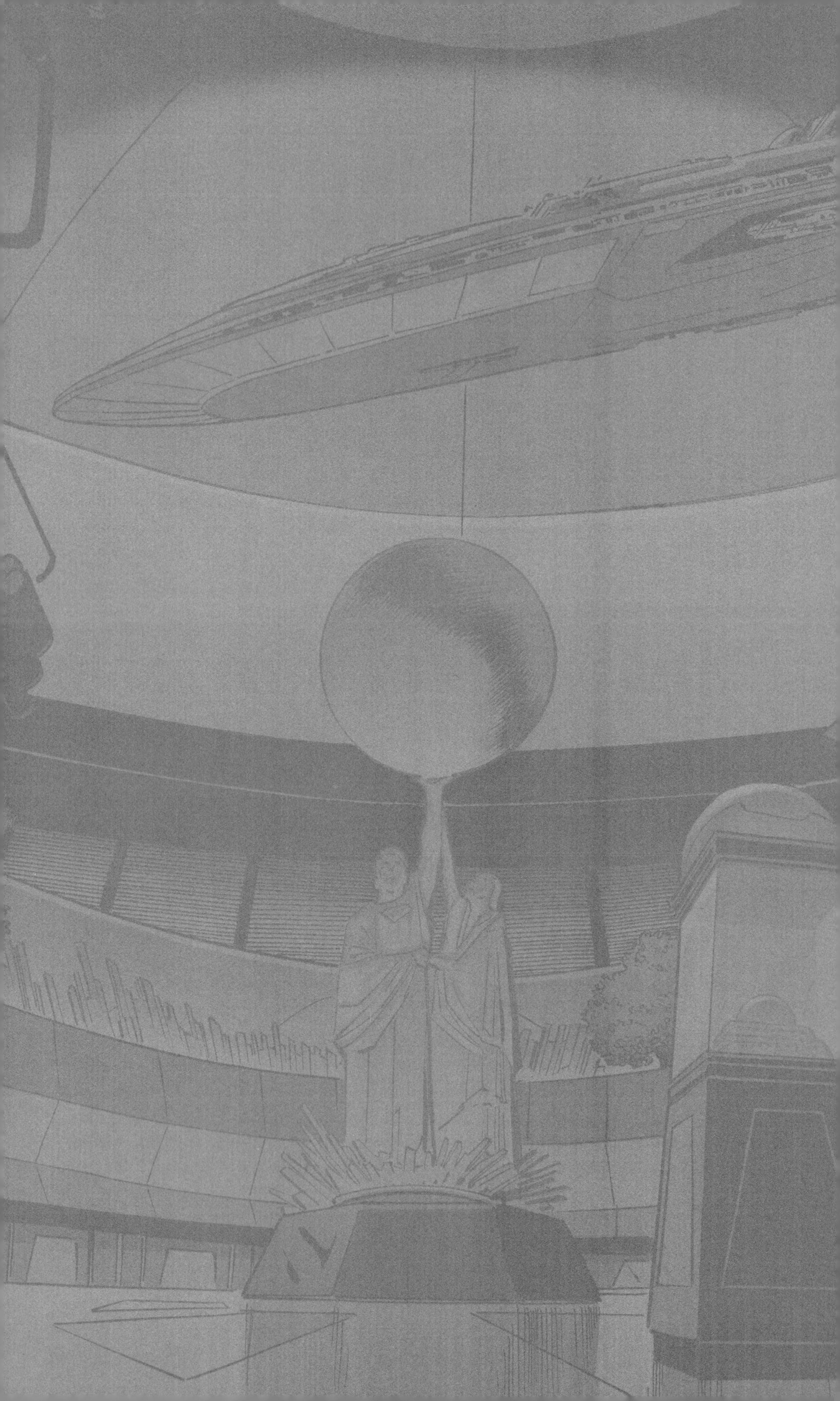

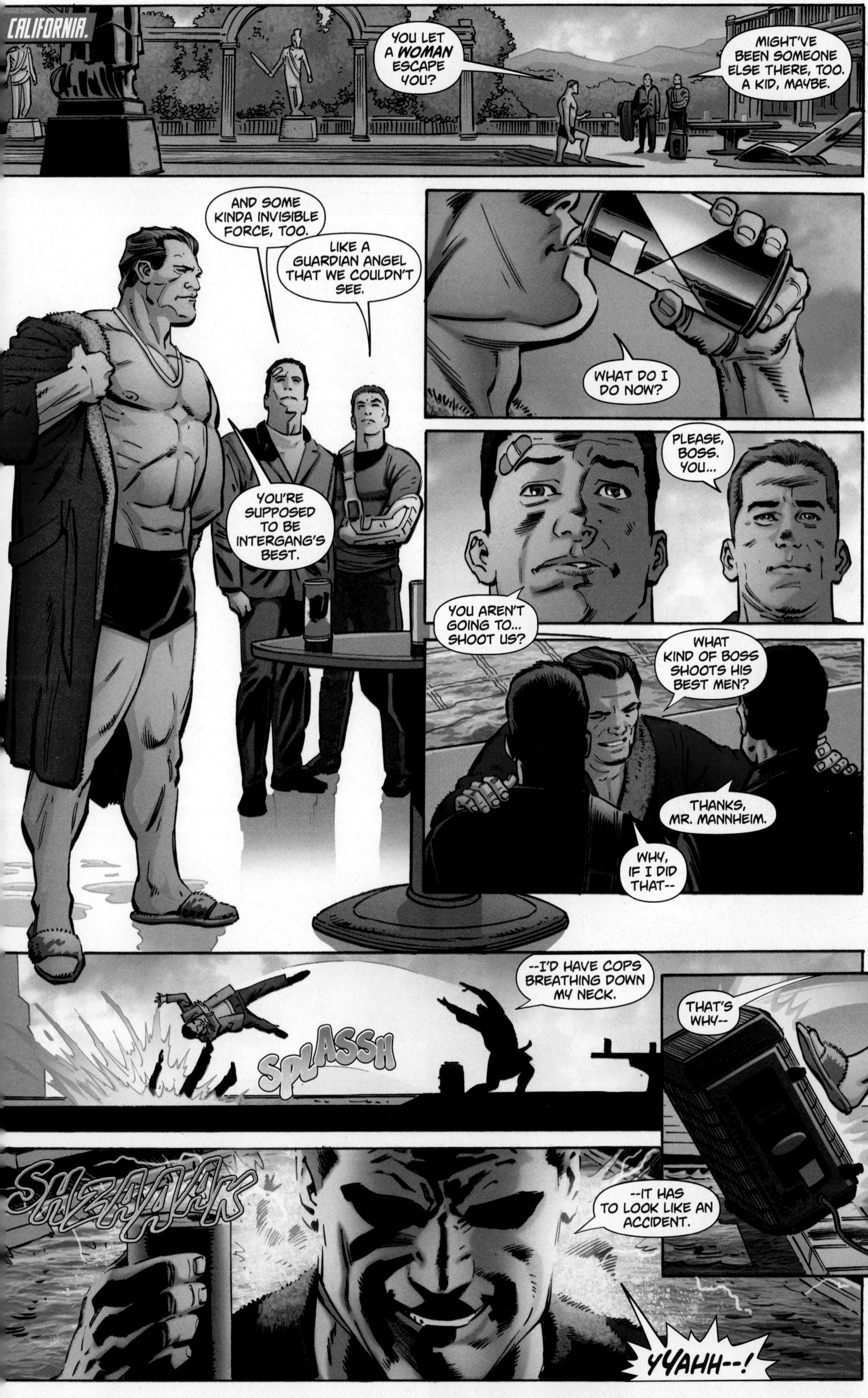
CALIFORNIA.
YOU LET A WOMAN ESCAPE YOU?
MIGHT'VE BEEN SOMEONE ELSE THERE, TOO. A KID, MAYBE.
AND SOME KINDA INVISIBLE FORCE, TOO.
LIKE A GUARDIAN ANGEL THAT WE COULDN'T SEE.
YOU'RE SUPPOSED TO BE INTERGANG'S BEST.
WHAT DO I DO NOW?
PLEASE, BOSS. YOU...
YOU AREN'T GOING TO... SHOOT US?
WHAT KIND OF BOSS SHOOTS HIS BEST MEN?
THANKS, MR. MANNHEIM.
WHY, IF I DID THAT--
--I'D HAVE COPS BREATHING DOWN MY NECK.
SPLASSH
THAT'S WHY--
SHZAAAK
--IT HAS TO LOOK LIKE AN ACCIDENT.
YYAHH--!

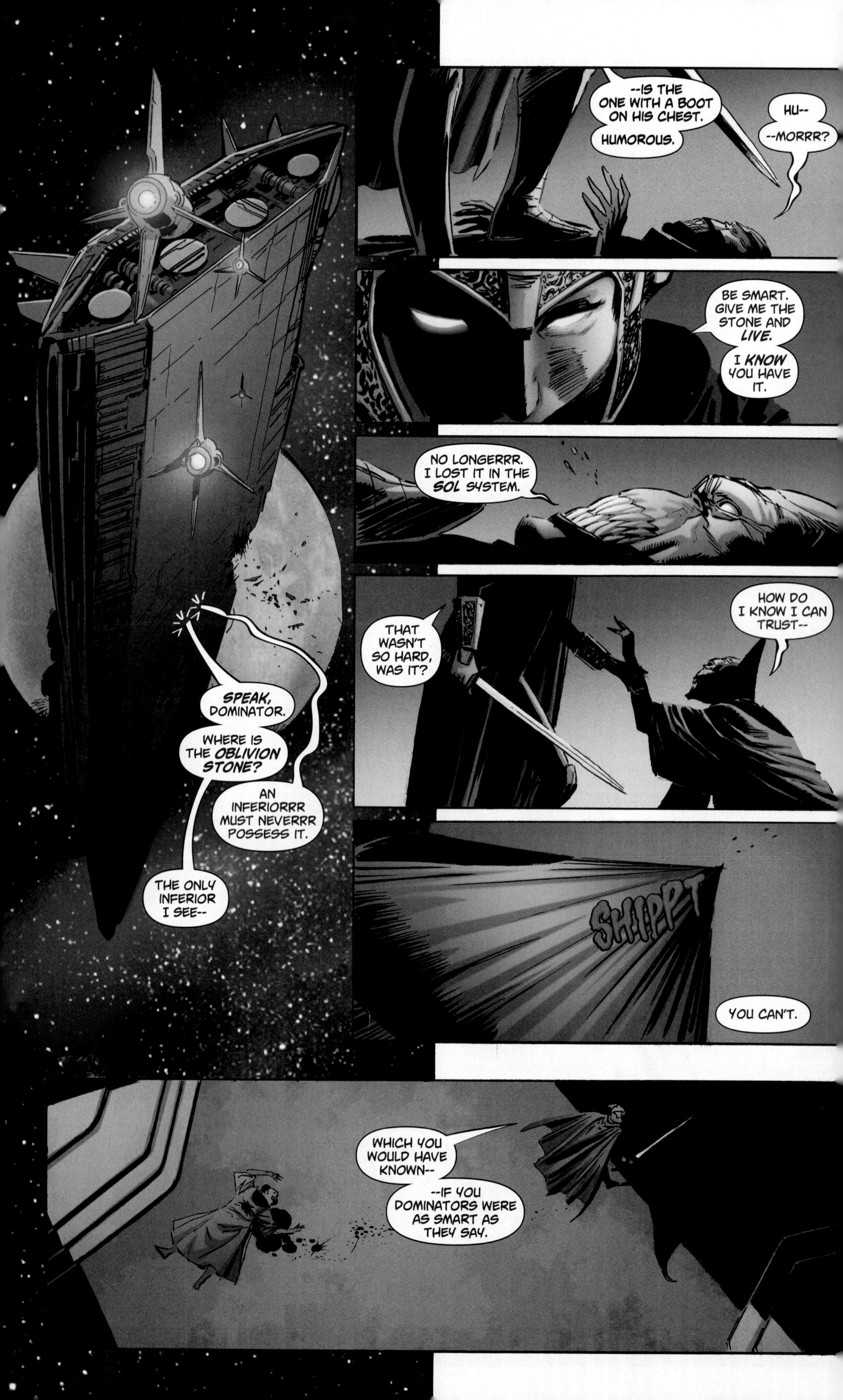
SPEAK, DOMINATOR.
WHERE IS THE OBLIVION STONE?
AN INFERIORRR MUST NEVERRR POSSESS IT.
THE ONLY INFERIOR I SEE--
--IS THE ONE WITH A BOOT ON HIS CHEST.
HUMOROUS.
HU--
--MORRR?
BE SMART. GIVE ME THE STONE AND LIVE.
I KNOW YOU HAVE IT.
NO LONGERRR. I LOST IT IN THE SOL SYSTEM.
THAT WASN'T SO HARD, WAS IT?
HOW DO I KNOW I CAN TRUST--
SHIPPT
YOU CAN'T.
WHICH YOU WOULD HAVE KNOWN--
--IF YOU DOMINATORS WERE AS SMART AS THEY SAY.

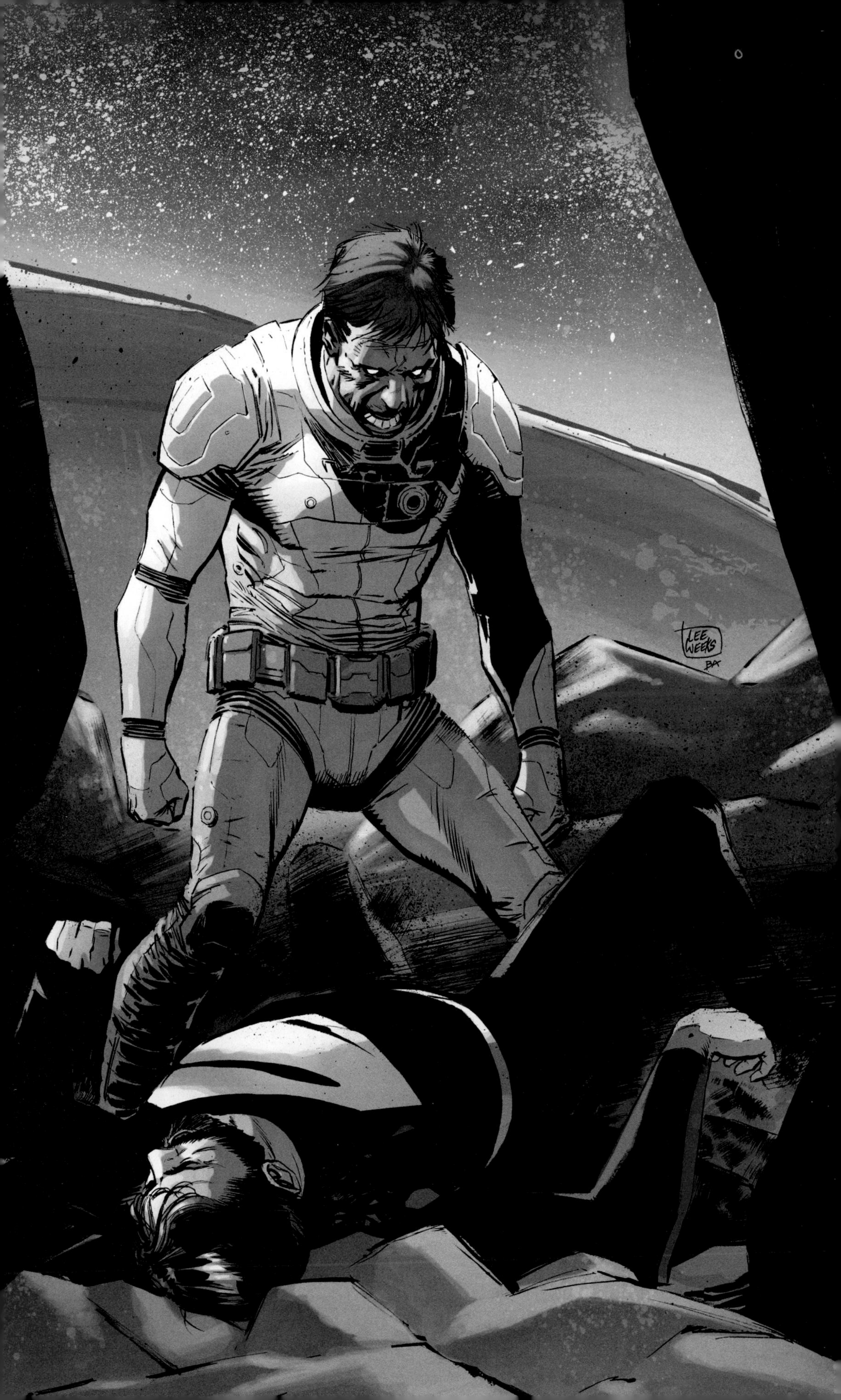
LEE WEEKS
BA

ARRIVAL: PART IV

DAN JURGENS writer LEE WEEKS MARCO SANTUCCI pencillers SERGIO CARIELLO SCOTT HANNA inkers JEROMY COX colorist A LARGER WORLD STUDIOS letterer LEE WEEKS BRAD ANDERSON cover artists

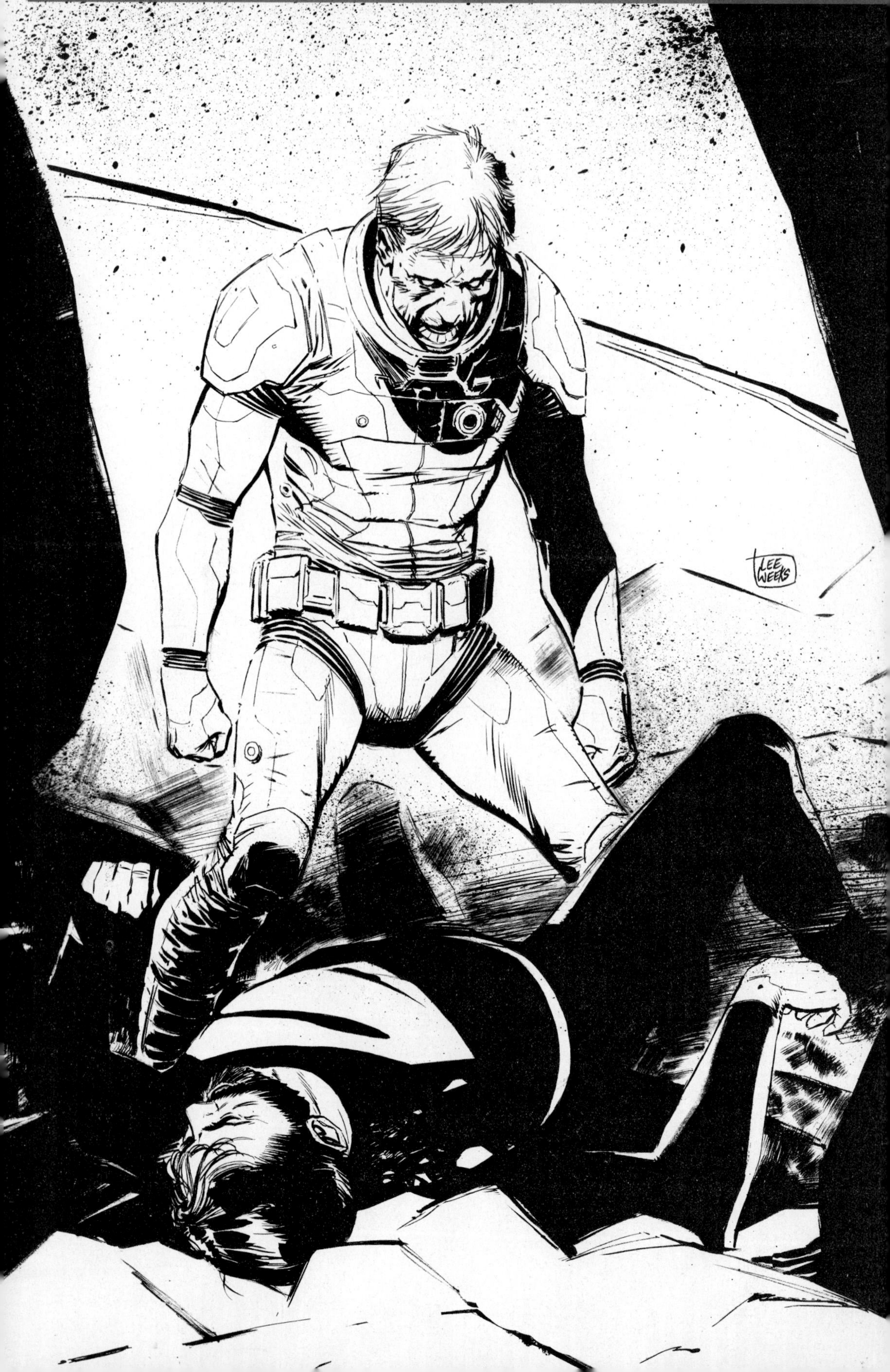
LEE WEEKS

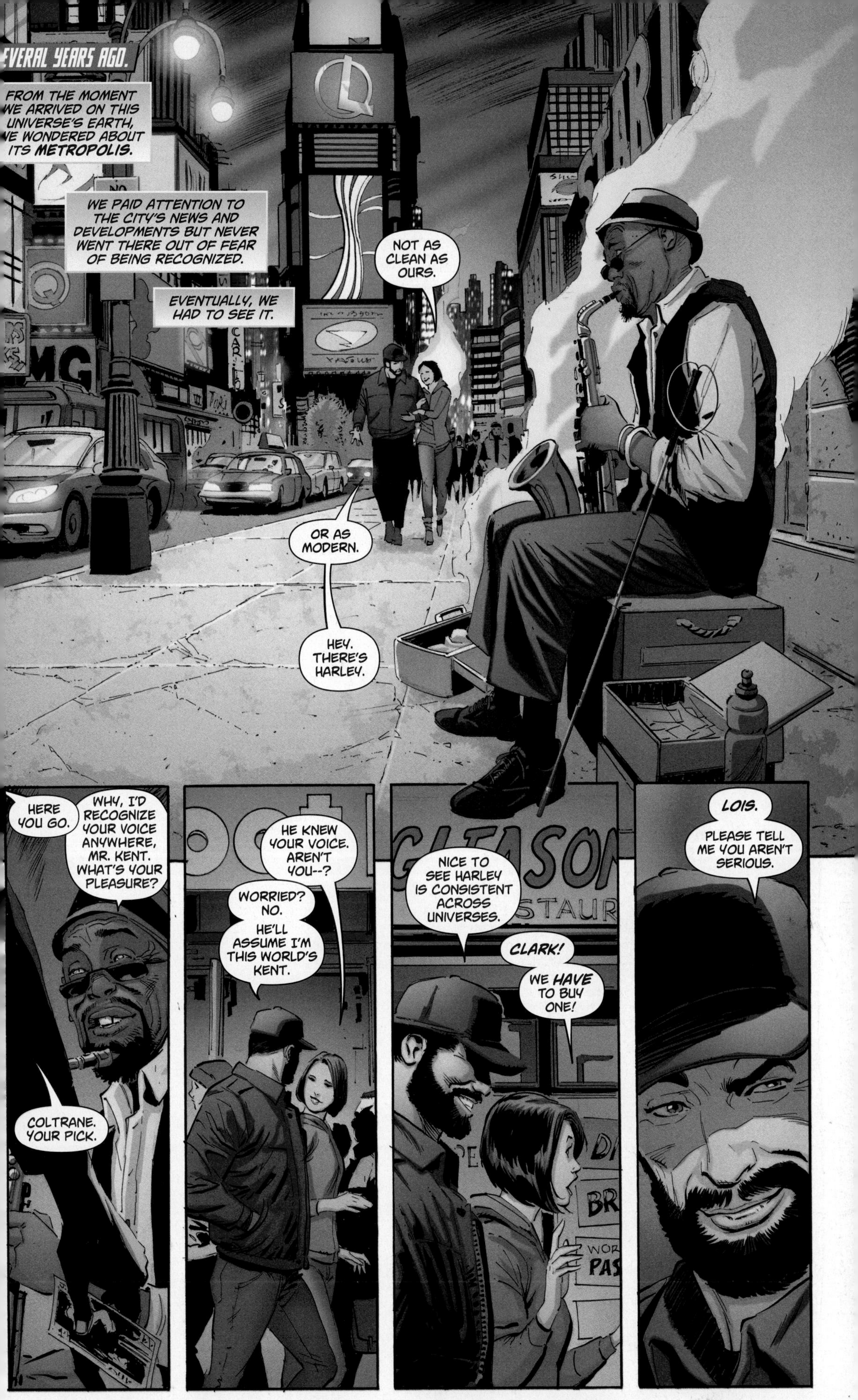

EVERAL YEARS AGO.
FROM THE MOMENT WE ARRIVED ON THIS UNIVERSE'S EARTH, WE WONDERED ABOUT ITS METROPOLIS.
WE PAID ATTENTION TO THE CITY'S NEWS AND DEVELOPMENTS BUT NEVER WENT THERE OUT OF FEAR OF BEING RECOGNIZED.
EVENTUALLY, WE HAD TO SEE IT.
NOT AS CLEAN AS OURS.
OR AS MODERN.
HEY. THERE'S HARLEY.
HERE YOU GO.
WHY, I'D RECOGNIZE YOUR VOICE ANYWHERE, MR. KENT. WHAT'S YOUR PLEASURE?
COLTRANE. YOUR PICK.
HE KNEW YOUR VOICE. AREN'T YOU--?
WORRIED? NO.
HE'LL ASSUME I'M THIS WORLD'S KENT.
NICE TO SEE HARLEY IS CONSISTENT ACROSS UNIVERSES.
CLARK!
WE HAVE TO BUY ONE!
LOIS.
PLEASE TELL ME YOU AREN'T SERIOUS.

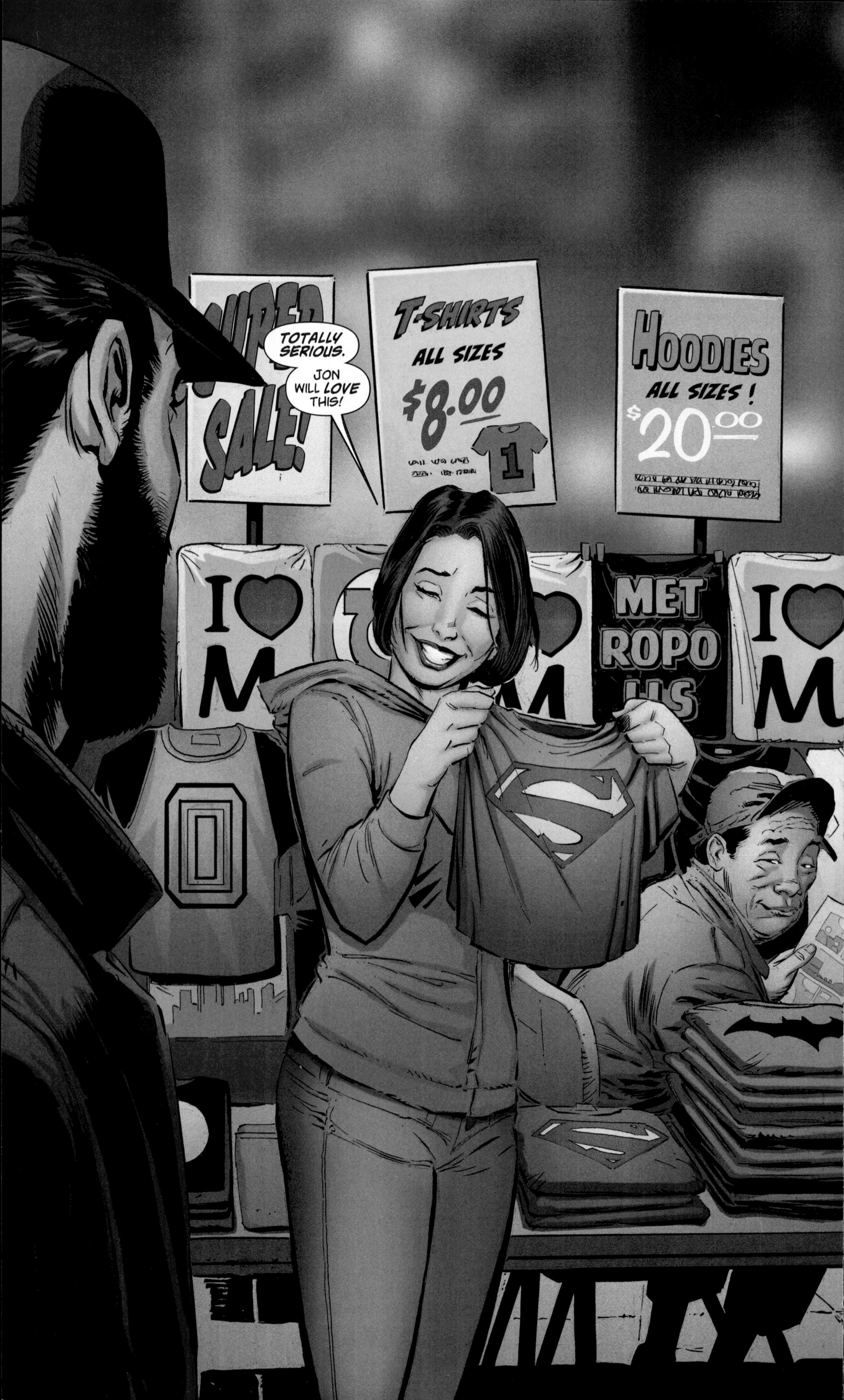
TOTALLY SERIOUS.
JON WILL LOVE THIS!
SALE!
T-SHIRTS
ALL SIZES
$8.00
HOODIES
ALL SIZES !
$20.00
MET
ROPO

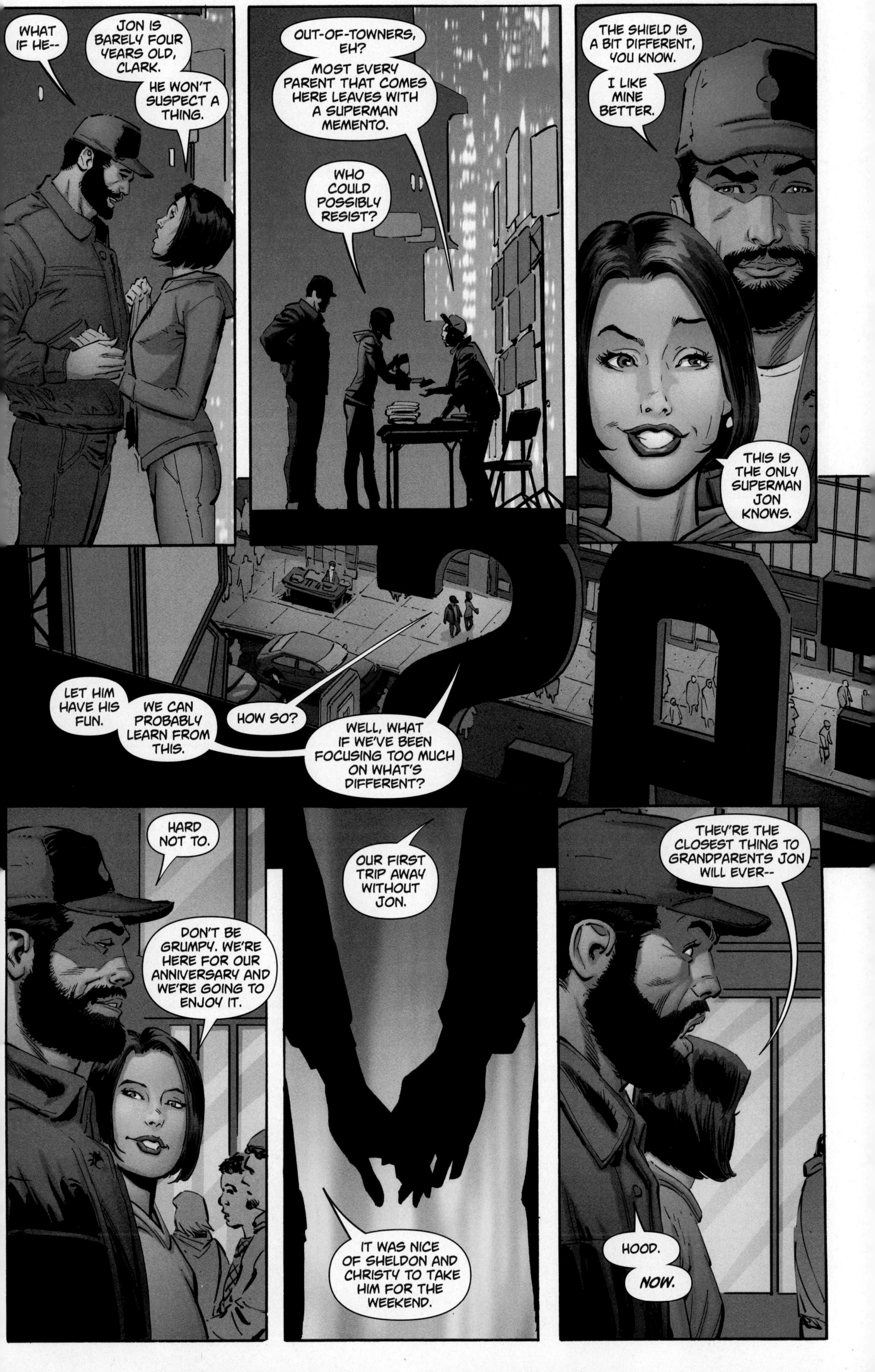

WHAT IF HE--
JON IS BARELY FOUR YEARS OLD, CLARK.
HE WON'T SUSPECT A THING.
OUT-OF-TOWNERS, EH?
MOST EVERY PARENT THAT COMES HERE LEAVES WITH A SUPERMAN MEMENTO.
WHO COULD POSSIBLY RESIST?
THE SHIELD IS A BIT DIFFERENT, YOU KNOW.
I LIKE MINE BETTER.
THIS IS THE ONLY SUPERMAN JON KNOWS.
LET HIM HAVE HIS FUN.
WE CAN PROBABLY LEARN FROM THIS.
HOW SO?
WELL, WHAT IF WE'VE BEEN FOCUSING TOO MUCH ON WHAT'S DIFFERENT?
HARD NOT TO.
DON'T BE GRUMPY. WE'RE HERE FOR OUR ANNIVERSARY AND WE'RE GOING TO ENJOY IT.
OUR FIRST TRIP AWAY WITHOUT JON.
IT WAS NICE OF SHELDON AND CHRISTY TO TAKE HIM FOR THE WEEKEND.
THEY'RE THE CLOSEST THING TO GRANDPARENTS JON WILL EVER--
HOOD.
NOW.

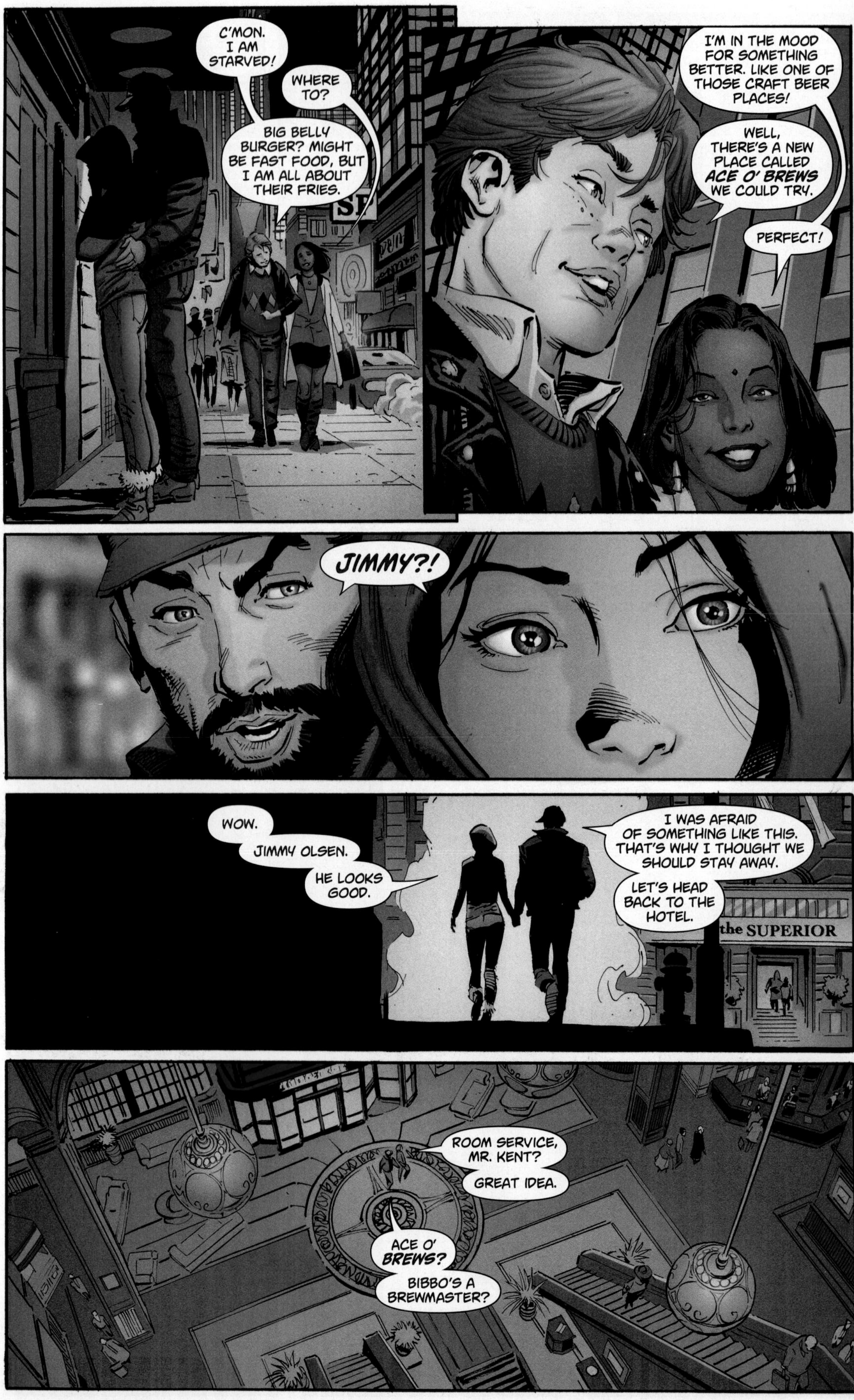

C'MON. I AM STARVED!
WHERE TO?
BIG BELLY BURGER? MIGHT BE FAST FOOD, BUT I AM ALL ABOUT THEIR FRIES.
I'M IN THE MOOD FOR SOMETHING BETTER. LIKE ONE OF THOSE CRAFT BEER PLACES!
WELL, THERE'S A NEW PLACE CALLED ACE O' BREWS WE COULD TRY.
PERFECT!
JIMMY?!
WOW.
JIMMY OLSEN.
HE LOOKS GOOD.
I WAS AFRAID OF SOMETHING LIKE THIS. THAT'S WHY I THOUGHT WE SHOULD STAY AWAY.
LET'S HEAD BACK TO THE HOTEL.
the SUPERIOR
ROOM SERVICE, MR. KENT?
GREAT IDEA.
ACE O' BREWS?
BIBBO'S A BREWMASTER?

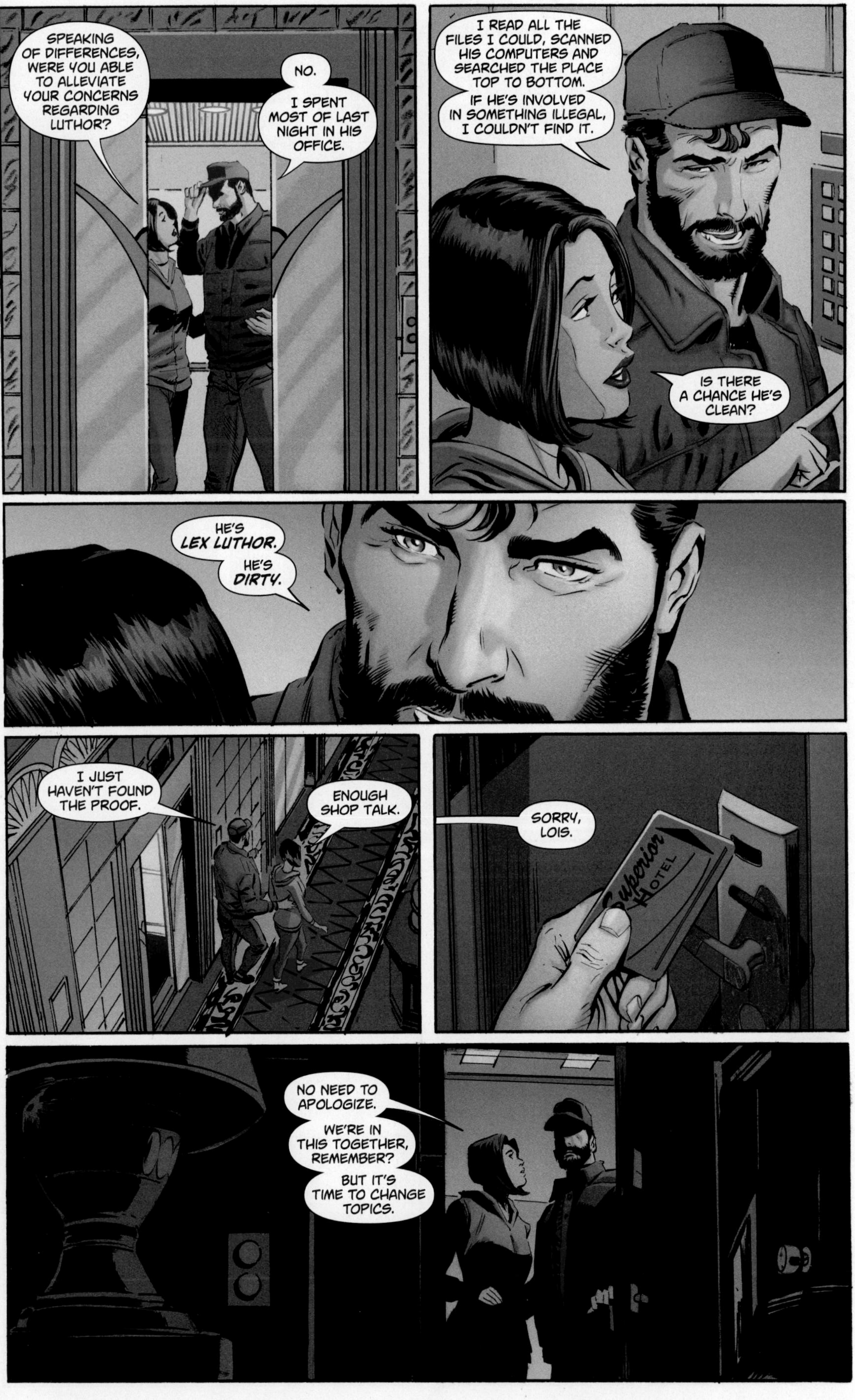
SPEAKING OF DIFFERENCES, WERE YOU ABLE TO ALLEVIATE YOUR CONCERNS REGARDING LUTHOR?
NO.
I SPENT MOST OF LAST NIGHT IN HIS OFFICE.
I READ ALL THE FILES I COULD, SCANNED HIS COMPUTERS AND SEARCHED THE PLACE TOP TO BOTTOM.
IF HE'S INVOLVED IN SOMETHING ILLEGAL, I COULDN'T FIND IT.
IS THERE A CHANCE HE'S CLEAN?
HE'S LEX LUTHOR.
HE'S DIRTY.
I JUST HAVEN'T FOUND THE PROOF.
ENOUGH SHOP TALK.
SORRY, LOIS.
Superior HOTEL
NO NEED TO APOLOGIZE.
WE'RE IN THIS TOGETHER, REMEMBER?
BUT IT'S TIME TO CHANGE TOPICS.

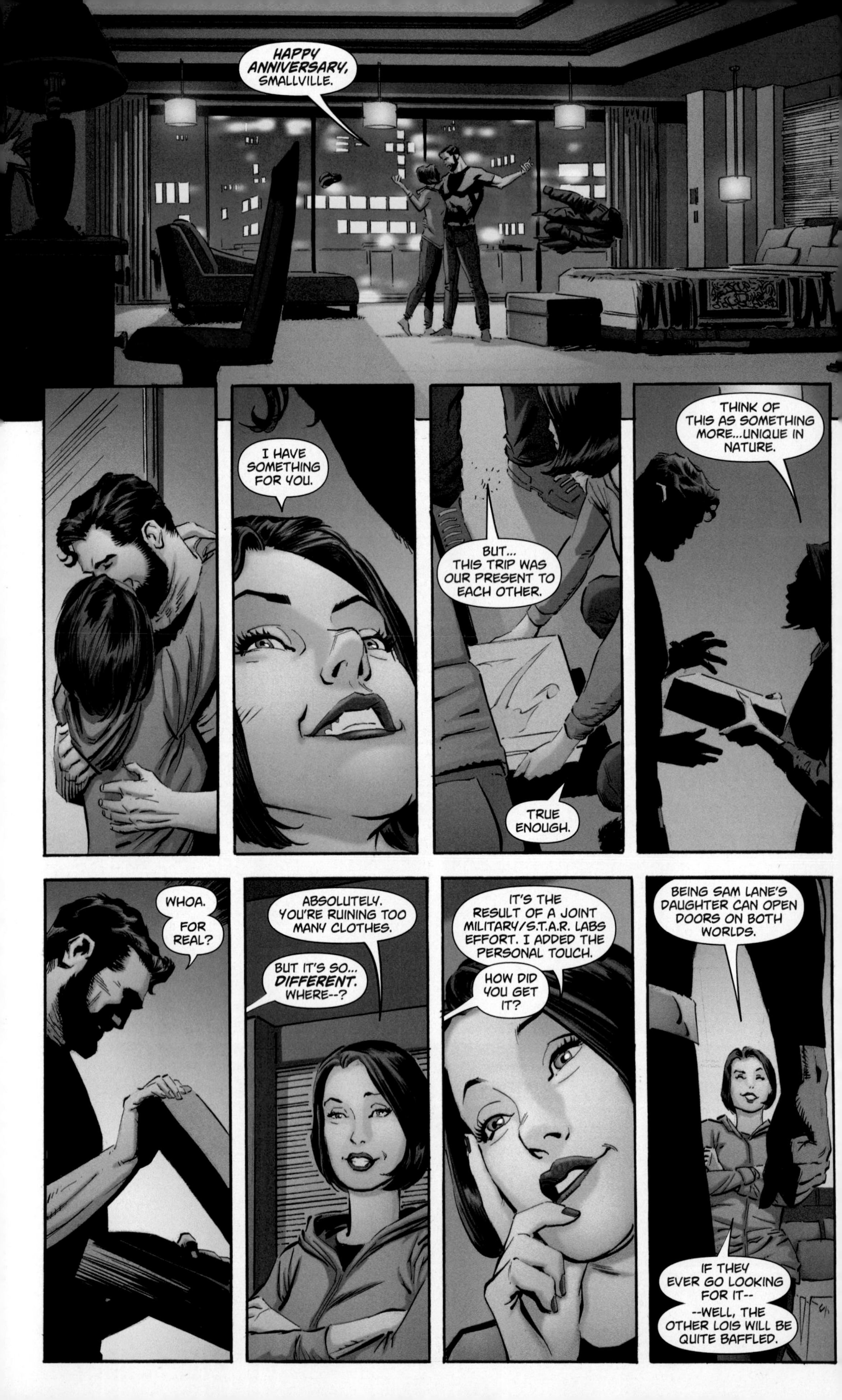
HAPPY ANNIVERSARY, SMALLVILLE.
I HAVE SOMETHING FOR YOU.
BUT... THIS TRIP WAS OUR PRESENT TO EACH OTHER.
TRUE ENOUGH.
THINK OF THIS AS SOMETHING MORE...UNIQUE IN NATURE.
WHOA.
FOR REAL?
ABSOLUTELY. YOU'RE RUINING TOO MANY CLOTHES.
BUT IT'S SO... DIFFERENT. WHERE--?
IT'S THE RESULT OF A JOINT MILITARY/S.T.A.R. LABS EFFORT. I ADDED THE PERSONAL TOUCH.
HOW DID YOU GET IT?
BEING SAM LANE'S DAUGHTER CAN OPEN DOORS ON BOTH WORLDS.
IF THEY EVER GO LOOKING FOR IT--
--WELL, THE OTHER LOIS WILL BE QUITE BAFFLED.

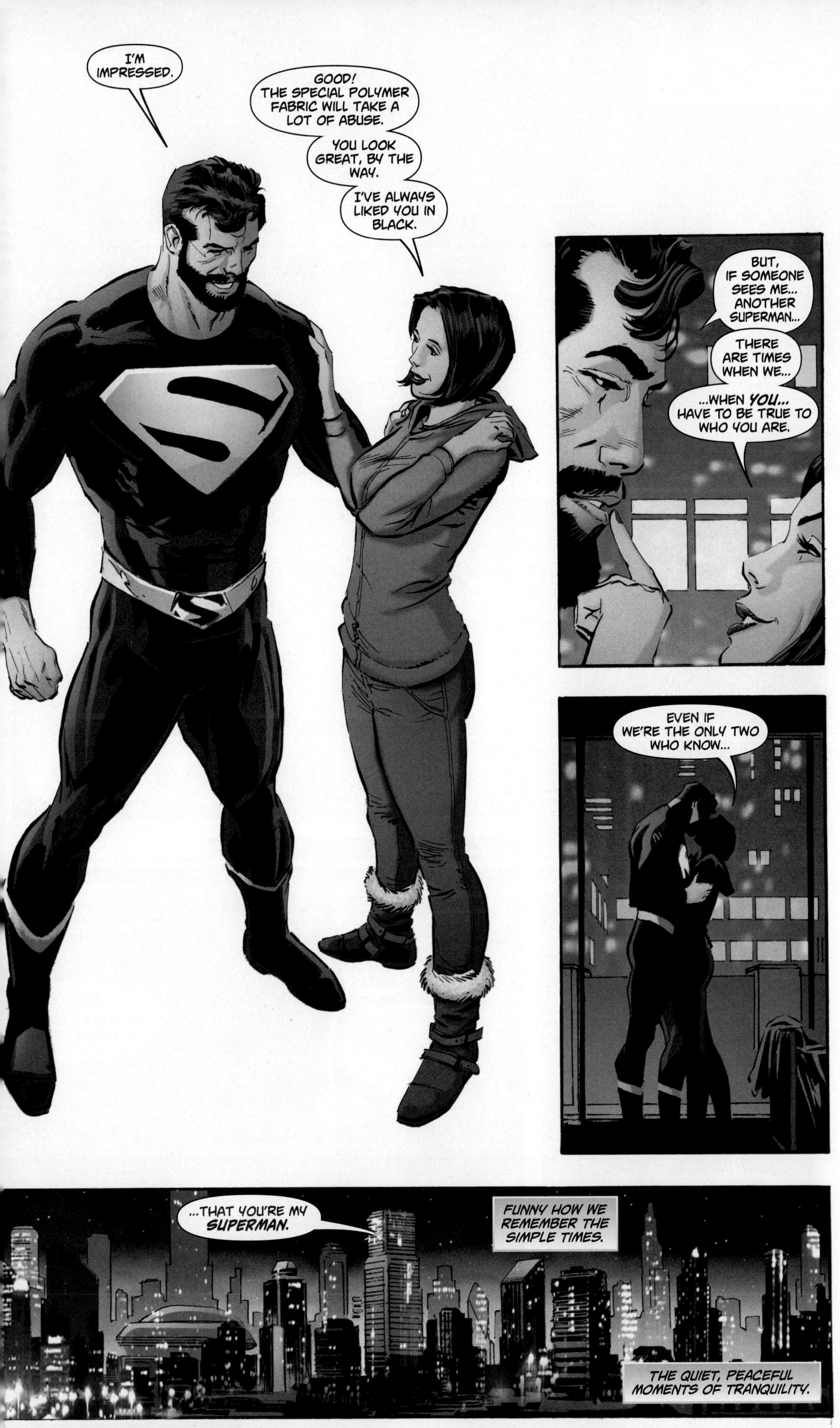
I'M IMPRESSED.
GOOD! THE SPECIAL POLYMER FABRIC WILL TAKE A LOT OF ABUSE.
YOU LOOK GREAT, BY THE WAY.
I'VE ALWAYS LIKED YOU IN BLACK.
BUT, IF SOMEONE SEES ME... ANOTHER SUPERMAN...
THERE ARE TIMES WHEN WE...
...WHEN *YOU*... HAVE TO BE TRUE TO WHO YOU ARE.
EVEN IF WE'RE THE ONLY TWO WHO KNOW...
...THAT YOU'RE MY **SUPERMAN.**
FUNNY HOW WE REMEMBER THE SIMPLE TIMES.
THE QUIET, PEACEFUL MOMENTS OF TRANQUILITY.

PROBABLY BECAUSE, RIGHT NOW, THOSE TIMES SEEM SO DISTANT.

HEY, MOM.

YES, HON?

I'VE BEEN LOOKING FOR NEWS ABOUT THAT HIGHWAY GANG THAT CAME AFTER US, AND YOU KNOW WHAT?

WHAT, JON?

THERE IS, LIKE, *ZERO* NEWS ABOUT 'EM ANYWHERE.

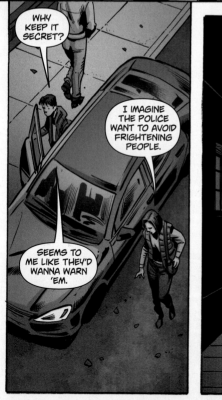

WHY KEEP IT SECRET?

I IMAGINE THE POLICE WANT TO AVOID FRIGHTENING PEOPLE.

SEEMS TO ME LIKE THEY'D WANNA WARN 'EM.

WHY'RE WE HERE SO LATE, MOM? SEEMS KINDA WEIRD.

I'M CHECKING ON A FRIEND, JON. I WANT TO MAKE SURE SHE'S OKAY.

WHO?

CORA. YOU REMEMBER HER... SHE'S BEEN TO THE HOUSE SEVERAL TIMES.

BRINGING JON WASN'T MY FIRST CHOICE, BUT I COULDN' LEAVE HIM HOME ALONE.

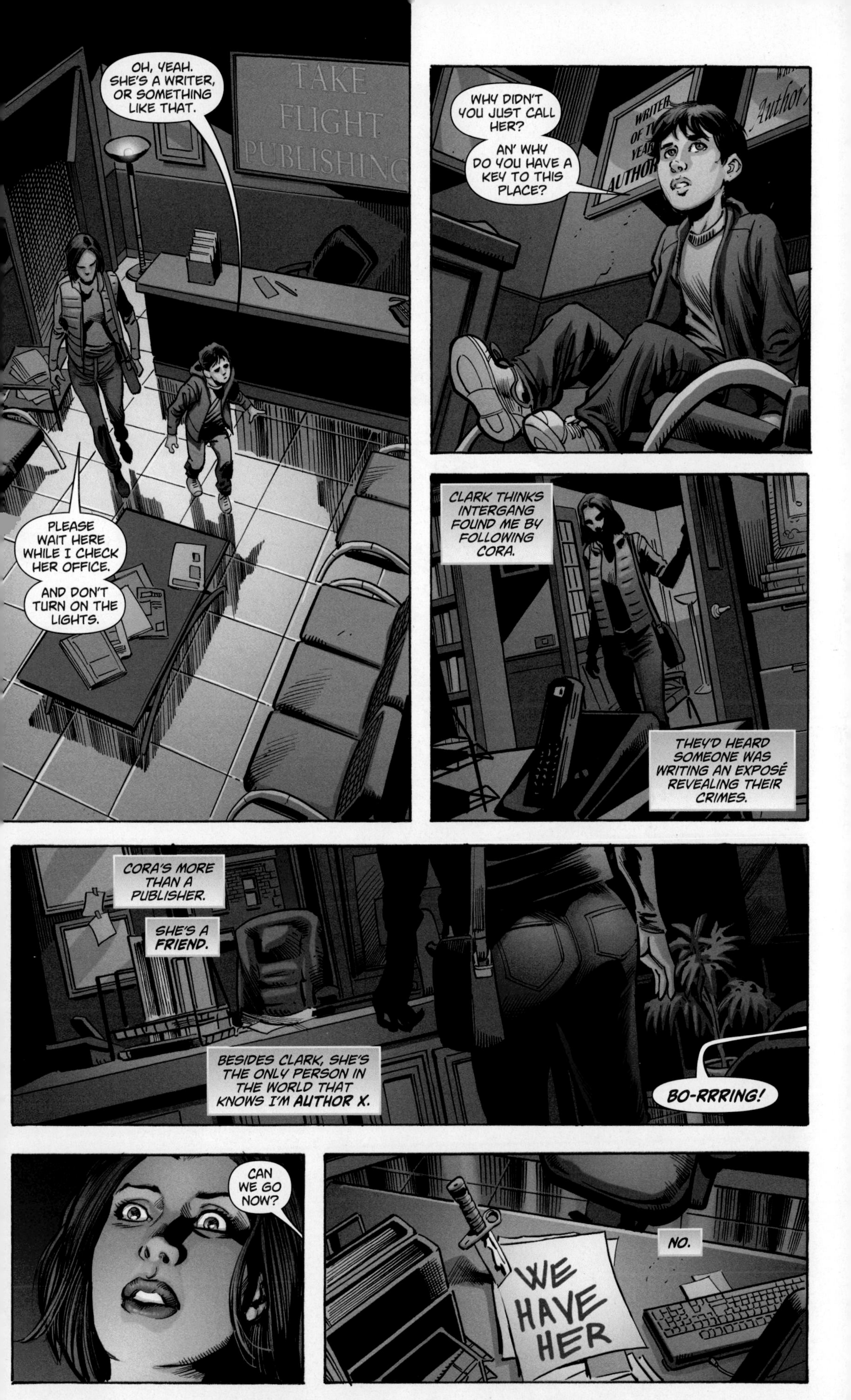
TAKE FLIGHT PUBLISHING
OH, YEAH. SHE'S A WRITER, OR SOMETHING LIKE THAT.
PLEASE WAIT HERE WHILE I CHECK HER OFFICE.
AND DON'T TURN ON THE LIGHTS.
WHY DIDN'T YOU JUST CALL HER?
AN' WHY DO YOU HAVE A KEY TO THIS PLACE?
CLARK THINKS INTERGANG FOUND ME BY FOLLOWING CORA.
THEY'D HEARD SOMEONE WAS WRITING AN EXPOSÉ REVEALING THEIR CRIMES.
CORA'S MORE THAN A PUBLISHER.
SHE'S A **FRIEND**.
BESIDES CLARK, SHE'S THE ONLY PERSON IN THE WORLD THAT KNOWS I'M **AUTHOR X**.
BO-RRRING!
CAN WE GO NOW?
NO.
WE HAVE HER

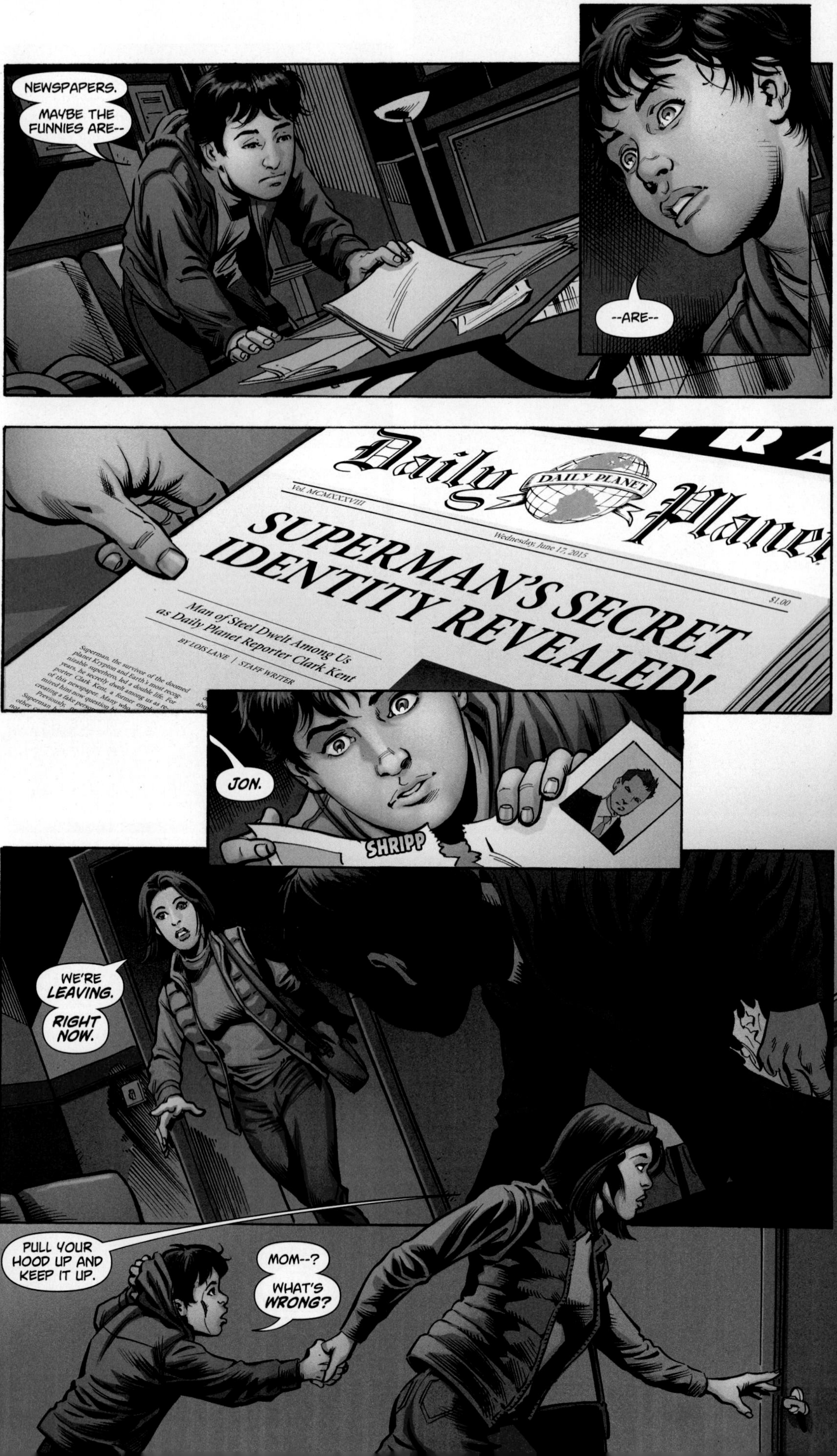

NEWSPAPERS.
MAYBE THE FUNNIES ARE--
--ARE--
Daily Planet
DAILY PLANET
Vol. MCMXXXVIII
Wednesday, June 17, 2015
$1.00
SUPERMAN'S SECRET IDENTITY REVEALED!
Man of Steel Dwelt Among Us as Daily Planet Reporter Clark Kent
BY LOIS LANE | STAFF WRITER
JON.
SHRIPP
WE'RE LEAVING.
RIGHT NOW.
PULL YOUR HOOD UP AND KEEP IT UP.
MOM--?
WHAT'S WRONG?

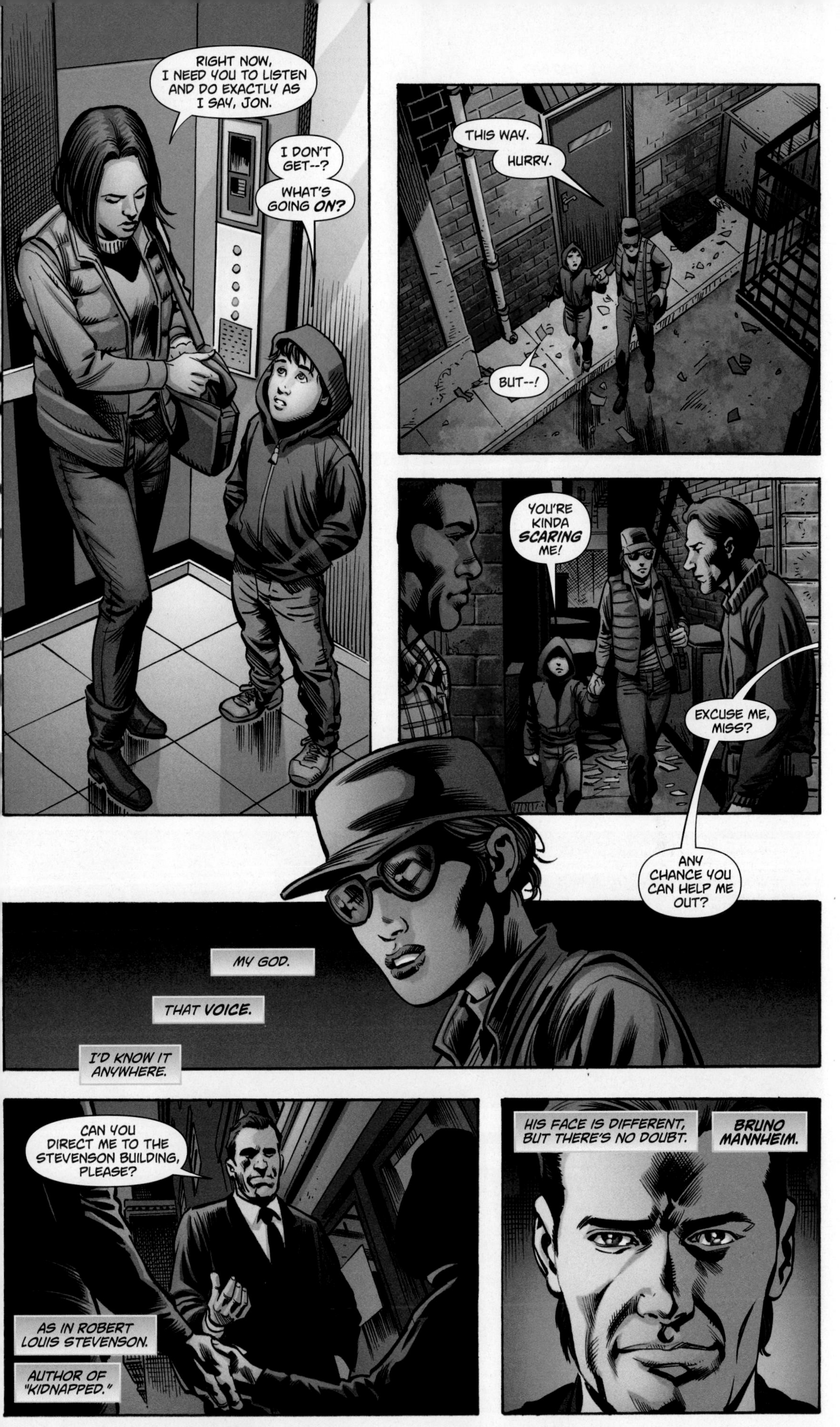

RIGHT NOW, I NEED YOU TO LISTEN AND DO EXACTLY AS I SAY, JON.
I DON'T GET--?
WHAT'S GOING ON?
THIS WAY.
HURRY.
BUT--!
YOU'RE KINDA SCARING ME!
EXCUSE ME, MISS?
ANY CHANCE YOU CAN HELP ME OUT?
MY GOD.
THAT VOICE.
I'D KNOW IT ANYWHERE.
CAN YOU DIRECT ME TO THE STEVENSON BUILDING, PLEASE?
AS IN ROBERT LOUIS STEVENSON.
AUTHOR OF "KIDNAPPED."
HIS FACE IS DIFFERENT, BUT THERE'S NO DOUBT.
BRUNO MANNHEIM.

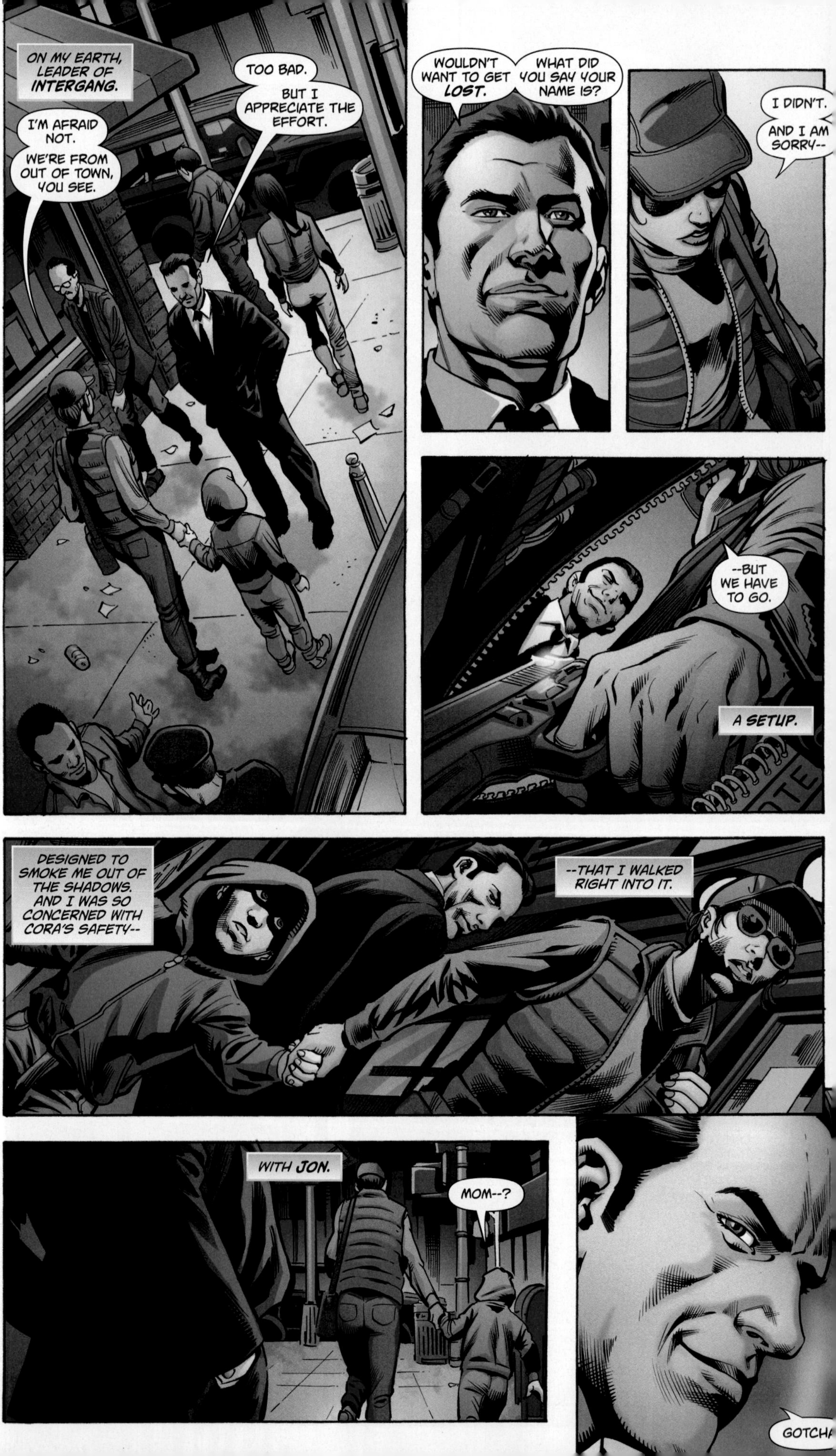
ON MY EARTH, LEADER OF INTERGANG.
I'M AFRAID NOT.
WE'RE FROM OUT OF TOWN, YOU SEE.
TOO BAD.
BUT I APPRECIATE THE EFFORT.
WOULDN'T WANT TO GET LOST.
WHAT DID YOU SAY YOUR NAME IS?
I DIDN'T.
AND I AM SORRY--
--BUT WE HAVE TO GO.
A SETUP.
DESIGNED TO SMOKE ME OUT OF THE SHADOWS. AND I WAS SO CONCERNED WITH CORA'S SAFETY--
--THAT I WALKED RIGHT INTO IT.
WITH JON.
MOM--?
GOTCHA

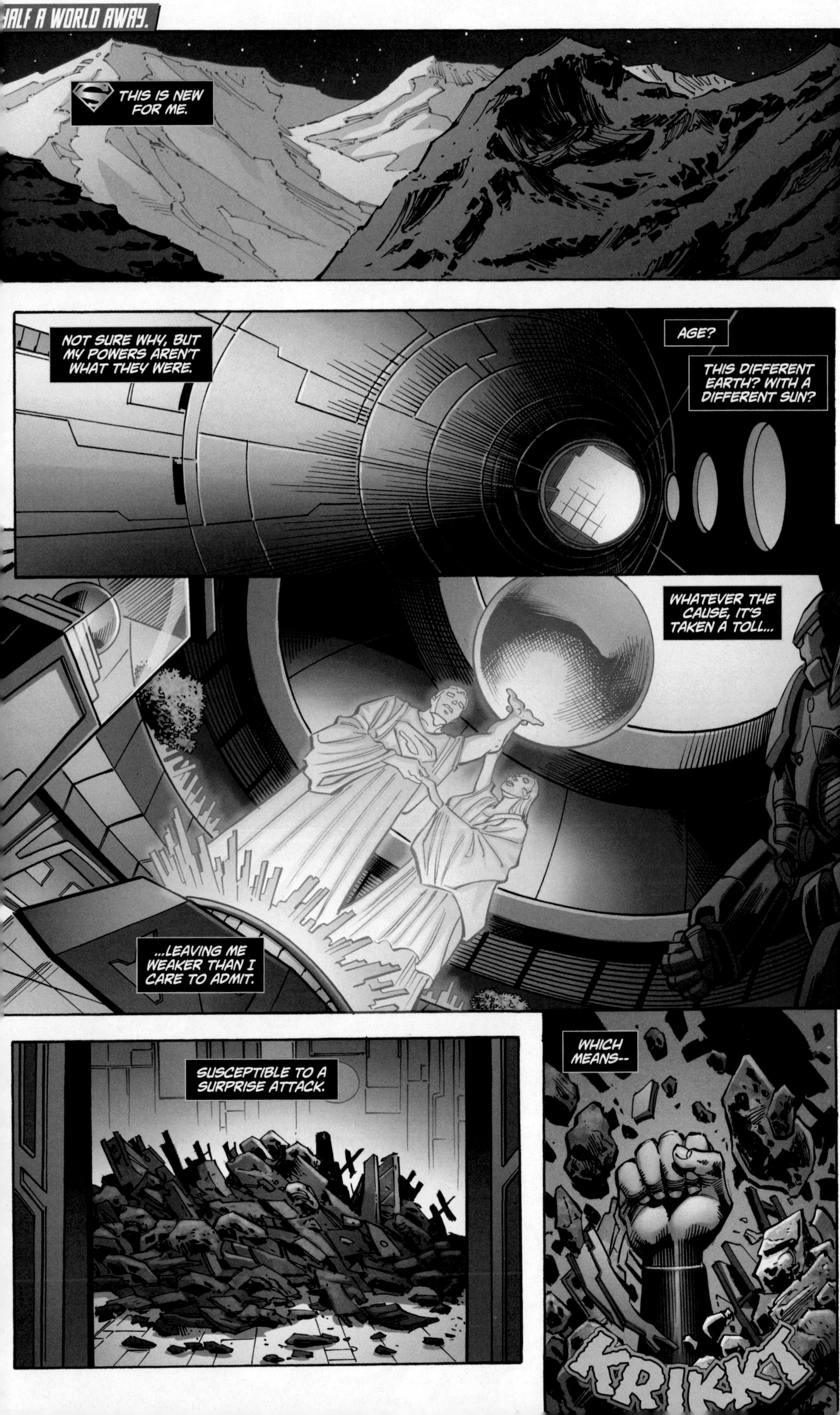
HALF A WORLD AWAY.
THIS IS NEW FOR ME.
NOT SURE WHY, BUT MY POWERS AREN'T WHAT THEY WERE.
AGE?
THIS DIFFERENT EARTH? WITH A DIFFERENT SUN?
WHATEVER THE CAUSE, IT'S TAKEN A TOLL...
...LEAVING ME WEAKER THAN I CARE TO ADMIT.
SUSCEPTIBLE TO A SURPRISE ATTACK.
WHICH MEANS--
KRIKK!

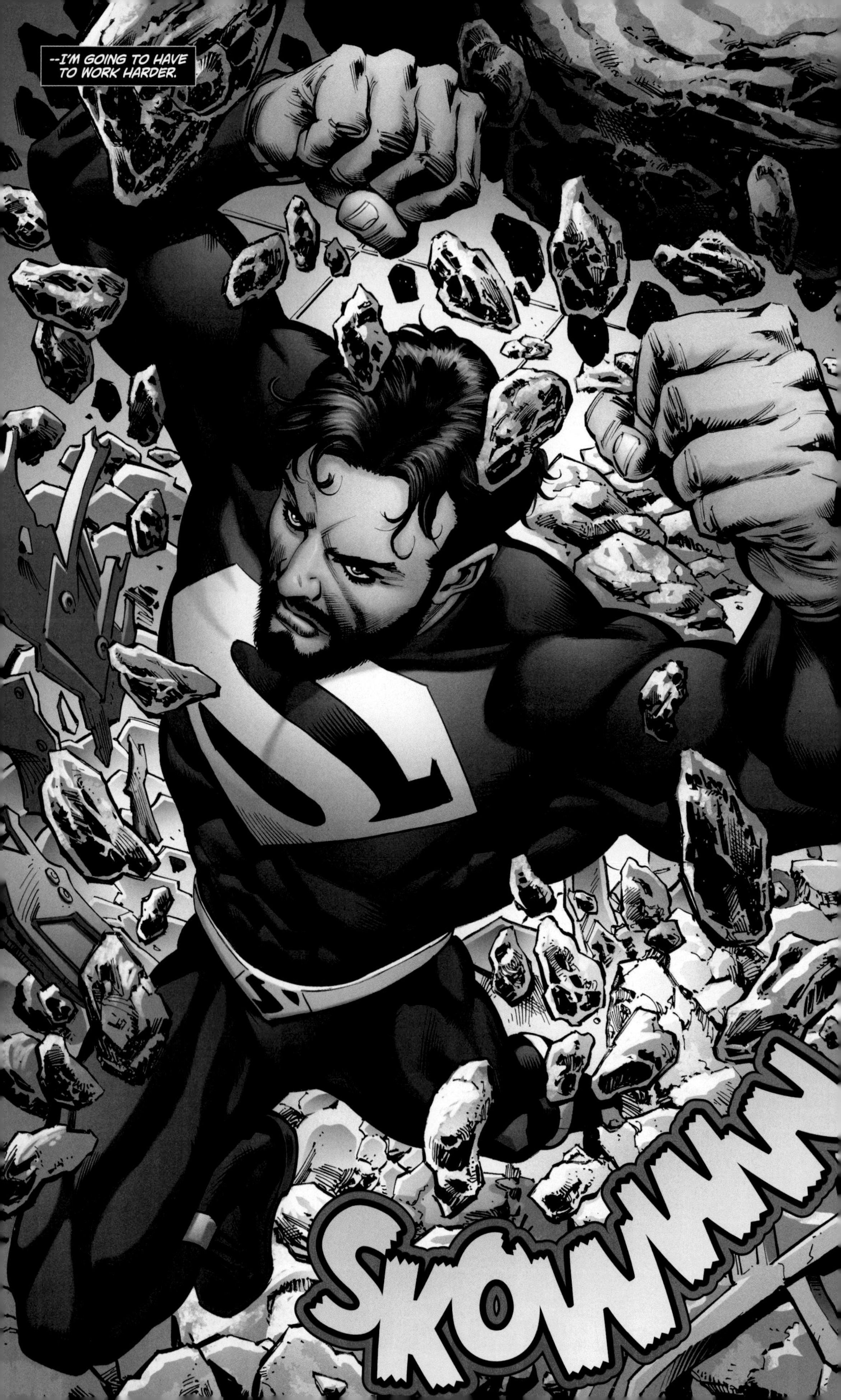
--I'M GOING TO HAVE TO WORK HARDER.
SKOWW

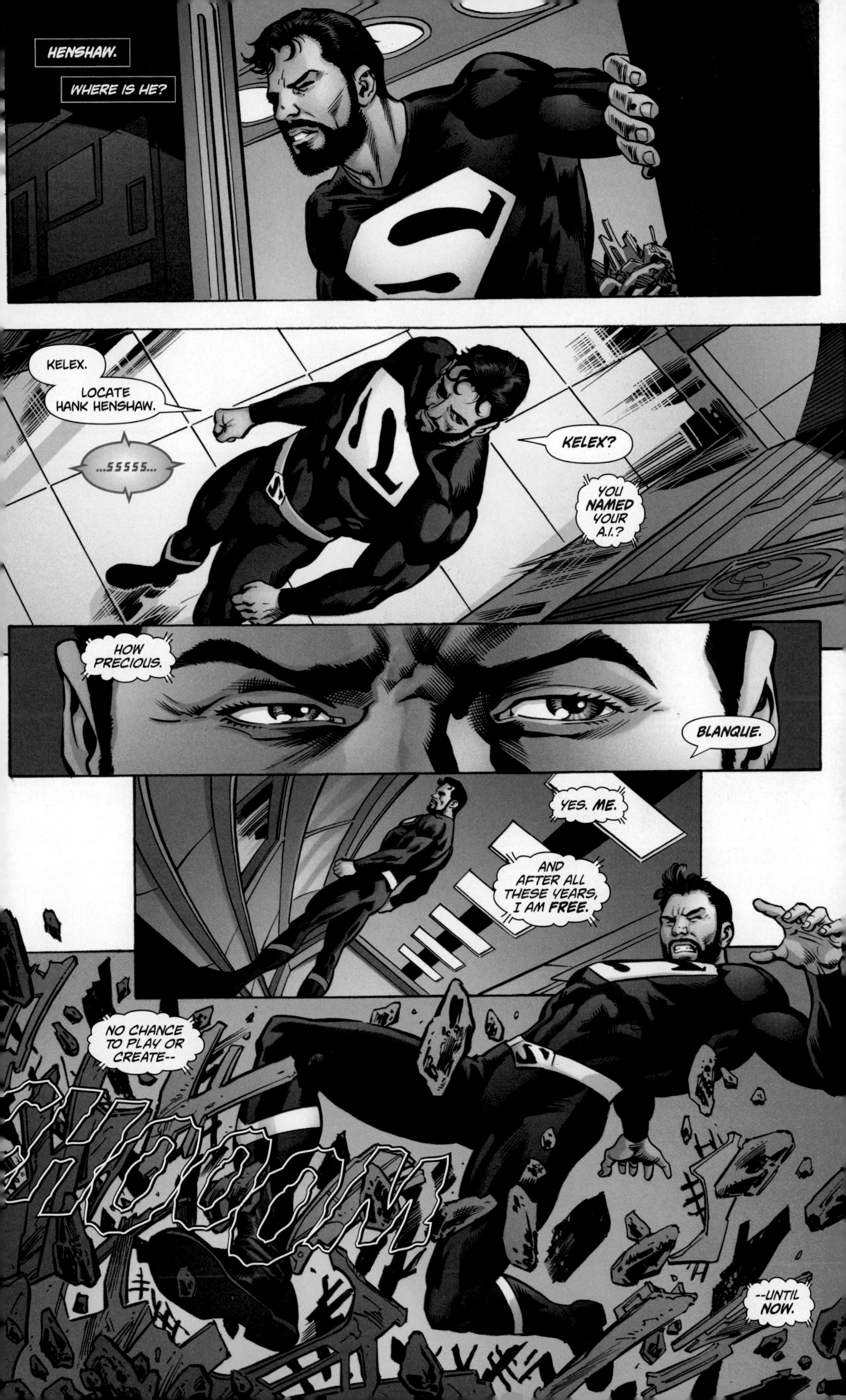
HENSHAW.
WHERE IS HE?
KELEX.
LOCATE HANK HENSHAW.
...SSSSS...
KELEX?
YOU NAMED YOUR A.I.?
HOW PRECIOUS.
BLANQUE.
YES. ME.
AND AFTER ALL THESE YEARS, I AM FREE.
NO CHANCE TO PLAY OR CREATE--
KROOOM
--UNTIL NOW.

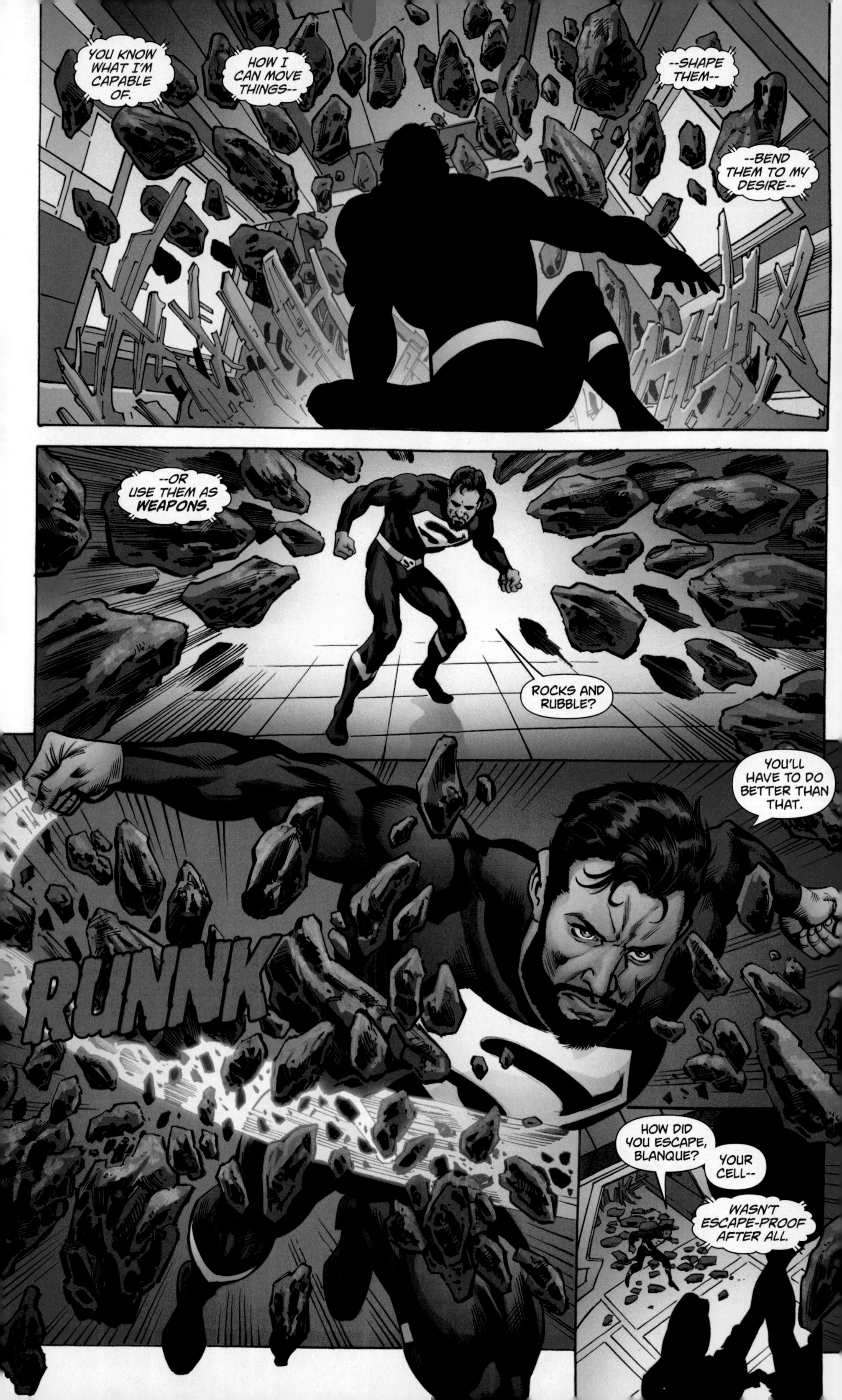
YOU KNOW WHAT I'M CAPABLE OF.
HOW I CAN MOVE THINGS--
--SHAPE THEM--
--BEND THEM TO MY DESIRE--
--OR USE THEM AS WEAPONS.
ROCKS AND RUBBLE?
YOU'LL HAVE TO DO BETTER THAN THAT.
RUNNK
HOW DID YOU ESCAPE, BLANQUE?
YOUR CELL--
WASN'T ESCAPE-PROOF AFTER ALL.

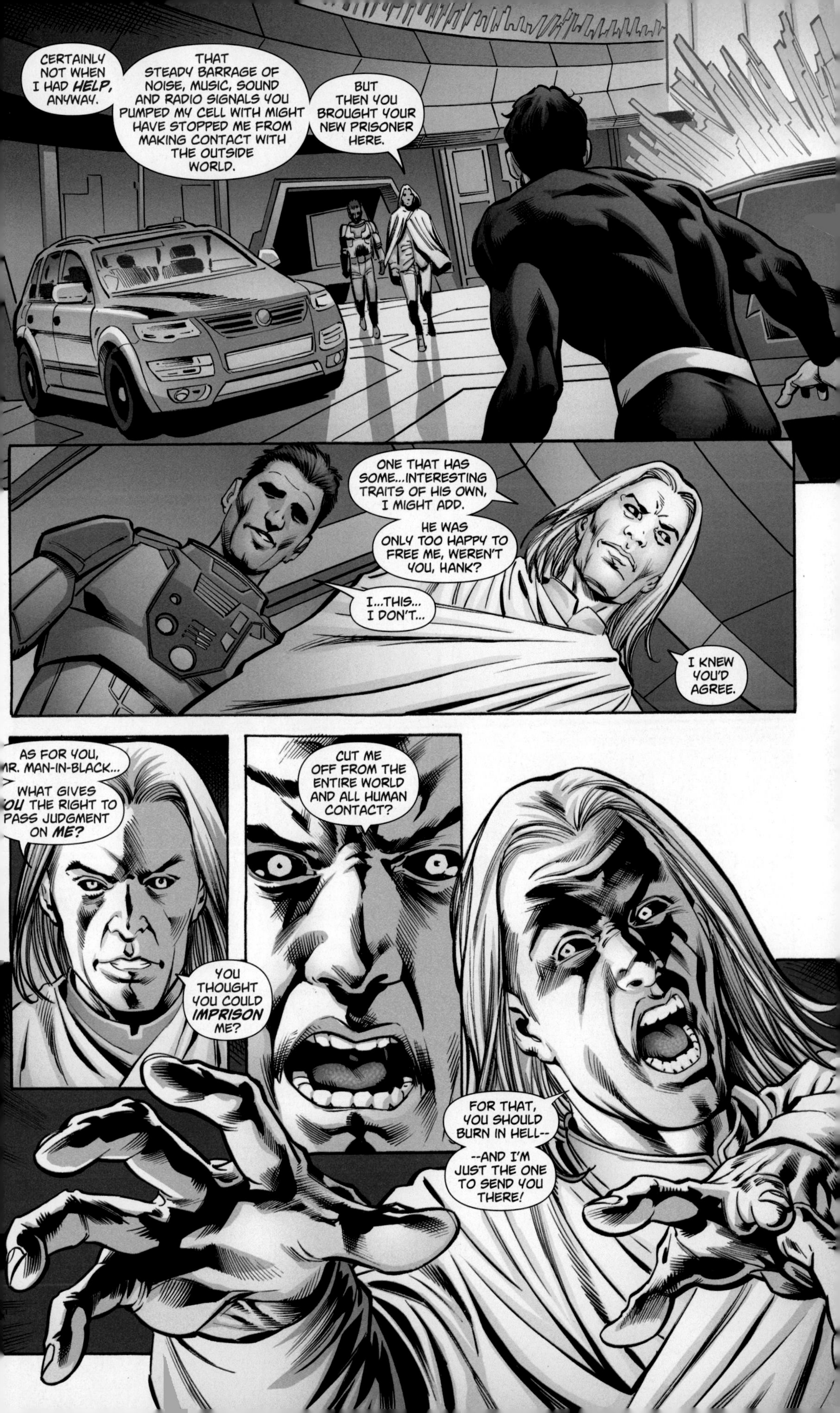
CERTAINLY NOT WHEN I HAD HELP, ANYWAY.
THAT STEADY BARRAGE OF NOISE, MUSIC, SOUND AND RADIO SIGNALS YOU PUMPED MY CELL WITH MIGHT HAVE STOPPED ME FROM MAKING CONTACT WITH THE OUTSIDE WORLD.
BUT THEN YOU BROUGHT YOUR NEW PRISONER HERE.
ONE THAT HAS SOME...INTERESTING TRAITS OF HIS OWN, I MIGHT ADD.
HE WAS ONLY TOO HAPPY TO FREE ME, WEREN'T YOU, HANK?
I...THIS... I DON'T...
I KNEW YOU'D AGREE.
AS FOR YOU, MR. MAN-IN-BLACK...
WHAT GIVES YOU THE RIGHT TO PASS JUDGMENT ON ME?
YOU THOUGHT YOU COULD IMPRISON ME?
CUT ME OFF FROM THE ENTIRE WORLD AND ALL HUMAN CONTACT?
FOR THAT, YOU SHOULD BURN IN HELL--
--AND I'M JUST THE ONE TO SEND YOU THERE!

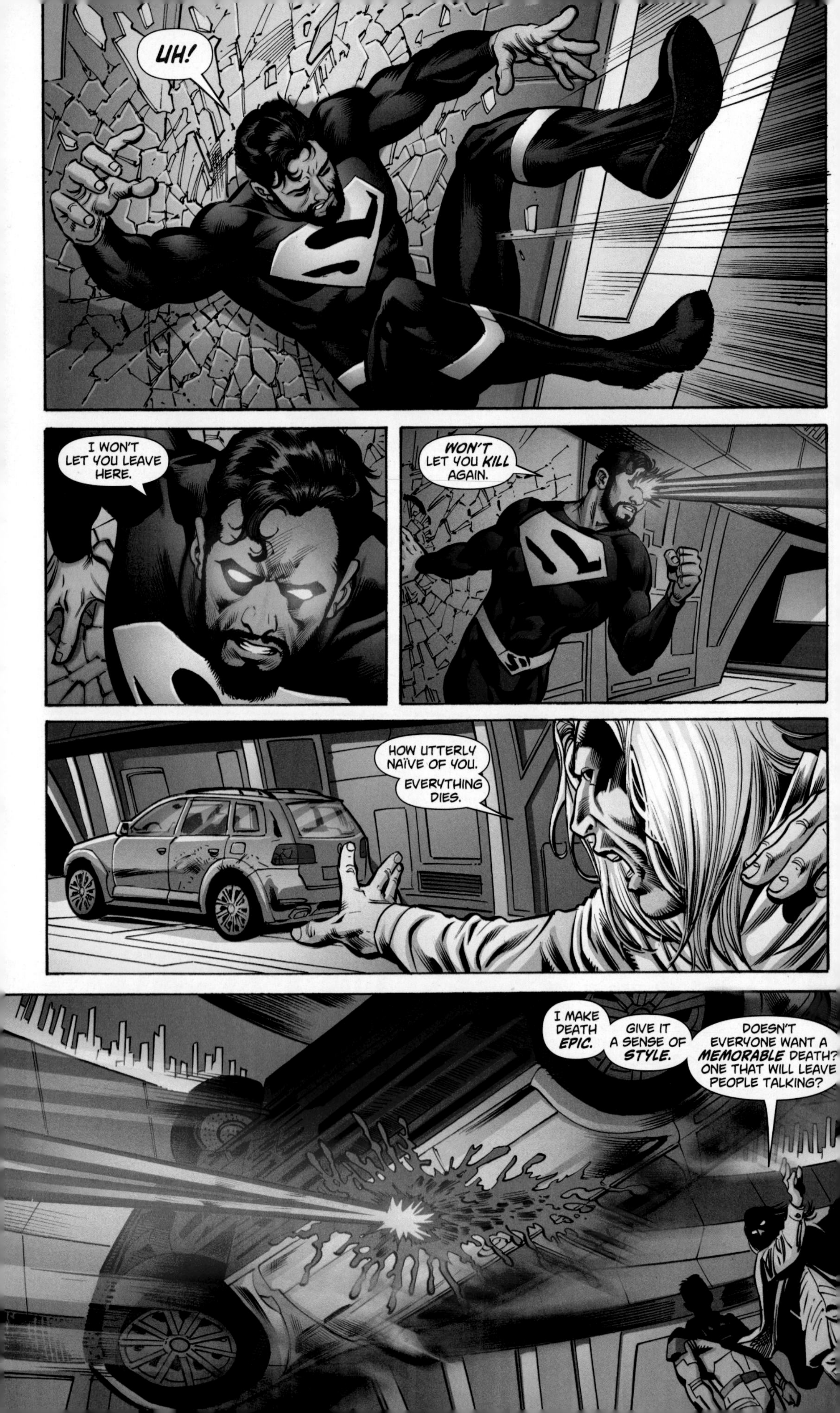
UH!
I WON'T LET YOU LEAVE HERE.
WON'T LET YOU KILL AGAIN.
HOW UTTERLY NAÏVE OF YOU.
EVERYTHING DIES.
I MAKE DEATH EPIC.
GIVE IT A SENSE OF STYLE.
DOESN'T EVERYONE WANT A MEMORABLE DEATH? ONE THAT WILL LEAVE PEOPLE TALKING?

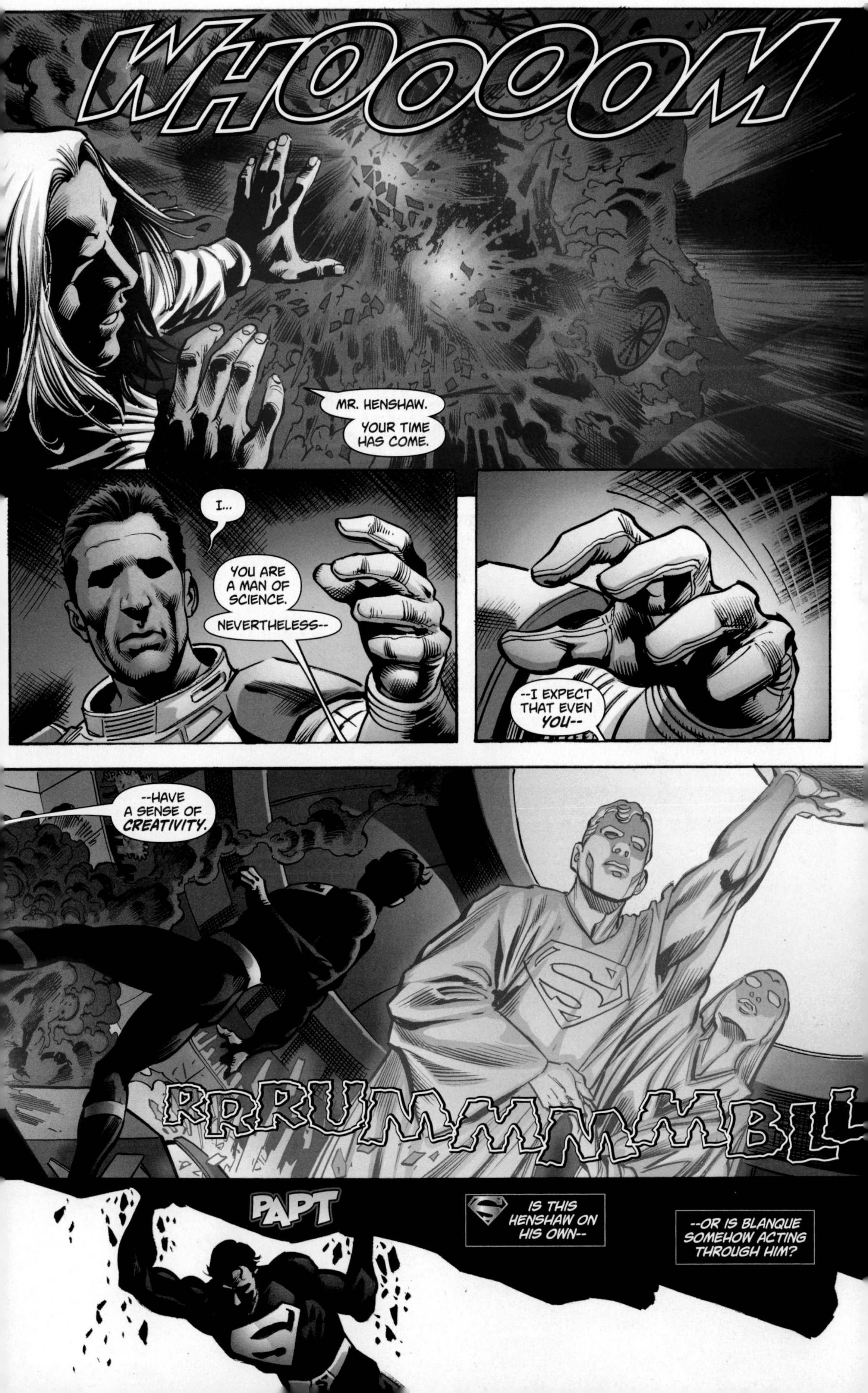
WHOOOOOM
MR. HENSHAW.
YOUR TIME HAS COME.
I...
YOU ARE A MAN OF SCIENCE.
NEVERTHELESS--
--I EXPECT THAT EVEN YOU--
--HAVE A SENSE OF CREATIVITY.
RRRUMMMMBL
PAPT
IS THIS HENSHAW ON HIS OWN--
--OR IS BLANQUE SOMEHOW ACTING THROUGH HIM?

BEING LOCKED UP HAS PREVENTED ME FROM EXERCISING MY SENSE OF CREATIVE EXPRESSION.

BUT IN ALL THAT TIME, I'VE HAD ONE IDEA-- --ONE VISION I WANT TO SE REALIZED.

YOUR DEATH!

BOO OM

"AND THOSE PEOPLE I SENSE IN YOUR MIND?"

KRAKA-CHAKKT

"THAT WOMAN?"

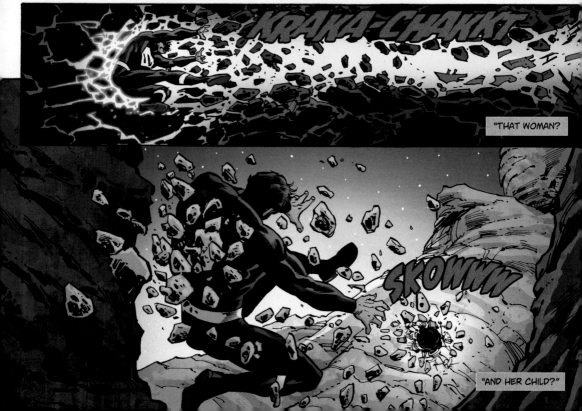

SKOWWW

"AND HER CHILD?"

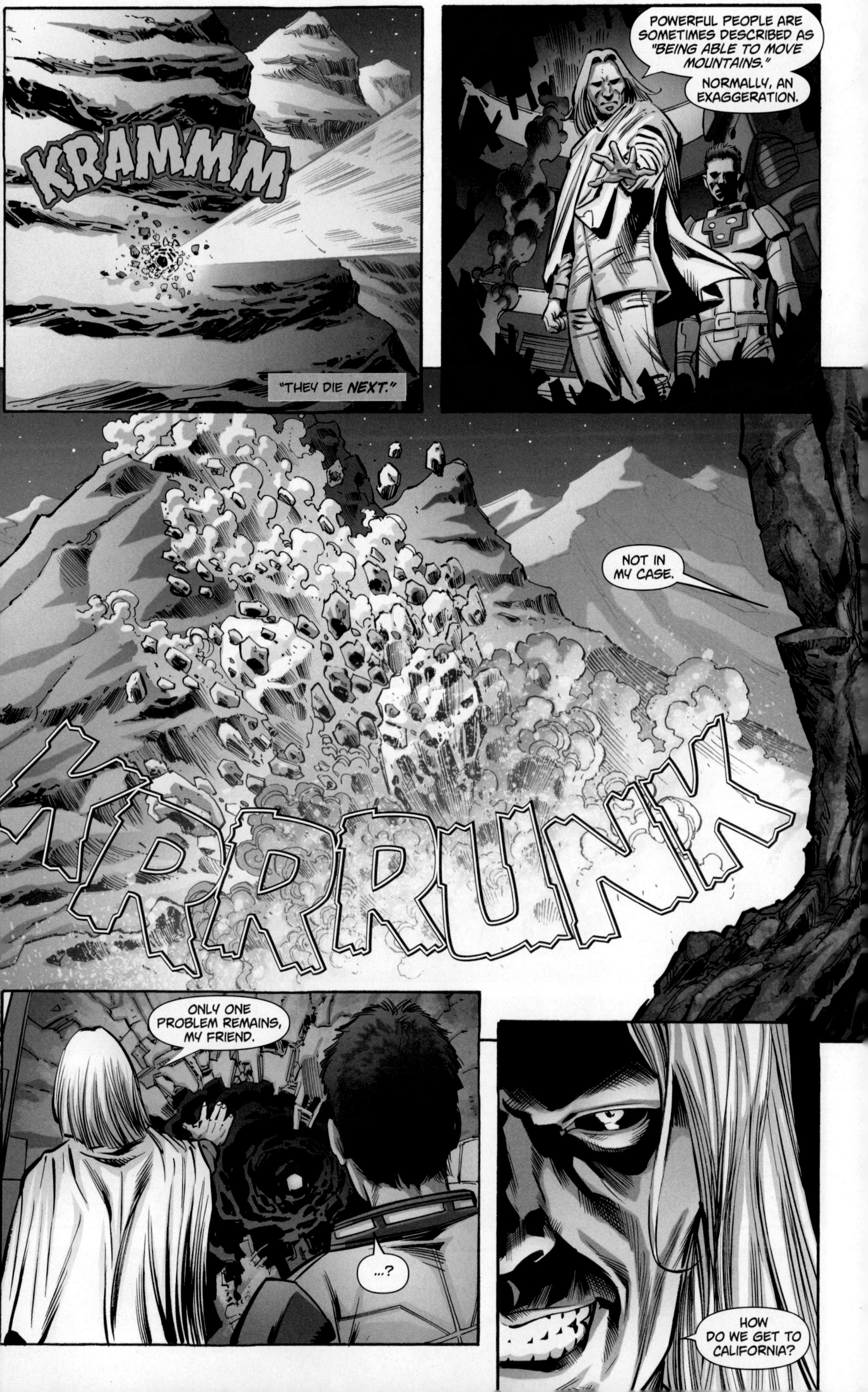
KRAMMMM
"THEY DIE NEXT."
POWERFUL PEOPLE ARE SOMETIMES DESCRIBED AS "BEING ABLE TO MOVE MOUNTAINS."
NORMALLY, AN EXAGGERATION.
NOT IN MY CASE.
KRRRUNK
ONLY ONE PROBLEM REMAINS, MY FRIEND.
...?
HOW DO WE GET TO CALIFORNIA?

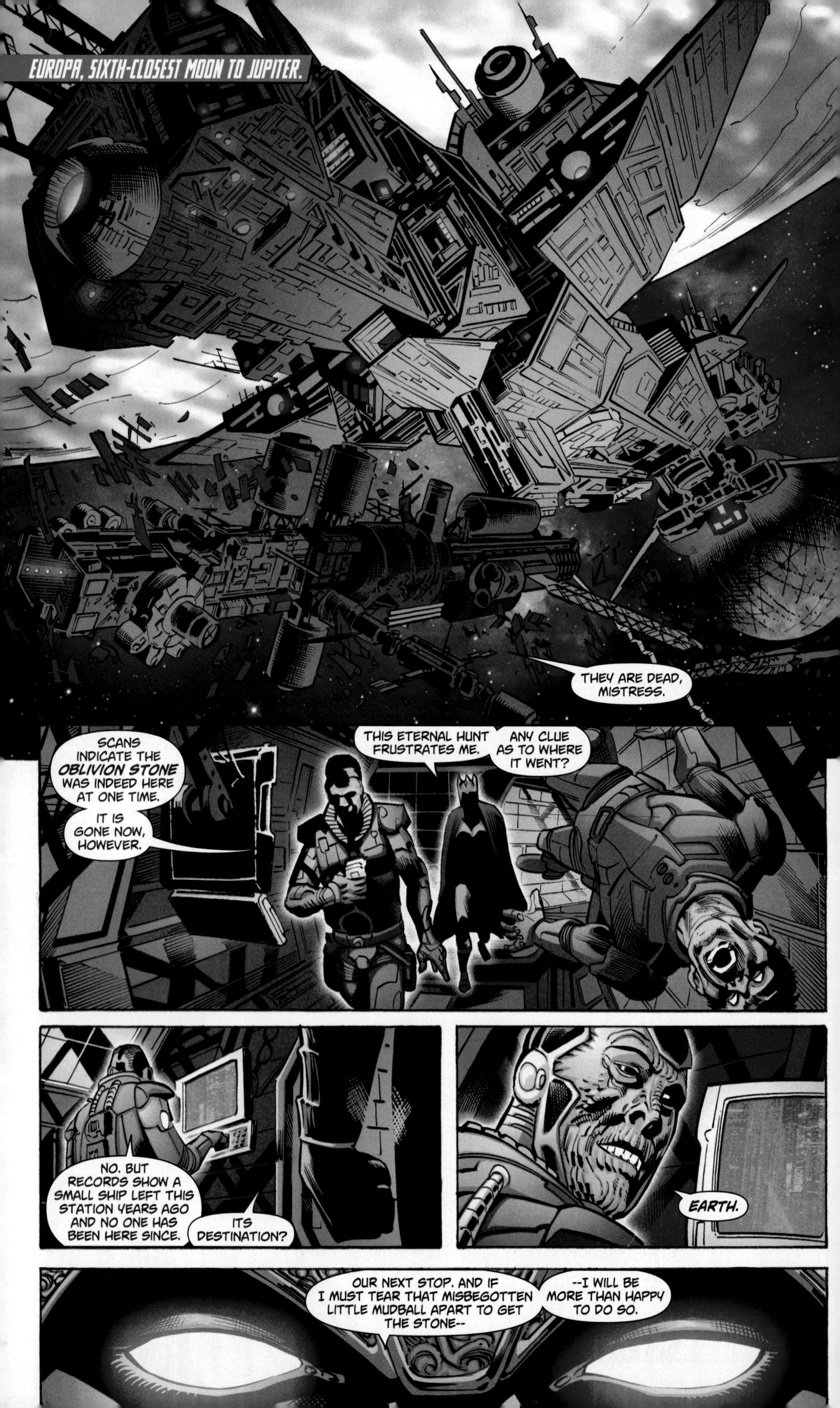
EUROPA, SIXTH-CLOSEST MOON TO JUPITER.
THEY ARE DEAD, MISTRESS.
SCANS INDICATE THE OBLIVION STONE WAS INDEED HERE AT ONE TIME.
IT IS GONE NOW, HOWEVER.
THIS ETERNAL HUNT FRUSTRATES ME.
ANY CLUE AS TO WHERE IT WENT?
NO. BUT RECORDS SHOW A SMALL SHIP LEFT THIS STATION YEARS AGO AND NO ONE HAS BEEN HERE SINCE.
ITS DESTINATION?
EARTH.
OUR NEXT STOP. AND IF I MUST TEAR THAT MISBEGOTTEN LITTLE MUDBALL APART TO GET THE STONE--
--I WILL BE MORE THAN HAPPY TO DO SO.

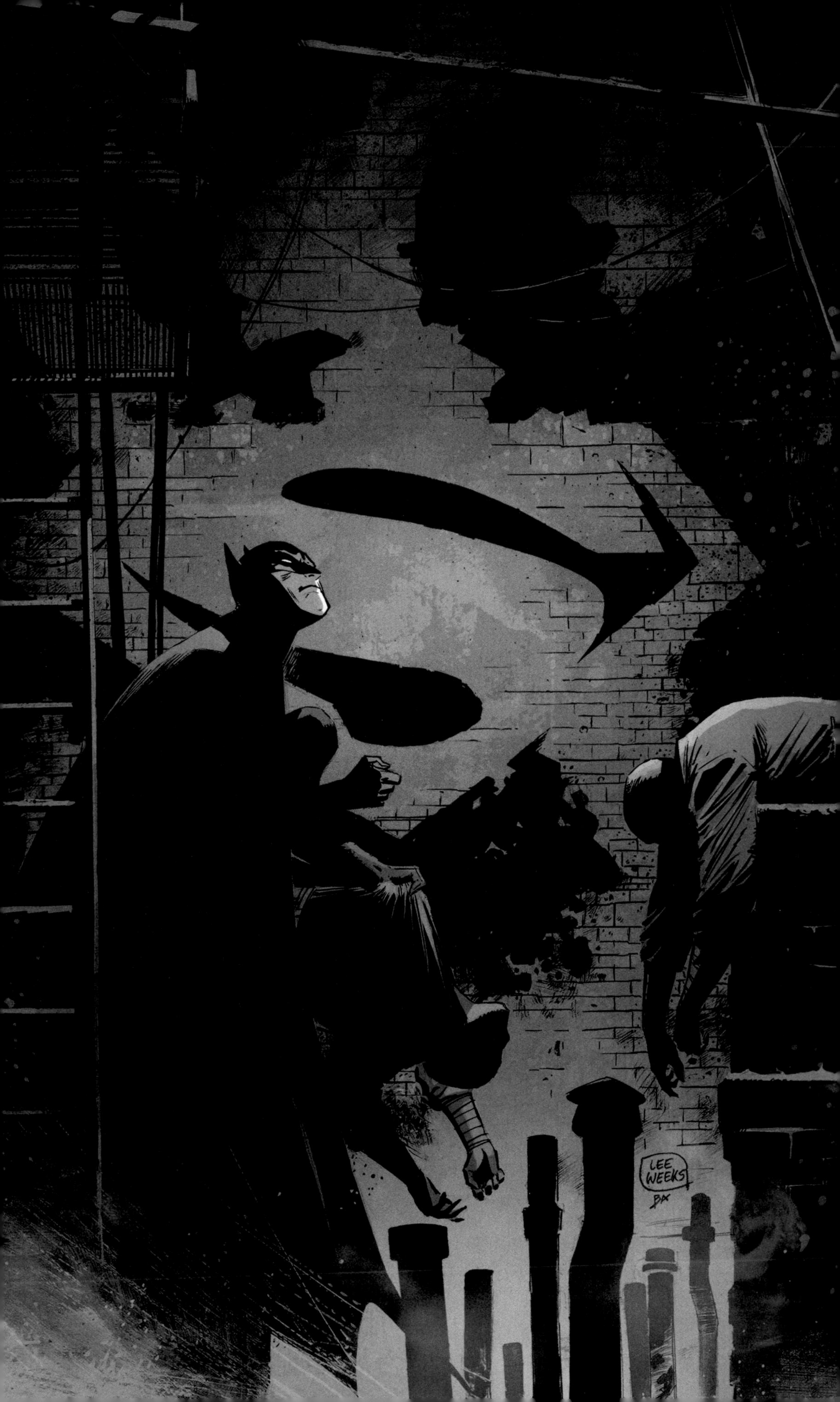
LEE WEEKS

ARRIVAL: PART V

DAN JURGENS writer **NEIL EDWARDS** penciller **SCOTT HANNA NEIL EDWARDS** inkers **JEROMY COX** colorist **A LARGER WORLD STUDIOS** letterer
LEE WEEKS BRAD ANDERSON cover artists

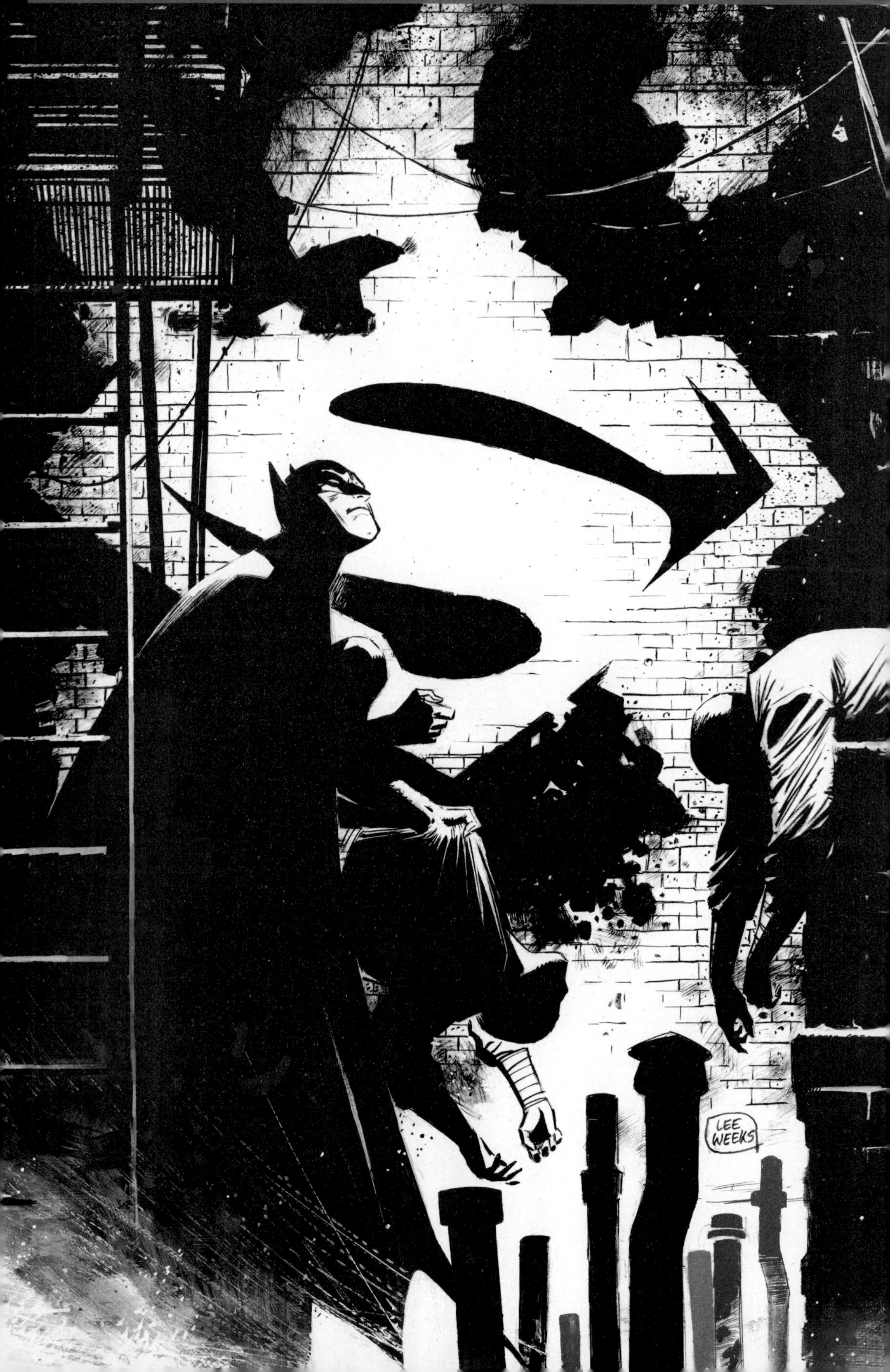
LEE
WEEKS

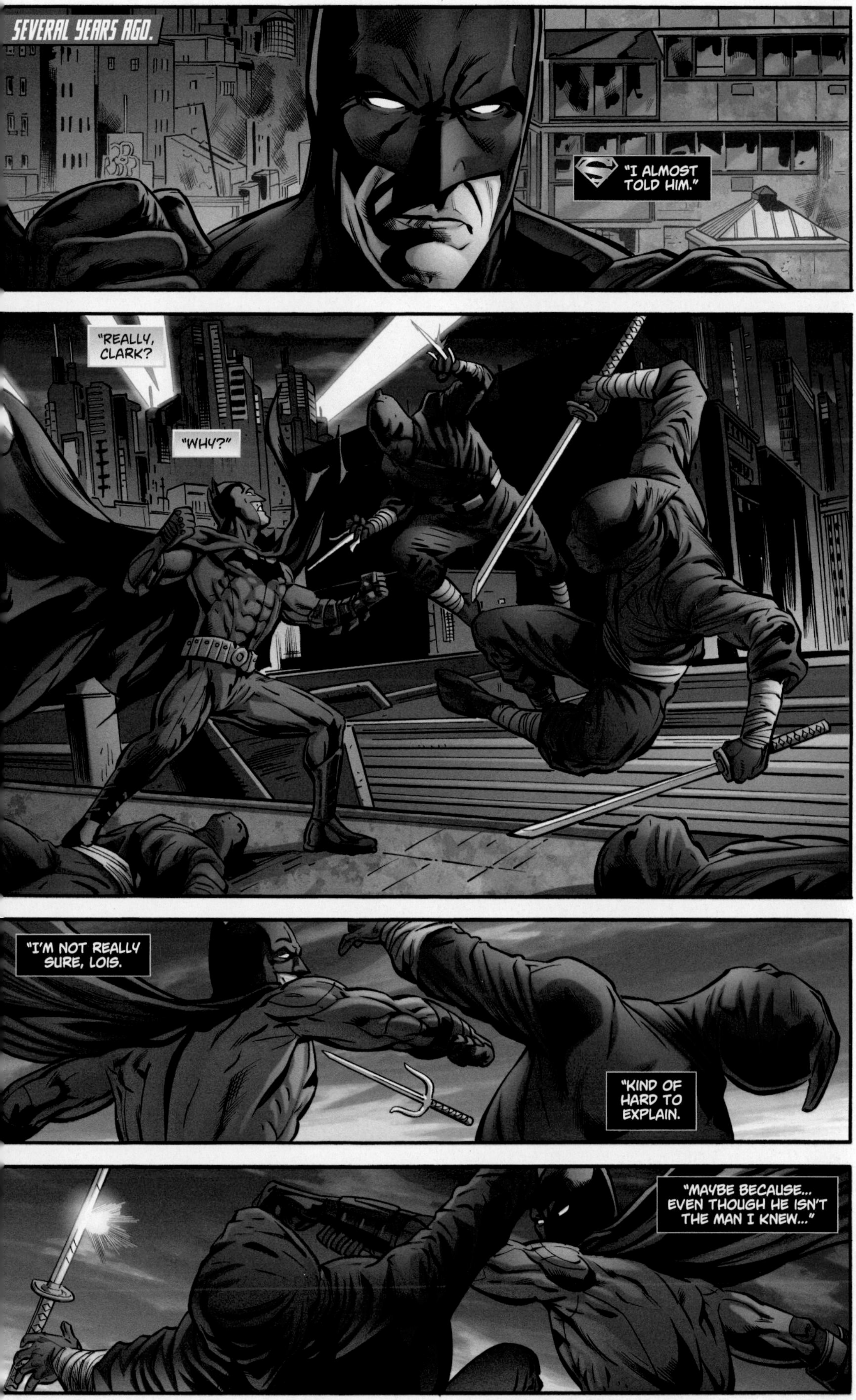
SEVERAL YEARS AGO.
"I ALMOST TOLD HIM."
"REALLY, CLARK?
"WHY?"
"I'M NOT REALLY SURE, LOIS.
"KIND OF HARD TO EXPLAIN.
"MAYBE BECAUSE... EVEN THOUGH HE ISN'T THE MAN I KNEW..."

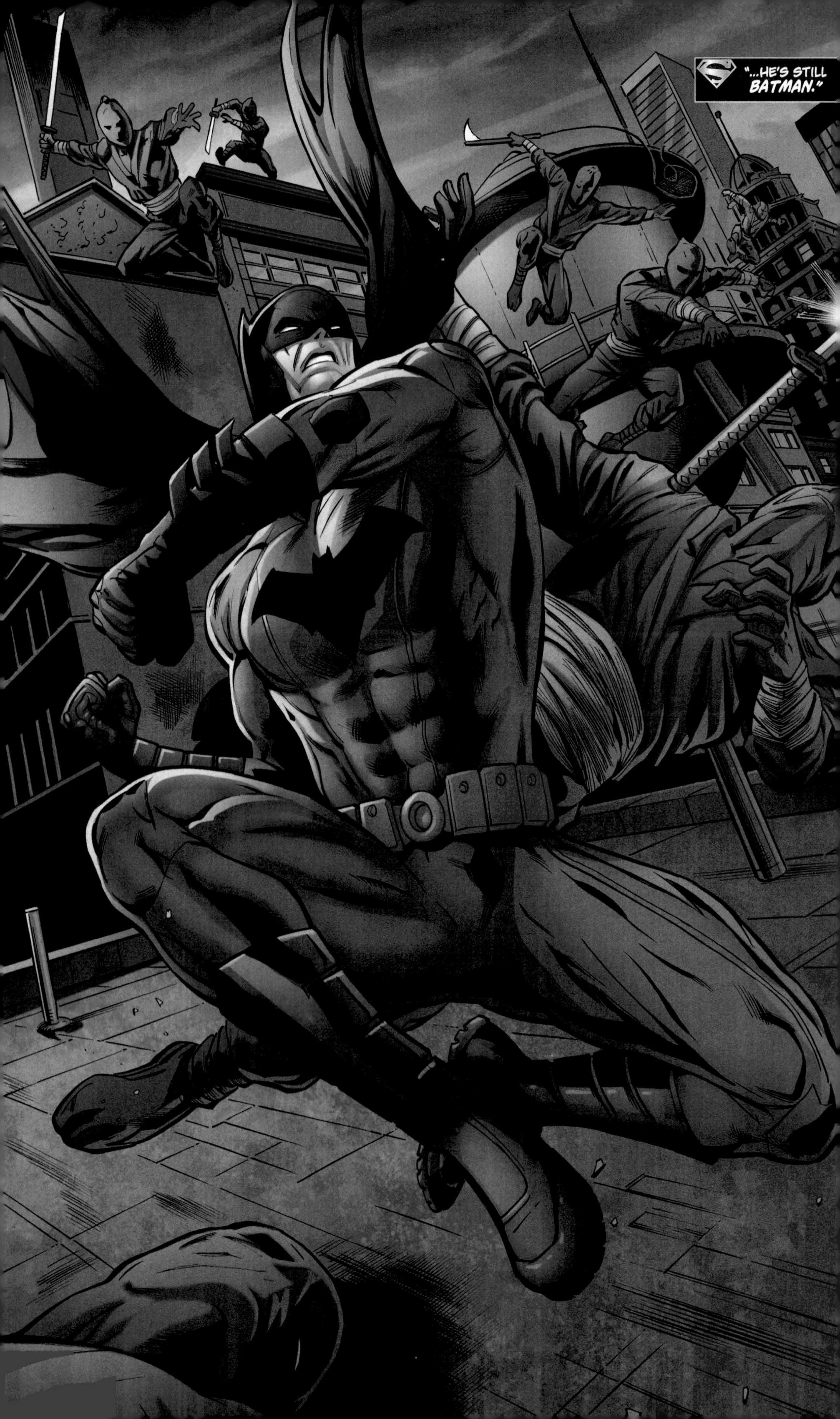
"...HE'S STILL BATMAN."

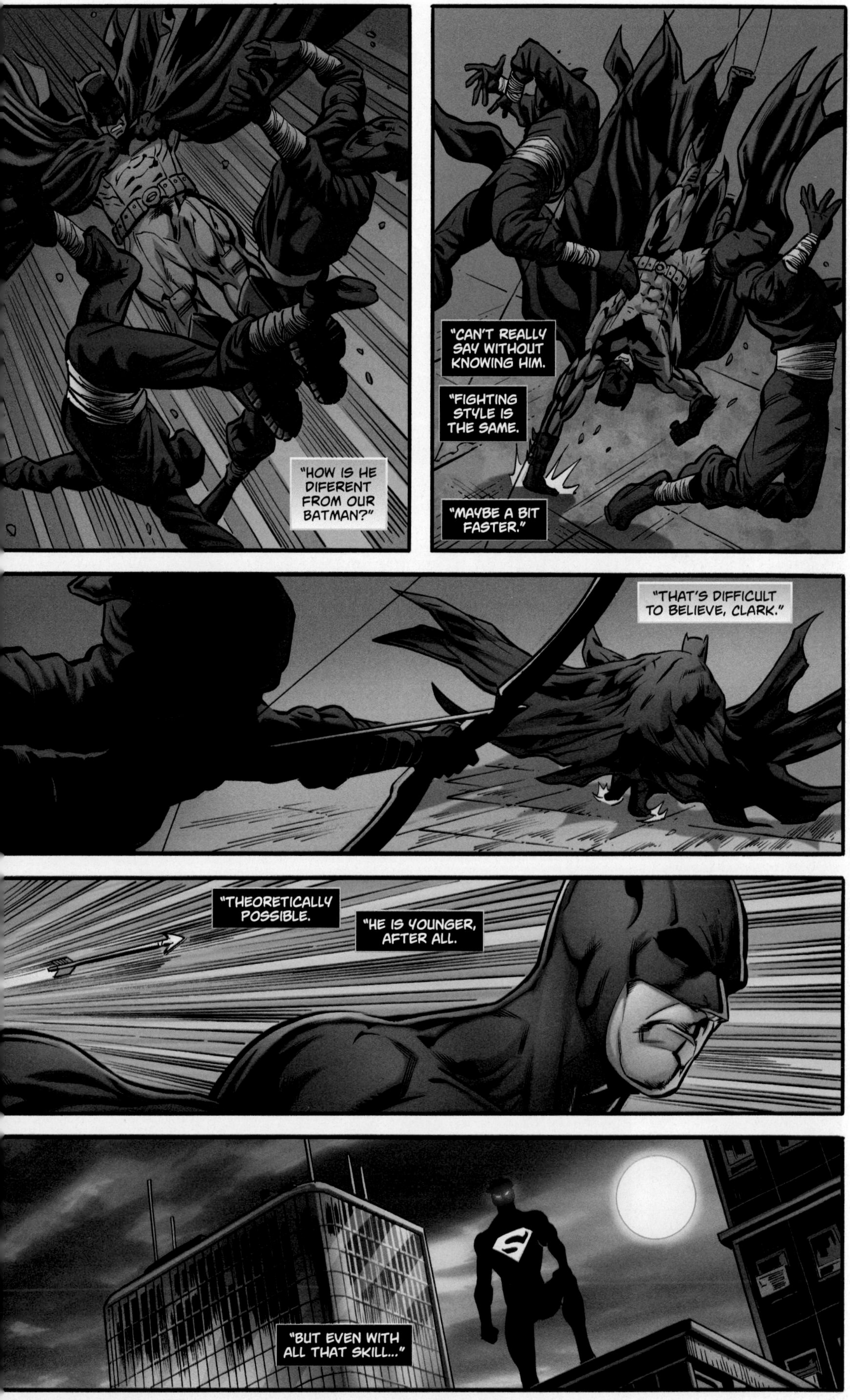
"HOW IS HE
DIFERENT
FROM OUR
BATMAN?"
"CAN'T REALLY
SAY WITHOUT
KNOWING HIM.
"FIGHTING
STYLE IS
THE SAME.
"MAYBE A BIT
FASTER."
"THAT'S DIFFICULT
TO BELIEVE, CLARK."
"THEORETICALLY
POSSIBLE.
"HE IS YOUNGER,
AFTER ALL.
"BUT EVEN WITH
ALL THAT SKILL..."

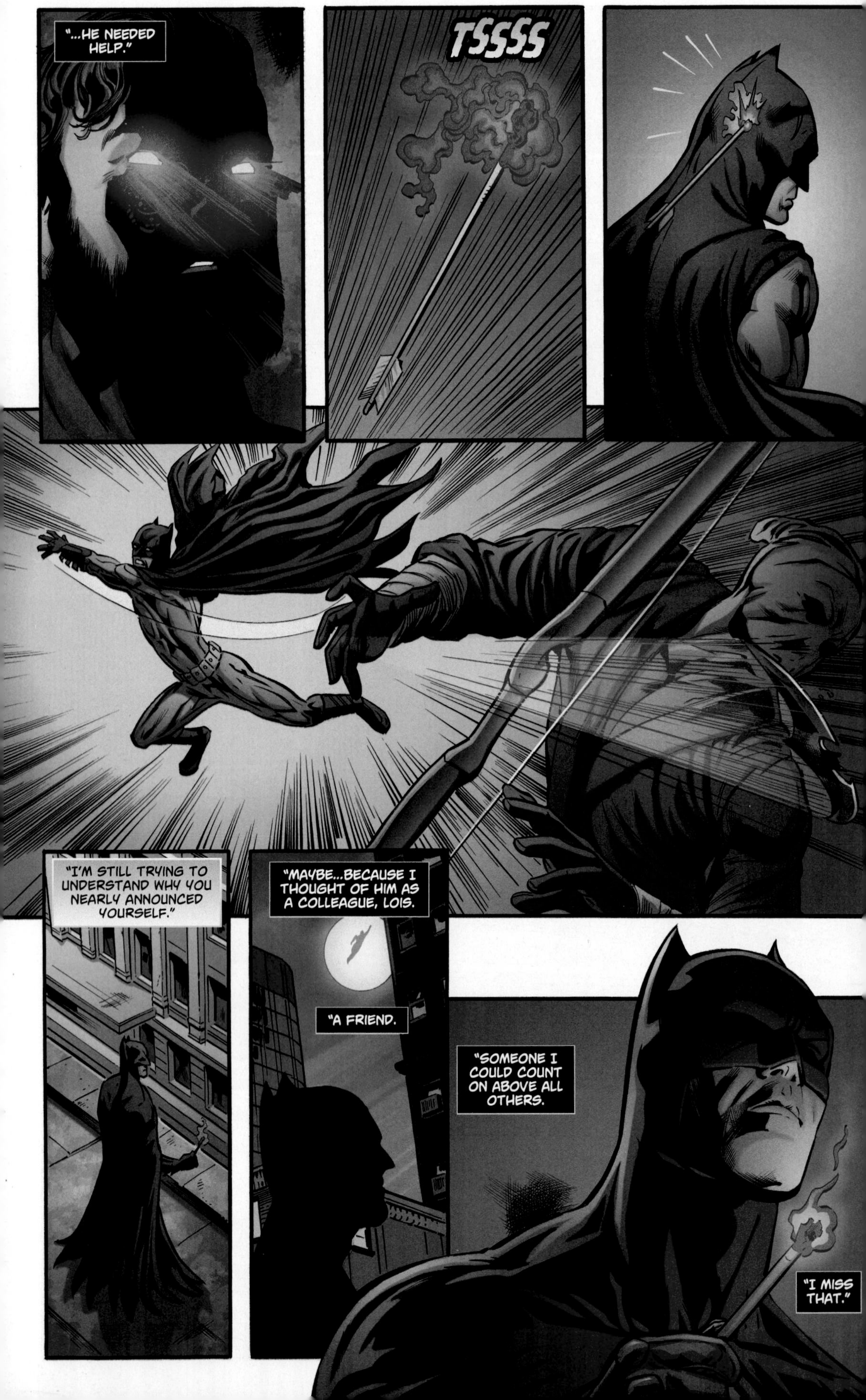
"...HE NEEDED HELP."
TSSSS
"I'M STILL TRYING TO UNDERSTAND WHY YOU NEARLY ANNOUNCED YOURSELF."
"MAYBE...BECAUSE I THOUGHT OF HIM AS A COLLEAGUE, LOIS.
"A FRIEND.
"SOMEONE I COULD COUNT ON ABOVE ALL OTHERS.
"I MISS THAT."

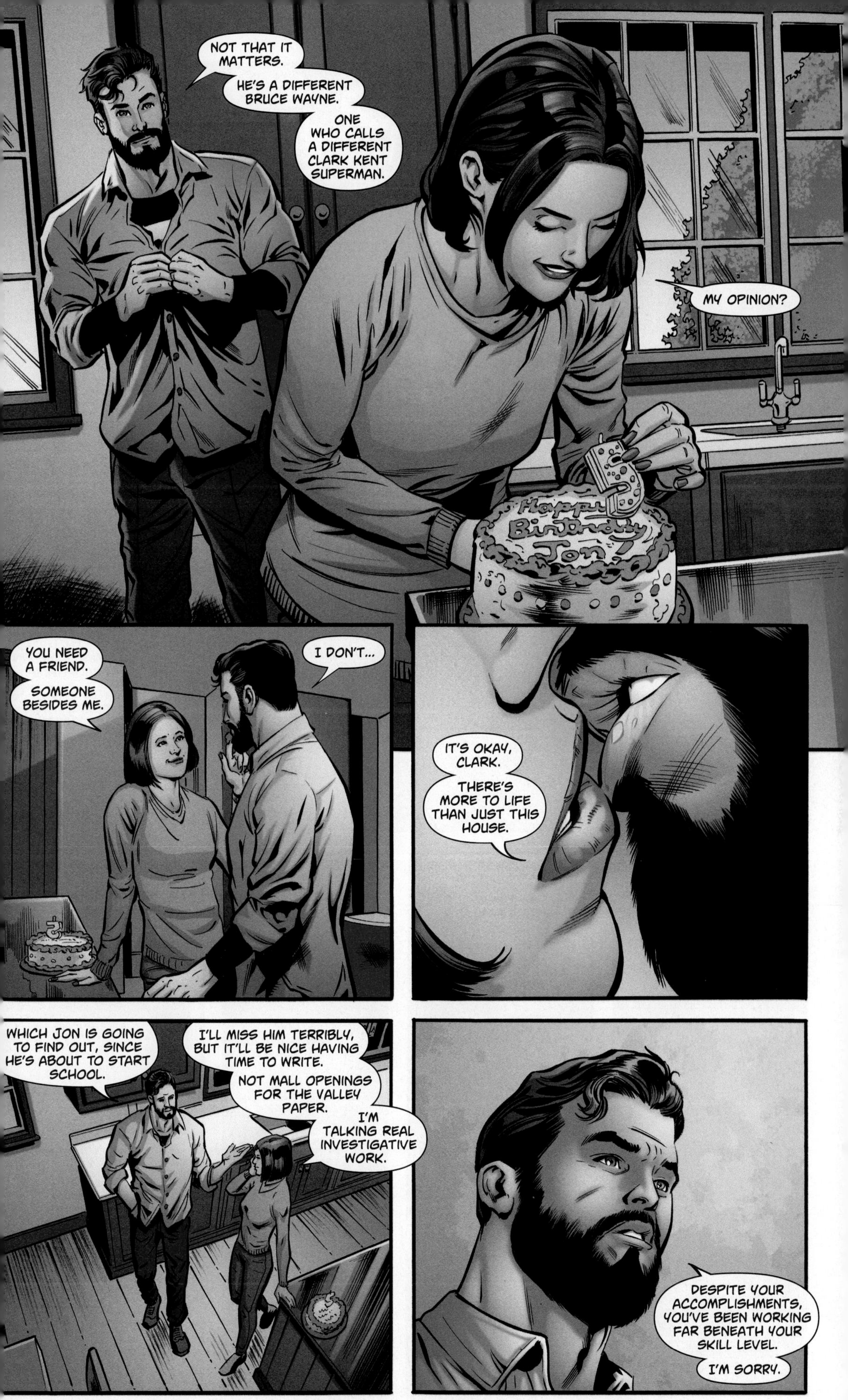
NOT THAT IT MATTERS.
HE'S A DIFFERENT BRUCE WAYNE.
ONE WHO CALLS A DIFFERENT CLARK KENT SUPERMAN.
MY OPINION?
Happy Birthday Jon!
YOU NEED A FRIEND.
SOMEONE BESIDES ME.
I DON'T...
IT'S OKAY, CLARK.
THERE'S MORE TO LIFE THAN JUST THIS HOUSE.
WHICH JON IS GOING TO FIND OUT, SINCE HE'S ABOUT TO START SCHOOL.
I'LL MISS HIM TERRIBLY, BUT IT'LL BE NICE HAVING TIME TO WRITE.
NOT MALL OPENINGS FOR THE VALLEY PAPER.
I'M TALKING REAL INVESTIGATIVE WORK.
DESPITE YOUR ACCOMPLISHMENTS, YOU'VE BEEN WORKING FAR BENEATH YOUR SKILL LEVEL.
I'M SORRY.

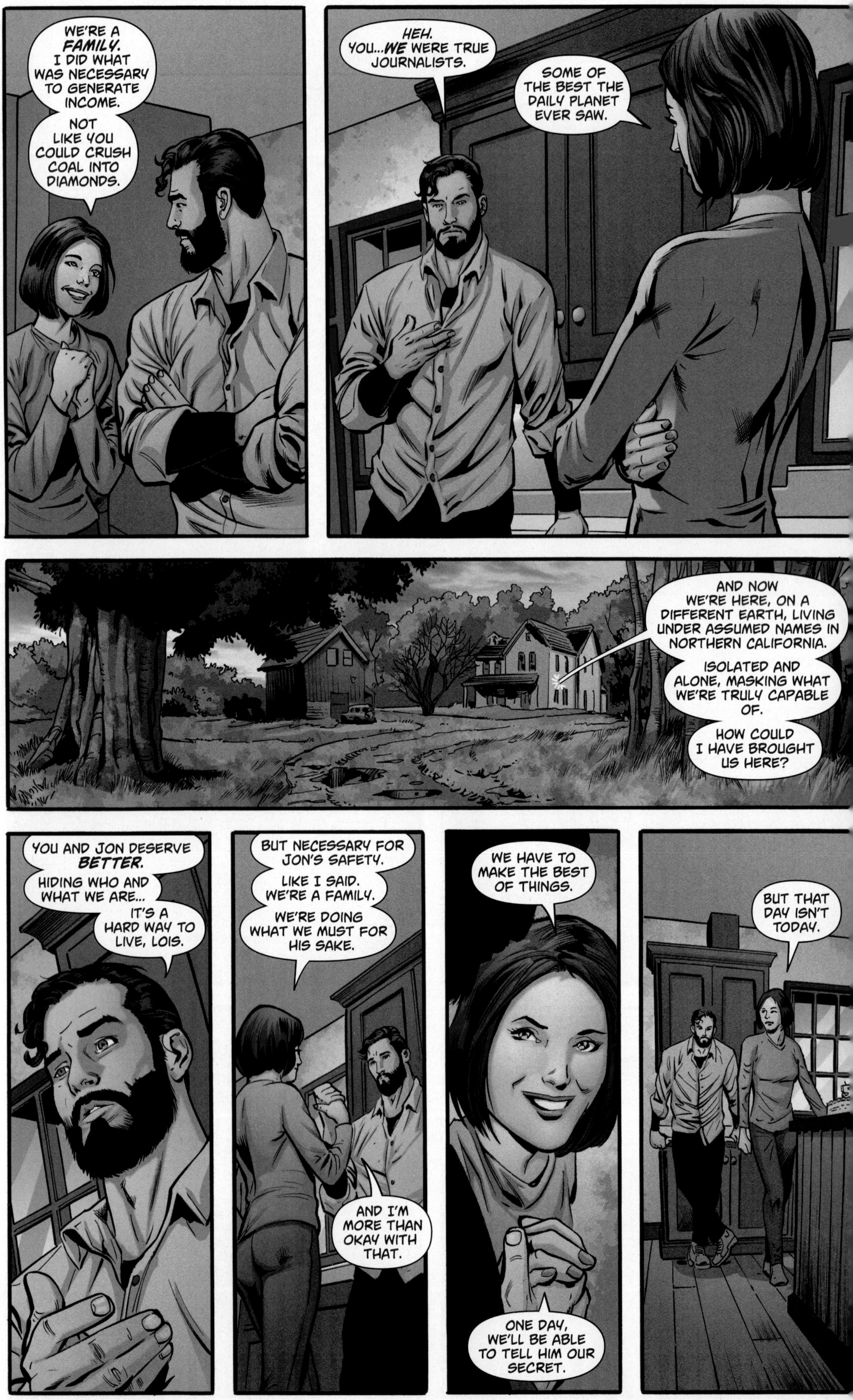
WE'RE A FAMILY. I DID WHAT WAS NECESSARY TO GENERATE INCOME.
NOT LIKE YOU COULD CRUSH COAL INTO DIAMONDS.
HEH. YOU...WE WERE TRUE JOURNALISTS.
SOME OF THE BEST THE DAILY PLANET EVER SAW.
AND NOW WE'RE HERE, ON A DIFFERENT EARTH, LIVING UNDER ASSUMED NAMES IN NORTHERN CALIFORNIA.
ISOLATED AND ALONE, MASKING WHAT WE'RE TRULY CAPABLE OF.
HOW COULD I HAVE BROUGHT US HERE?
YOU AND JON DESERVE BETTER.
HIDING WHO AND WHAT WE ARE...
IT'S A HARD WAY TO LIVE, LOIS.
BUT NECESSARY FOR JON'S SAFETY.
LIKE I SAID. WE'RE A FAMILY.
WE'RE DOING WHAT WE MUST FOR HIS SAKE.
AND I'M MORE THAN OKAY WITH THAT.
WE HAVE TO MAKE THE BEST OF THINGS.
ONE DAY, WE'LL BE ABLE TO TELL HIM OUR SECRET.
BUT THAT DAY ISN'T TODAY.

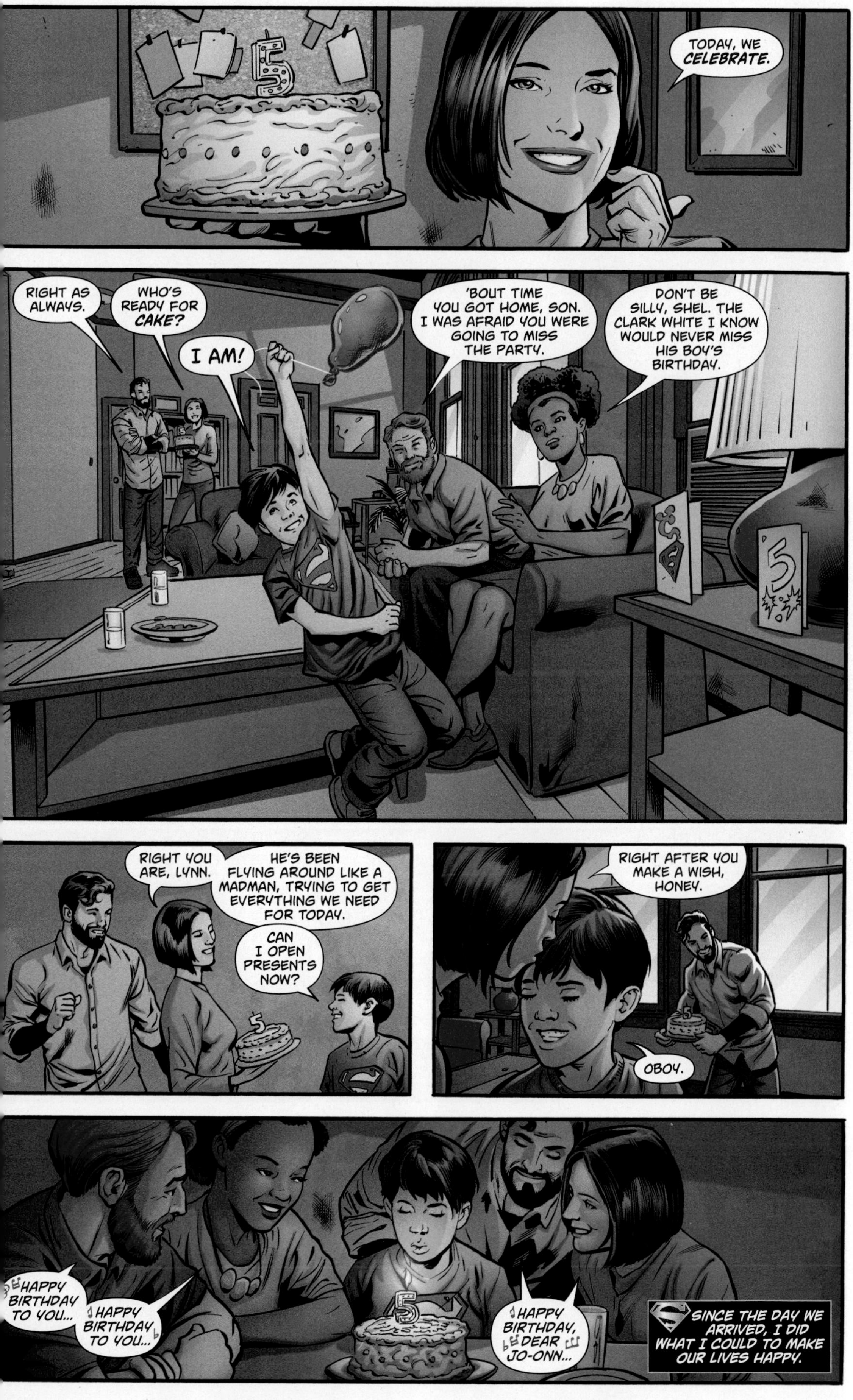
TODAY, WE CELEBRATE.
RIGHT AS ALWAYS.
WHO'S READY FOR CAKE?
I AM!
'BOUT TIME YOU GOT HOME, SON. I WAS AFRAID YOU WERE GOING TO MISS THE PARTY.
DON'T BE SILLY, SHEL. THE CLARK WHITE I KNOW WOULD NEVER MISS HIS BOY'S BIRTHDAY.
RIGHT YOU ARE, LYNN.
HE'S BEEN FLYING AROUND LIKE A MADMAN, TRYING TO GET EVERYTHING WE NEED FOR TODAY.
CAN I OPEN PRESENTS NOW?
RIGHT AFTER YOU MAKE A WISH, HONEY.
OBOY.
HAPPY BIRTHDAY TO YOU...
HAPPY BIRTHDAY TO YOU...
HAPPY BIRTHDAY, DEAR JO-ONN...
SINCE THE DAY WE ARRIVED, I DID WHAT I COULD TO MAKE OUR LIVES HAPPY.

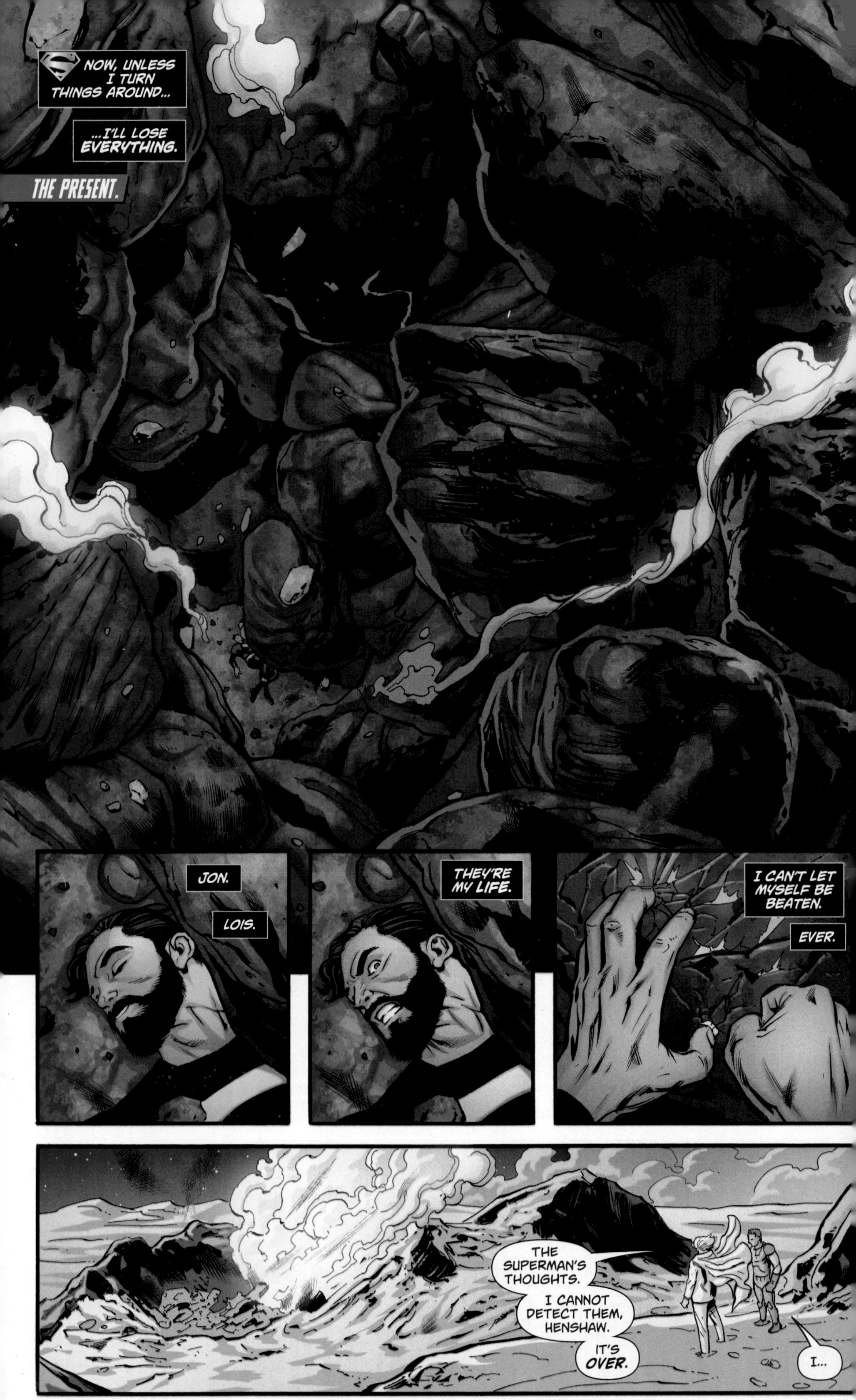

NOW, UNLESS I TURN THINGS AROUND...
...I'LL LOSE EVERYTHING.
THE PRESENT.
JON.
LOIS.
THEY'RE MY LIFE.
I CAN'T LET MYSELF BE BEATEN.
EVER.
THE SUPERMAN'S THOUGHTS.
I CANNOT DETECT THEM, HENSHAW.
IT'S OVER.
I...

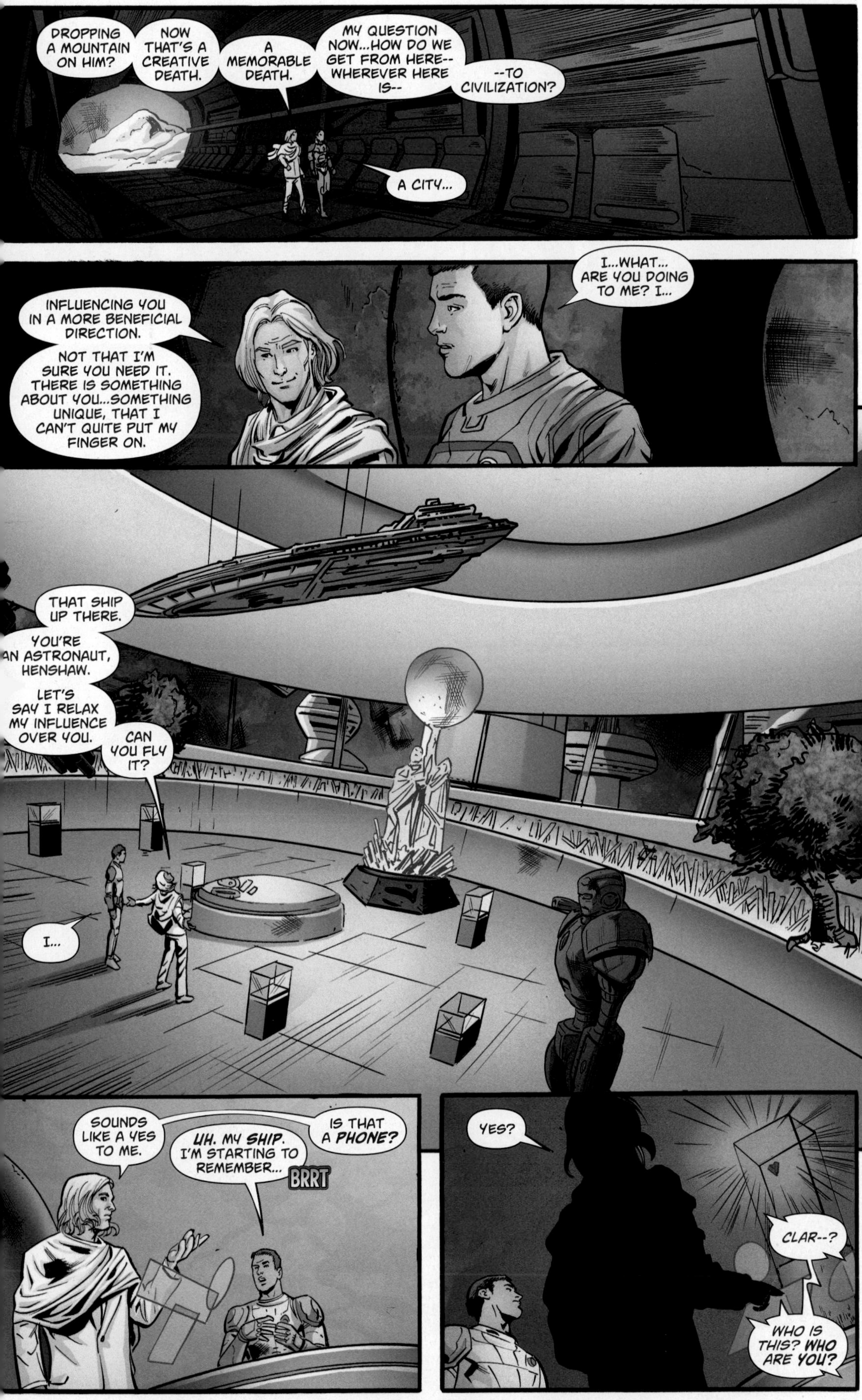
DROPPING A MOUNTAIN ON HIM?
NOW THAT'S A CREATIVE DEATH.
A MEMORABLE DEATH.
MY QUESTION NOW...HOW DO WE GET FROM HERE--WHEREVER HERE IS--
--TO CIVILIZATION?
A CITY...
INFLUENCING YOU IN A MORE BENEFICIAL DIRECTION.
NOT THAT I'M SURE YOU NEED IT. THERE IS SOMETHING ABOUT YOU...SOMETHING UNIQUE, THAT I CAN'T QUITE PUT MY FINGER ON.
I...WHAT...ARE YOU DOING TO ME? I...
THAT SHIP UP THERE.
YOU'RE AN ASTRONAUT, HENSHAW.
LET'S SAY I RELAX MY INFLUENCE OVER YOU.
CAN YOU FLY IT?
I...
SOUNDS LIKE A YES TO ME.
UH. MY SHIP. I'M STARTING TO REMEMBER...
BRRT
IS THAT A PHONE?
YES?
CLAR--?
WHO IS THIS? WHO ARE YOU?

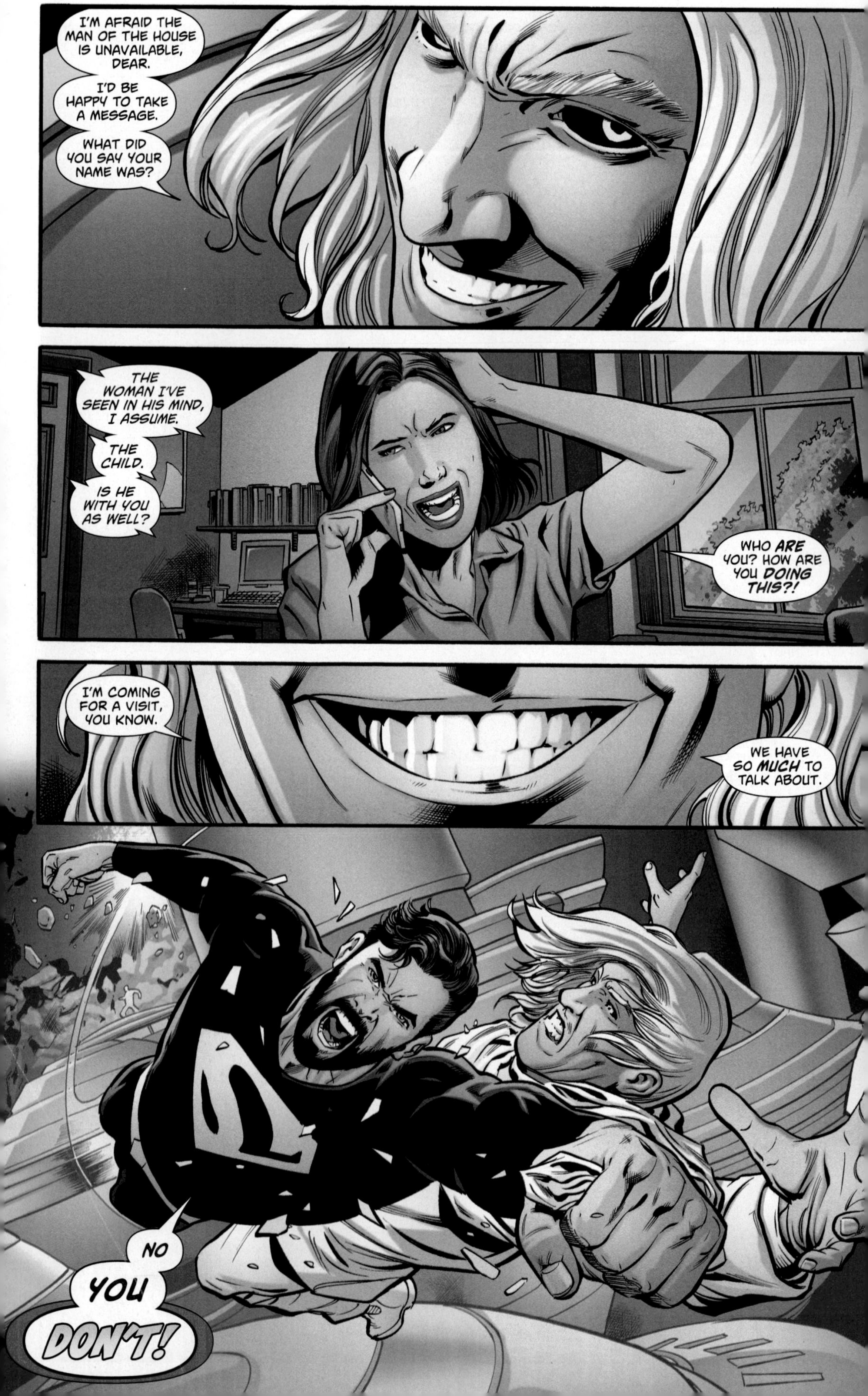
I'M AFRAID THE MAN OF THE HOUSE IS UNAVAILABLE, DEAR.
I'D BE HAPPY TO TAKE A MESSAGE.
WHAT DID YOU SAY YOUR NAME WAS?
THE WOMAN I'VE SEEN IN HIS MIND, I ASSUME.
THE CHILD.
IS HE WITH YOU AS WELL?
WHO ARE YOU? HOW ARE YOU DOING THIS?!
I'M COMING FOR A VISIT, YOU KNOW.
WE HAVE SO MUCH TO TALK ABOUT.
NO
YOU
DON'T!

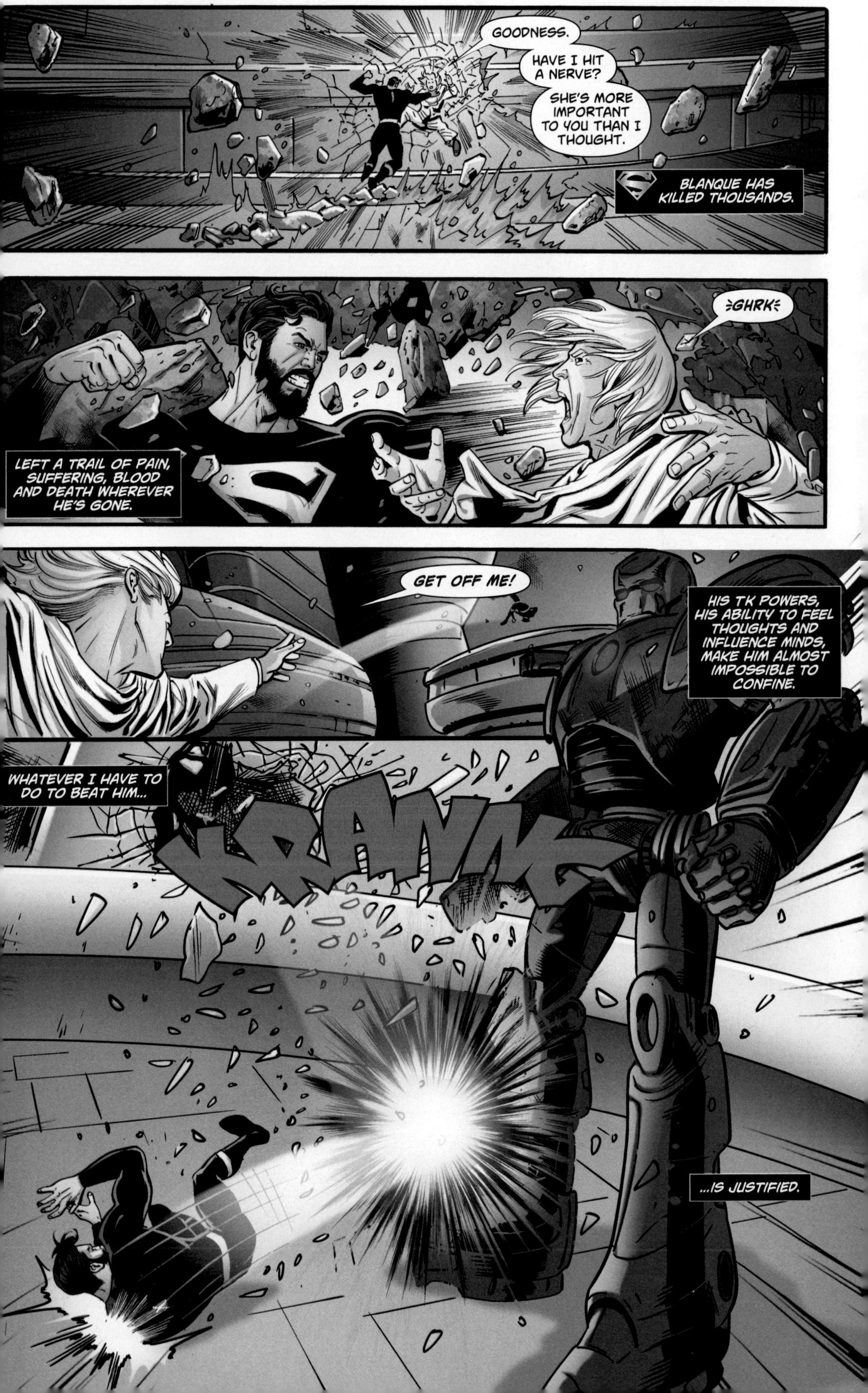
GOODNESS.
HAVE I HIT A NERVE?
SHE'S MORE IMPORTANT TO YOU THAN I THOUGHT.
BLANQUE HAS KILLED THOUSANDS.
GHRK
LEFT A TRAIL OF PAIN, SUFFERING, BLOOD AND DEATH WHEREVER HE'S GONE.
GET OFF ME!
HIS TK POWERS, HIS ABILITY TO FEEL THOUGHTS AND INFLUENCE MINDS, MAKE HIM ALMOST IMPOSSIBLE TO CONFINE.
WHATEVER I HAVE TO DO TO BEAT HIM...
KRANK
...IS JUSTIFIED.

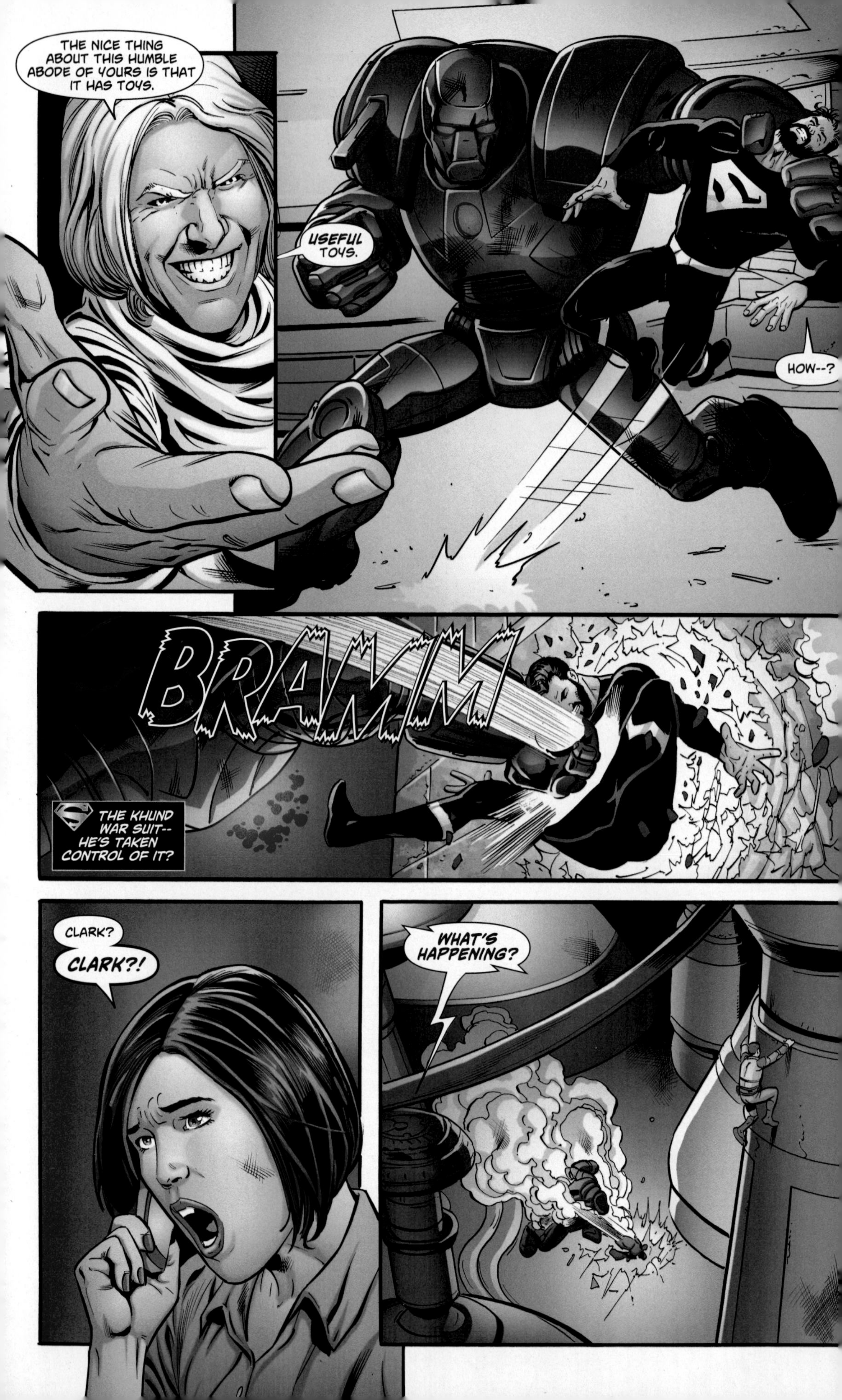
THE NICE THING ABOUT THIS HUMBLE ABODE OF YOURS IS THAT IT HAS TOYS.
USEFUL TOYS.
HOW--?
BRAMM
THE KHUND WAR SUIT-- HE'S TAKEN CONTROL OF IT?
CLARK? CLARK?!
WHAT'S HAPPENING?

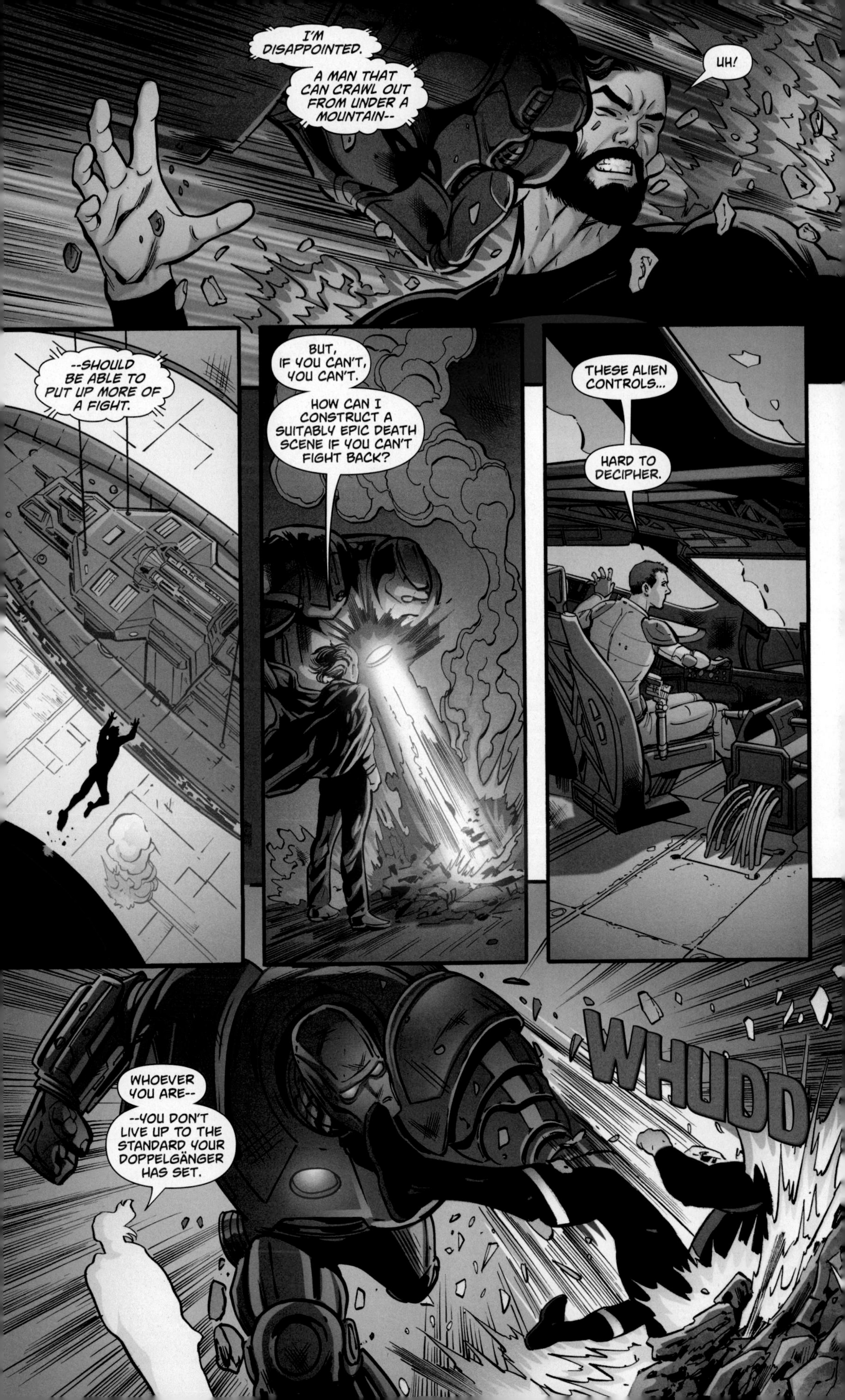
I'M DISAPPOINTED.
A MAN THAT CAN CRAWL OUT FROM UNDER A MOUNTAIN--
UH!
--SHOULD BE ABLE TO PUT UP MORE OF A FIGHT.
BUT, IF YOU CAN'T, YOU CAN'T.
HOW CAN I CONSTRUCT A SUITABLY EPIC DEATH SCENE IF YOU CAN'T FIGHT BACK?
THESE ALIEN CONTROLS...
HARD TO DECIPHER.
WHUDD
WHOEVER YOU ARE--
--YOU DON'T LIVE UP TO THE STANDARD YOUR DOPPELGÄNGER HAS SET.

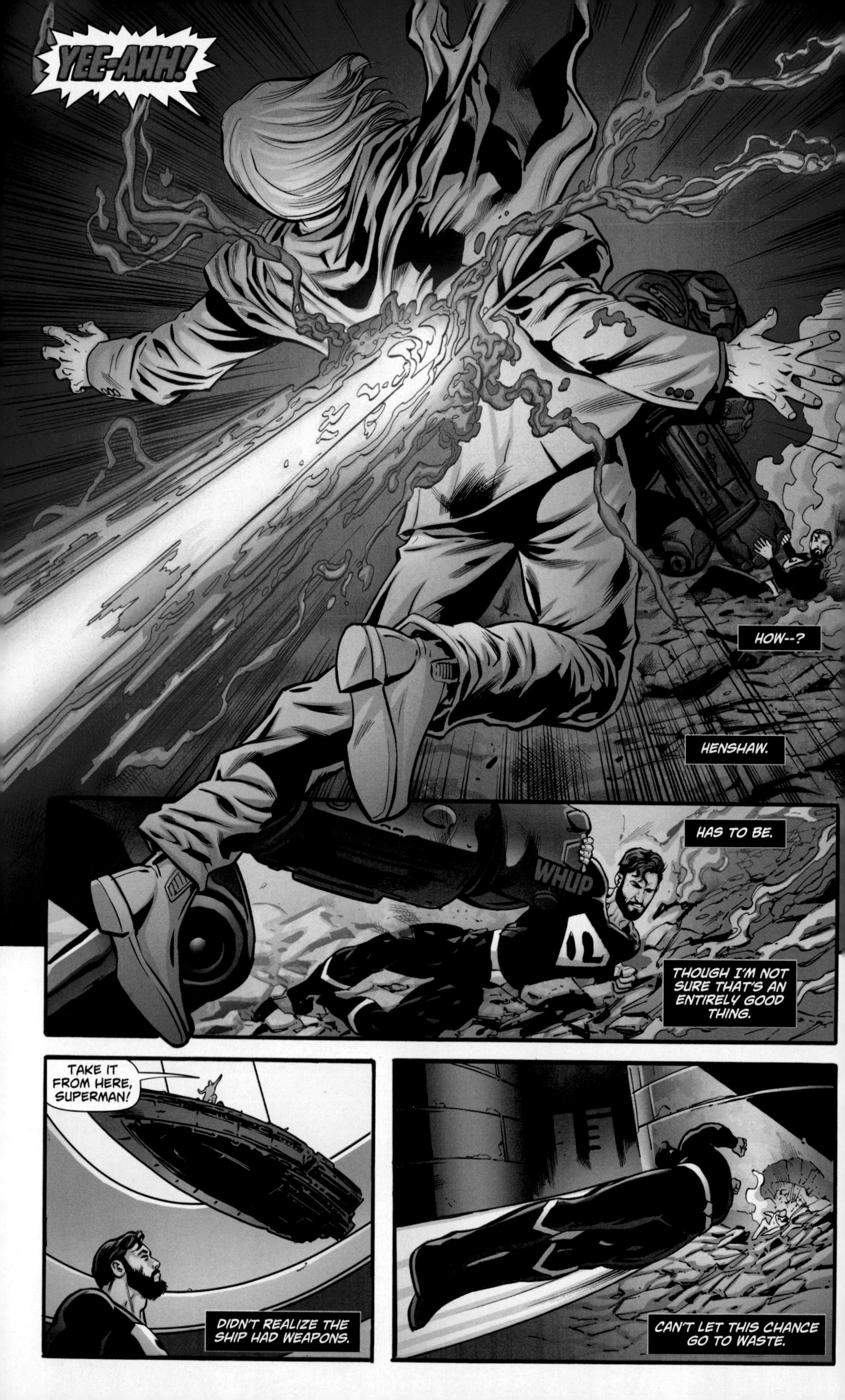
YEE-AHH!
HOW--?
HENSHAW.
HAS TO BE.
WHUP
THOUGH I'M NOT SURE THAT'S AN ENTIRELY GOOD THING.
TAKE IT FROM HERE, SUPERMAN!
DIDN'T REALIZE THE SHIP HAD WEAPONS.
CAN'T LET THIS CHANCE GO TO WASTE.

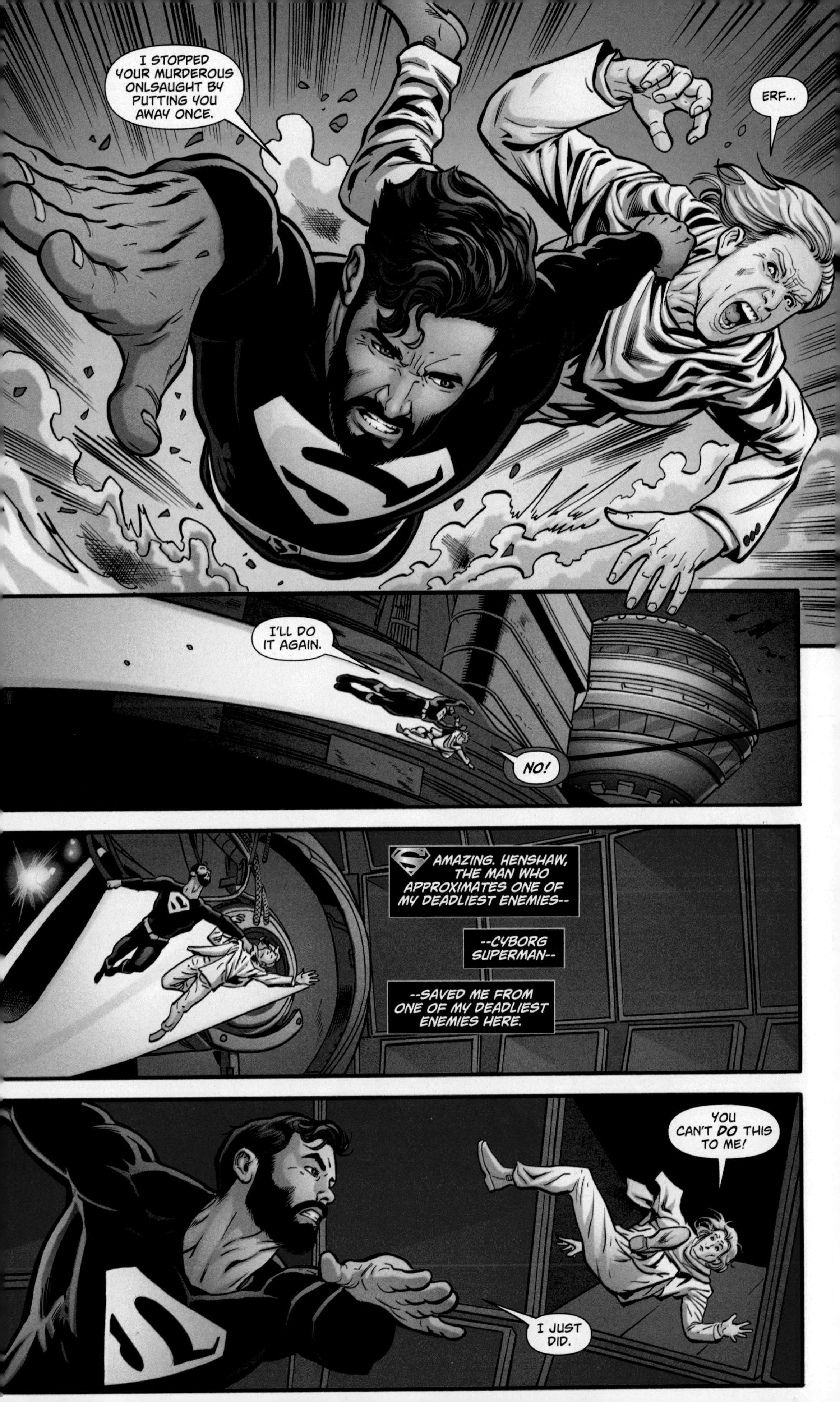
I STOPPED YOUR MURDEROUS ONLSAUGHT BY PUTTING YOU AWAY ONCE.
ERF...
I'LL DO IT AGAIN.
NO!
AMAZING. HENSHAW, THE MAN WHO APPROXIMATES ONE OF MY DEADLIEST ENEMIES--
--CYBORG SUPERMAN--
--SAVED ME FROM ONE OF MY DEADLIEST ENEMIES HERE.
YOU CAN'T DO THIS TO ME!
I JUST DID.

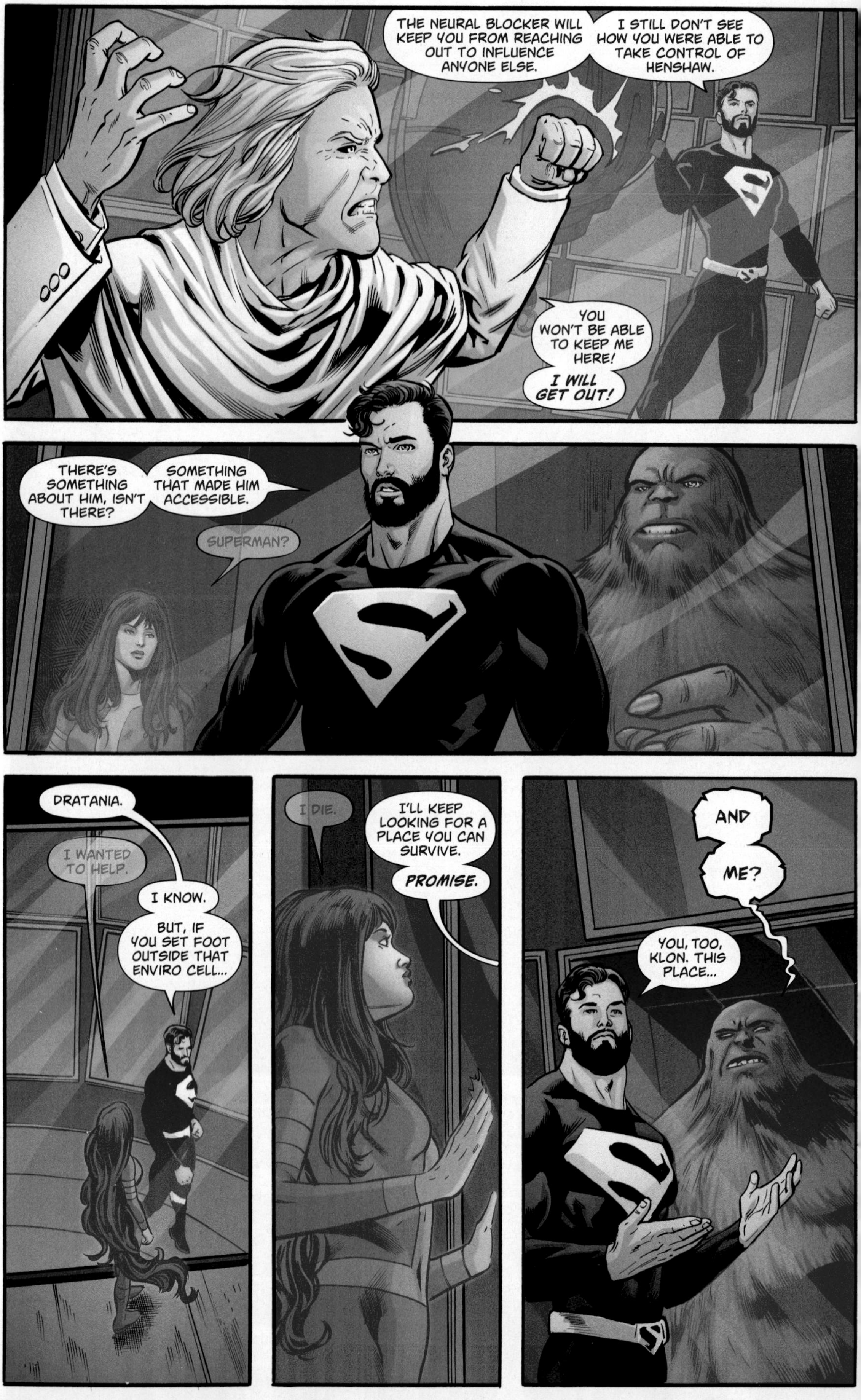
THE NEURAL BLOCKER WILL KEEP YOU FROM REACHING OUT TO INFLUENCE ANYONE ELSE.
I STILL DON'T SEE HOW YOU WERE ABLE TO TAKE CONTROL OF HENSHAW.
YOU WON'T BE ABLE TO KEEP ME HERE!
I WILL GET OUT!
THERE'S SOMETHING ABOUT HIM, ISN'T THERE?
SOMETHING THAT MADE HIM ACCESSIBLE.
SUPERMAN?
DRATANIA.
I WANTED TO HELP.
I KNOW.
BUT, IF YOU SET FOOT OUTSIDE THAT ENVIRO CELL...
I DIE.
I'LL KEEP LOOKING FOR A PLACE YOU CAN SURVIVE.
PROMISE.
AND
ME?
YOU, TOO, KLON. THIS PLACE...

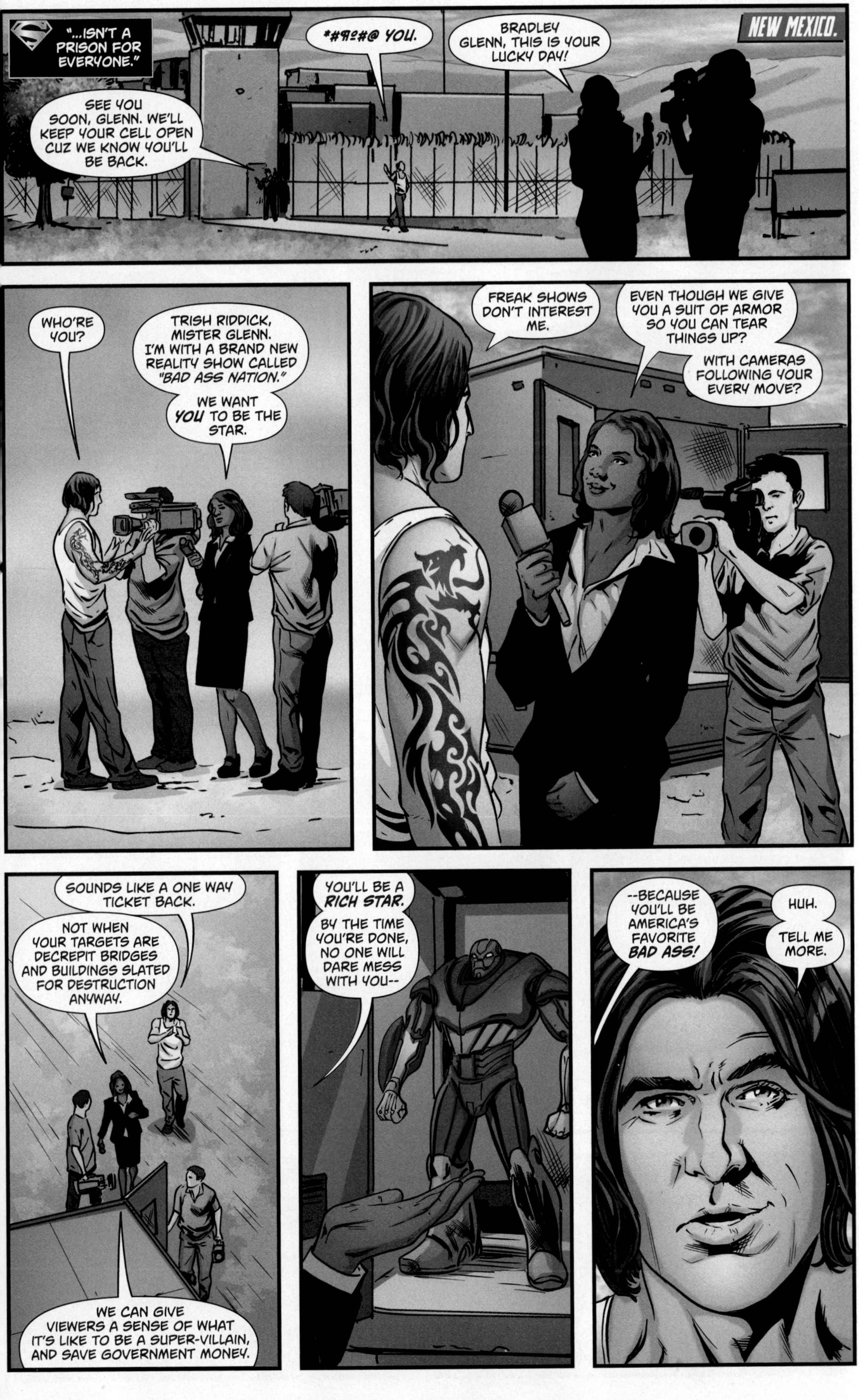
"...ISN'T A PRISON FOR EVERYONE."
SEE YOU SOON, GLENN. WE'LL KEEP YOUR CELL OPEN CUZ WE KNOW YOU'LL BE BACK.
*#%@#@ YOU.
BRADLEY GLENN, THIS IS YOUR LUCKY DAY!
NEW MEXICO.
WHO'RE YOU?
TRISH RIDDICK, MISTER GLENN. I'M WITH A BRAND NEW REALITY SHOW CALLED "BAD ASS NATION."
WE WANT YOU TO BE THE STAR.
FREAK SHOWS DON'T INTEREST ME.
EVEN THOUGH WE GIVE YOU A SUIT OF ARMOR SO YOU CAN TEAR THINGS UP?
WITH CAMERAS FOLLOWING YOUR EVERY MOVE?
SOUNDS LIKE A ONE WAY TICKET BACK.
NOT WHEN YOUR TARGETS ARE DECREPIT BRIDGES AND BUILDINGS SLATED FOR DESTRUCTION ANYWAY.
WE CAN GIVE VIEWERS A SENSE OF WHAT IT'S LIKE TO BE A SUPER-VILLAIN, AND SAVE GOVERNMENT MONEY.
YOU'LL BE A RICH STAR.
BY THE TIME YOU'RE DONE, NO ONE WILL DARE MESS WITH YOU--
--BECAUSE YOU'LL BE AMERICA'S FAVORITE BAD ASS!
HUH.
TELL ME MORE.

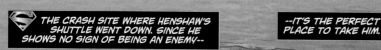

THE CRASH SITE WHERE HENSHAW'S SHUTTLE WENT DOWN. SINCE HE SHOWS NO SIGN OF BEING AN ENEMY--

--IT'S THE PERFECT PLACE TO TAKE HIM.

DESPITE THE FACT THAT THERE IS SOMETHING... UNSETTLING ABOUT HIM.

I STILL DON'T UNDERSTAND WHY YOU BROUGHT ME TO THAT WEIRD PLACE OF YOURS.

THE *EXCALIBUR* ARRIVED WITH NO COMMUNICATION AND YOUR CREW MISSING.

I HAD TO VERIFY YOU WEREN'T CARRYING A CONTAMINANT.

HAVE TO HOPE HE BUYS THAT.

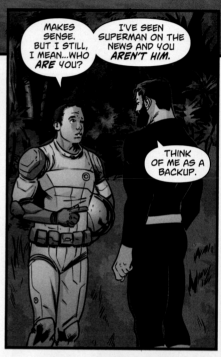

MAKES SENSE. BUT I STILL, I MEAN...WHO *ARE* YOU?

I'VE SEEN SUPERMAN ON THE NEWS AND YOU *AREN'T HIM.*

THINK OF ME AS A BACKUP.

A STRATEGIC SECRET.

ONE I HOPE YOU'LL KEEP TO YOURSELF.

IF IT'S IMPORTANT...

EVERY BIT AS IMPORTANT AS YOU USING THE SHIP'S WEAPONS TO TAKE DOWN BLANQUE.

I'LL TELL THE SEARCHERS THAT I WAS CONCUSSED IN THE CRASH, STUMBLED AWAY AND PASSED OUT.

THAT'LL WORK.

SO LONG.

EH.

SHIP'S WEAPONS.

HARDLY.

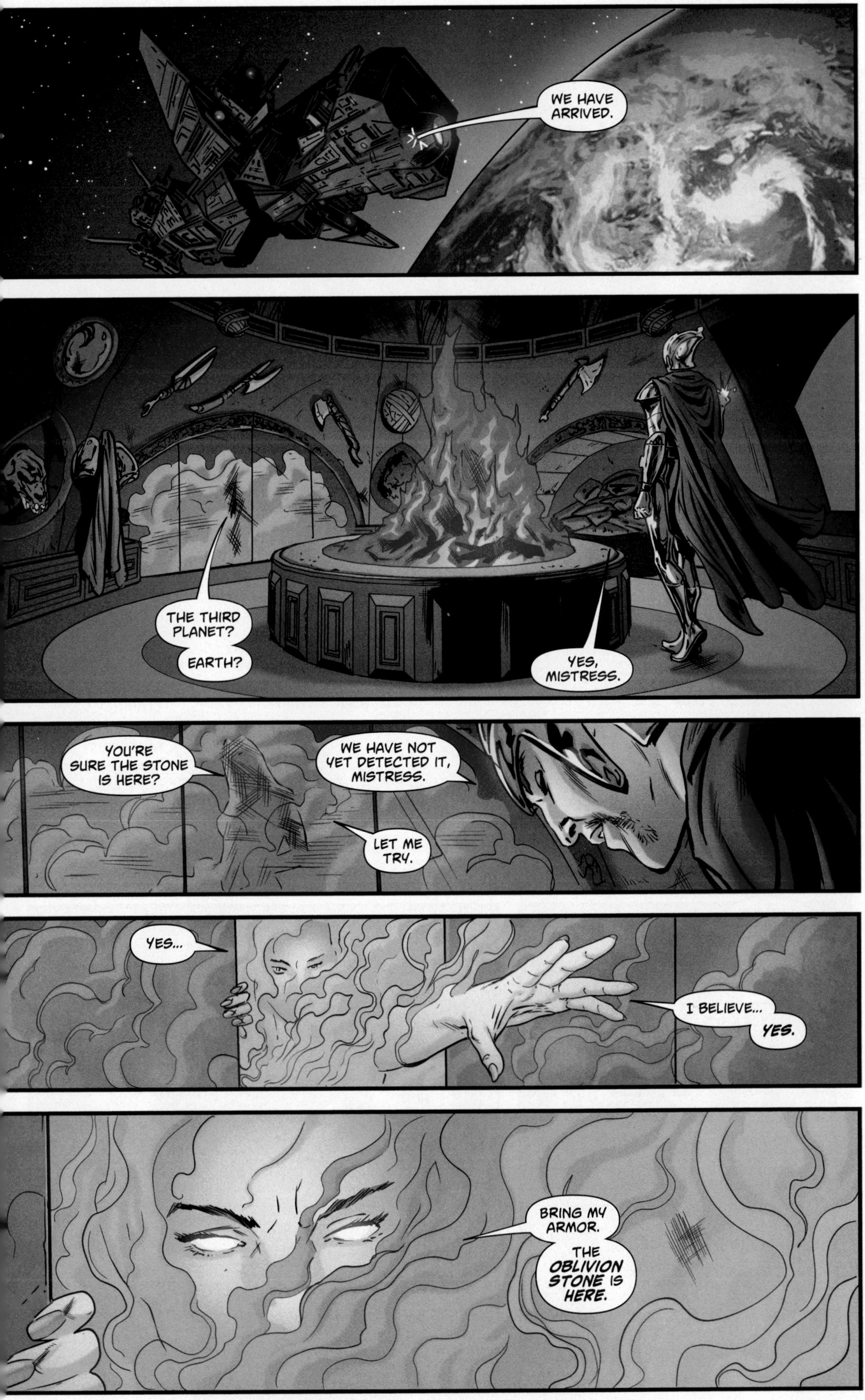
WE HAVE ARRIVED.
THE THIRD PLANET?
EARTH?
YES, MISTRESS.
YOU'RE SURE THE STONE IS HERE?
WE HAVE NOT YET DETECTED IT, MISTRESS.
LET ME TRY.
YES...
I BELIEVE... YES.
BRING MY ARMOR.
THE OBLIVION STONE IS HERE.

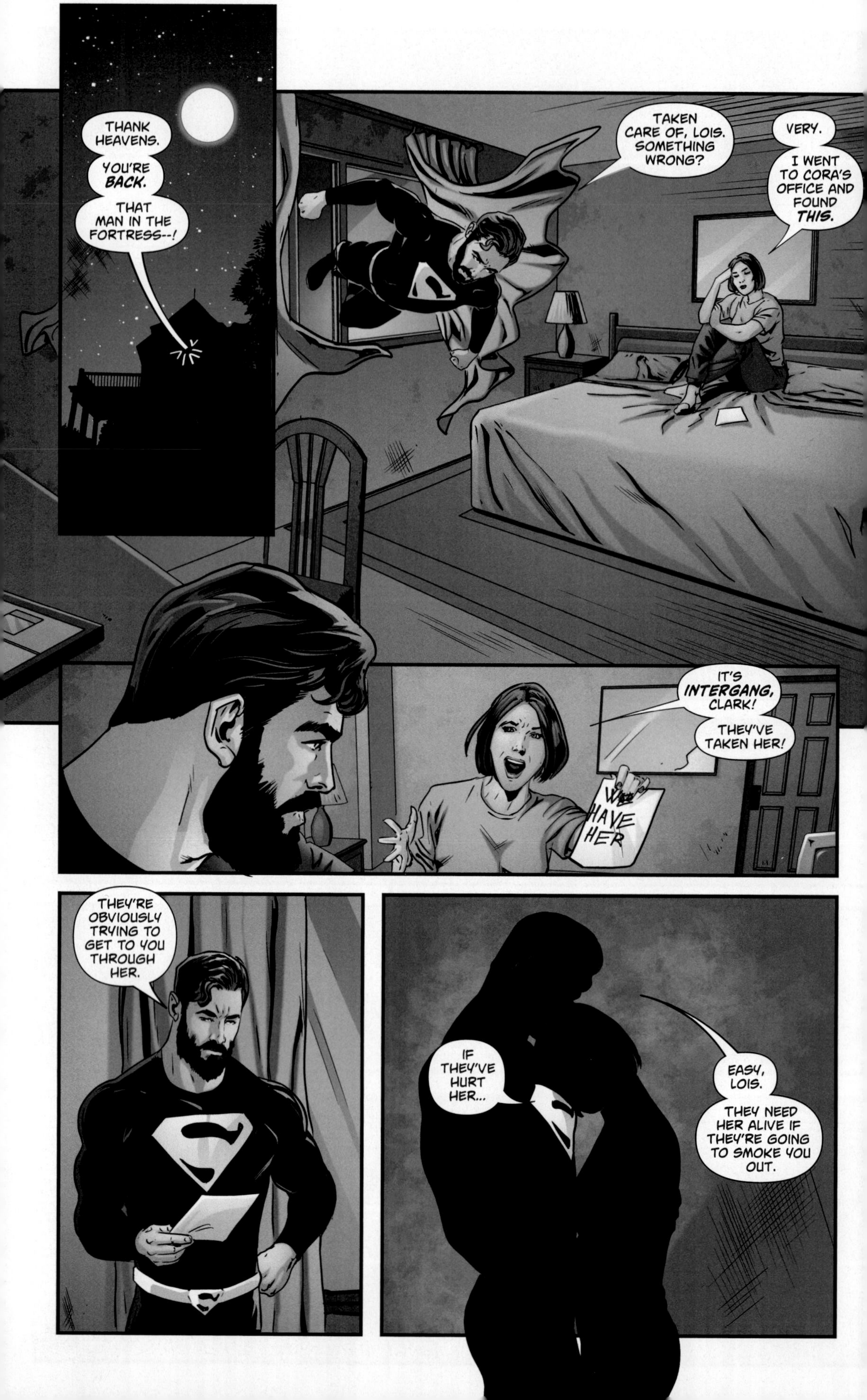
THANK HEAVENS.
YOU'RE BACK.
THAT MAN IN THE FORTRESS--!
TAKEN CARE OF, LOIS. SOMETHING WRONG?
VERY.
I WENT TO CORA'S OFFICE AND FOUND THIS.
IT'S INTERGANG, CLARK!
THEY'VE TAKEN HER!
WE HAVE HER
THEY'RE OBVIOUSLY TRYING TO GET TO YOU THROUGH HER.
IF THEY'VE HURT HER...
EASY, LOIS.
THEY NEED HER ALIVE IF THEY'RE GOING TO SMOKE YOU OUT.

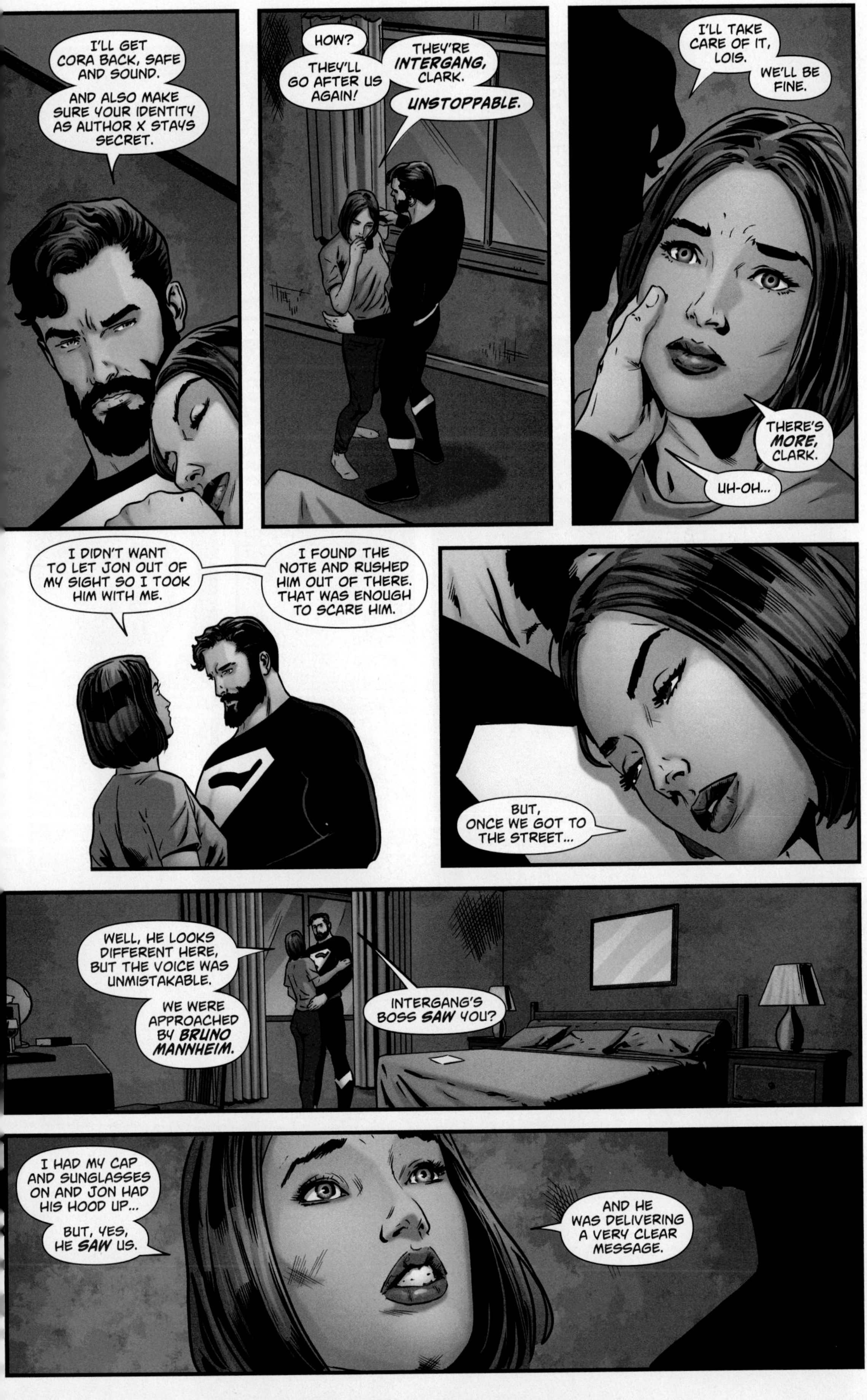

I'LL GET CORA BACK, SAFE AND SOUND.
AND ALSO MAKE SURE YOUR IDENTITY AS AUTHOR X STAYS SECRET.
HOW?
THEY'LL GO AFTER US AGAIN!
THEY'RE INTERGANG, CLARK.
UNSTOPPABLE.
I'LL TAKE CARE OF IT, LOIS.
WE'LL BE FINE.
THERE'S MORE, CLARK.
UH-OH...
I DIDN'T WANT TO LET JON OUT OF MY SIGHT SO I TOOK HIM WITH ME.
I FOUND THE NOTE AND RUSHED HIM OUT OF THERE. THAT WAS ENOUGH TO SCARE HIM.
BUT, ONCE WE GOT TO THE STREET...
WELL, HE LOOKS DIFFERENT HERE, BUT THE VOICE WAS UNMISTAKABLE.
WE WERE APPROACHED BY BRUNO MANNHEIM.
INTERGANG'S BOSS SAW YOU?
I HAD MY CAP AND SUNGLASSES ON AND JON HAD HIS HOOD UP...
BUT, YES, HE SAW US.
AND HE WAS DELIVERING A VERY CLEAR MESSAGE.

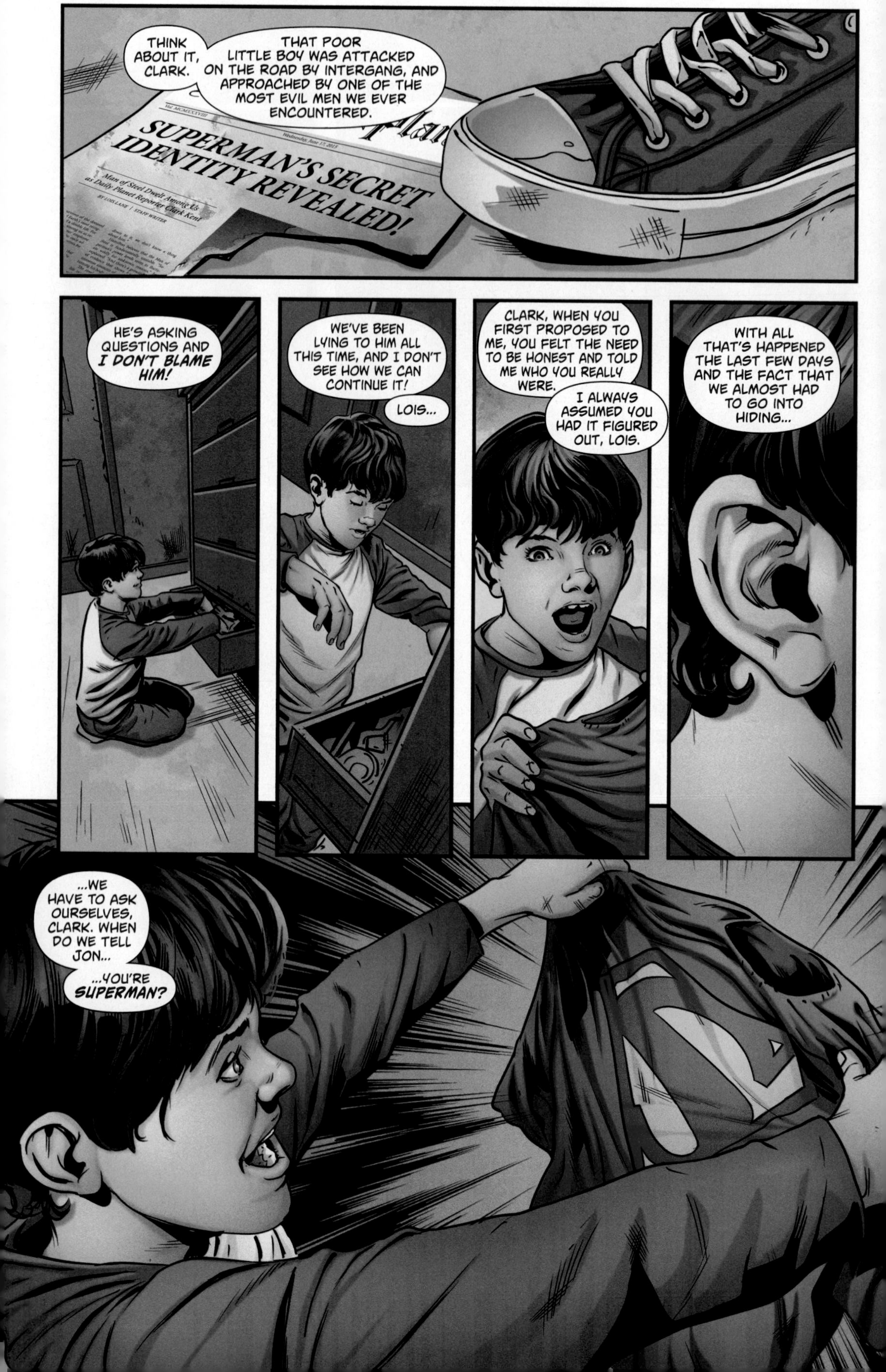
THINK ABOUT IT, CLARK.
THAT POOR LITTLE BOY WAS ATTACKED ON THE ROAD BY INTERGANG, AND APPROACHED BY ONE OF THE MOST EVIL MEN WE EVER ENCOUNTERED.
SUPERMAN'S SECRET IDENTITY REVEALED!
Man of Steel Dwelt Among Us as Daily Planet Reporter Clark Kent
BY LOIS LANE | STAFF WRITER
HE'S ASKING QUESTIONS AND I DON'T BLAME HIM!
WE'VE BEEN LYING TO HIM ALL THIS TIME, AND I DON'T SEE HOW WE CAN CONTINUE IT!
LOIS...
CLARK, WHEN YOU FIRST PROPOSED TO ME, YOU FELT THE NEED TO BE HONEST AND TOLD ME WHO YOU REALLY WERE.
I ALWAYS ASSUMED YOU HAD IT FIGURED OUT, LOIS.
WITH ALL THAT'S HAPPENED THE LAST FEW DAYS AND THE FACT THAT WE ALMOST HAD TO GO INTO HIDING...
...WE HAVE TO ASK OURSELVES, CLARK. WHEN DO WE TELL JON...
...YOU'RE SUPERMAN?

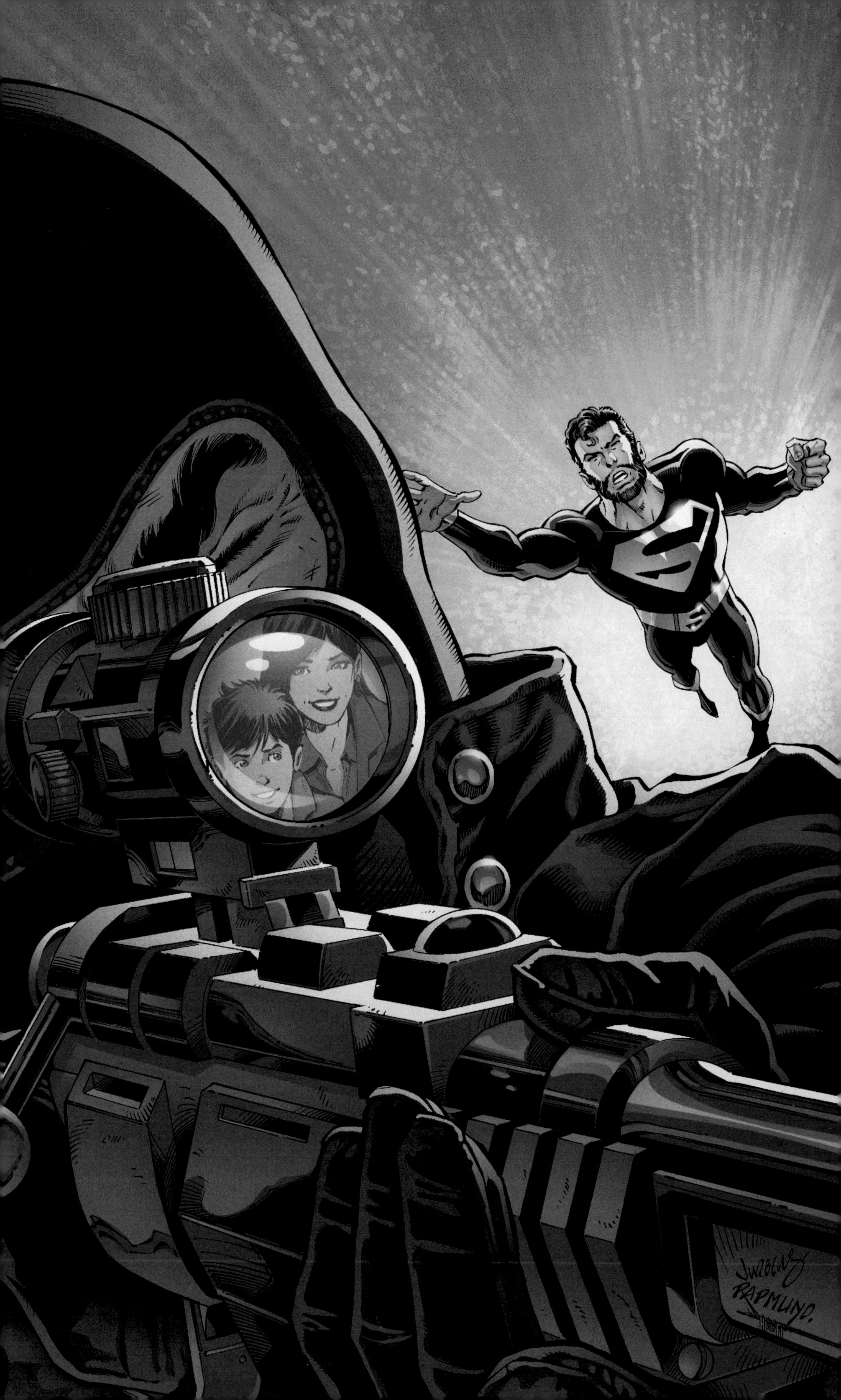

ARRIVAL: PART VI

DAN JURGENS writer LEE WEEKS penciller SCOTT HANNA inker JEROMY COX colorist A LARGER WORLD STUDIOS letterer DAN JURGENS HI-FI cover artists

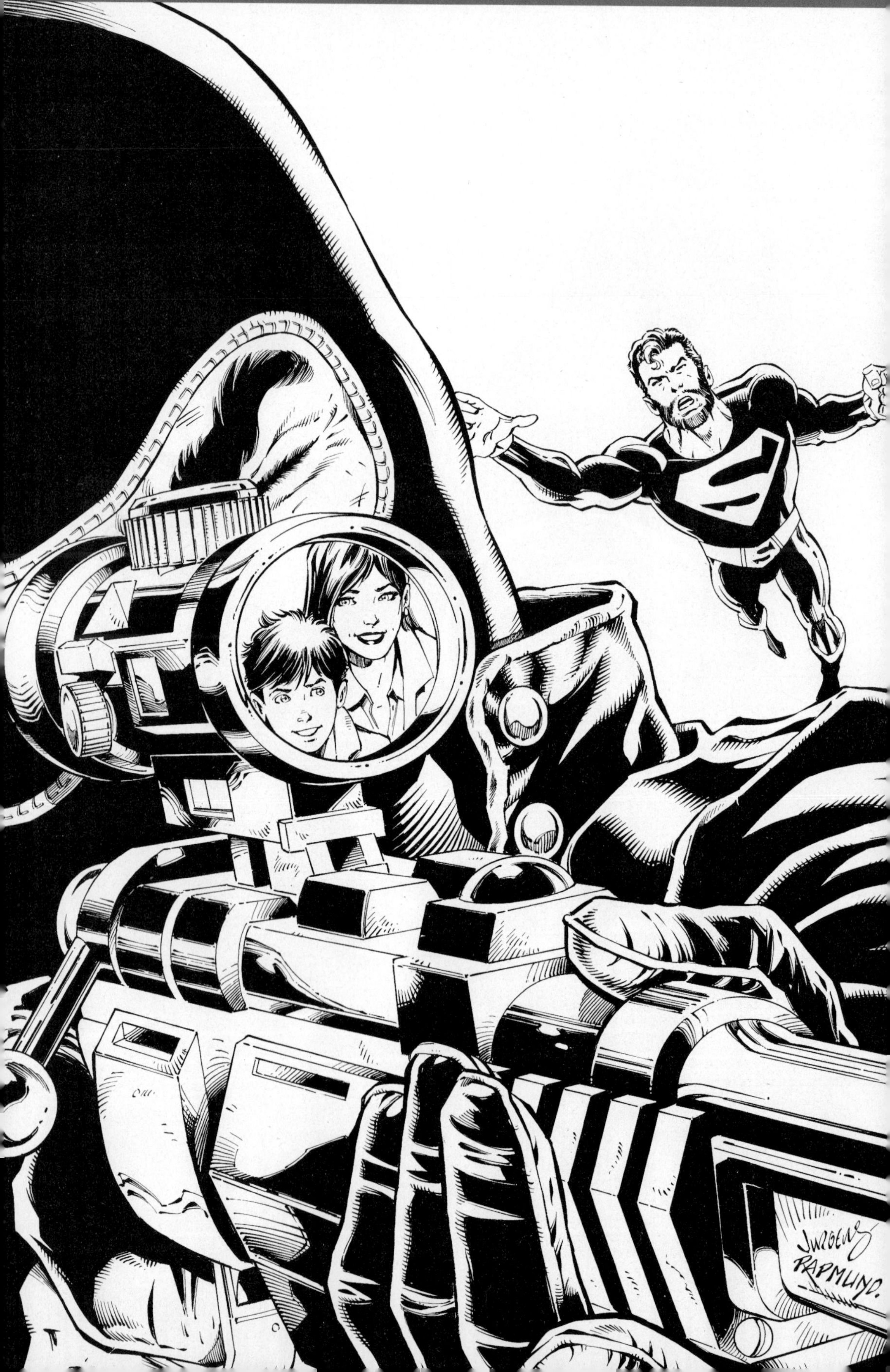

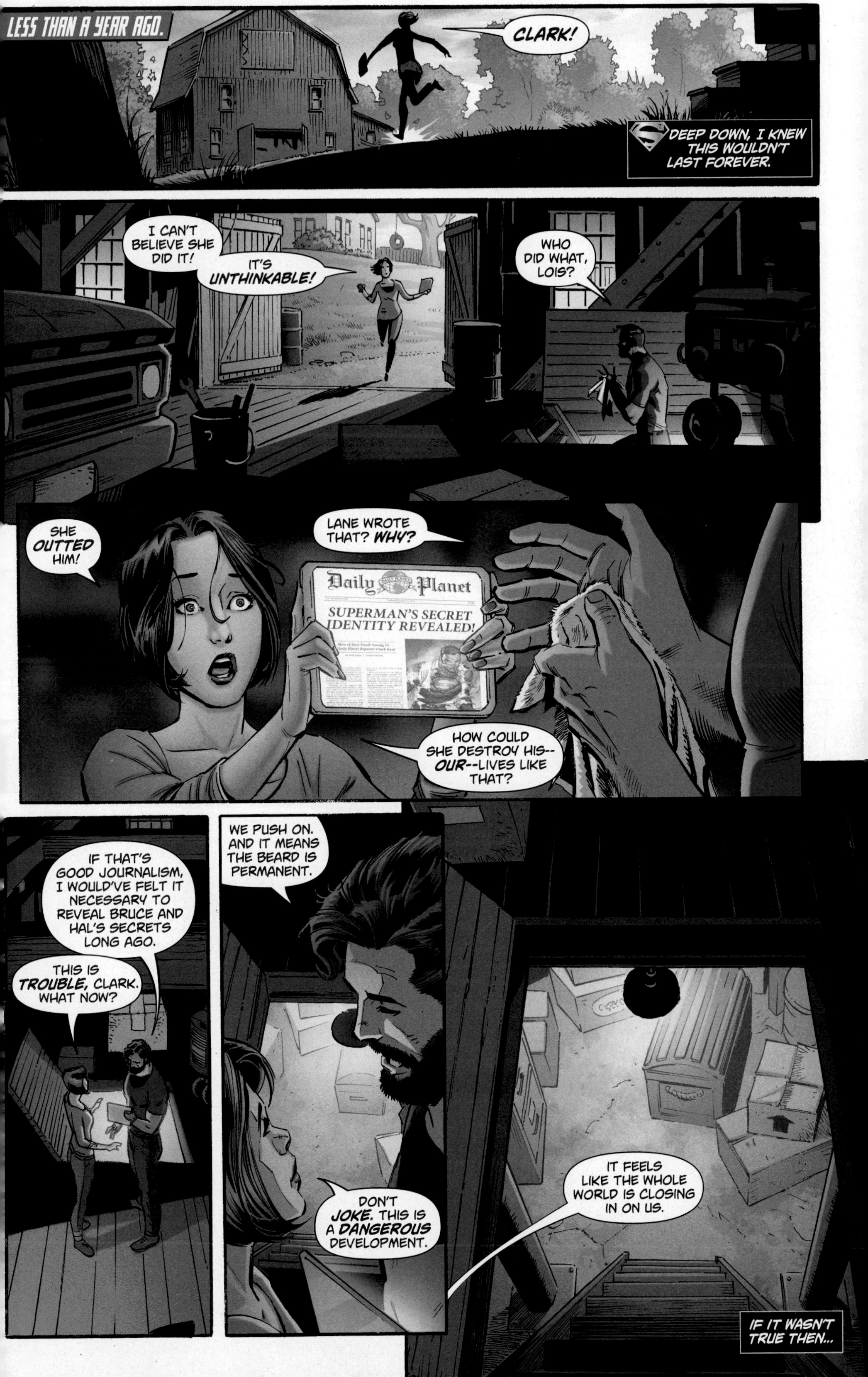

LESS THAN A YEAR AGO.
CLARK!
DEEP DOWN, I KNEW THIS WOULDN'T LAST FOREVER.
I CAN'T BELIEVE SHE DID IT!
IT'S UNTHINKABLE!
WHO DID WHAT, LOIS?
SHE OUTTED HIM!
LANE WROTE THAT? WHY?
Daily Planet
SUPERMAN'S SECRET IDENTITY REVEALED!
HOW COULD SHE DESTROY HIS--OUR--LIVES LIKE THAT?
IF THAT'S GOOD JOURNALISM, I WOULD'VE FELT IT NECESSARY TO REVEAL BRUCE AND HAL'S SECRETS LONG AGO.
THIS IS TROUBLE, CLARK. WHAT NOW?
WE PUSH ON. AND IT MEANS THE BEARD IS PERMANENT.
DON'T JOKE. THIS IS A DANGEROUS DEVELOPMENT.
IT FEELS LIKE THE WHOLE WORLD IS CLOSING IN ON US.
IF IT WASN'T TRUE THEN...

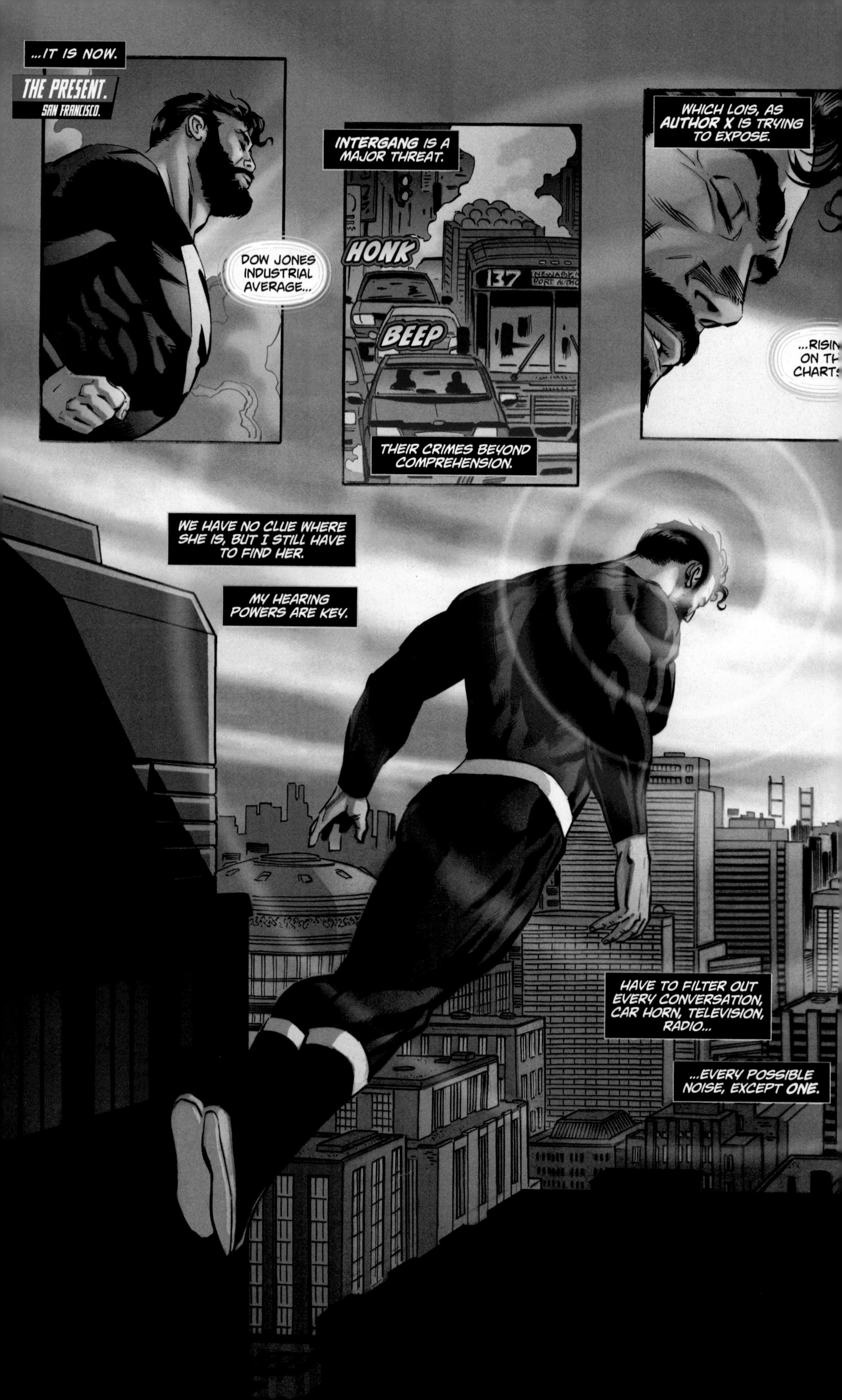
...IT IS NOW.
THE PRESENT.
SAN FRANCISCO.
DOW JONES INDUSTRIAL AVERAGE...
INTERGANG IS A MAJOR THREAT.
HONK
BEEP
137
THEIR CRIMES BEYOND COMPREHENSION.
WHICH LOIS, AS AUTHOR X IS TRYING TO EXPOSE.
WE HAVE NO CLUE WHERE SHE IS, BUT I STILL HAVE TO FIND HER.
MY HEARING POWERS ARE KEY.
HAVE TO FILTER OUT EVERY CONVERSATION, CAR HORN, TELEVISION, RADIO...
...EVERY POSSIBLE NOISE, EXCEPT ONE.

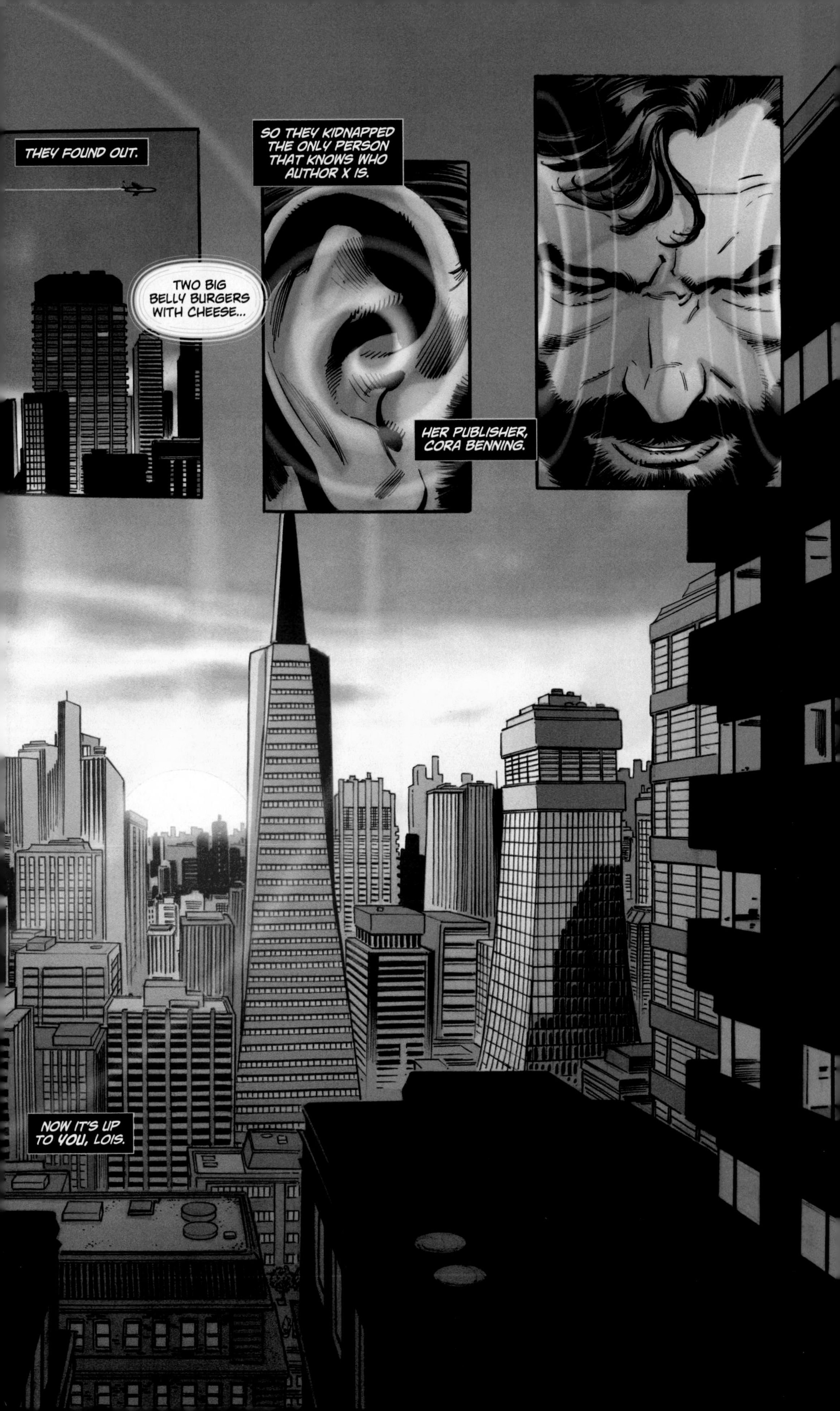
THEY FOUND OUT.
TWO BIG BELLY BURGERS WITH CHEESE...
SO THEY KIDNAPPED THE ONLY PERSON THAT KNOWS WHO AUTHOR X IS.
HER PUBLISHER, CORA BENNING.
NOW IT'S UP TO YOU, LOIS.

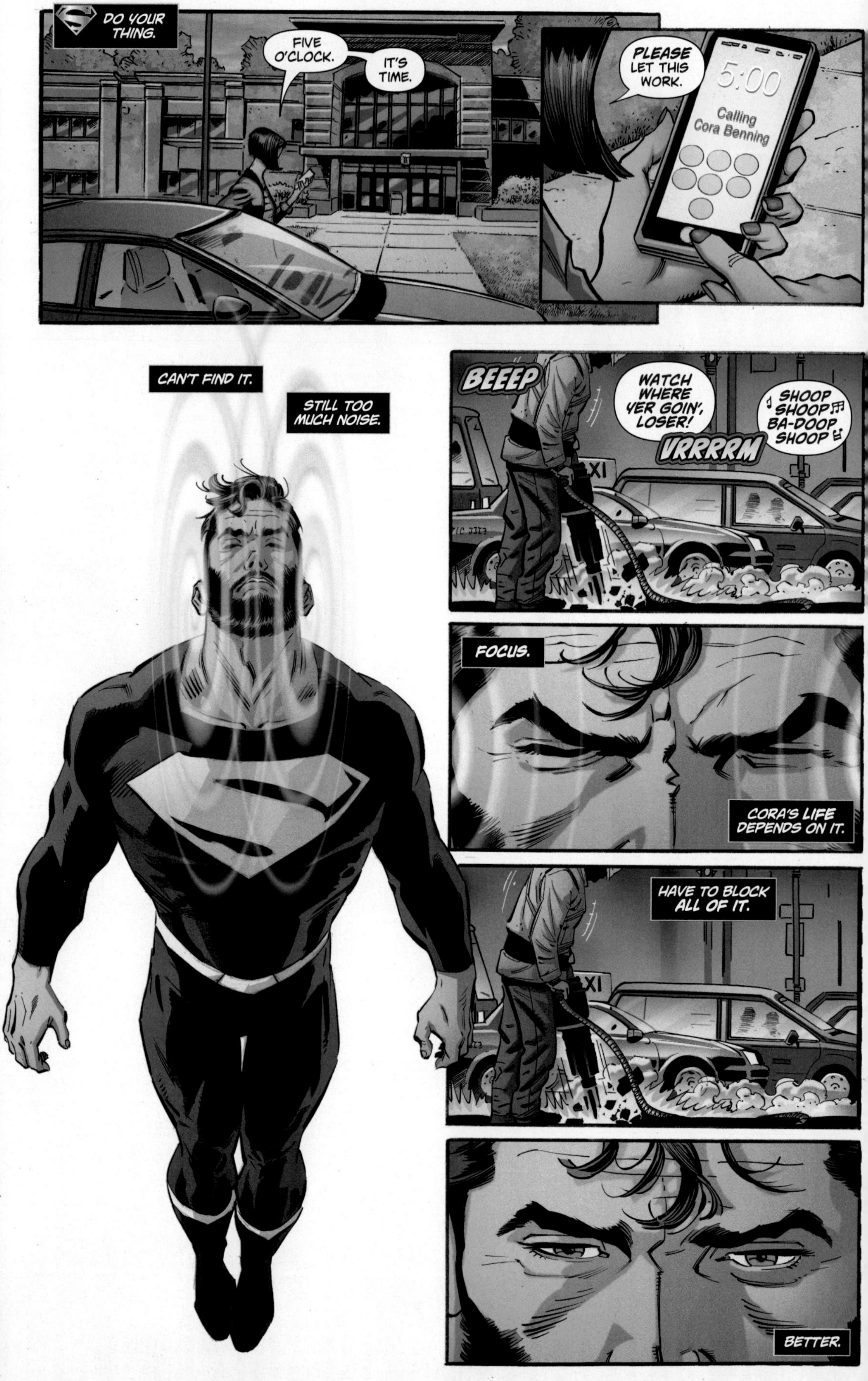
DO YOUR THING.
FIVE O'CLOCK.
IT'S TIME.
PLEASE LET THIS WORK.
5:00
Calling Cora Benning
CAN'T FIND IT.
STILL TOO MUCH NOISE.
BEEEP
WATCH WHERE YER GOIN', LOSER!
VRRRRM
SHOOP SHOOP BA-DOOP SHOOP
XI
FOCUS.
CORA'S LIFE DEPENDS ON IT.
HAVE TO BLOCK ALL OF IT.
XI
BETTER.

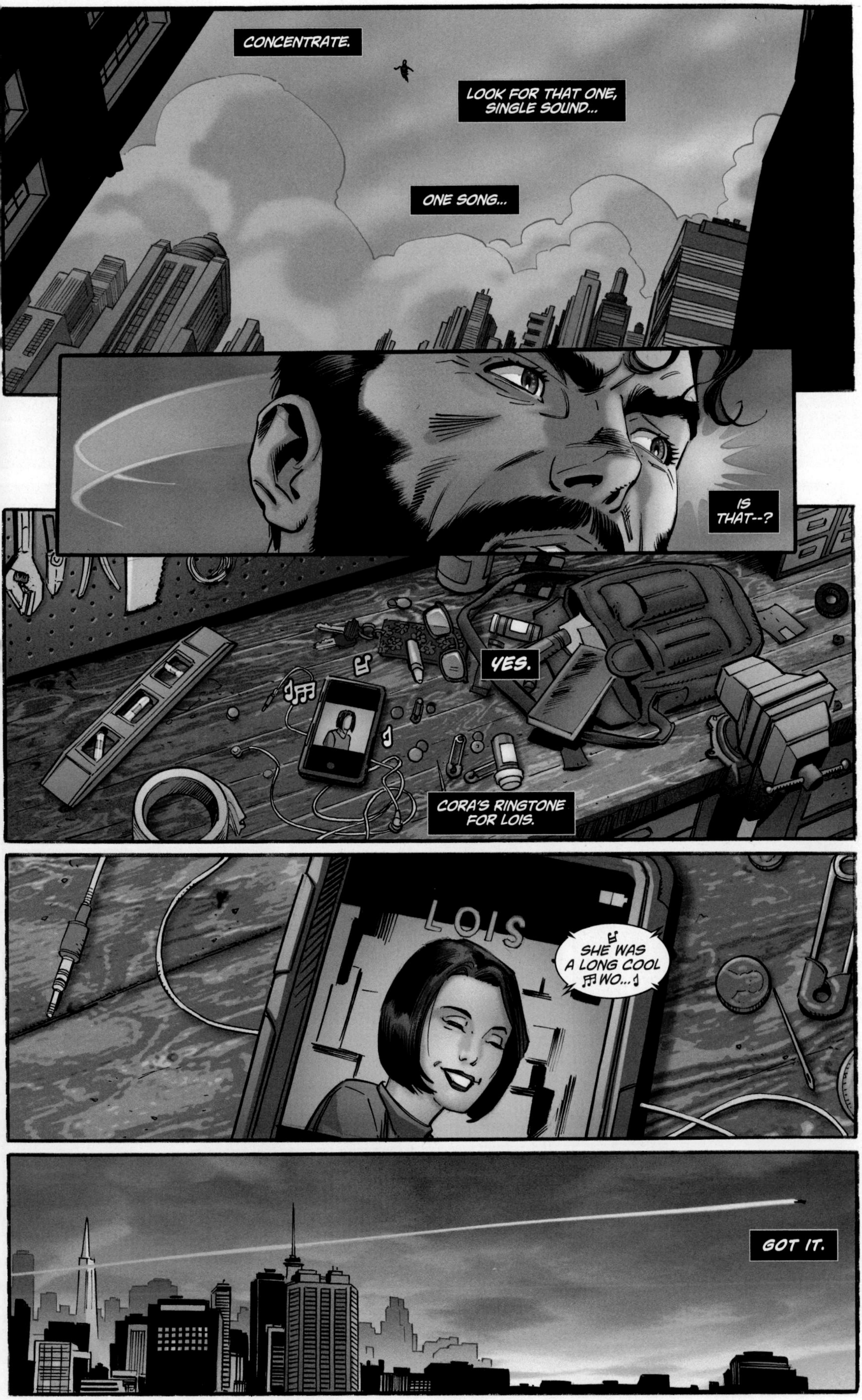
CONCENTRATE.
LOOK FOR THAT ONE, SINGLE SOUND...
ONE SONG...
IS THAT--?
YES.
CORA'S RINGTONE FOR LOIS.
LOIS
SHE WAS A LONG COOL WO...
GOT IT.

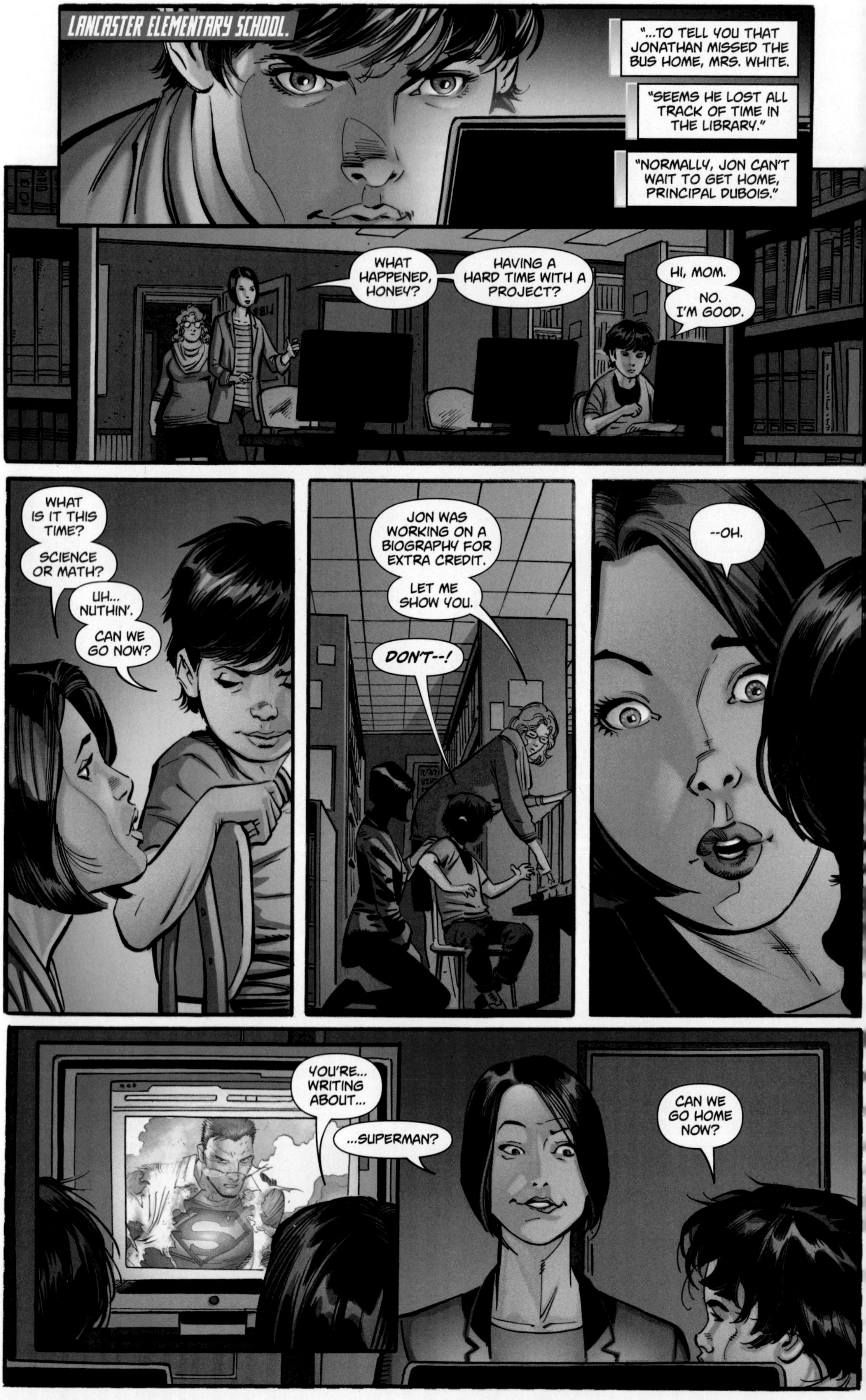
LANCASTER ELEMENTARY SCHOOL.
"...TO TELL YOU THAT JONATHAN MISSED THE BUS HOME, MRS. WHITE.
"SEEMS HE LOST ALL TRACK OF TIME IN THE LIBRARY."
"NORMALLY, JON CAN'T WAIT TO GET HOME, PRINCIPAL DUBOIS."
WHAT HAPPENED, HONEY?
HAVING A HARD TIME WITH A PROJECT?
HI, MOM.
NO. I'M GOOD.
WHAT IS IT THIS TIME?
SCIENCE OR MATH?
UH... NUTHIN'.
CAN WE GO NOW?
JON WAS WORKING ON A BIOGRAPHY FOR EXTRA CREDIT.
LET ME SHOW YOU.
DON'T--!
--OH.
YOU'RE... WRITING ABOUT...
...SUPERMAN?
CAN WE GO HOME NOW?

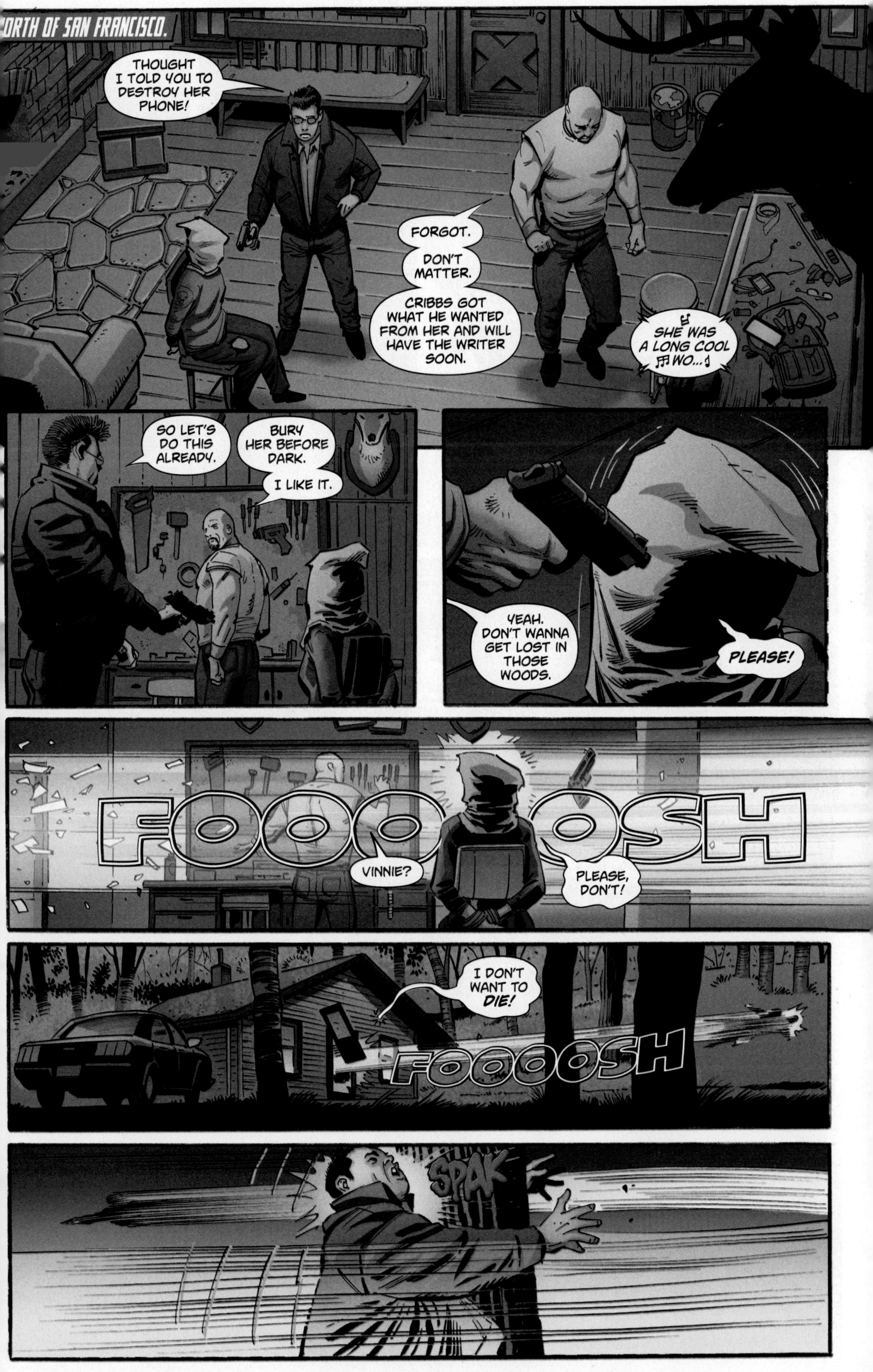
ORTH OF SAN FRANCISCO.
THOUGHT I TOLD YOU TO DESTROY HER PHONE!
FORGOT.
DON'T MATTER.
CRIBBS GOT WHAT HE WANTED FROM HER AND WILL HAVE THE WRITER SOON.
SHE WAS A LONG COOL WO...
SO LET'S DO THIS ALREADY.
BURY HER BEFORE DARK.
I LIKE IT.
YEAH. DON'T WANNA GET LOST IN THOSE WOODS.
PLEASE!
FOOOOOSH
VINNIE?
PLEASE, DON'T!
I DON'T WANT TO DIE!
FOOOOOSH
SPAK

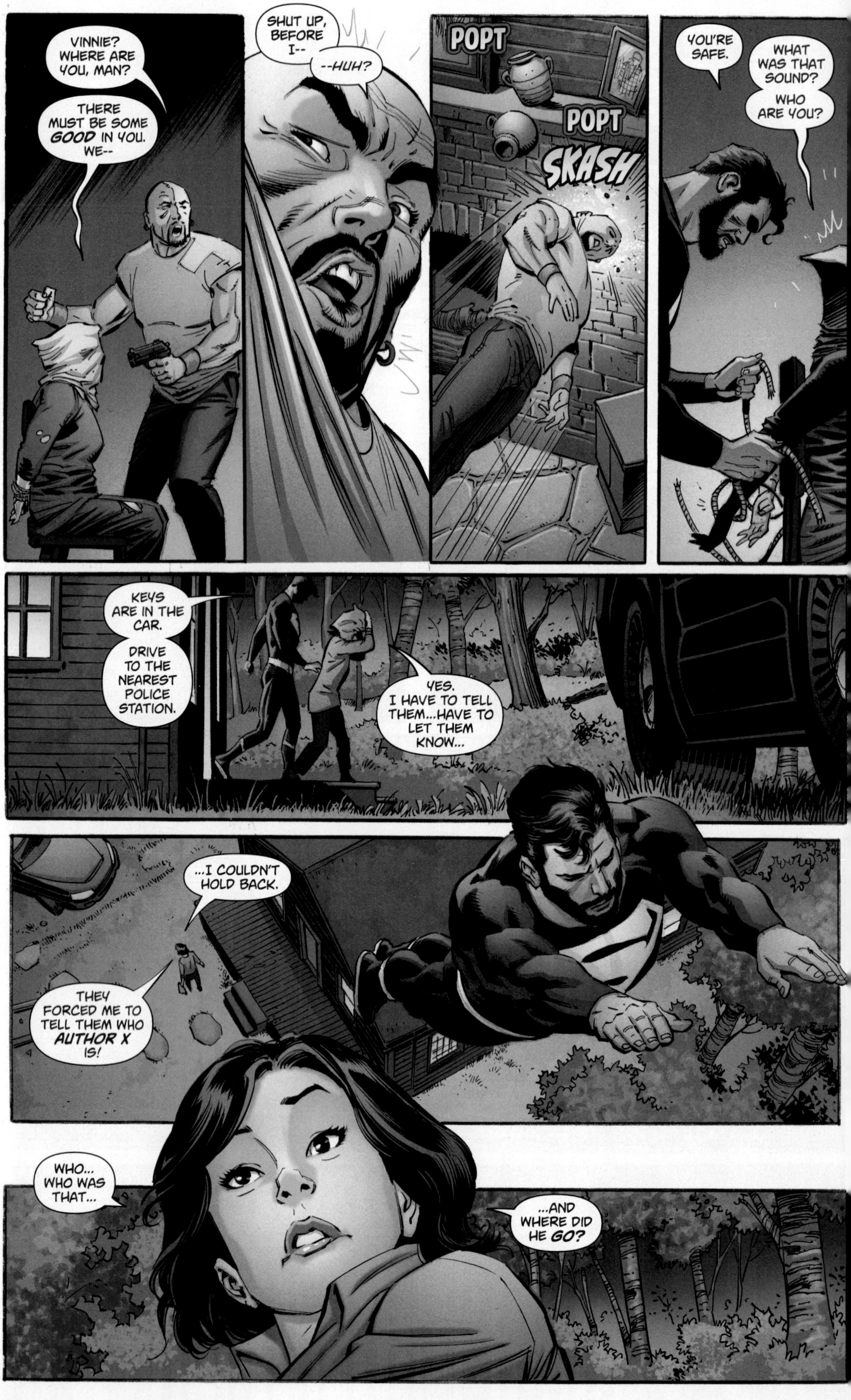
VINNIE? WHERE ARE YOU, MAN?
THERE MUST BE SOME GOOD IN YOU. WE--
SHUT UP, BEFORE I--
--HUH?
POPT
POPT
SKASH
YOU'RE SAFE.
WHAT WAS THAT SOUND?
WHO ARE YOU?
KEYS ARE IN THE CAR.
DRIVE TO THE NEAREST POLICE STATION.
YES. I HAVE TO TELL THEM...HAVE TO LET THEM KNOW...
...I COULDN'T HOLD BACK.
THEY FORCED ME TO TELL THEM WHO AUTHOR X IS!
WHO... WHO WAS THAT...
...AND WHERE DID HE GO?

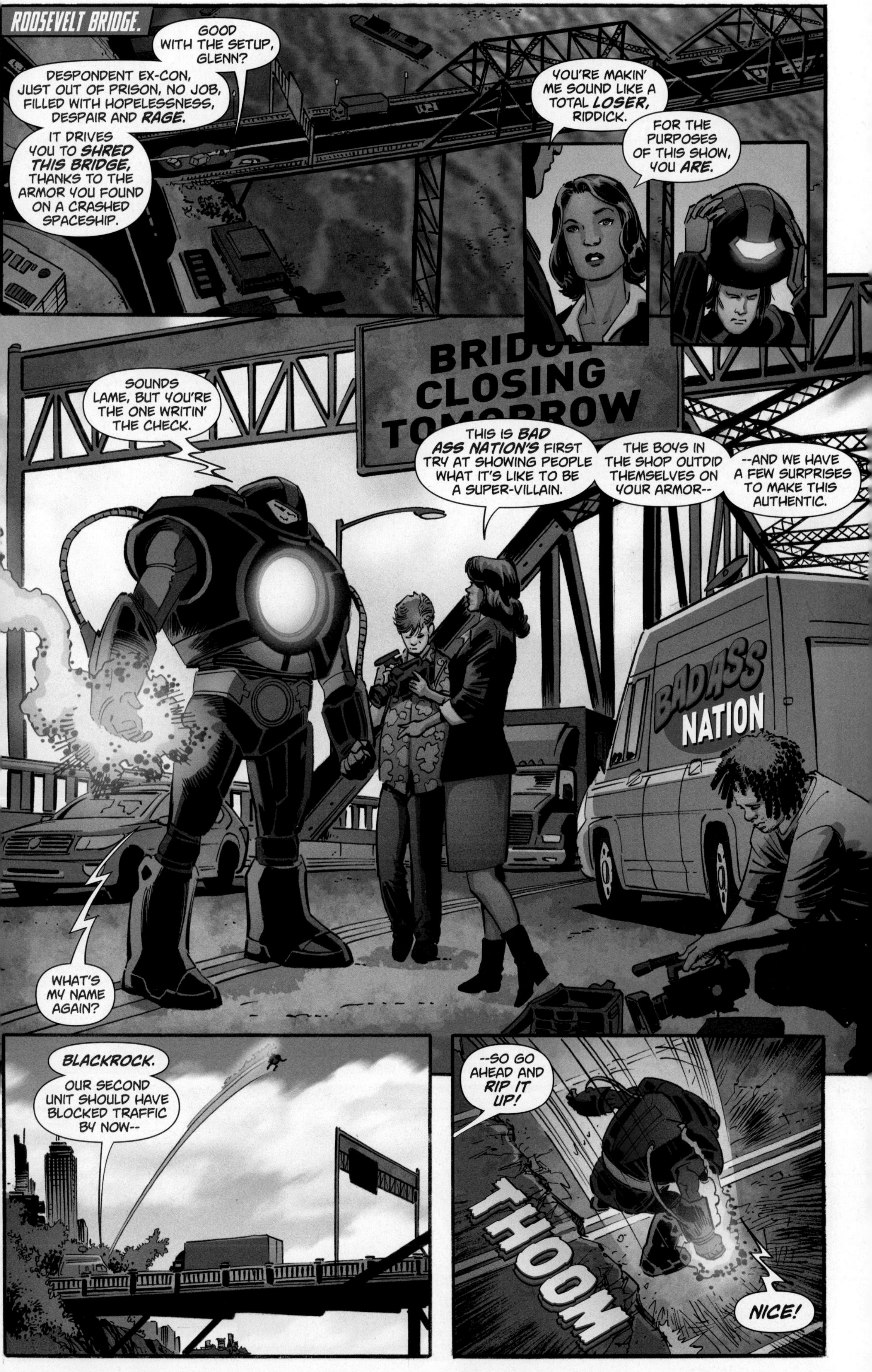

ROOSEVELT BRIDGE.
GOOD WITH THE SETUP, GLENN?
DESPONDENT EX-CON, JUST OUT OF PRISON, NO JOB, FILLED WITH HOPELESSNESS, DESPAIR AND RAGE.
IT DRIVES YOU TO SHRED THIS BRIDGE, THANKS TO THE ARMOR YOU FOUND ON A CRASHED SPACESHIP.
YOU'RE MAKIN' ME SOUND LIKE A TOTAL LOSER, RIDDICK.
FOR THE PURPOSES OF THIS SHOW, YOU ARE.
BRIDGE CLOSING TOMORROW
SOUNDS LAME, BUT YOU'RE THE ONE WRITIN' THE CHECK.
THIS IS BAD ASS NATION'S FIRST TRY AT SHOWING PEOPLE WHAT IT'S LIKE TO BE A SUPER-VILLAIN.
THE BOYS IN THE SHOP OUTDID THEMSELVES ON YOUR ARMOR--
--AND WE HAVE A FEW SURPRISES TO MAKE THIS AUTHENTIC.
BAD ASS NATION
WHAT'S MY NAME AGAIN?
BLACKROCK.
OUR SECOND UNIT SHOULD HAVE BLOCKED TRAFFIC BY NOW--
--SO GO AHEAD AND RIP IT UP!
THOOM
NICE!

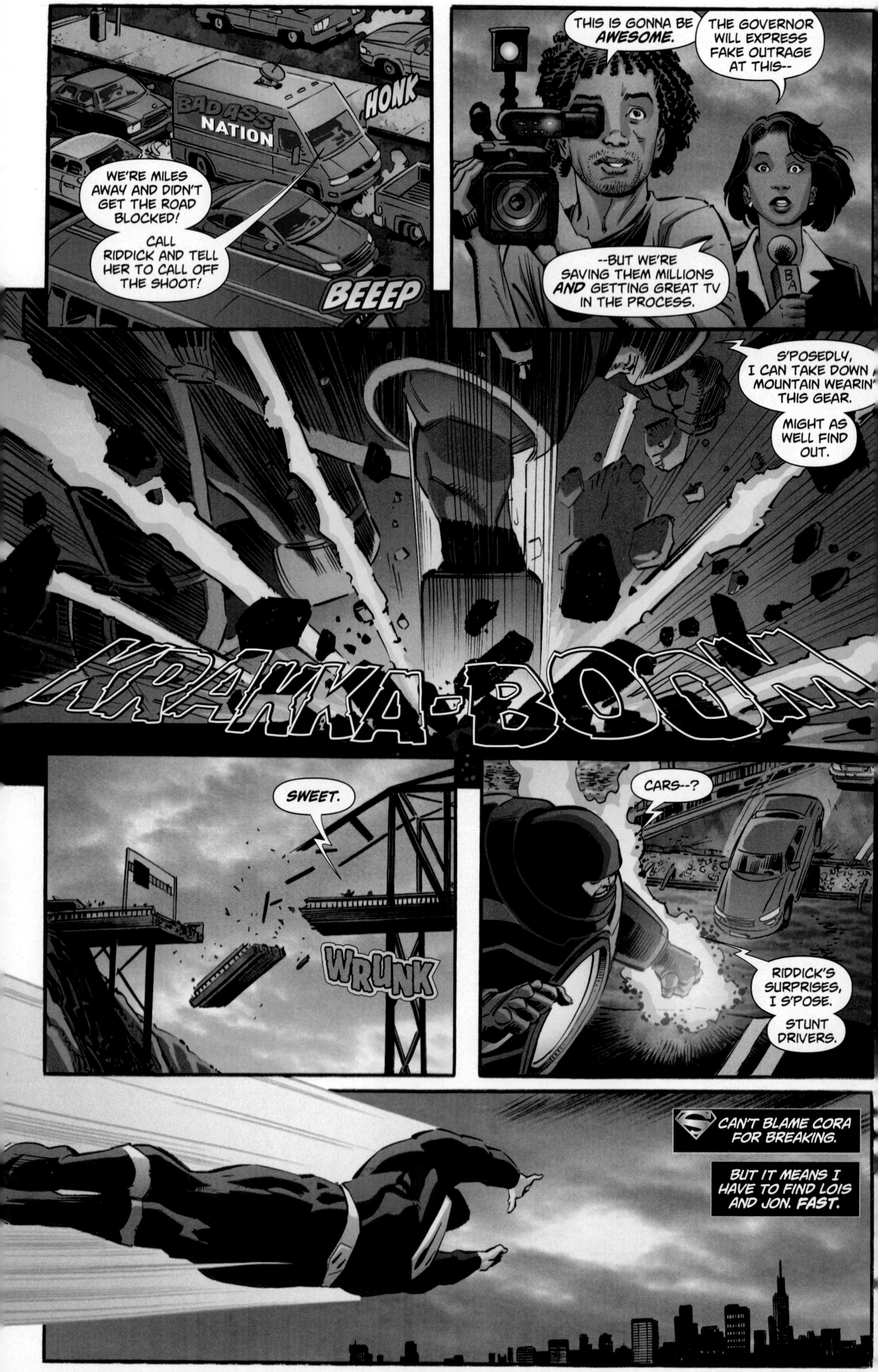

HONK
BADASS NATION
WE'RE MILES AWAY AND DIDN'T GET THE ROAD BLOCKED!
CALL RIDDICK AND TELL HER TO CALL OFF THE SHOOT!
BEEEP
THIS IS GONNA BE AWESOME.
THE GOVERNOR WILL EXPRESS FAKE OUTRAGE AT THIS--
--BUT WE'RE SAVING THEM MILLIONS AND GETTING GREAT TV IN THE PROCESS.
S'POSEDLY, I CAN TAKE DOWN MOUNTAIN WEARIN' THIS GEAR.
MIGHT AS WELL FIND OUT.
KRAKKA-BOOM
SWEET.
WRUNK
CARS--?
RIDDICK'S SURPRISES, I S'POSE.
STUNT DRIVERS.
CAN'T BLAME CORA FOR BREAKING.
BUT IT MEANS I HAVE TO FIND LOIS AND JON. FAST.

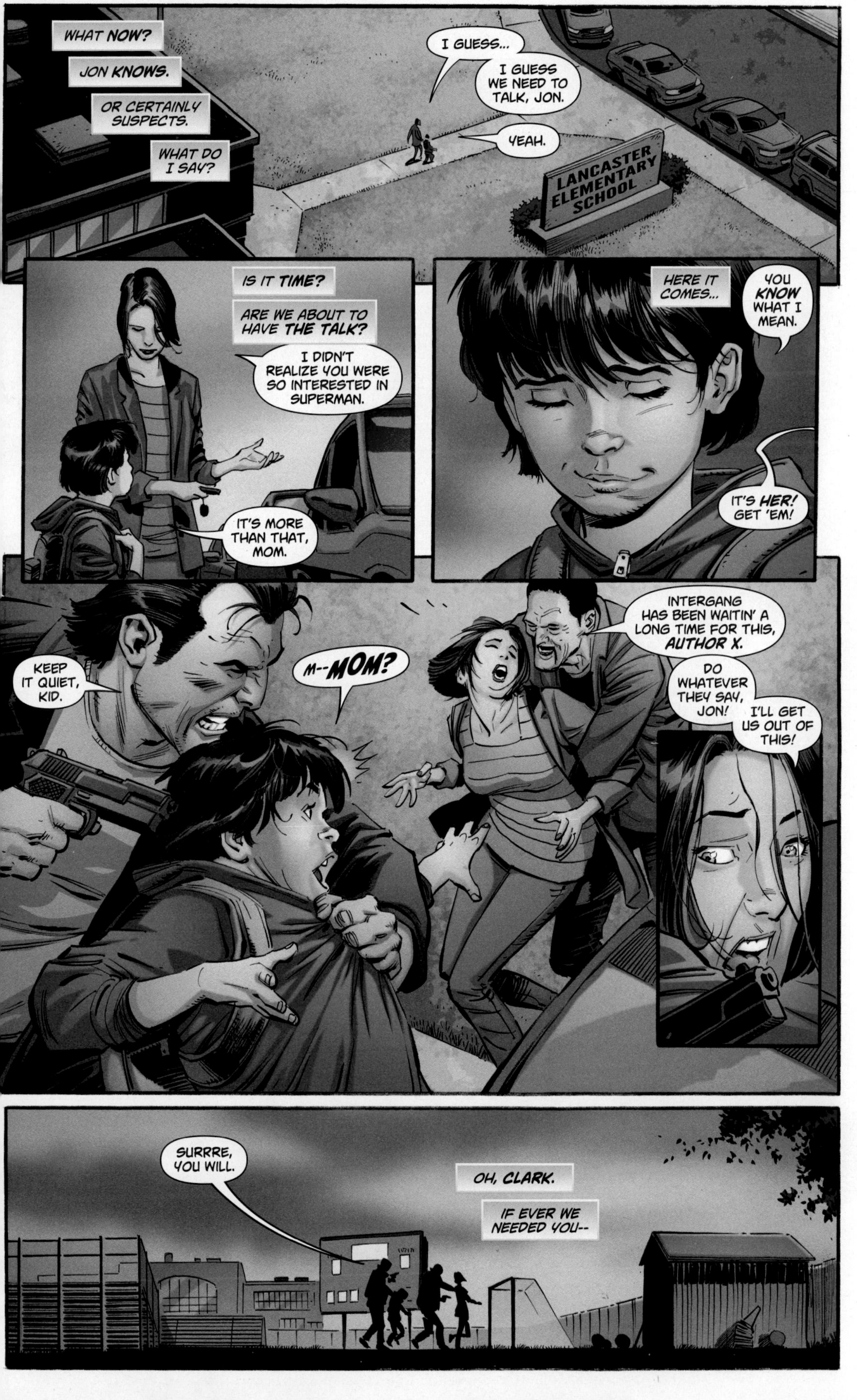

WHAT NOW?
JON KNOWS.
OR CERTAINLY SUSPECTS.
WHAT DO I SAY?
I GUESS...
I GUESS WE NEED TO TALK, JON.
YEAH.
LANCASTER ELEMENTARY SCHOOL
IS IT TIME?
ARE WE ABOUT TO HAVE THE TALK?
I DIDN'T REALIZE YOU WERE SO INTERESTED IN SUPERMAN.
IT'S MORE THAN THAT, MOM.
HERE IT COMES...
YOU KNOW WHAT I MEAN.
IT'S HER! GET 'EM!
KEEP IT QUIET, KID.
M--MOM?
INTERGANG HAS BEEN WAITIN' A LONG TIME FOR THIS, AUTHOR X.
DO WHATEVER THEY SAY, JON!
I'LL GET US OUT OF THIS!
SURRRE, YOU WILL.
OH, CLARK.
IF EVER WE NEEDED YOU--

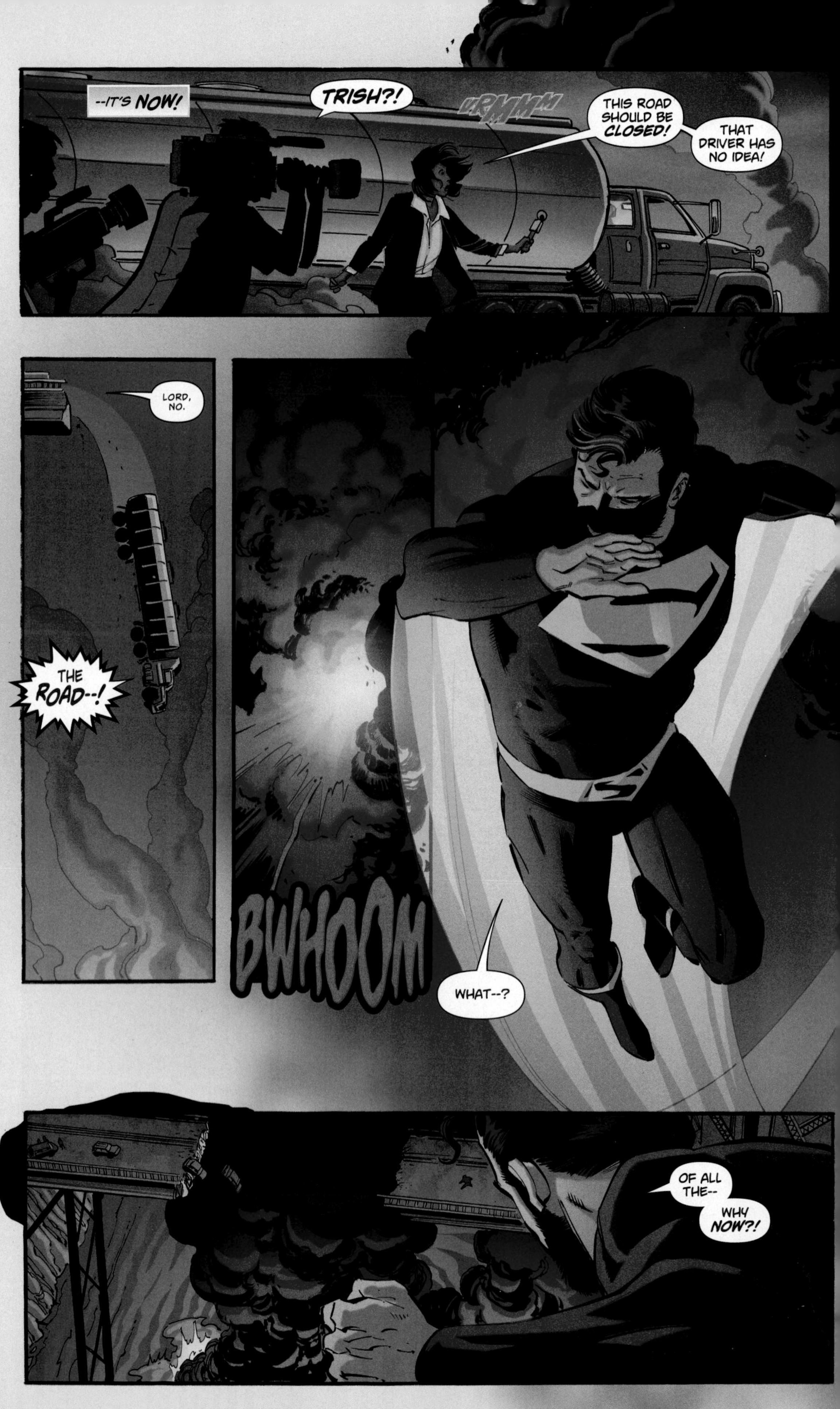
--IT'S NOW!
TRISH?!
VRMMM
THIS ROAD SHOULD BE CLOSED!
THAT DRIVER HAS NO IDEA!
LORD, NO.
THE ROAD--!
BWHOOM
WHAT--?
OF ALL THE--
WHY NOW?!

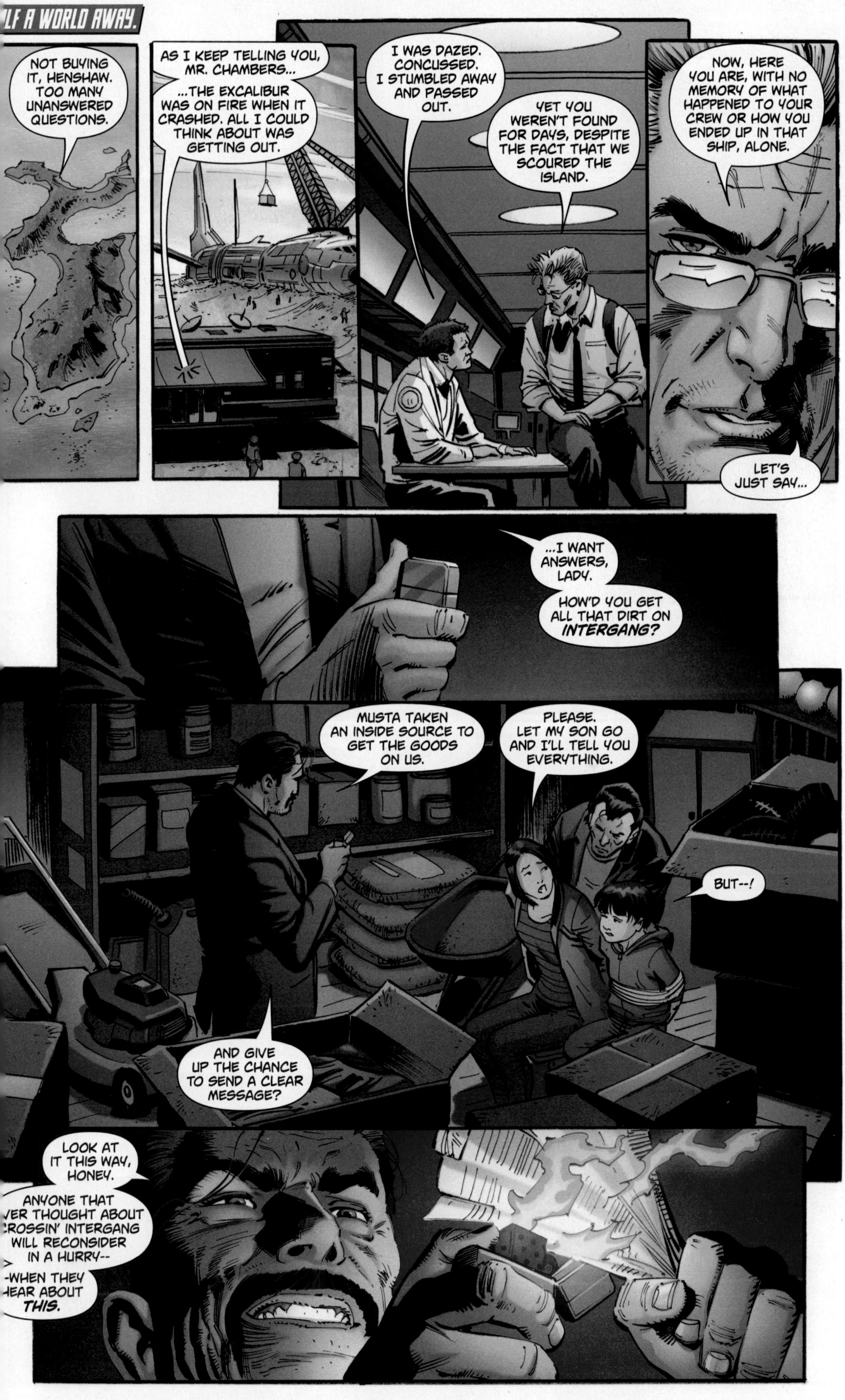

LF A WORLD AWAY.
NOT BUYING IT, HENSHAW. TOO MANY UNANSWERED QUESTIONS.
AS I KEEP TELLING YOU, MR. CHAMBERS...
...THE EXCALIBUR WAS ON FIRE WHEN IT CRASHED. ALL I COULD THINK ABOUT WAS GETTING OUT.
I WAS DAZED. CONCUSSED. I STUMBLED AWAY AND PASSED OUT.
YET YOU WEREN'T FOUND FOR DAYS, DESPITE THE FACT THAT WE SCOURED THE ISLAND.
NOW, HERE YOU ARE, WITH NO MEMORY OF WHAT HAPPENED TO YOUR CREW OR HOW YOU ENDED UP IN THAT SHIP, ALONE.
LET'S JUST SAY...
...I WANT ANSWERS, LADY.
HOW'D YOU GET ALL THAT DIRT ON *INTERGANG?*
MUSTA TAKEN AN INSIDE SOURCE TO GET THE GOODS ON US.
PLEASE. LET MY SON GO AND I'LL TELL YOU EVERYTHING.
BUT--!
AND GIVE UP THE CHANCE TO SEND A CLEAR MESSAGE?
LOOK AT IT THIS WAY, HONEY.
ANYONE THAT VER THOUGHT ABOUT CROSSIN' INTERGANG WILL RECONSIDER IN A HURRY--
-WHEN THEY HEAR ABOUT *THIS.*

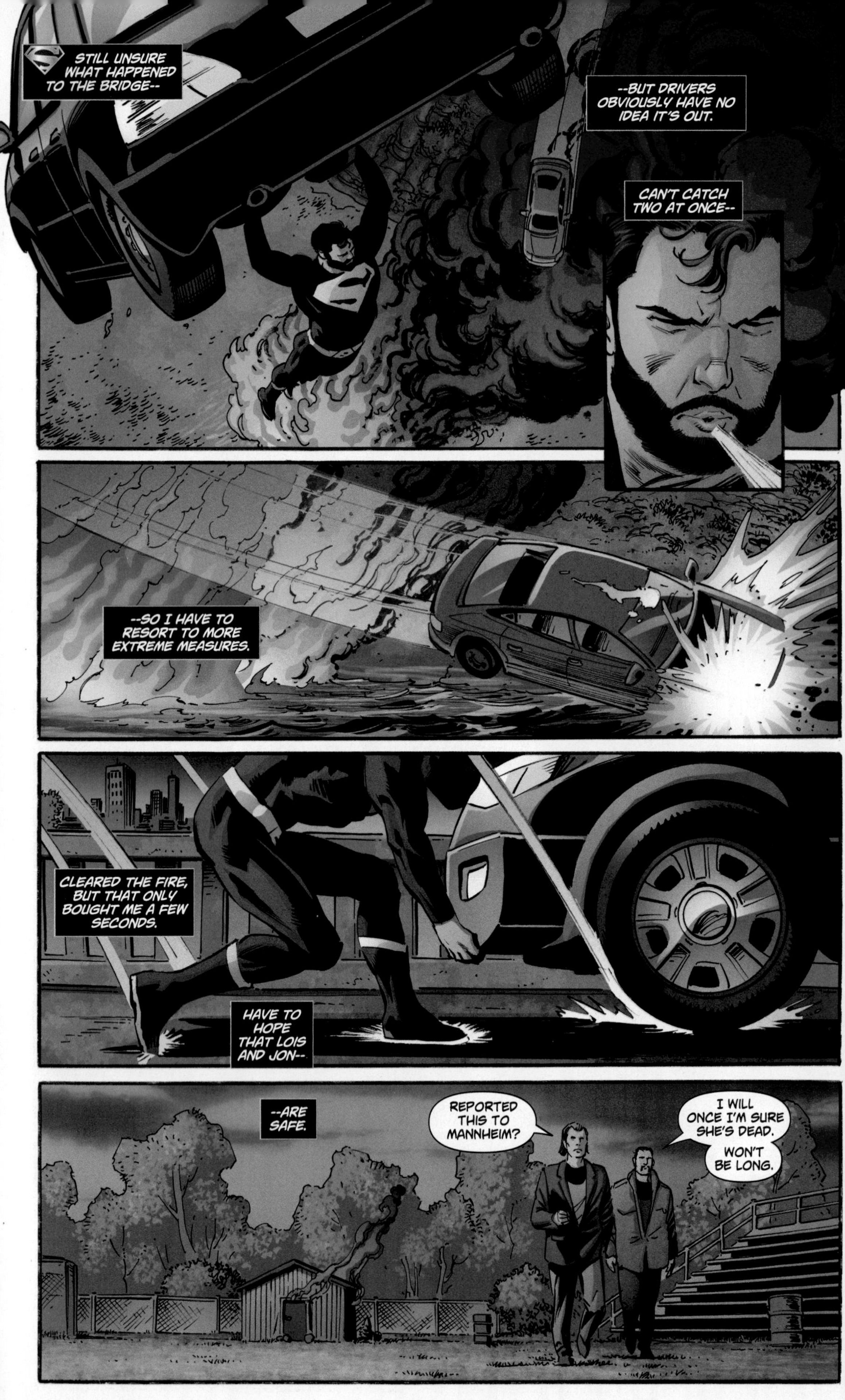
STILL UNSURE WHAT HAPPENED TO THE BRIDGE--
--BUT DRIVERS OBVIOUSLY HAVE NO IDEA IT'S OUT.
CAN'T CATCH TWO AT ONCE--
--SO I HAVE TO RESORT TO MORE EXTREME MEASURES.
CLEARED THE FIRE, BUT THAT ONLY BOUGHT ME A FEW SECONDS.
HAVE TO HOPE THAT LOIS AND JON--
--ARE SAFE.
REPORTED THIS TO MANNHEIM?
I WILL ONCE I'M SURE SHE'S DEAD.
WON'T BE LONG.

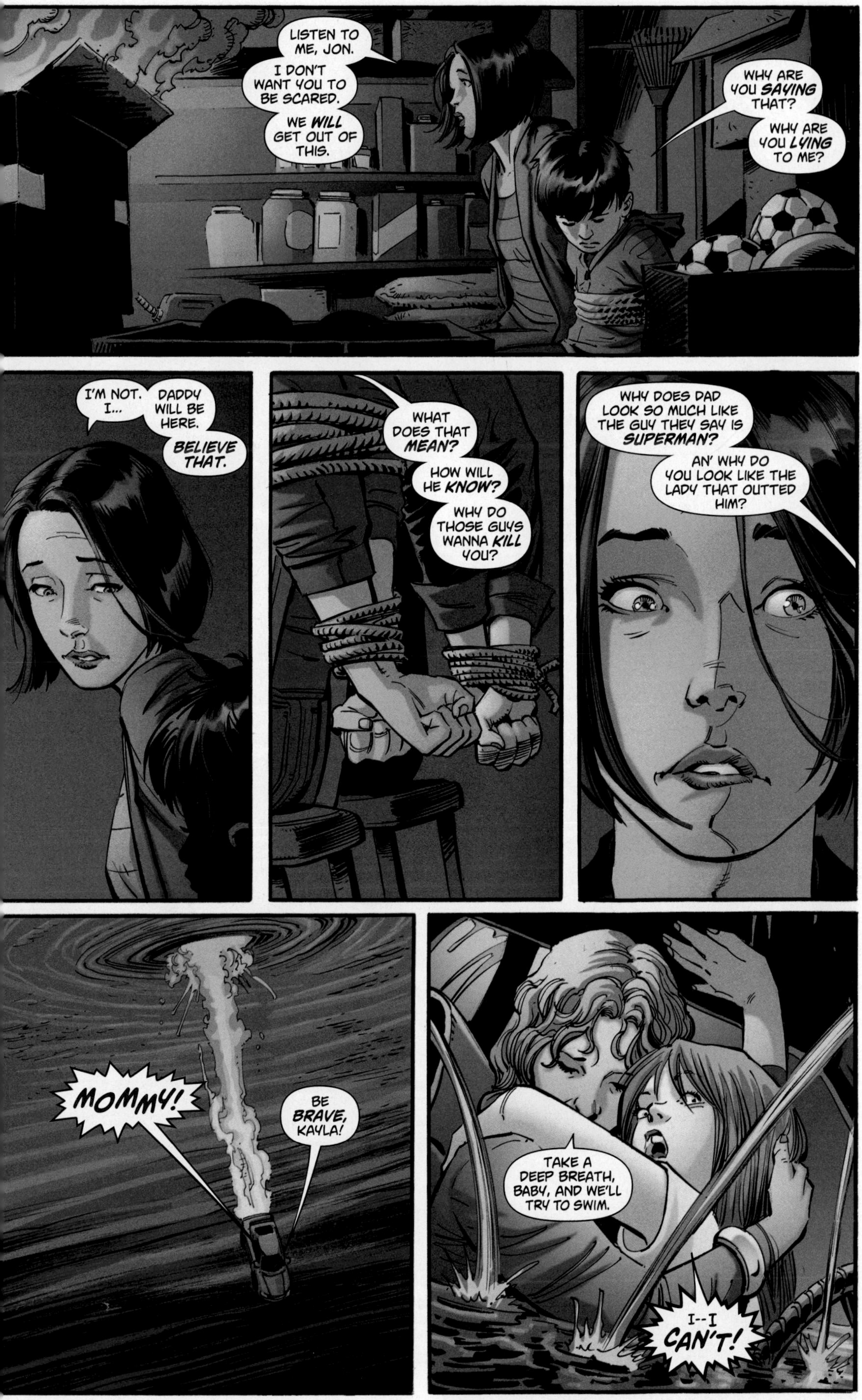
LISTEN TO ME, JON.
I DON'T WANT YOU TO BE SCARED.
WE WILL GET OUT OF THIS.
WHY ARE YOU SAYING THAT?
WHY ARE YOU LYING TO ME?
I'M NOT. I...
DADDY WILL BE HERE.
BELIEVE THAT.
WHAT DOES THAT MEAN?
HOW WILL HE KNOW?
WHY DO THOSE GUYS WANNA KILL YOU?
WHY DOES DAD LOOK SO MUCH LIKE THE GUY THEY SAY IS SUPERMAN?
AN' WHY DO YOU LOOK LIKE THE LADY THAT OUTTED HIM?
MOMMY!
BE BRAVE, KAYLA!
TAKE A DEEP BREATH, BABY, AND WE'LL TRY TO SWIM.
I--I CAN'T!

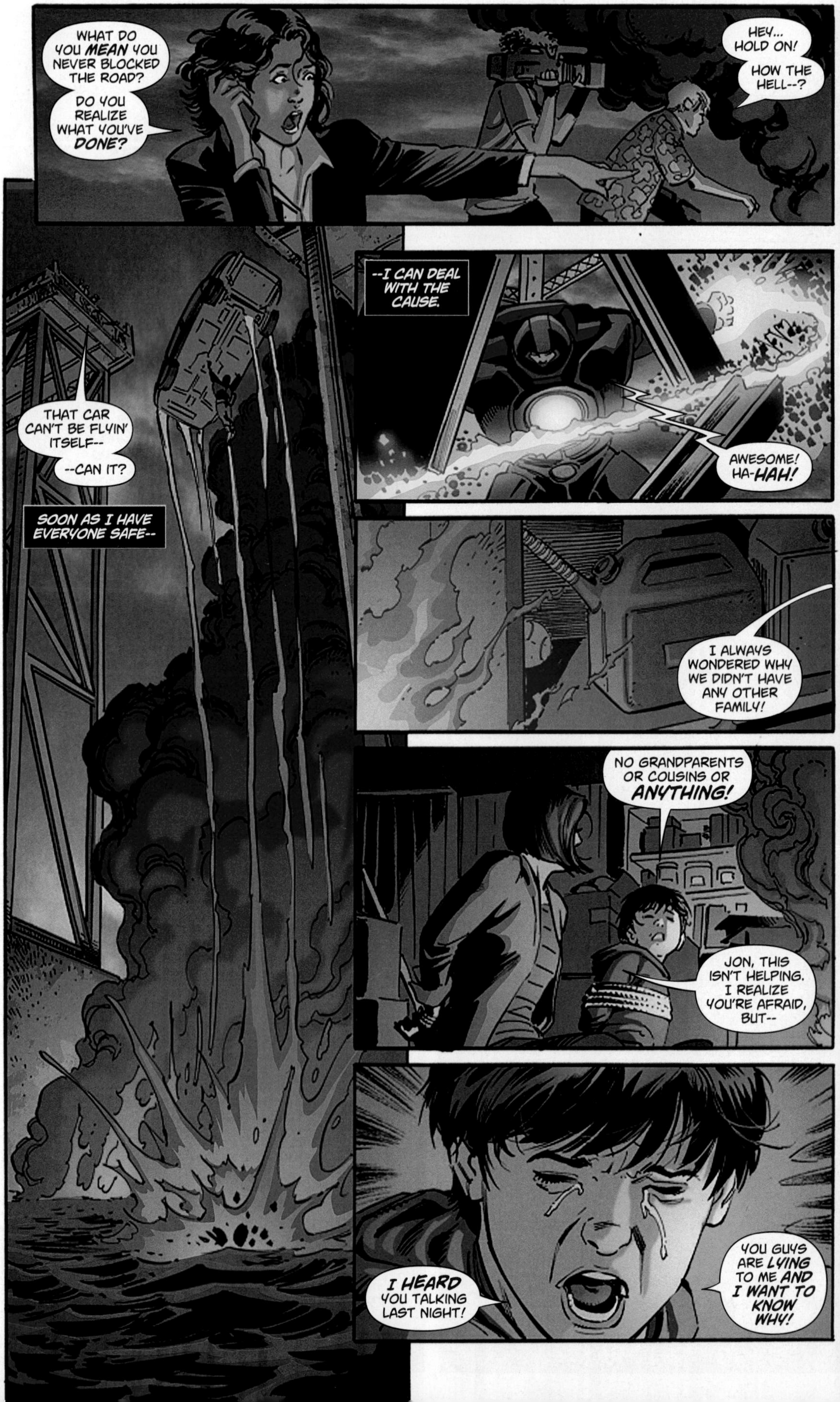
WHAT DO YOU MEAN YOU NEVER BLOCKED THE ROAD?
DO YOU REALIZE WHAT YOU'VE DONE?
HEY... HOLD ON!
HOW THE HELL--?
THAT CAR CAN'T BE FLYIN' ITSELF--
--CAN IT?
SOON AS I HAVE EVERYONE SAFE--
--I CAN DEAL WITH THE CAUSE.
AWESOME! HA-HAH!
I ALWAYS WONDERED WHY WE DIDN'T HAVE ANY OTHER FAMILY!
NO GRANDPARENTS OR COUSINS OR ANYTHING!
JON, THIS ISN'T HELPING. I REALIZE YOU'RE AFRAID, BUT--
I HEARD YOU TALKING LAST NIGHT!
YOU GUYS ARE LYING TO ME AND I WANT TO KNOW WHY!

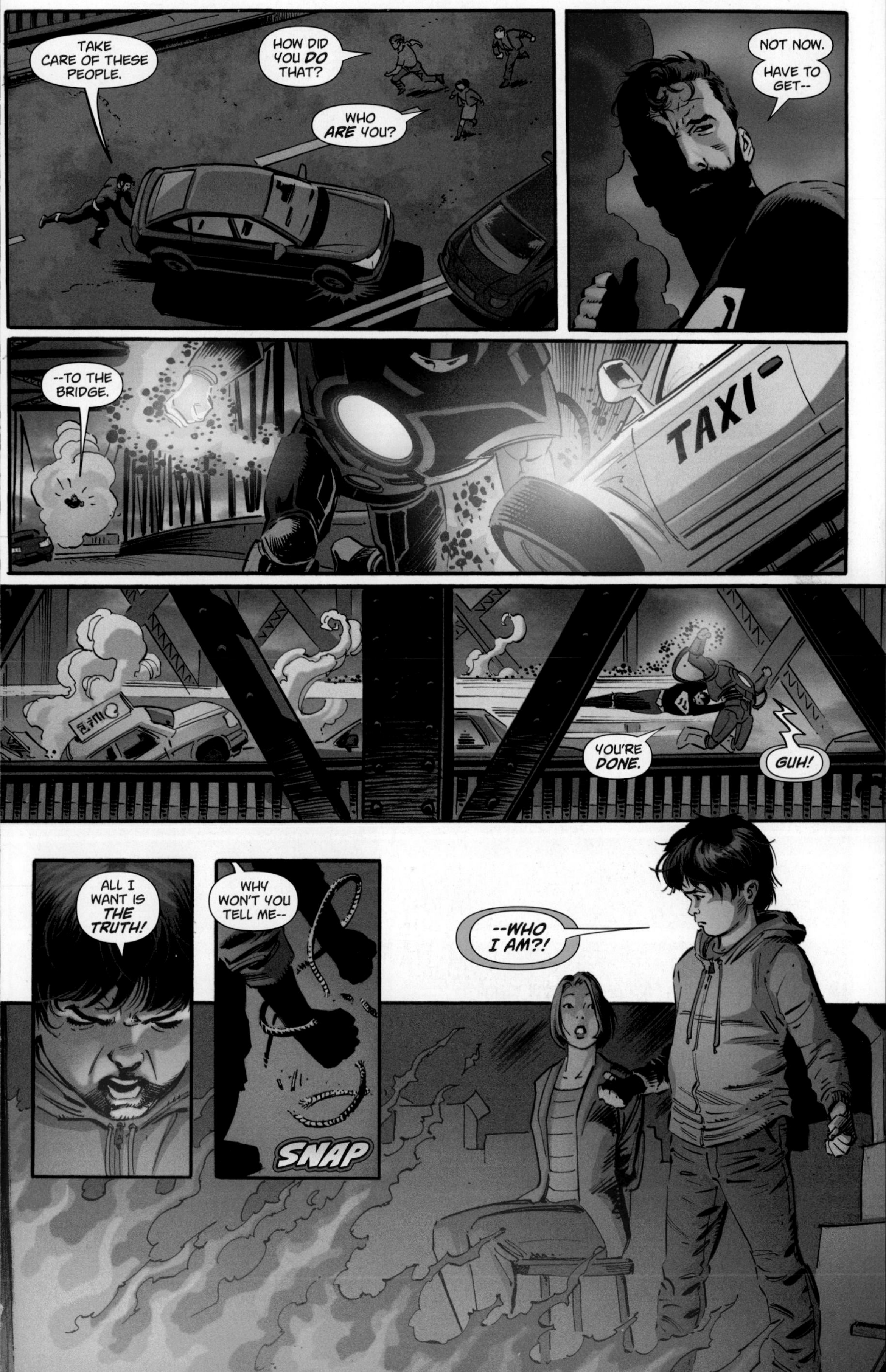
TAKE CARE OF THESE PEOPLE.
HOW DID YOU DO THAT?
WHO ARE YOU?
NOT NOW.
HAVE TO GET--
--TO THE BRIDGE.
TAXI
YOU'RE DONE.
GUH!
ALL I WANT IS THE TRUTH!
WHY WON'T YOU TELL ME--
SNAP
--WHO I AM?!

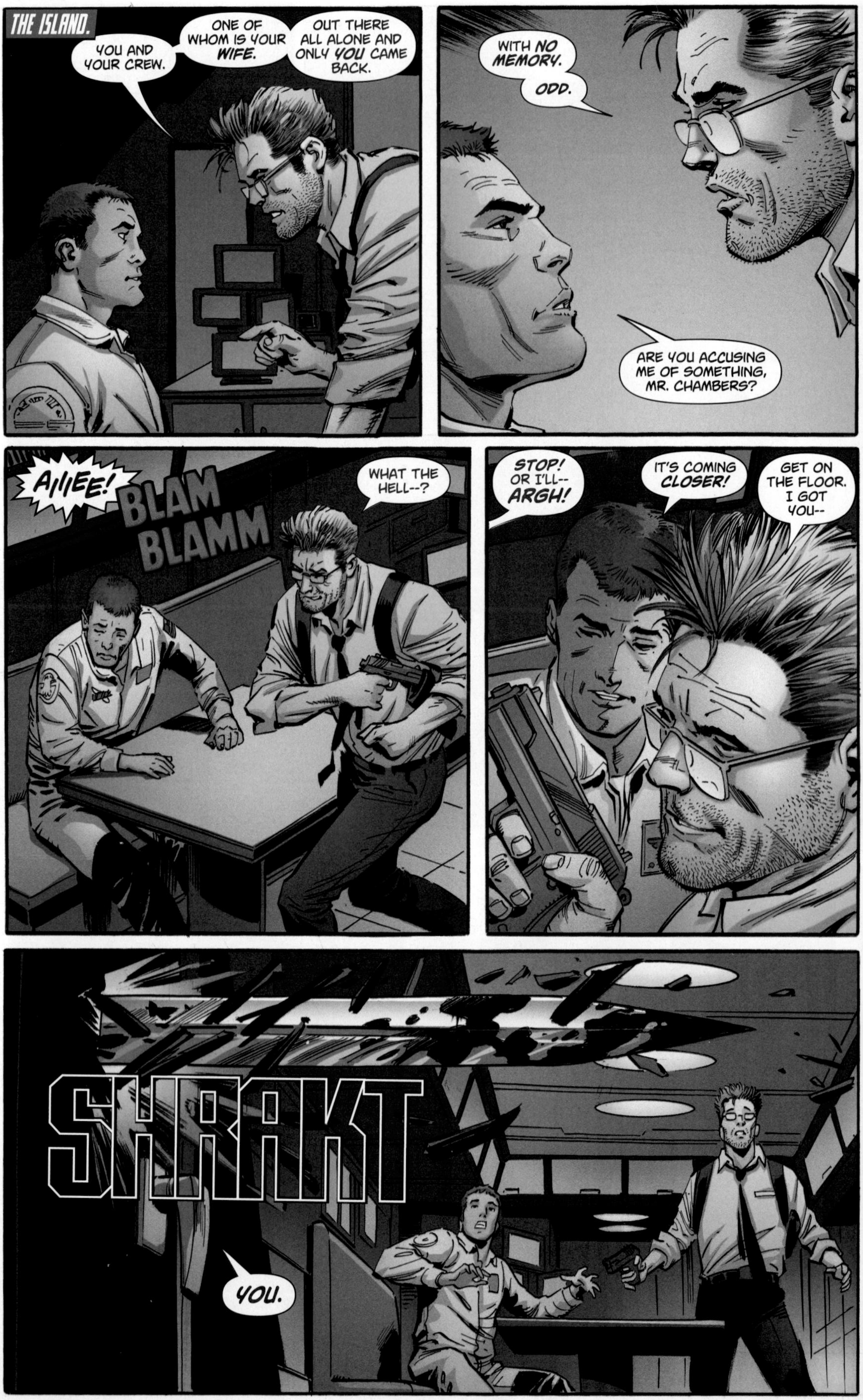
THE ISLAND.
YOU AND YOUR CREW.
ONE OF WHOM IS YOUR WIFE.
OUT THERE ALL ALONE AND ONLY YOU CAME BACK.
WITH NO MEMORY.
ODD.
ARE YOU ACCUSING ME OF SOMETHING, MR. CHAMBERS?
AIIIEE!
BLAM BLAMM
WHAT THE HELL--?
STOP! OR I'LL-- ARGH!
IT'S COMING CLOSER!
GET ON THE FLOOR. I GOT YOU--
SHRAKT
YOU.

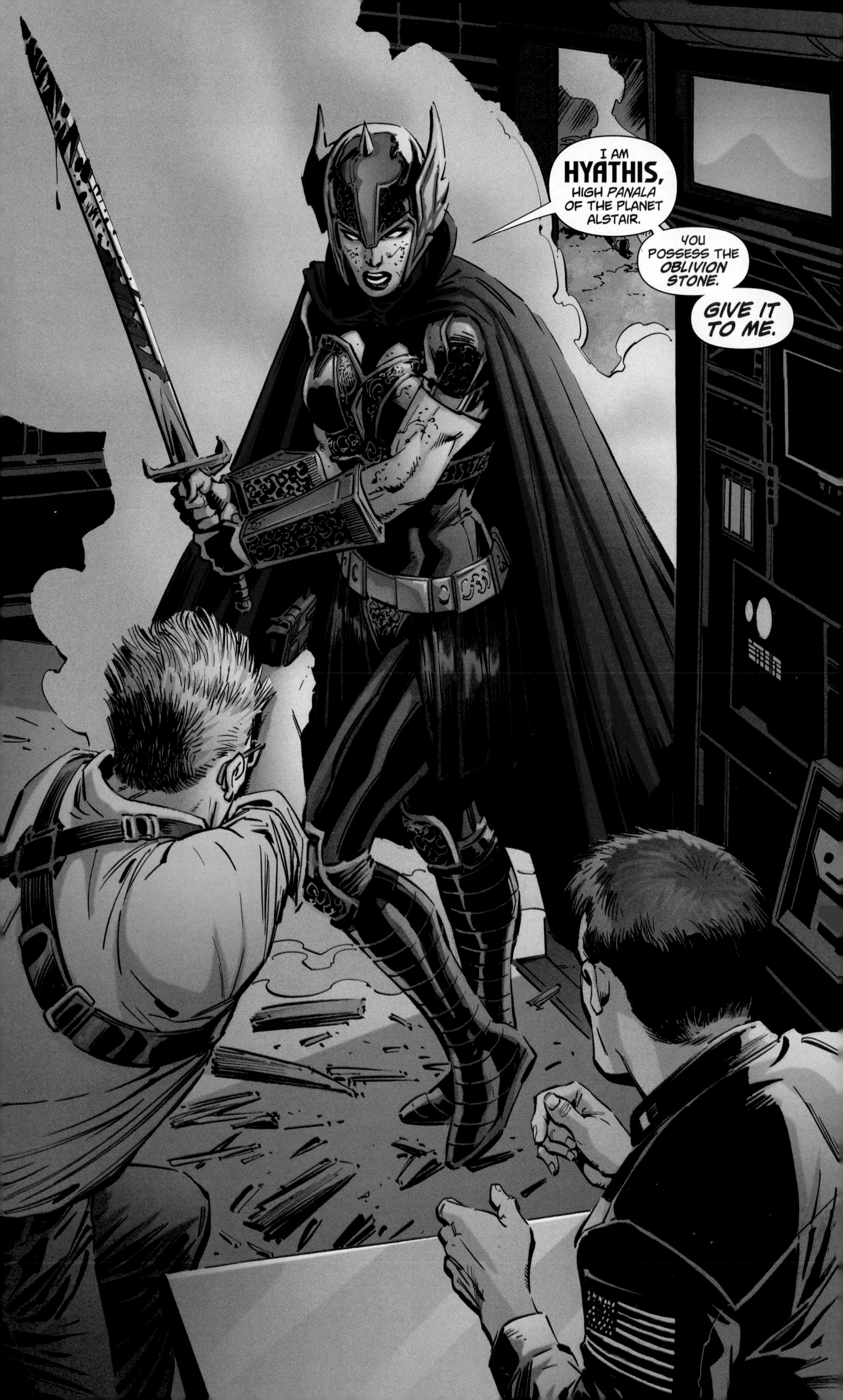
I AM **HYATHIS,** HIGH *PANALA* OF THE PLANET ALSTAIR.
YOU POSSESS THE *OBLIVION* STONE.
GIVE IT TO ME.

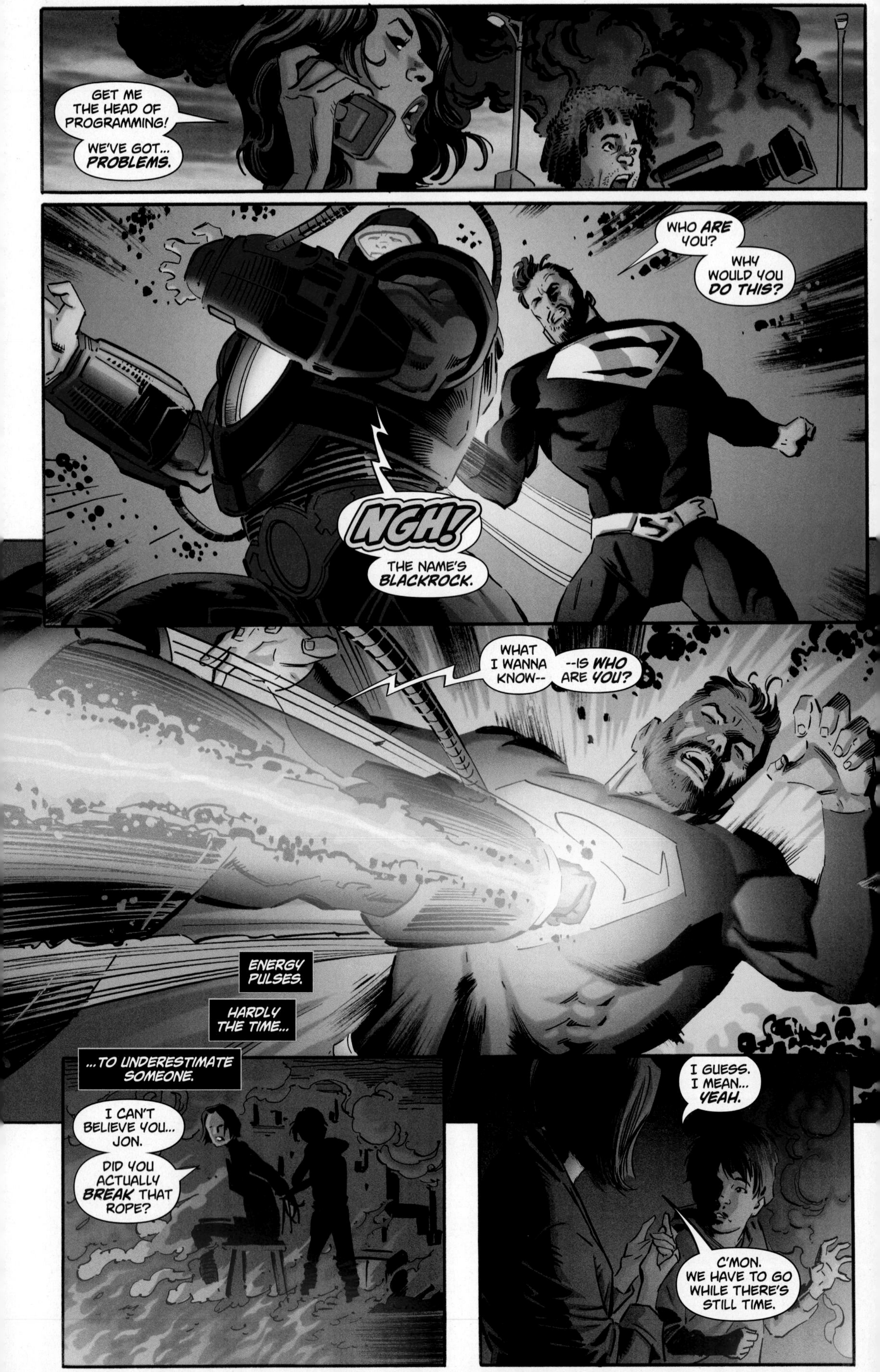
GET ME THE HEAD OF PROGRAMMING!
WE'VE GOT... PROBLEMS.
WHO ARE YOU?
WHY WOULD YOU DO THIS?
NGH!
THE NAME'S BLACKROCK.
WHAT I WANNA KNOW--
--IS WHO ARE YOU?
ENERGY PULSES.
HARDLY THE TIME...
...TO UNDERESTIMATE SOMEONE.
I CAN'T BELIEVE YOU... JON.
DID YOU ACTUALLY BREAK THAT ROPE?
I GUESS. I MEAN... YEAH.
C'MON. WE HAVE TO GO WHILE THERE'S STILL TIME.

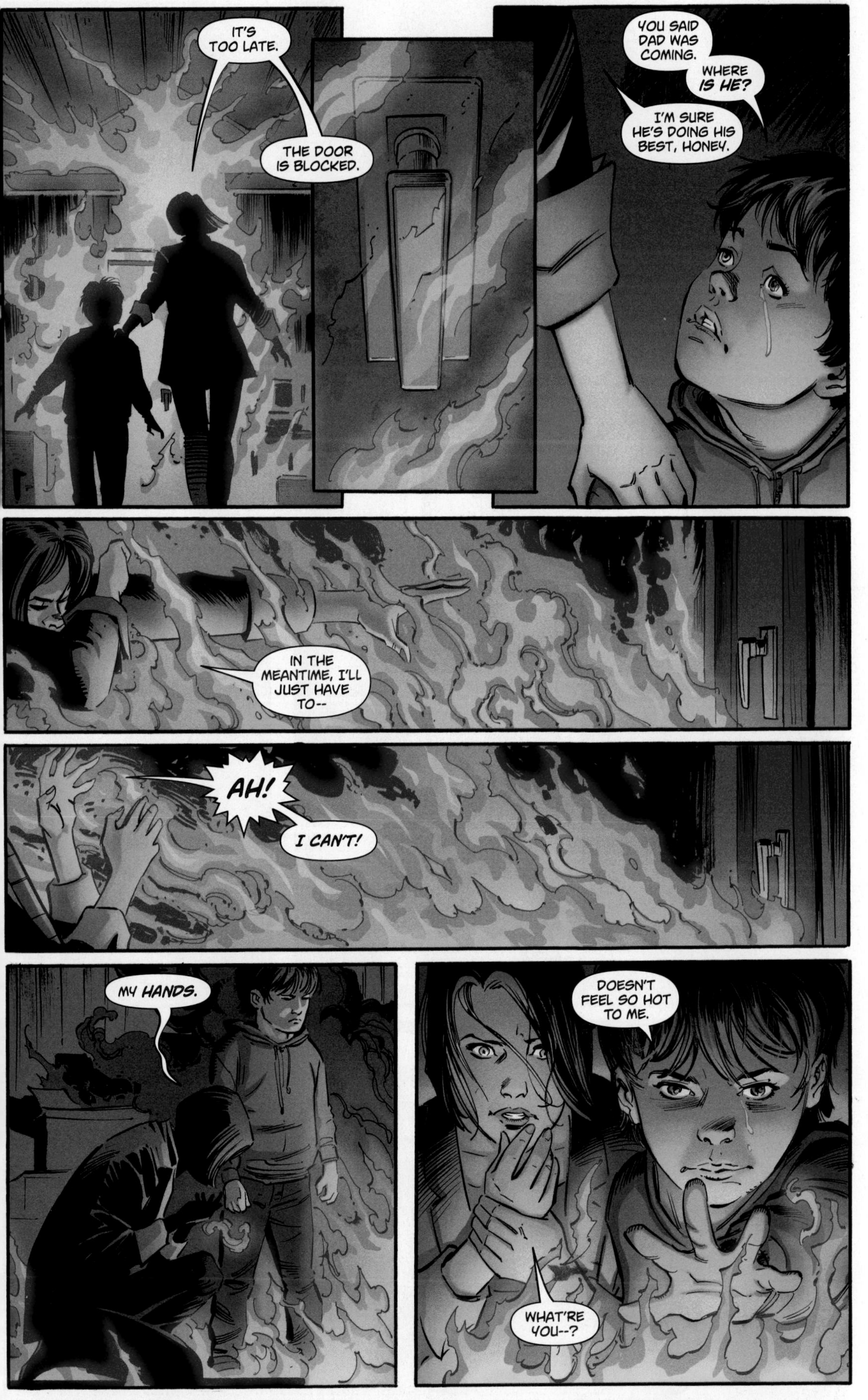
IT'S TOO LATE.
THE DOOR IS BLOCKED.
YOU SAID DAD WAS COMING.
WHERE IS HE?
I'M SURE HE'S DOING HIS BEST, HONEY.
IN THE MEANTIME, I'LL JUST HAVE TO--
AH!
I CAN'T!
MY HANDS.
DOESN'T FEEL SO HOT TO ME.
WHAT'RE YOU--?

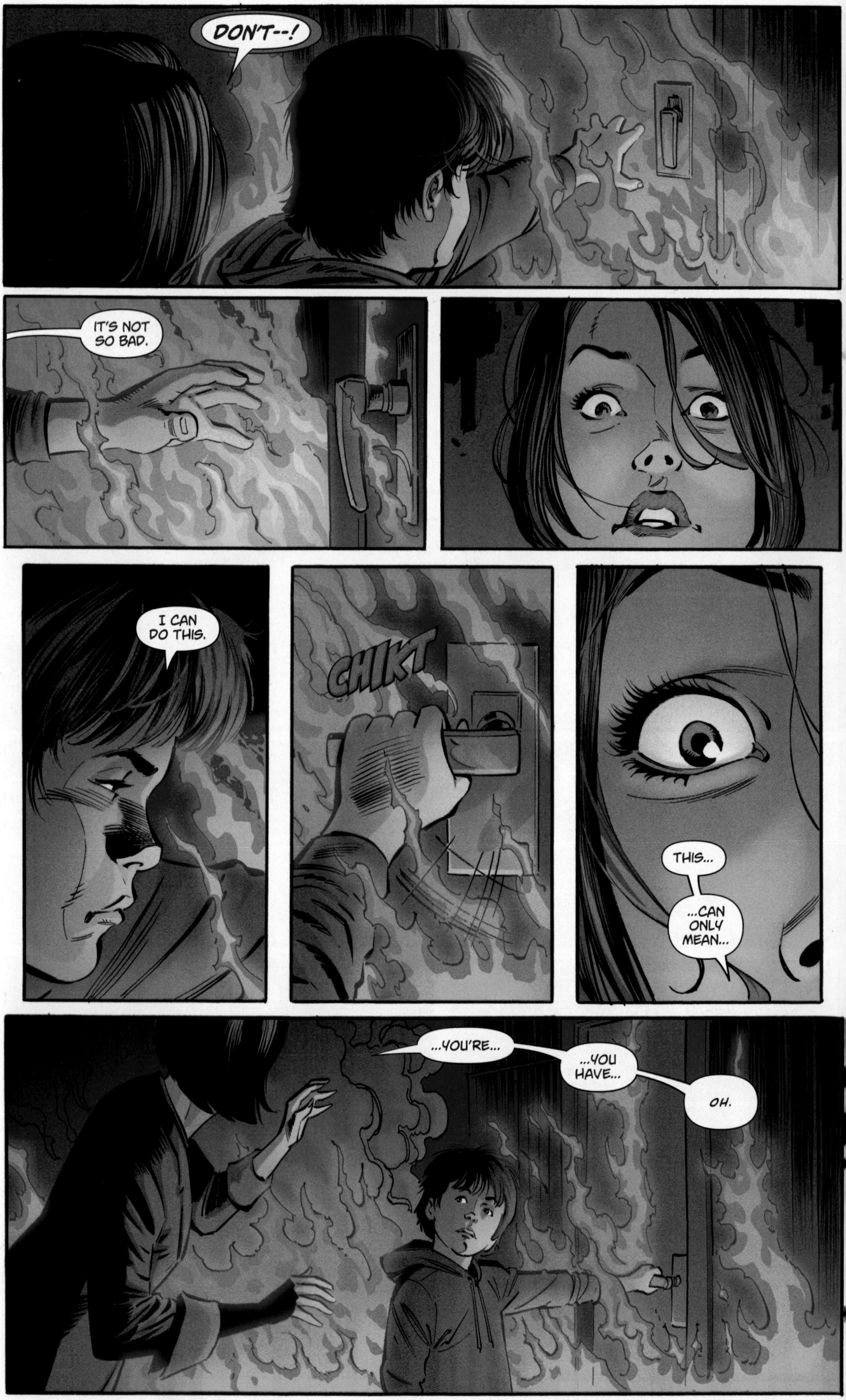
DON'T--!
IT'S NOT SO BAD.
I CAN DO THIS.
CHIKT
THIS...
...CAN ONLY MEAN...
...YOU'RE...
...YOU HAVE...
OH.

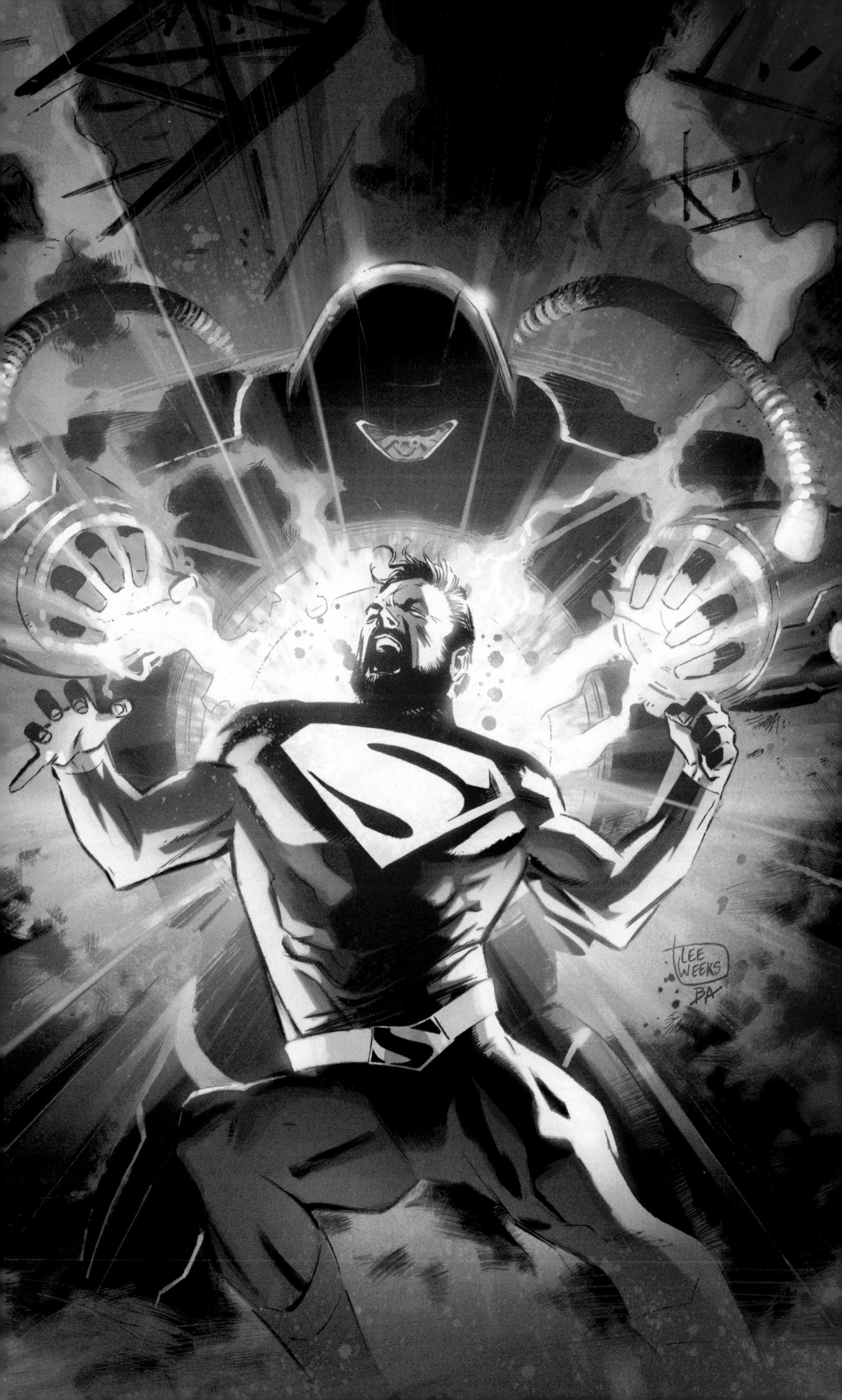
LEE WEEKS
BA

ARRIVAL: PART VII

DAN JURGENS writer **LEE WEEKS STEPHEN SEGOVIA** pencillers **SCOTT HANNA ART THIBERT JAY LEISTEN** inkers **JEROMY COX** colorist **A LARGER WORLD STUDIOS** letterer
LEE WEEKS BRAD ANDERSON cover artists

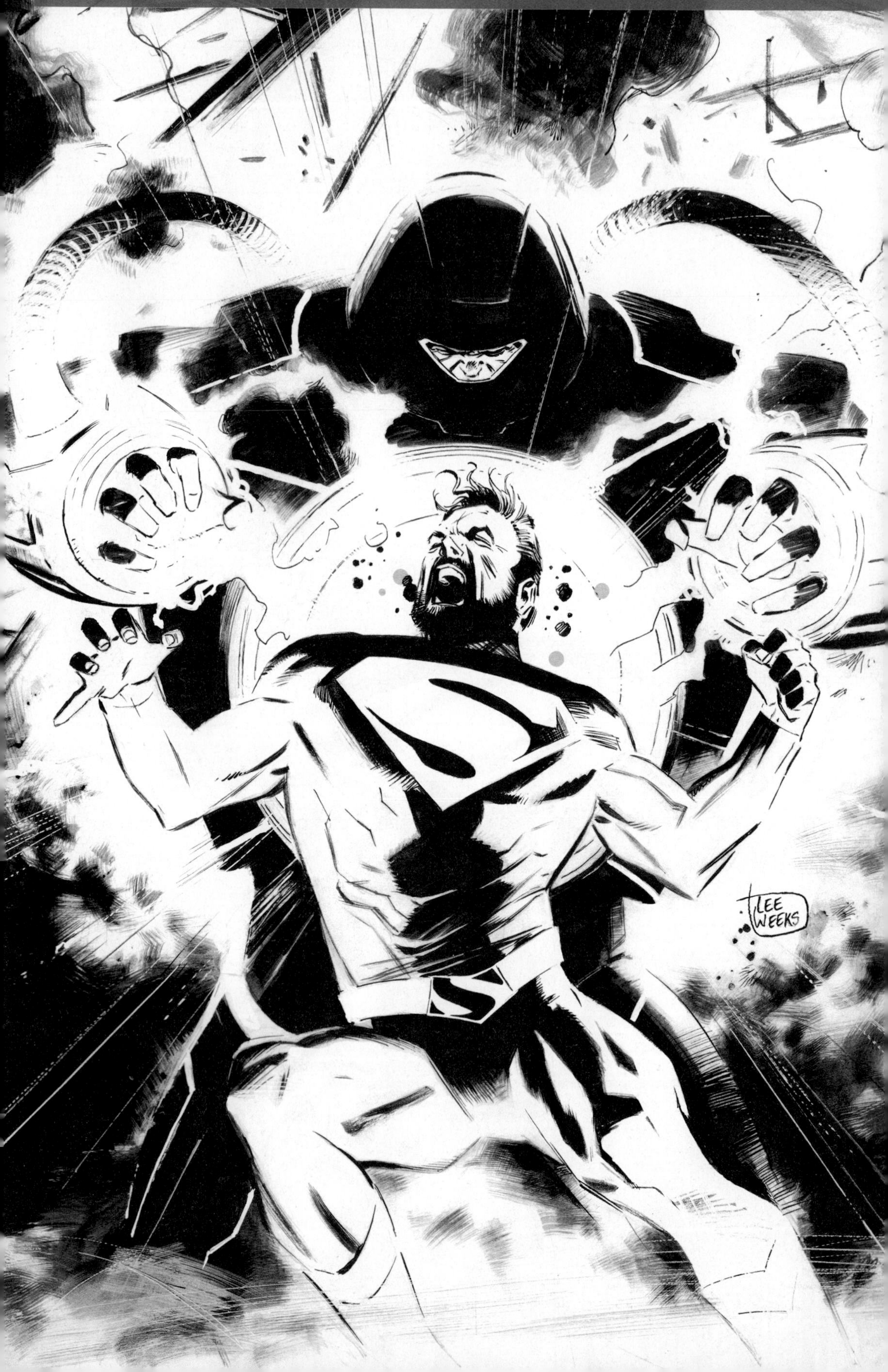
LEE WEEKS

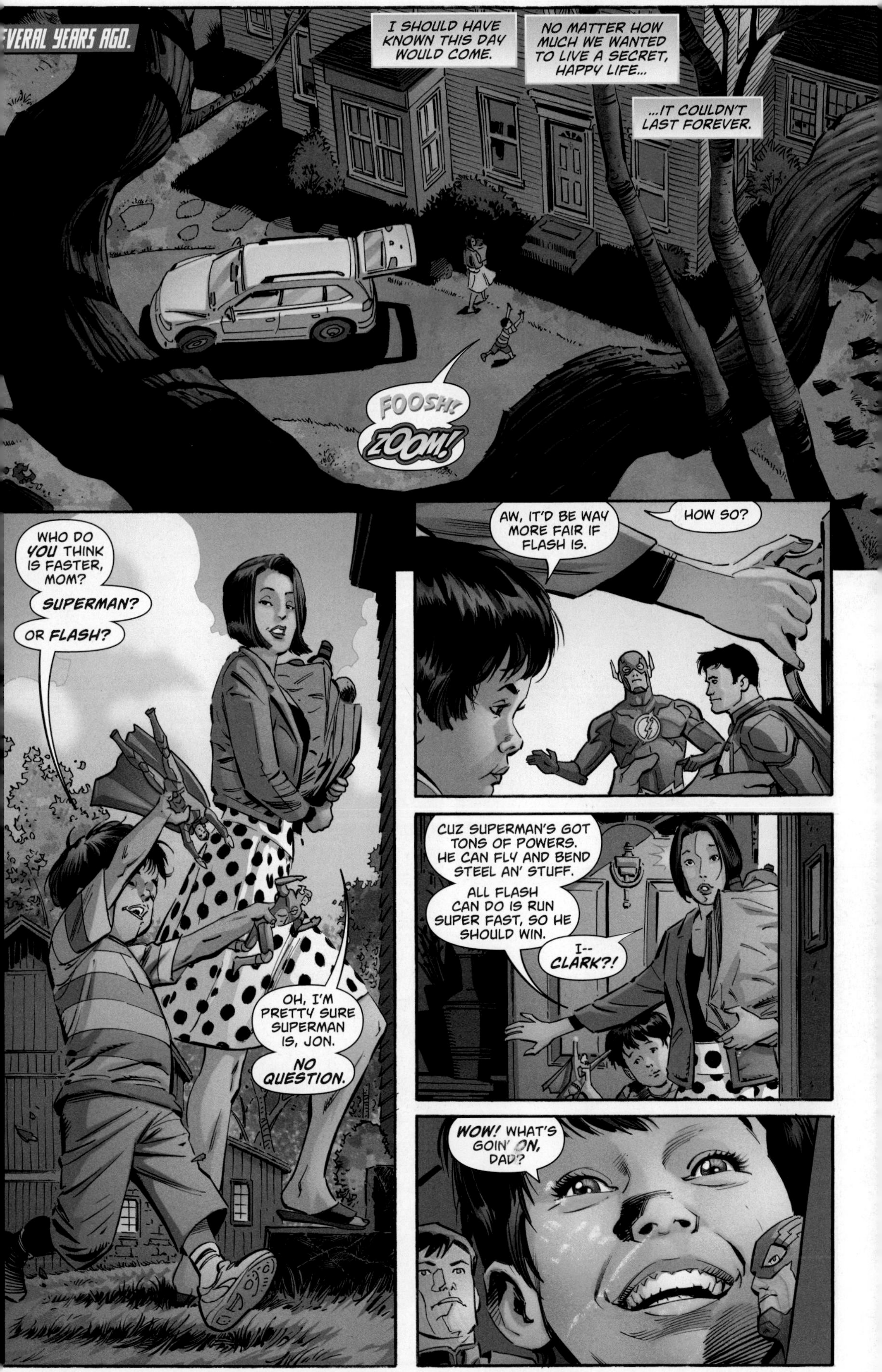

EVERAL YEARS AGO.
I SHOULD HAVE KNOWN THIS DAY WOULD COME.
NO MATTER HOW MUCH WE WANTED TO LIVE A SECRET, HAPPY LIFE...
...IT COULDN'T LAST FOREVER.
FOOSH!
ZOOM!
WHO DO YOU THINK IS FASTER, MOM?
SUPERMAN?
OR FLASH?
OH, I'M PRETTY SURE SUPERMAN IS, JON.
NO QUESTION.
AW, IT'D BE WAY MORE FAIR IF FLASH IS.
HOW SO?
CUZ SUPERMAN'S GOT TONS OF POWERS. HE CAN FLY AND BEND STEEL AN' STUFF.
ALL FLASH CAN DO IS RUN SUPER FAST, SO HE SHOULD WIN.
I-- CLARK?!
WOW! WHAT'S GOIN' ON, DAD?

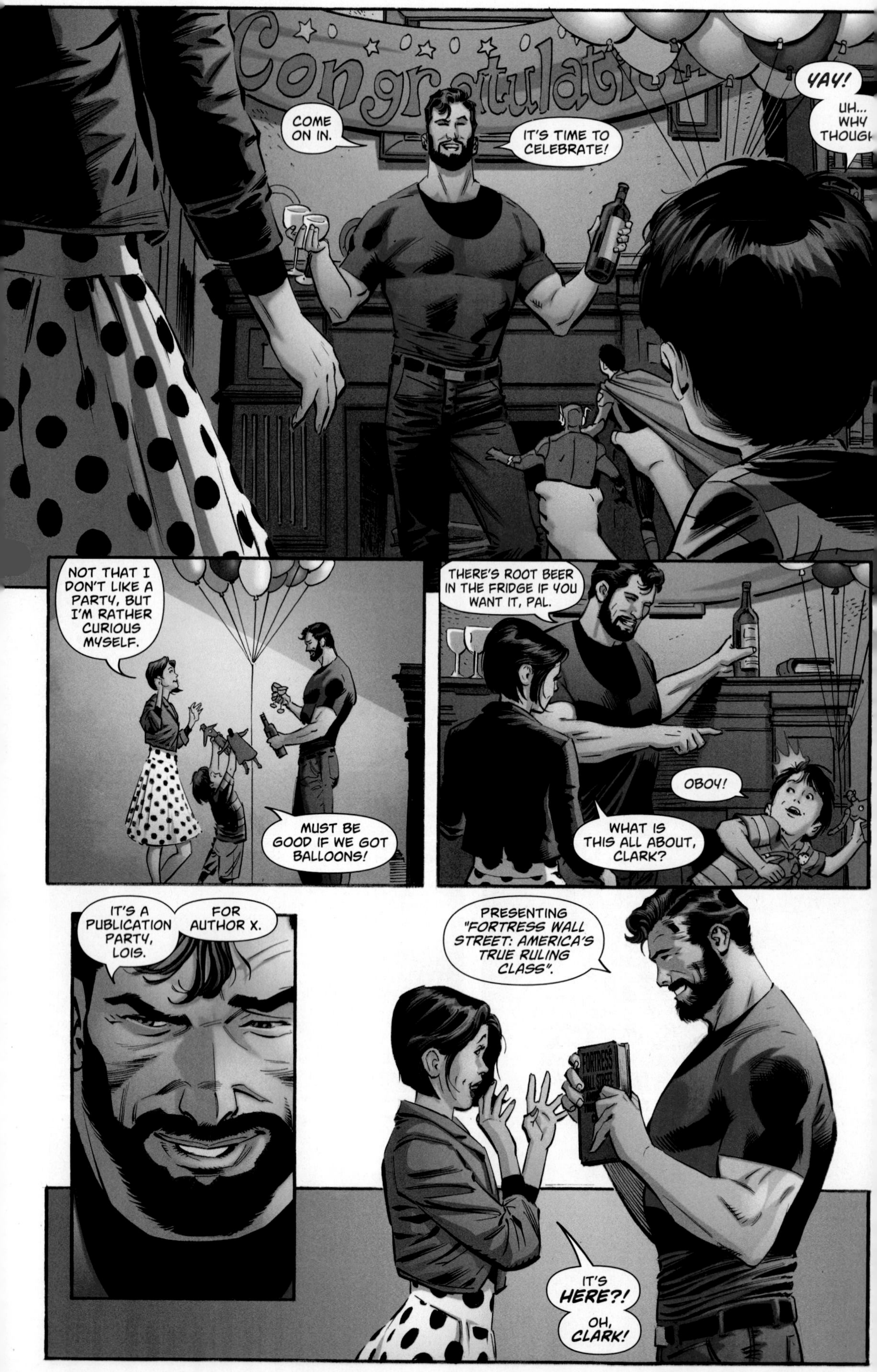
Congratulations
COME ON IN.
IT'S TIME TO CELEBRATE!
YAY!
UH... WHY THOUGH
NOT THAT I DON'T LIKE A PARTY, BUT I'M RATHER CURIOUS MYSELF.
MUST BE GOOD IF WE GOT BALLOONS!
THERE'S ROOT BEER IN THE FRIDGE IF YOU WANT IT, PAL.
OBOY!
WHAT IS THIS ALL ABOUT, CLARK?
IT'S A PUBLICATION PARTY, LOIS.
FOR AUTHOR X.
PRESENTING "FORTRESS WALL STREET: AMERICA'S TRUE RULING CLASS".
IT'S HERE?!
OH, CLARK!

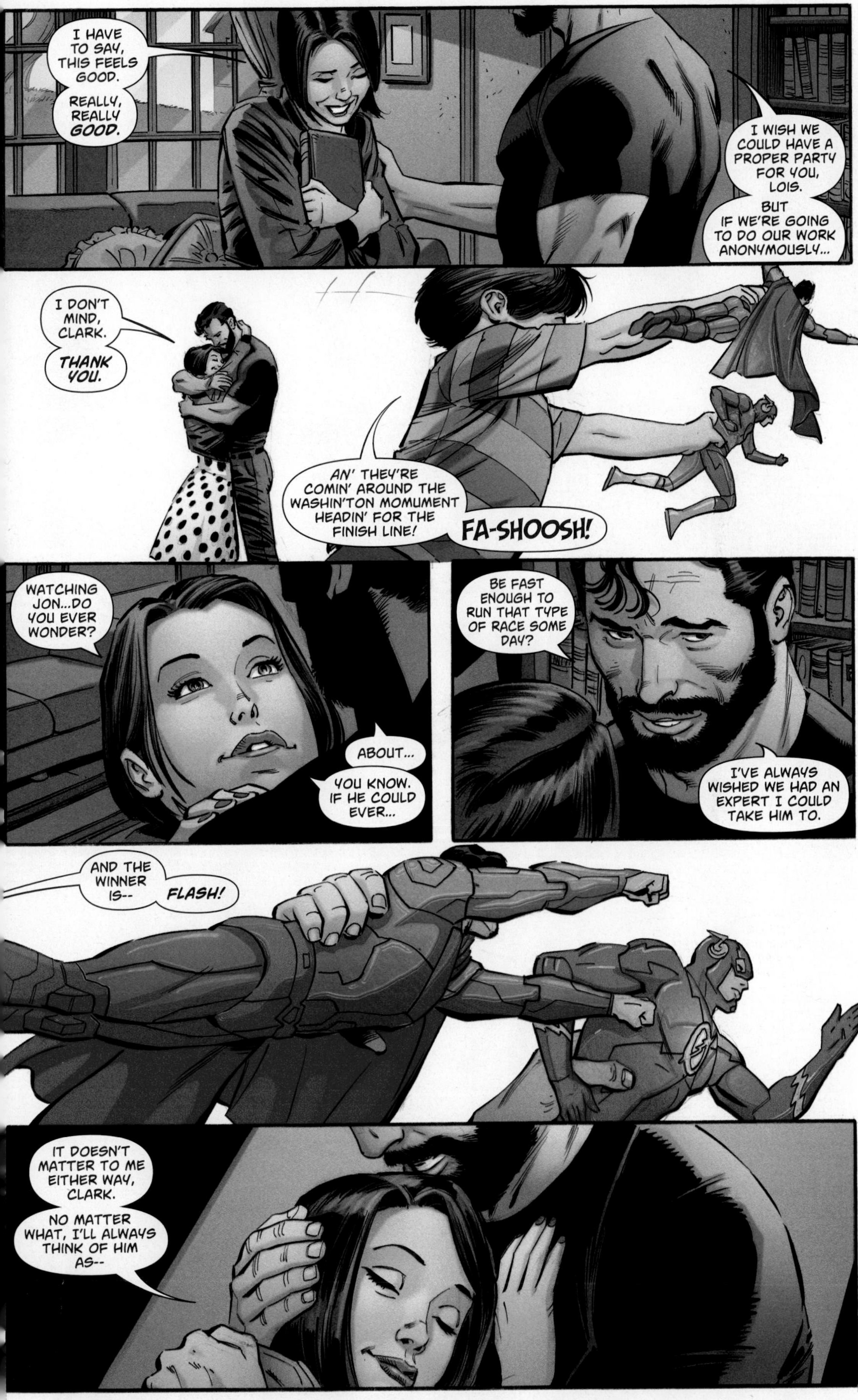
I HAVE TO SAY, THIS FEELS GOOD.
REALLY, REALLY GOOD.
I WISH WE COULD HAVE A PROPER PARTY FOR YOU, LOIS.
BUT IF WE'RE GOING TO DO OUR WORK ANONYMOUSLY...
I DON'T MIND, CLARK.
THANK YOU.
AN' THEY'RE COMIN' AROUND THE WASHIN'TON MOMUMENT HEADIN' FOR THE FINISH LINE!
FA-SHOOSH!
WATCHING JON...DO YOU EVER WONDER?
ABOUT...
YOU KNOW. IF HE COULD EVER...
BE FAST ENOUGH TO RUN THAT TYPE OF RACE SOME DAY?
I'VE ALWAYS WISHED WE HAD AN EXPERT I COULD TAKE HIM TO.
AND THE WINNER IS--
FLASH!
IT DOESN'T MATTER TO ME EITHER WAY, CLARK.
NO MATTER WHAT, I'LL ALWAYS THINK OF HIM AS--

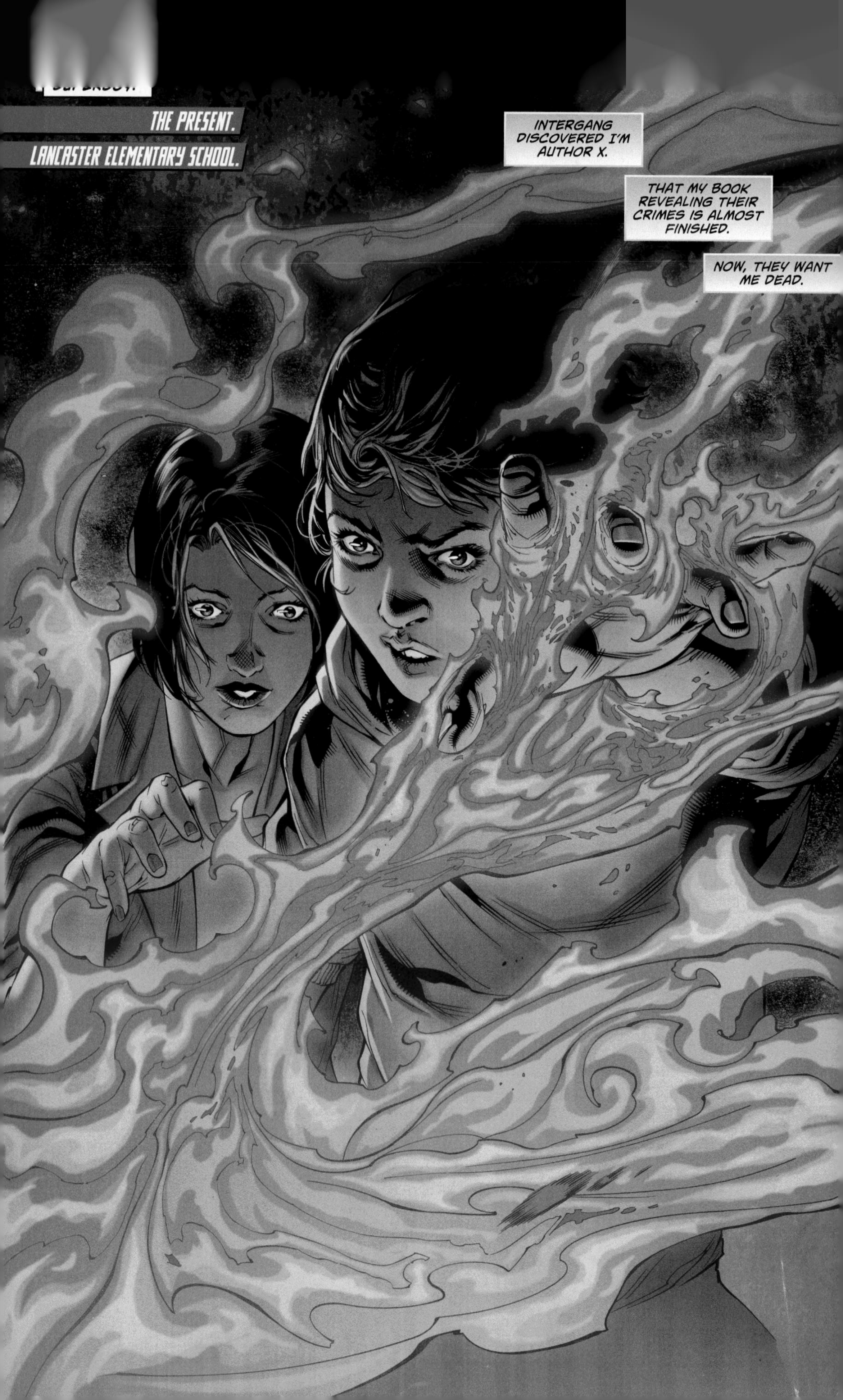

THE PRESENT.
LANCASTER ELEMENTARY SCHOOL.
INTERGANG DISCOVERED I'M AUTHOR X.
THAT MY BOOK REVEALING THEIR CRIMES IS ALMOST FINISHED.
NOW, THEY WANT ME DEAD.

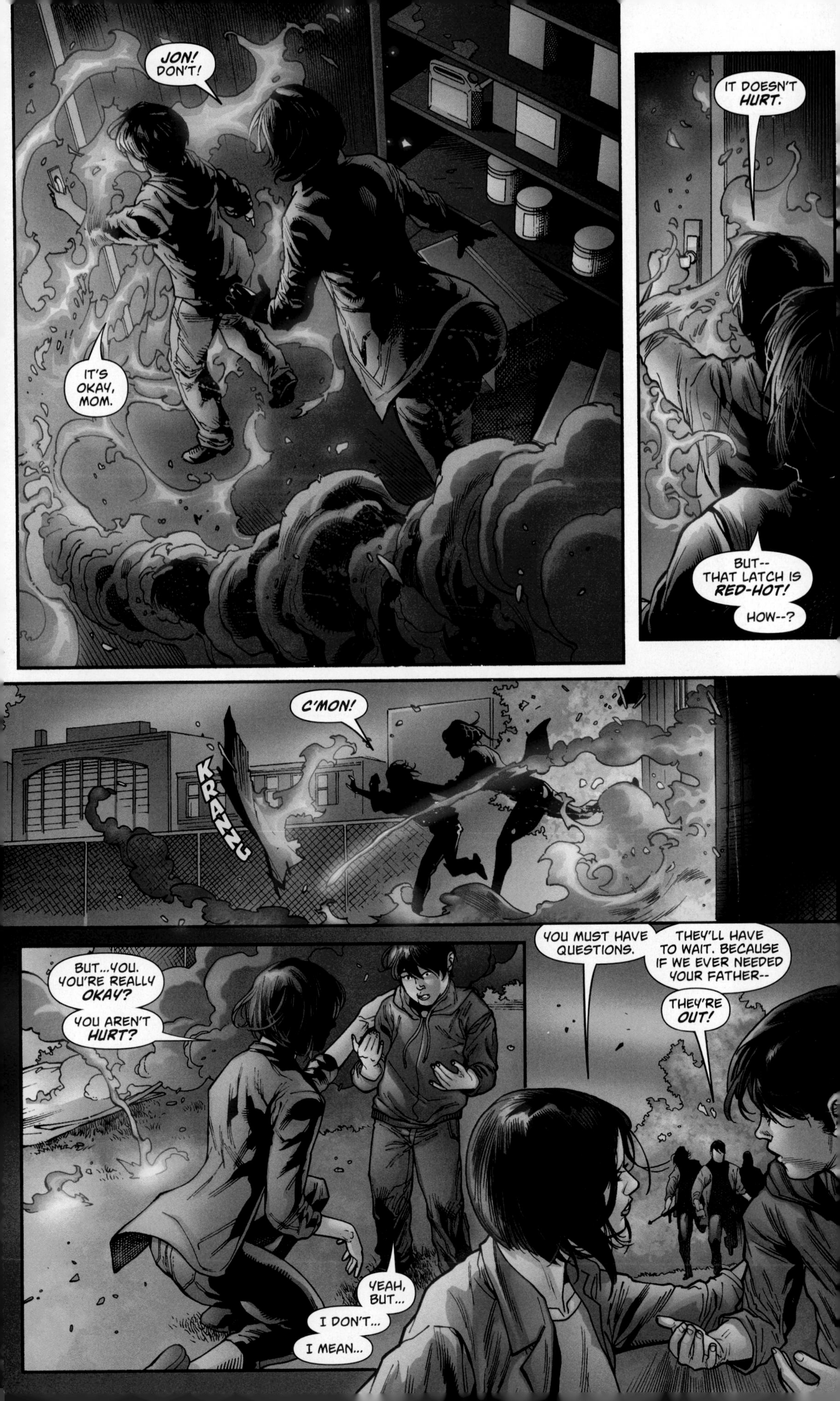
JON! DON'T!
IT'S OKAY, MOM.
IT DOESN'T HURT.
BUT-- THAT LATCH IS RED-HOT!
HOW--?
C'MON!
KRANNG
BUT...YOU. YOU'RE REALLY OKAY?
YOU AREN'T HURT?
YEAH, BUT...
I DON'T...
I MEAN...
YOU MUST HAVE QUESTIONS.
THEY'LL HAVE TO WAIT. BECAUSE IF WE EVER NEEDED YOUR FATHER--
THEY'RE OUT!

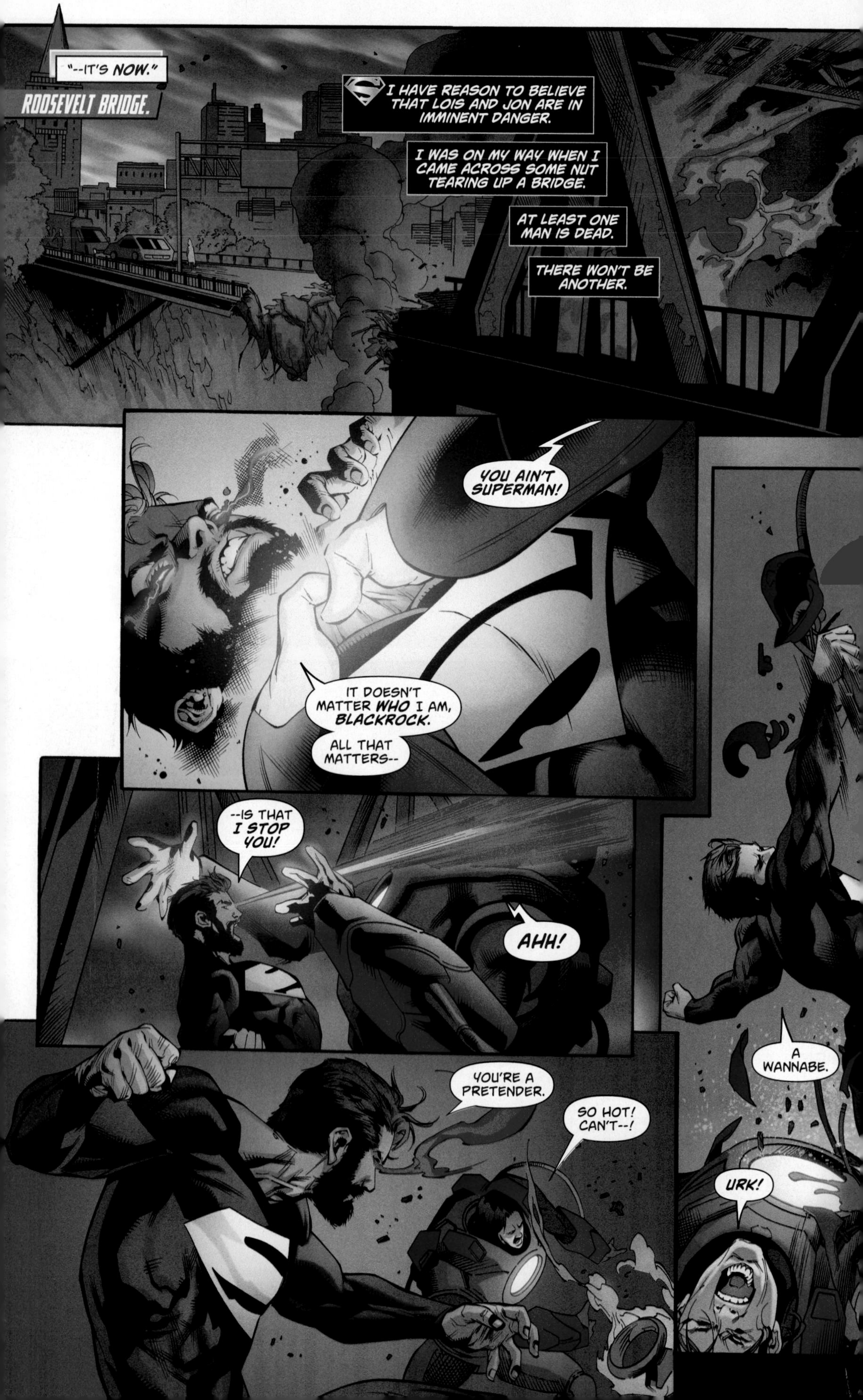
"--IT'S NOW."
ROOSEVELT BRIDGE.
I HAVE REASON TO BELIEVE THAT LOIS AND JON ARE IN IMMINENT DANGER.
I WAS ON MY WAY WHEN I CAME ACROSS SOME NUT TEARING UP A BRIDGE.
AT LEAST ONE MAN IS DEAD.
THERE WON'T BE ANOTHER.
YOU AIN'T SUPERMAN!
IT DOESN'T MATTER WHO I AM, BLACKROCK.
ALL THAT MATTERS--
--IS THAT I STOP YOU!
AHH!
YOU'RE A PRETENDER.
SO HOT! CAN'T--!
A WANNABE.
URK!

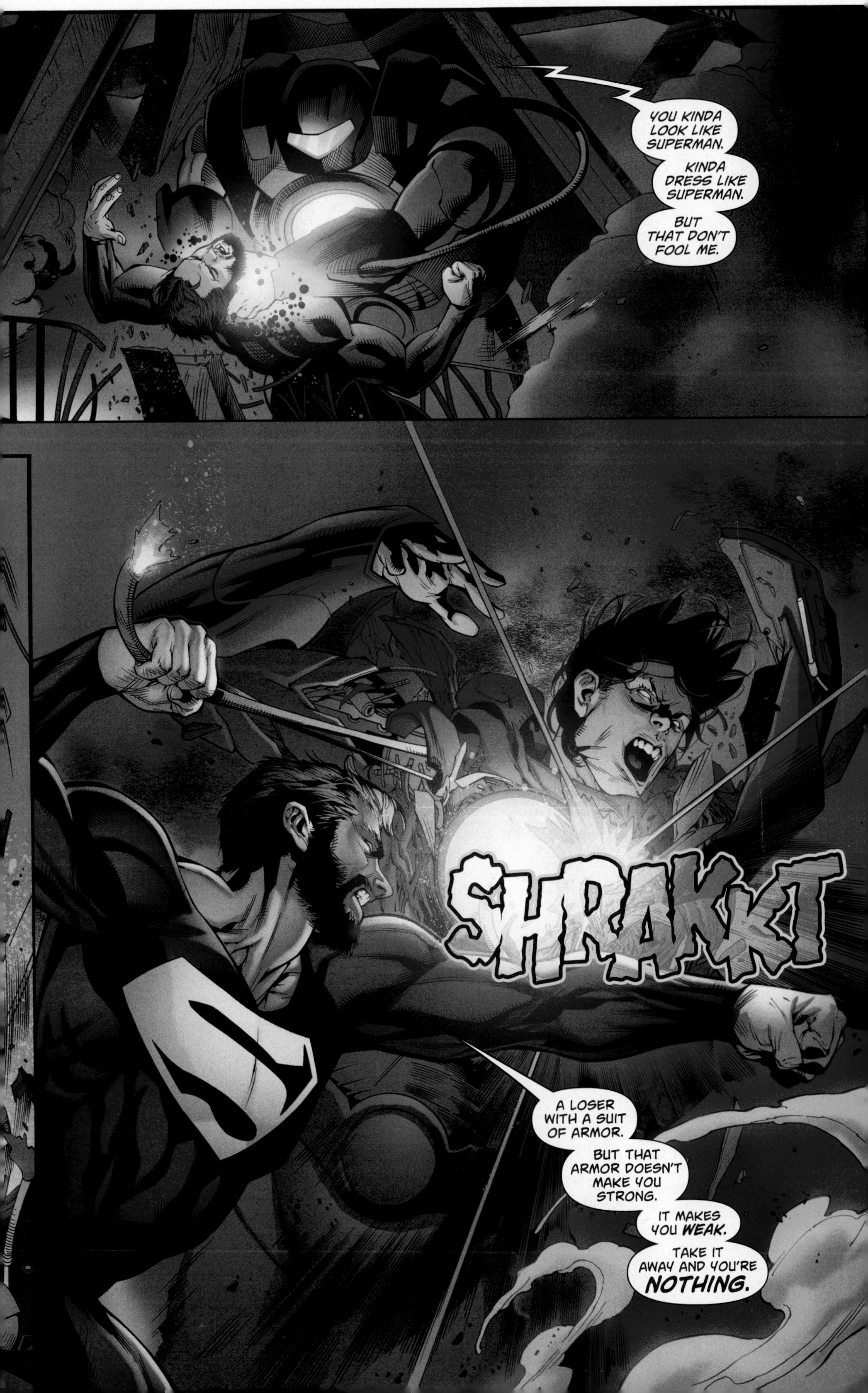

YOU KINDA LOOK LIKE SUPERMAN.
KINDA DRESS LIKE SUPERMAN.
BUT THAT DON'T FOOL ME.
SHRAKKT
A LOSER WITH A SUIT OF ARMOR.
BUT THAT ARMOR DOESN'T MAKE YOU STRONG.
IT MAKES YOU WEAK.
TAKE IT AWAY AND YOU'RE NOTHING.

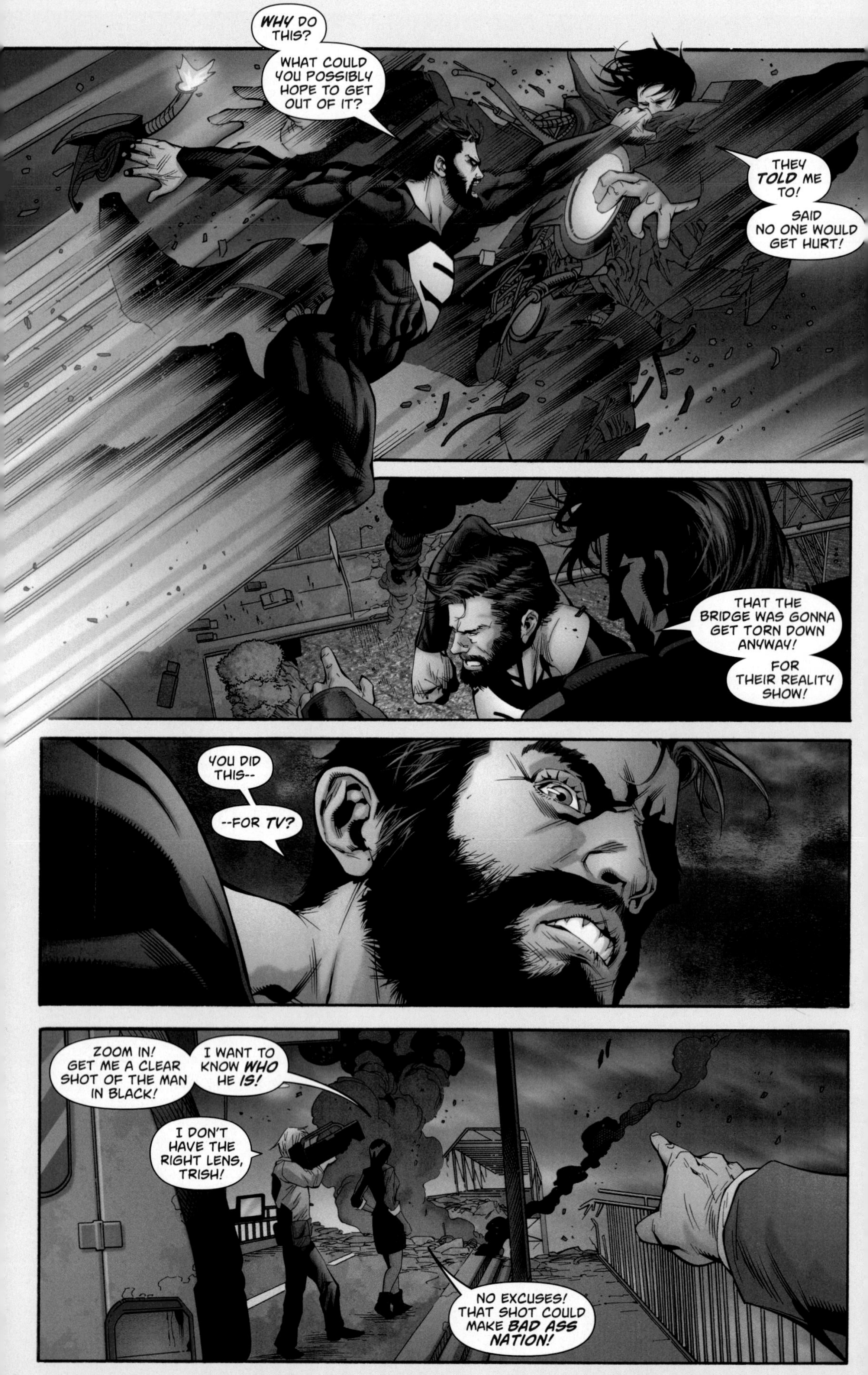
WHY DO THIS?
WHAT COULD YOU POSSIBLY HOPE TO GET OUT OF IT?
THEY TOLD ME TO!
SAID NO ONE WOULD GET HURT!
THAT THE BRIDGE WAS GONNA GET TORN DOWN ANYWAY!
FOR THEIR REALITY SHOW!
YOU DID THIS--
--FOR TV?
ZOOM IN! GET ME A CLEAR SHOT OF THE MAN IN BLACK!
I WANT TO KNOW WHO HE IS!
I DON'T HAVE THE RIGHT LENS, TRISH!
NO EXCUSES! THAT SHOT COULD MAKE BAD ASS NATION!

BAD ASS NATION?

YOU WERE [WILLING] TO *KILL* FOR [DEMENTED] GARBAGE [THAT] ONLY EXISTS TO [SELL] BEER AND ANTACID TABLETS?

IT WASN'T... MY...*FAULT!*

THEY WERE... SUPPOSED TO... BLOCK THE ROAD!

UNBELIEVABLE.

KRAKKT

AH! MY CAMERA!

MELTED?

GOOD THING THE VAN'S RECORDING EQUIPMENT HAS THE FOOTAGE.

UH...NOT ANYMORE, TRISH.

DO YOU REALIZE WHAT THIS MEANS TO MY CAREER?

I'M DONE!

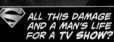

ALL THIS DAMAGE AND A MAN'S LIFE FOR A *TV SHOW?*

NO WONDER THIS WORLD STILL SEEMS FOREIGN.

THEY'RE LUCKY I HAVE TO GET TO LOIS AND JON.

IF I STAY, IT MIGHT GET UGLY.

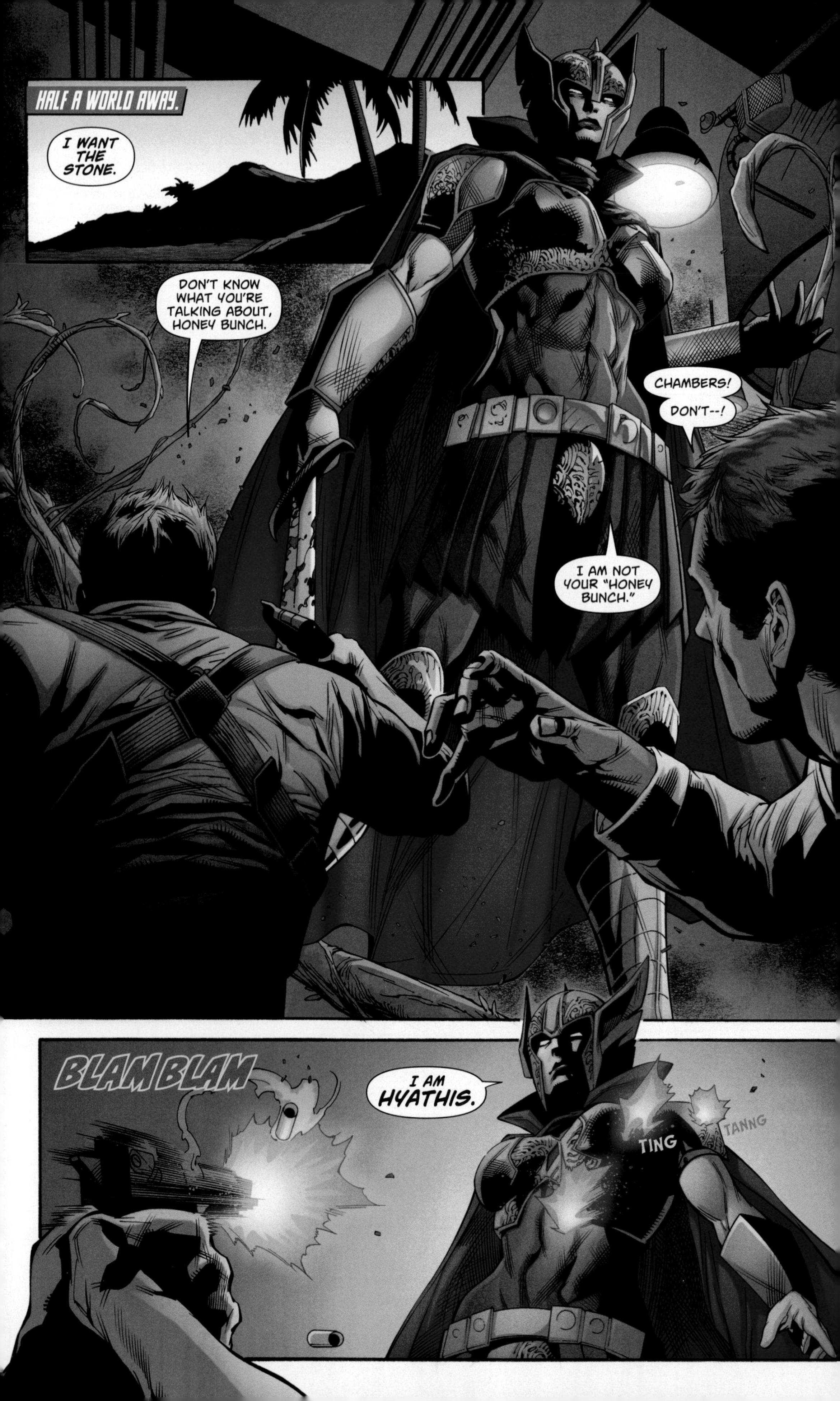
HALF A WORLD AWAY.
I WANT THE STONE.
DON'T KNOW WHAT YOU'RE TALKING ABOUT, HONEY BUNCH.
CHAMBERS!
DON'T--!
I AM NOT YOUR "HONEY BUNCH."
BLAM BLAM
I AM HYATHIS.
TING
TANNG

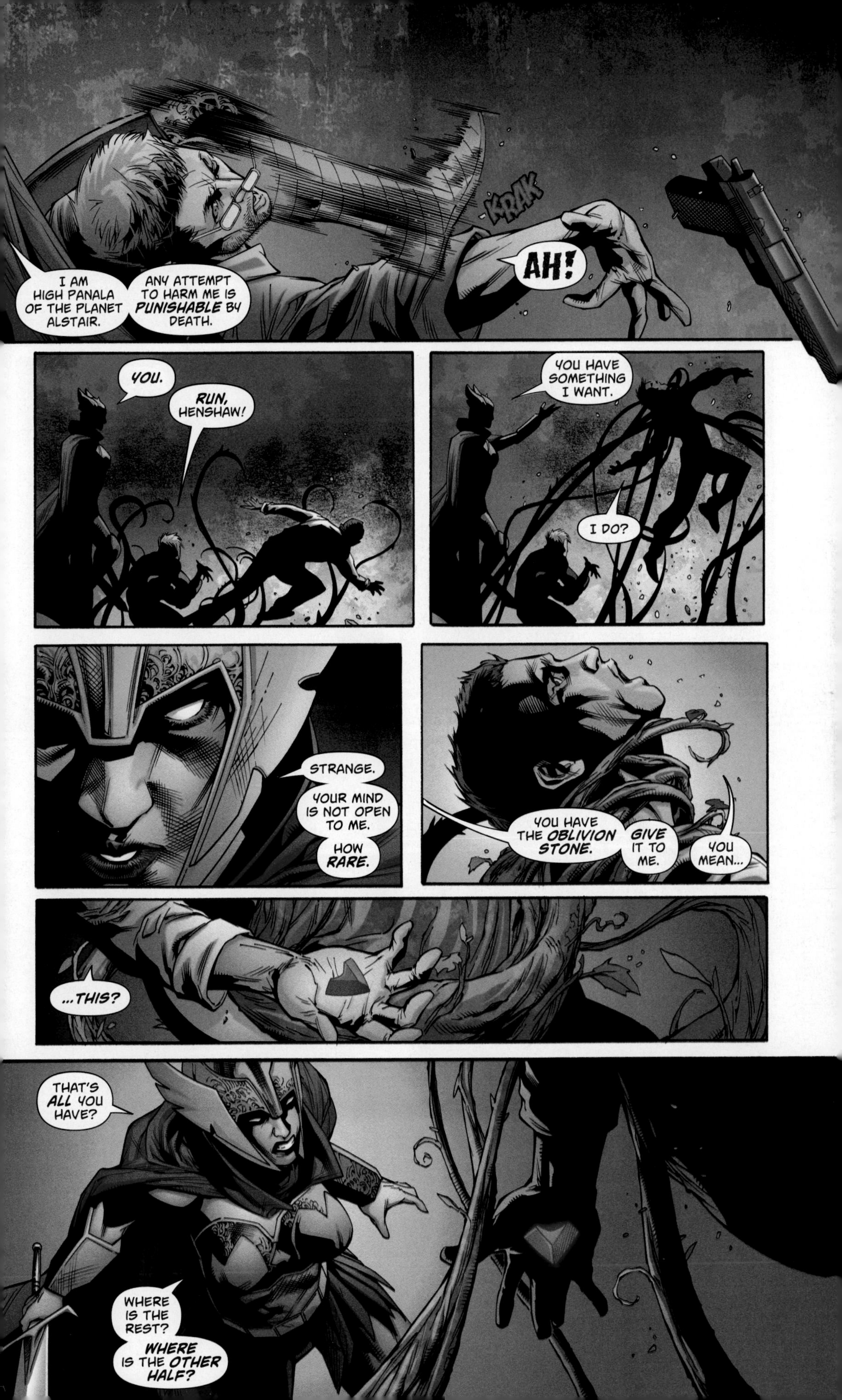
KRAK
AH!
I AM HIGH PANALA OF THE PLANET ALSTAIR.
ANY ATTEMPT TO HARM ME IS PUNISHABLE BY DEATH.
YOU.
RUN, HENSHAW!
YOU HAVE SOMETHING I WANT.
I DO?
STRANGE.
YOUR MIND IS NOT OPEN TO ME.
HOW RARE.
YOU HAVE THE OBLIVION STONE.
GIVE IT TO ME.
YOU MEAN...
...THIS?
THAT'S ALL YOU HAVE?
WHERE IS THE REST?
WHERE IS THE OTHER HALF?

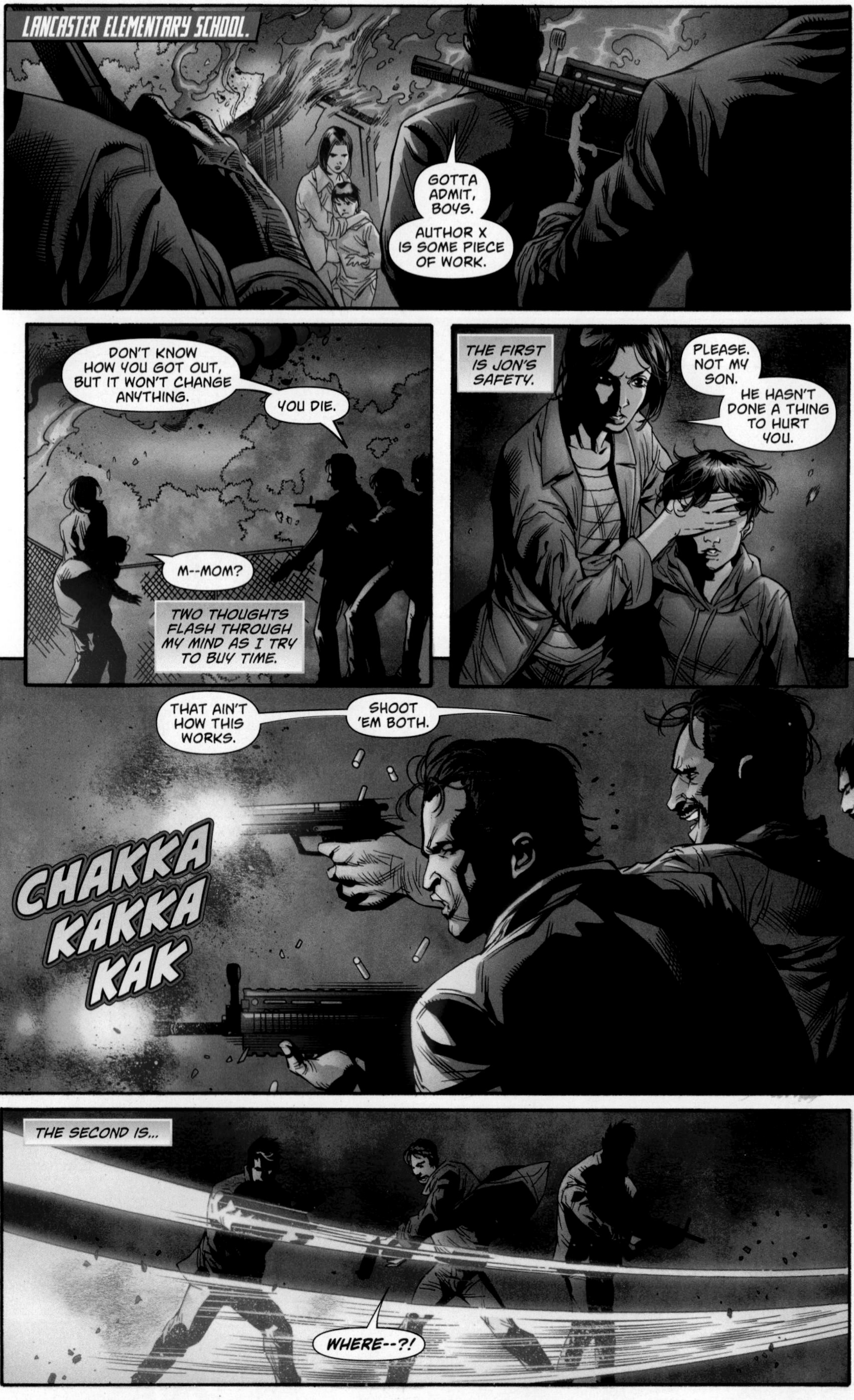
LANCASTER ELEMENTARY SCHOOL.
GOTTA ADMIT, BOYS.
AUTHOR X IS SOME PIECE OF WORK.
DON'T KNOW HOW YOU GOT OUT, BUT IT WON'T CHANGE ANYTHING.
YOU DIE.
M--MOM?
TWO THOUGHTS FLASH THROUGH MY MIND AS I TRY TO BUY TIME.
THE FIRST IS JON'S SAFETY.
PLEASE. NOT MY SON.
HE HASN'T DONE A THING TO HURT YOU.
THAT AIN'T HOW THIS WORKS.
SHOOT 'EM BOTH.
CHAKKA KAKKA KAK
THE SECOND IS...
WHERE--?!

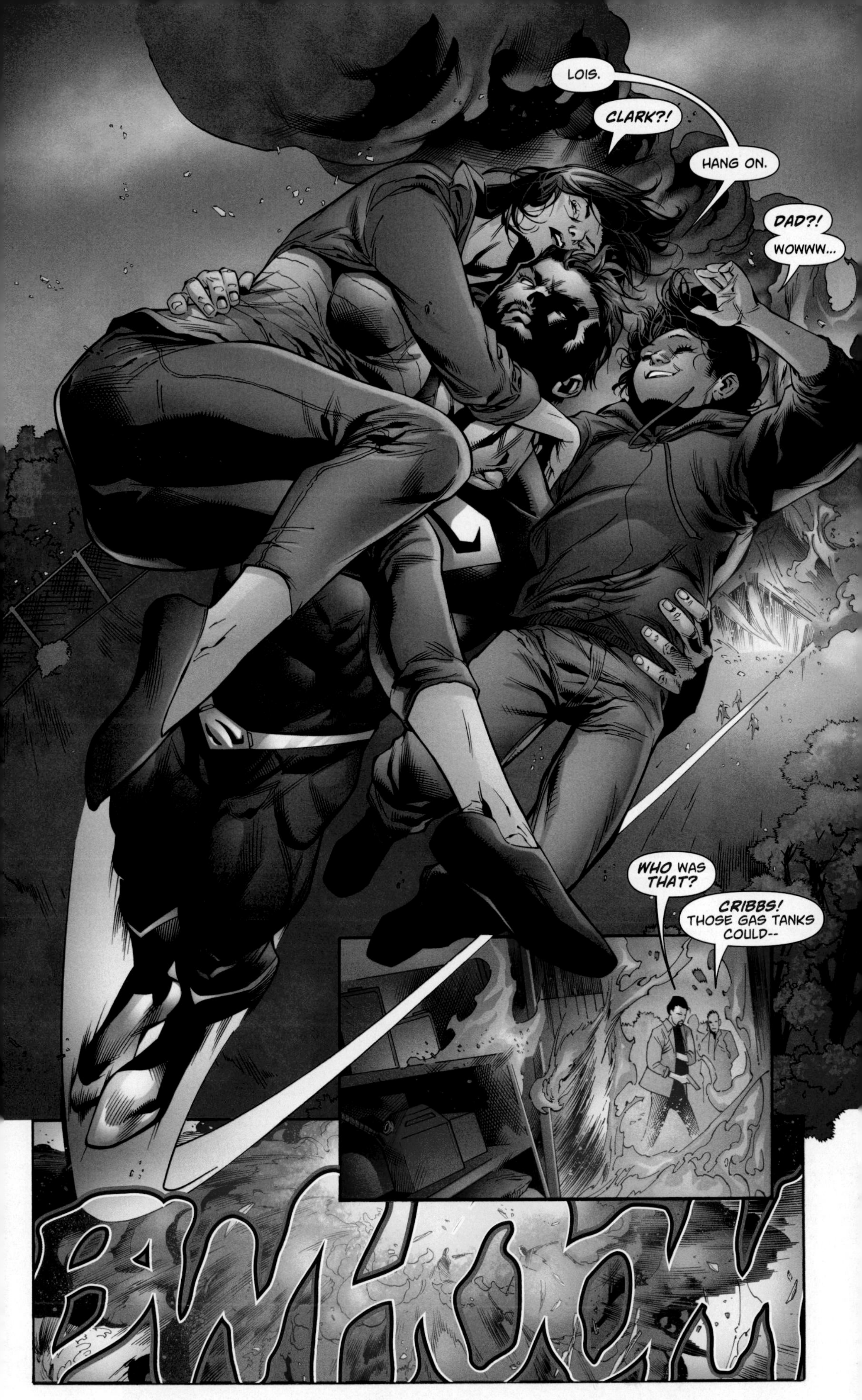
LOIS.
CLARK?!
HANG ON.
DAD?! WOWWW...
WHO WAS THAT?
CRIBBS! THOSE GAS TANKS COULD--

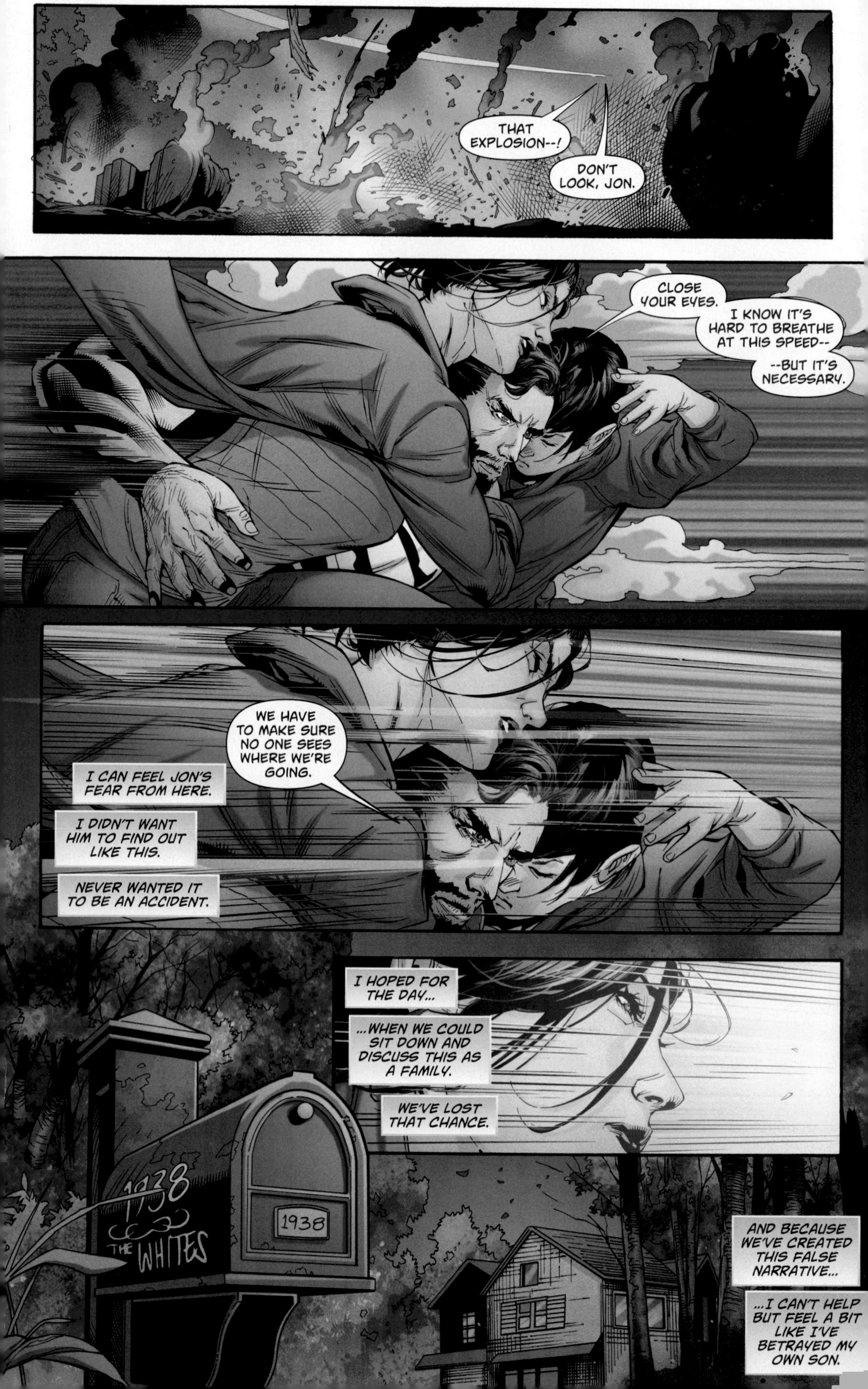
THAT EXPLOSION--!
DON'T LOOK, JON.
CLOSE YOUR EYES.
I KNOW IT'S HARD TO BREATHE AT THIS SPEED--
--BUT IT'S NECESSARY.
WE HAVE TO MAKE SURE NO ONE SEES WHERE WE'RE GOING.
I CAN FEEL JON'S FEAR FROM HERE.
I DIDN'T WANT HIM TO FIND OUT LIKE THIS.
NEVER WANTED IT TO BE AN ACCIDENT.
I HOPED FOR THE DAY...
...WHEN WE COULD SIT DOWN AND DISCUSS THIS AS A FAMILY.
WE'VE LOST THAT CHANCE.
1938
THE WHITES
1938
AND BECAUSE WE'VE CREATED THIS FALSE NARRATIVE...
...I CAN'T HELP BUT FEEL A BIT LIKE I'VE BETRAYED MY OWN SON.

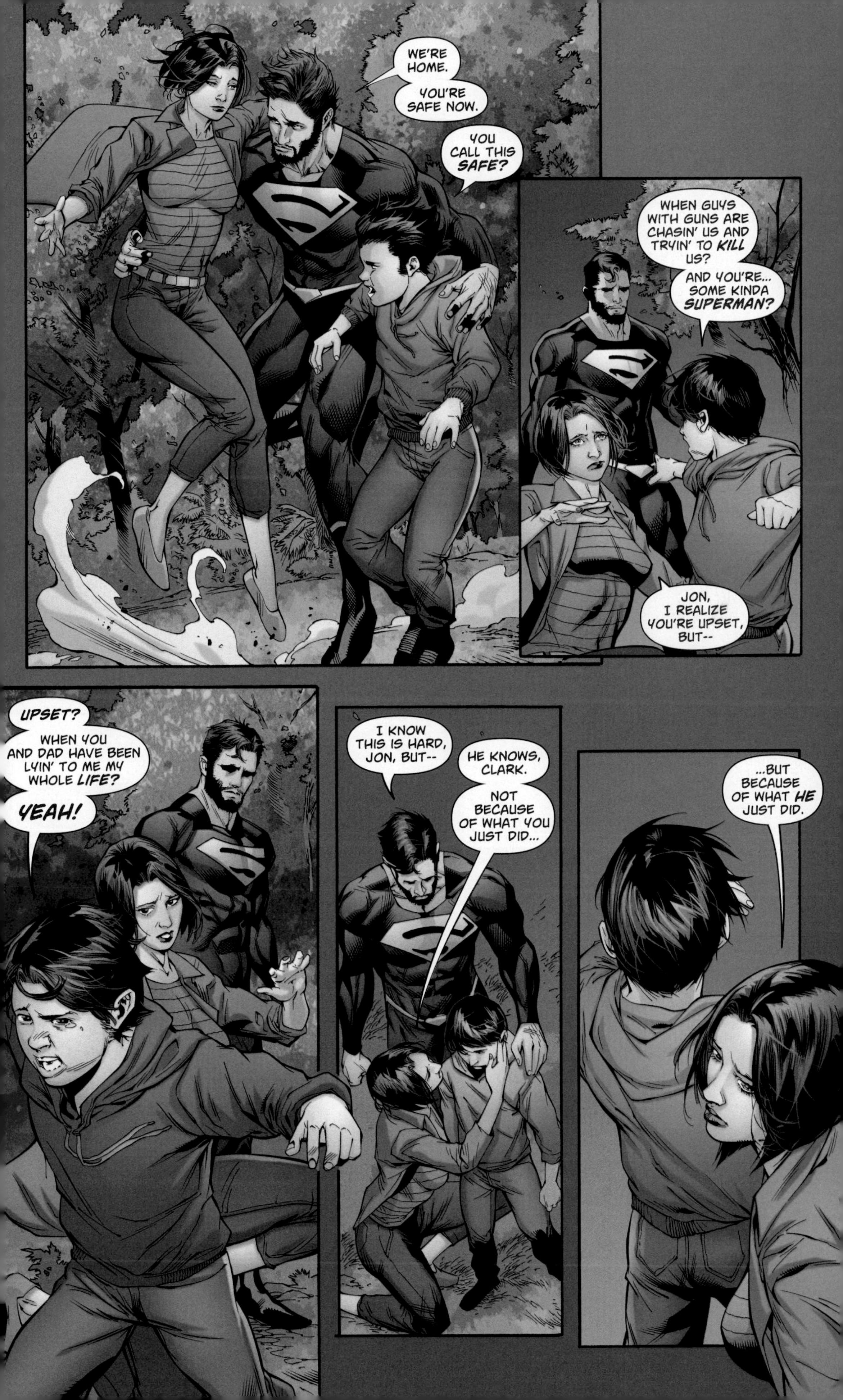

WE'RE HOME.
YOU'RE SAFE NOW.
YOU CALL THIS *SAFE?*
WHEN GUYS WITH GUNS ARE CHASIN' US AND TRYIN' TO *KILL* US?
AND YOU'RE... SOME KINDA *SUPERMAN?*
JON, I REALIZE YOU'RE UPSET, BUT--
UPSET?
WHEN YOU AND DAD HAVE BEEN LYIN' TO ME MY WHOLE *LIFE?*
YEAH!
I KNOW THIS IS HARD, JON, BUT--
HE KNOWS, CLARK.
NOT BECAUSE OF WHAT YOU JUST DID...
...BUT BECAUSE OF WHAT *HE* JUST DID.

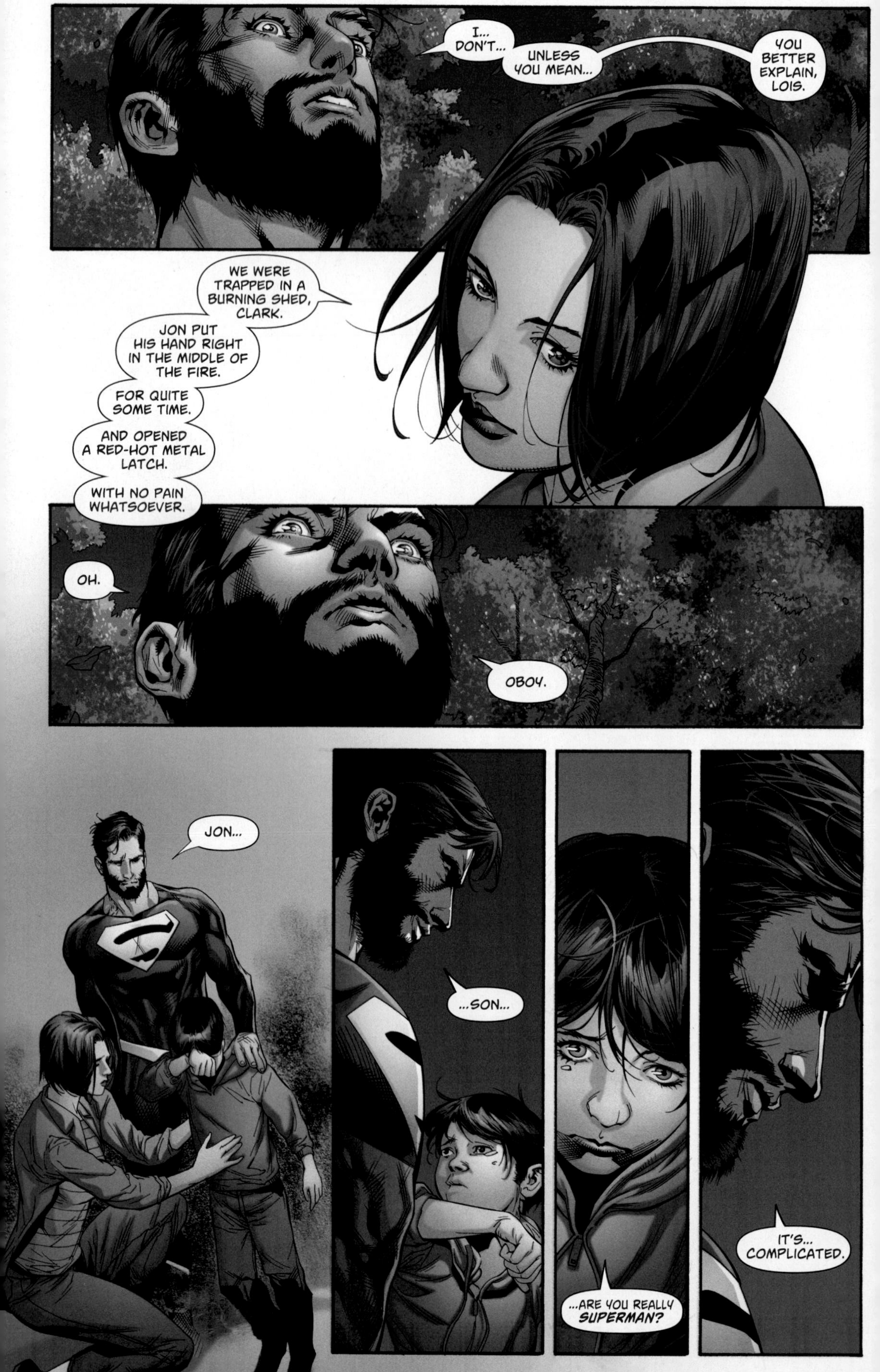
I... DON'T...
UNLESS YOU MEAN...
YOU BETTER EXPLAIN, LOIS.
WE WERE TRAPPED IN A BURNING SHED, CLARK.
JON PUT HIS HAND RIGHT IN THE MIDDLE OF THE FIRE.
FOR QUITE SOME TIME.
AND OPENED A RED-HOT METAL LATCH.
WITH NO PAIN WHATSOEVER.
OH.
OBOY.
JON...
...SON...
...ARE YOU REALLY *SUPERMAN?*
IT'S... COMPLICATED.

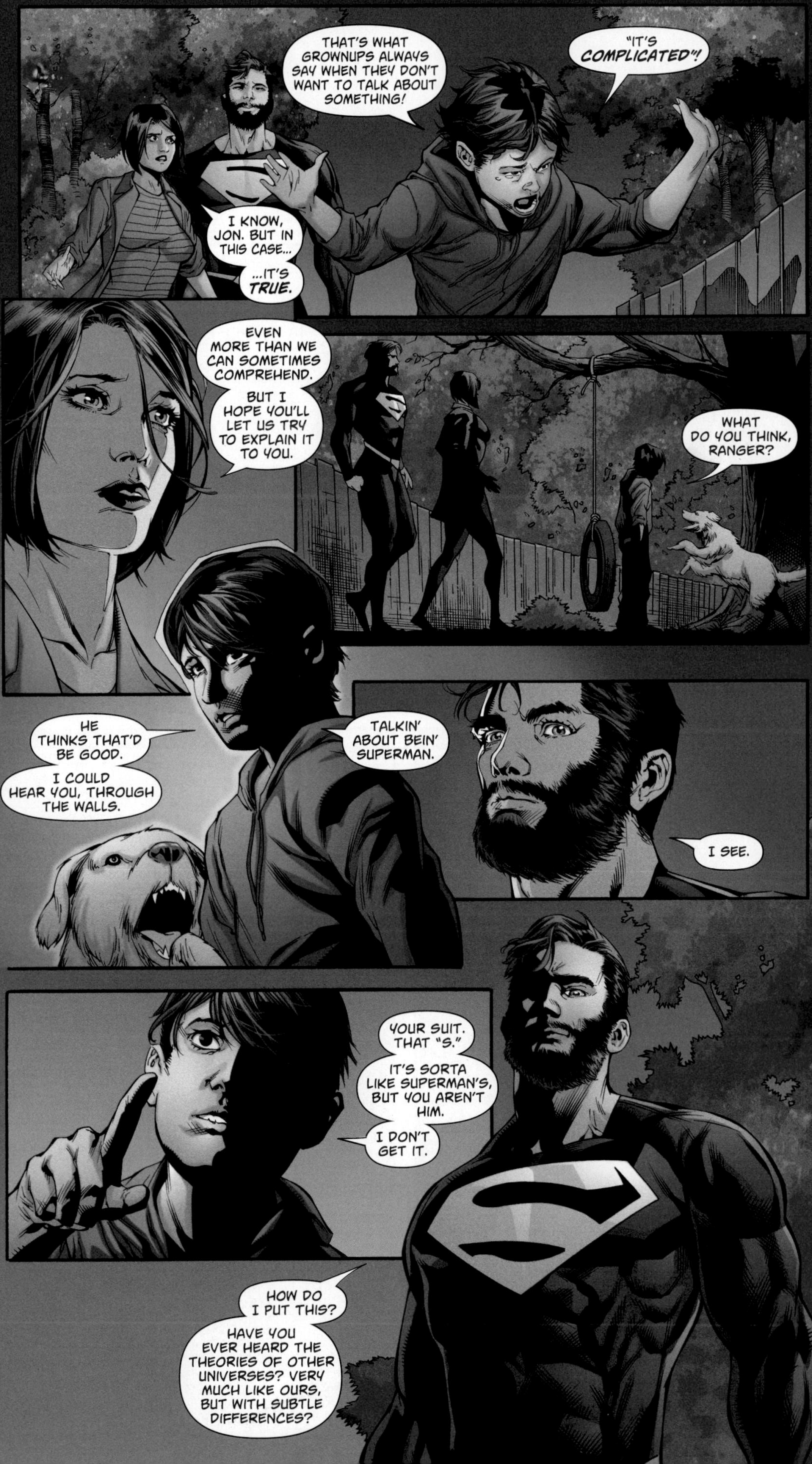
THAT'S WHAT GROWNUPS ALWAYS SAY WHEN THEY DON'T WANT TO TALK ABOUT SOMETHING!
"IT'S COMPLICATED"!
I KNOW, JON. BUT IN THIS CASE...
...IT'S TRUE.
EVEN MORE THAN WE CAN SOMETIMES COMPREHEND.
BUT I HOPE YOU'LL LET US TRY TO EXPLAIN IT TO YOU.
WHAT DO YOU THINK, RANGER?
HE THINKS THAT'D BE GOOD.
I COULD HEAR YOU, THROUGH THE WALLS.
TALKIN' ABOUT BEIN' SUPERMAN.
I SEE.
YOUR SUIT. THAT "S."
IT'S SORTA LIKE SUPERMAN'S, BUT YOU AREN'T HIM.
I DON'T GET IT.
HOW DO I PUT THIS?
HAVE YOU EVER HEARD THE THEORIES OF OTHER UNIVERSES? VERY MUCH LIKE OURS, BUT WITH SUBTLE DIFFERENCES?

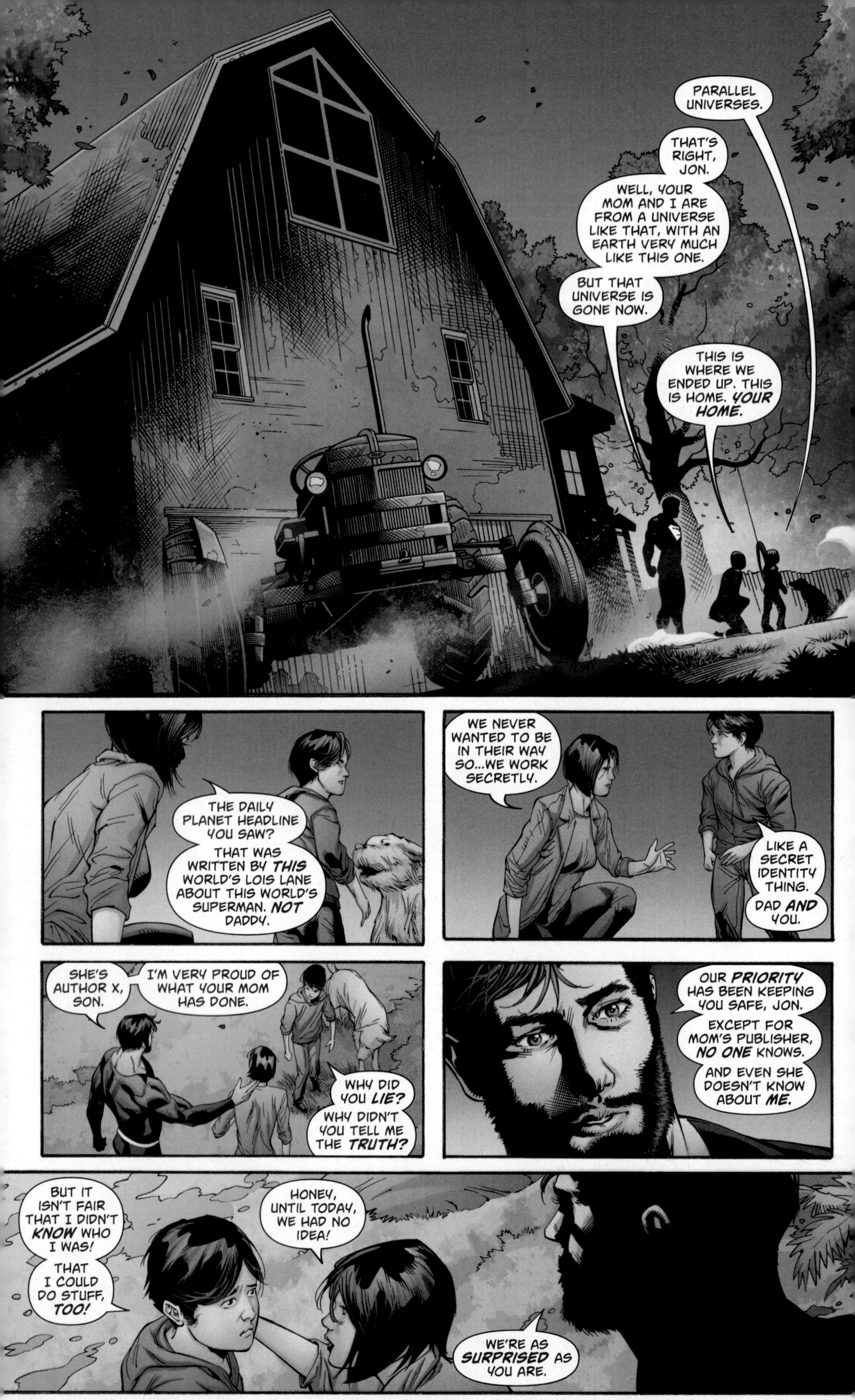
PARALLEL UNIVERSES.
THAT'S RIGHT, JON.
WELL, YOUR MOM AND I ARE FROM A UNIVERSE LIKE THAT, WITH AN EARTH VERY MUCH LIKE THIS ONE.
BUT THAT UNIVERSE IS GONE NOW.
THIS IS WHERE WE ENDED UP. THIS IS HOME. YOUR HOME.
THE DAILY PLANET HEADLINE YOU SAW?
THAT WAS WRITTEN BY THIS WORLD'S LOIS LANE ABOUT THIS WORLD'S SUPERMAN. NOT DADDY.
WE NEVER WANTED TO BE IN THEIR WAY SO...WE WORK SECRETLY.
LIKE A SECRET IDENTITY THING.
DAD AND YOU.
SHE'S AUTHOR X, SON.
I'M VERY PROUD OF WHAT YOUR MOM HAS DONE.
WHY DID YOU LIE?
WHY DIDN'T YOU TELL ME THE TRUTH?
OUR PRIORITY HAS BEEN KEEPING YOU SAFE, JON.
EXCEPT FOR MOM'S PUBLISHER, NO ONE KNOWS.
AND EVEN SHE DOESN'T KNOW ABOUT ME.
BUT IT ISN'T FAIR THAT I DIDN'T KNOW WHO I WAS!
THAT I COULD DO STUFF, TOO!
HONEY, UNTIL TODAY, WE HAD NO IDEA!
WE'RE AS SURPRISED AS YOU ARE.

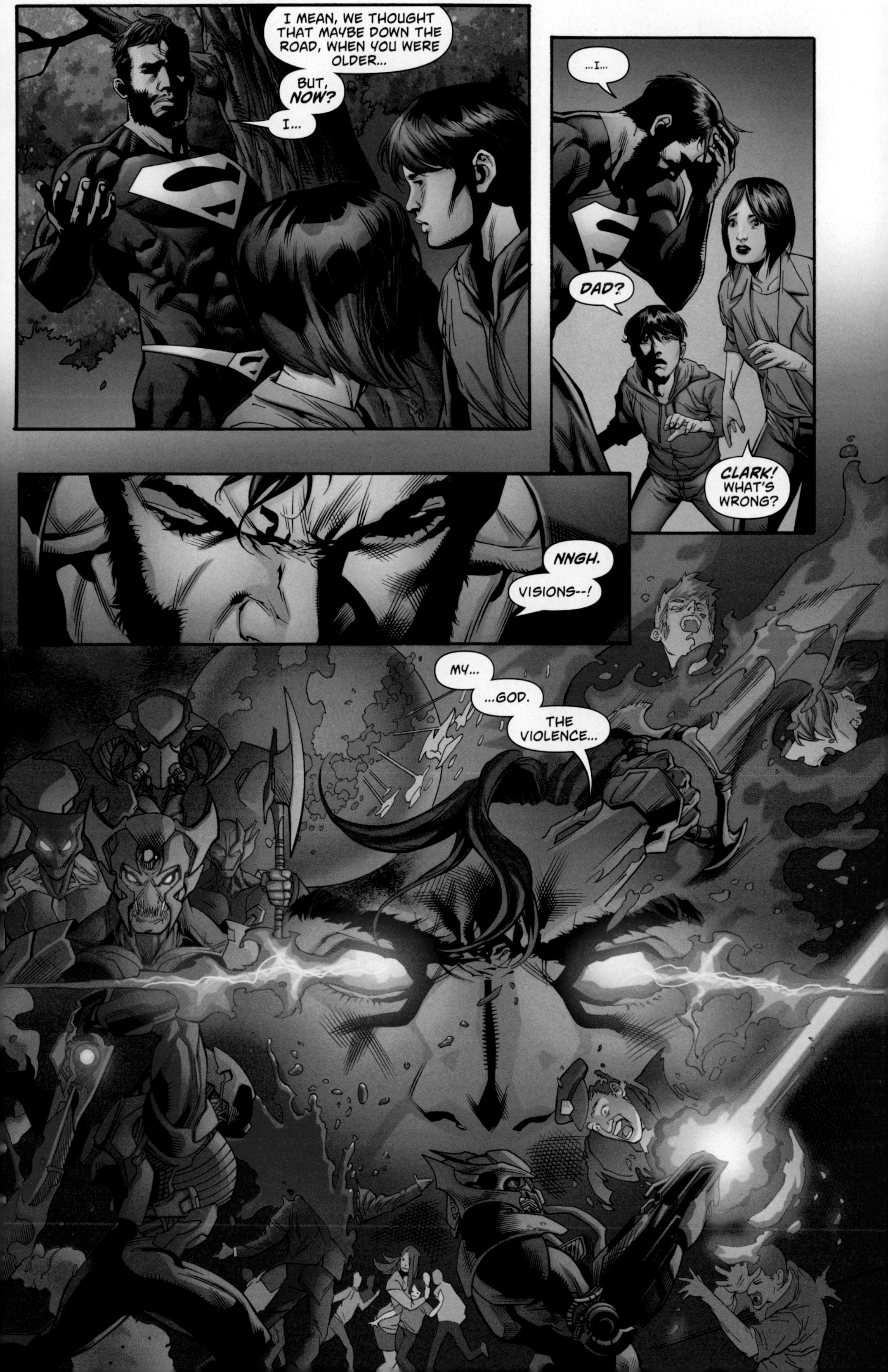
I MEAN, WE THOUGHT THAT MAYBE DOWN THE ROAD, WHEN YOU WERE OLDER...
BUT, NOW?
I...
...I...
DAD?
CLARK! WHAT'S WRONG?
NNGH.
VISIONS--!
MY...
...GOD.
THE VIOLENCE...

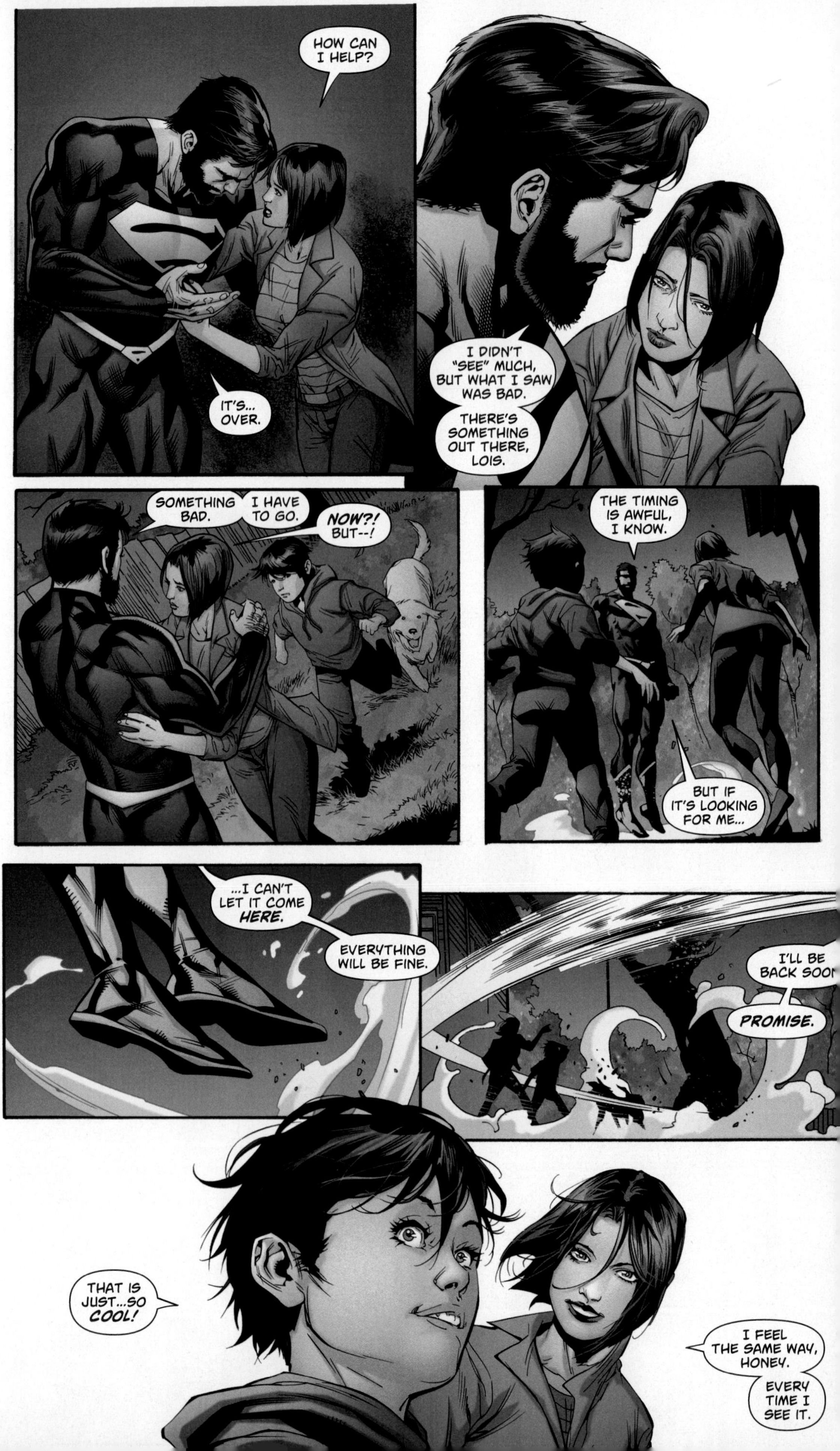

HOW CAN I HELP?
IT'S... OVER.
I DIDN'T "SEE" MUCH, BUT WHAT I SAW WAS BAD.
THERE'S SOMETHING OUT THERE, LOIS.
SOMETHING BAD.
I HAVE TO GO.
NOW?! BUT--!
THE TIMING IS AWFUL, I KNOW.
BUT IF IT'S LOOKING FOR ME...
...I CAN'T LET IT COME HERE.
EVERYTHING WILL BE FINE.
I'LL BE BACK SOO
PROMISE.
THAT IS JUST...SO COOL!
I FEEL THE SAME WAY, HONEY.
EVERY TIME I SEE IT.

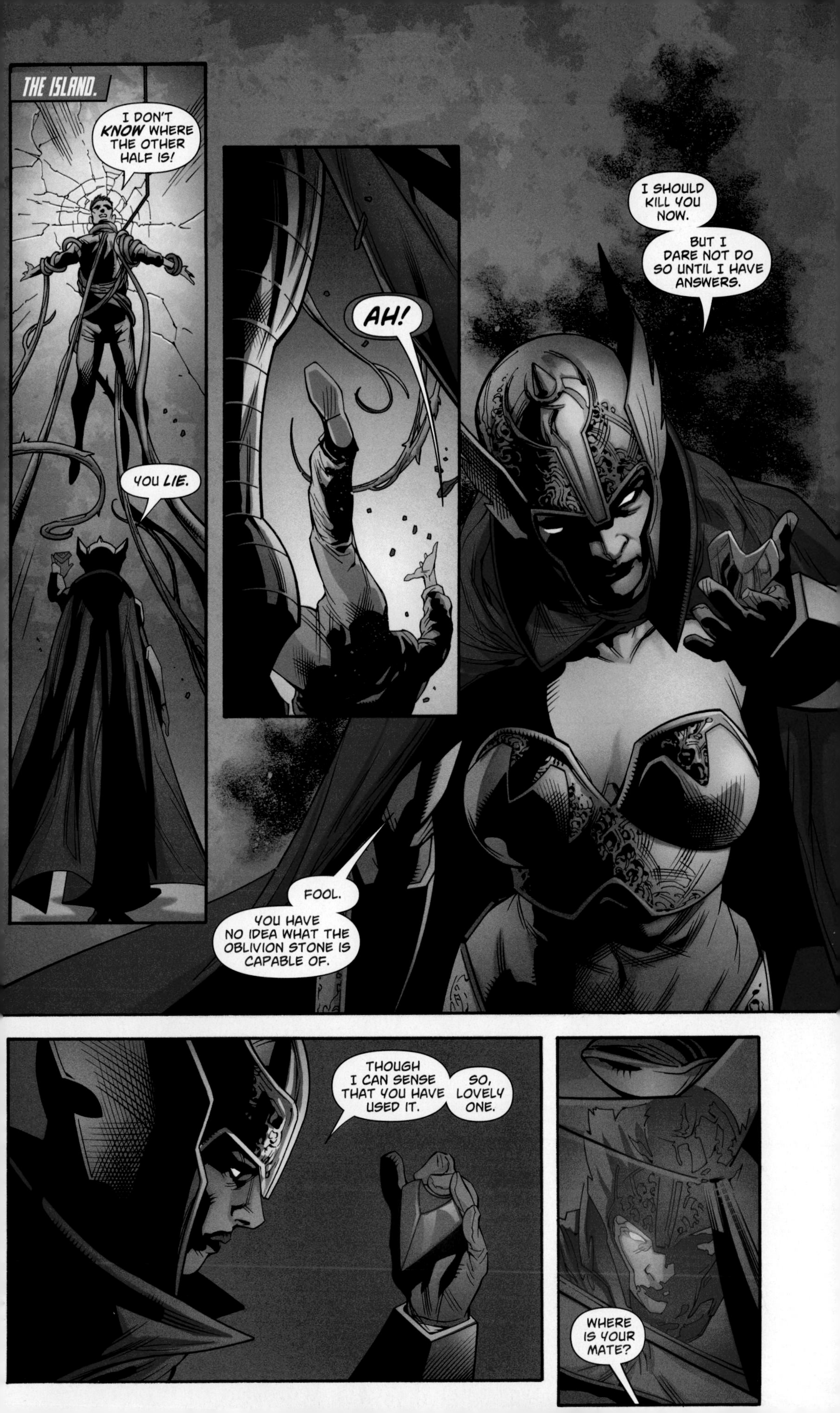
THE ISLAND.
I DON'T KNOW WHERE THE OTHER HALF IS!
YOU LIE.
AH!
I SHOULD KILL YOU NOW.
BUT I DARE NOT DO SO UNTIL I HAVE ANSWERS.
FOOL.
YOU HAVE NO IDEA WHAT THE OBLIVION STONE IS CAPABLE OF.
THOUGH I CAN SENSE THAT YOU HAVE USED IT.
SO, LOVELY ONE.
WHERE IS YOUR MATE?

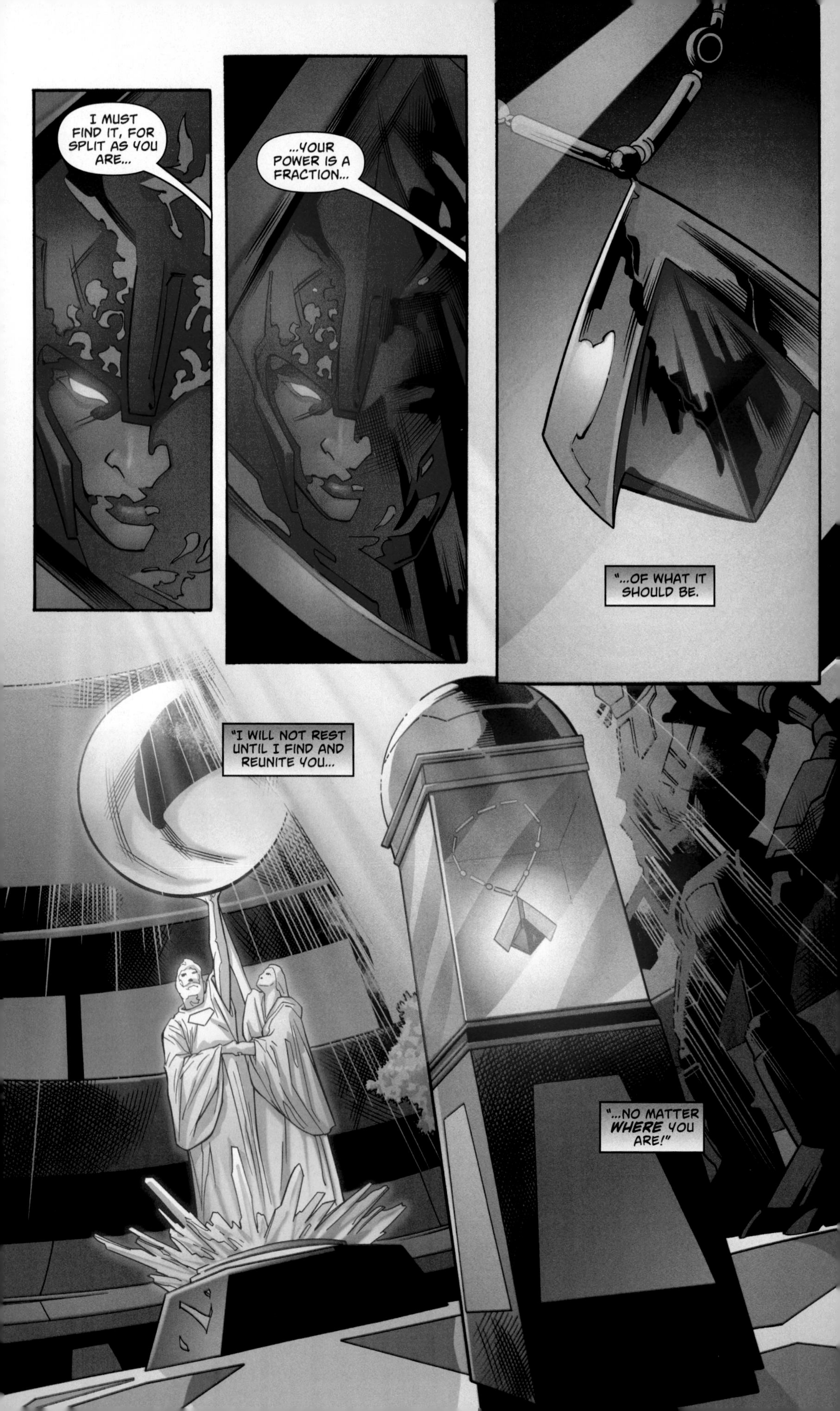
I MUST FIND IT, FOR SPLIT AS YOU ARE...
...YOUR POWER IS A FRACTION...
"...OF WHAT IT SHOULD BE.
"I WILL NOT REST UNTIL I FIND AND REUNITE YOU...
"...NO MATTER WHERE YOU ARE!"

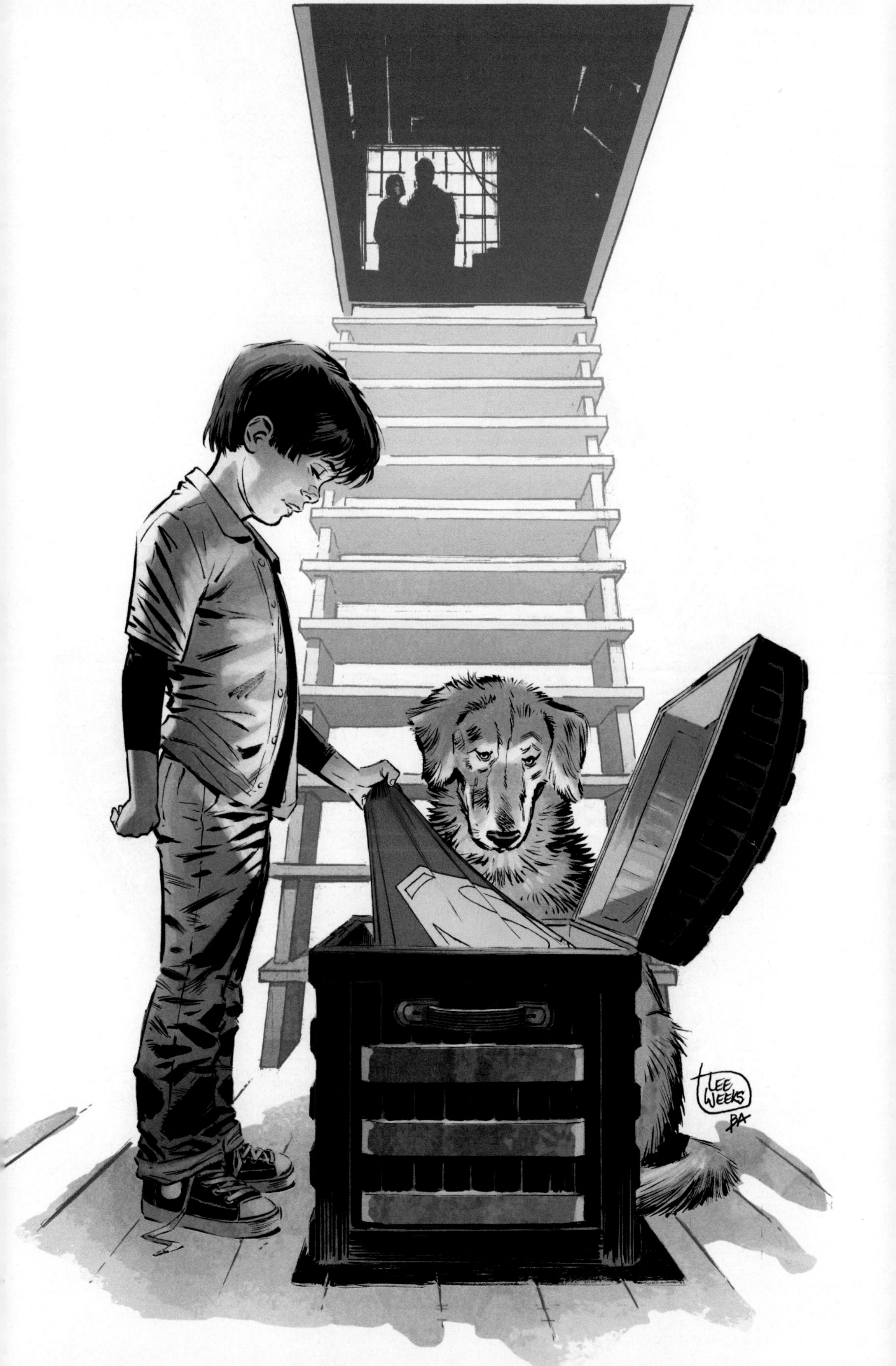
LEE WEEKS
BA

ARRIVAL: PART VIII

DAN JURGENS writer **LEE WEEKS** penciller **SCOTT HANNA** inker **JEROMY COX** colorist **A LARGER WORLD STUDIOS** letterer **BRAD ANDERSON LEE WEEKS** cover artists

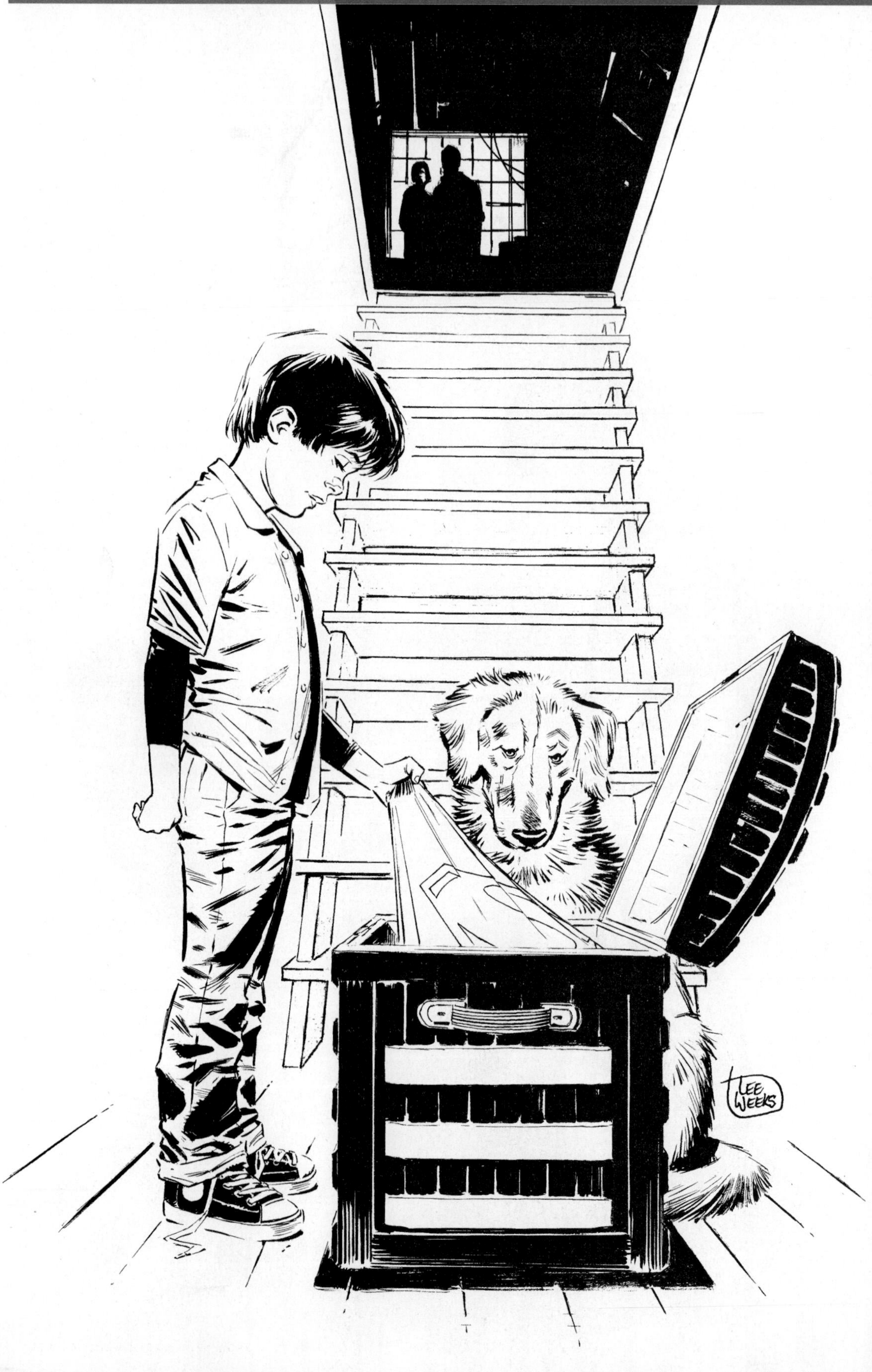
LEE WEEKS

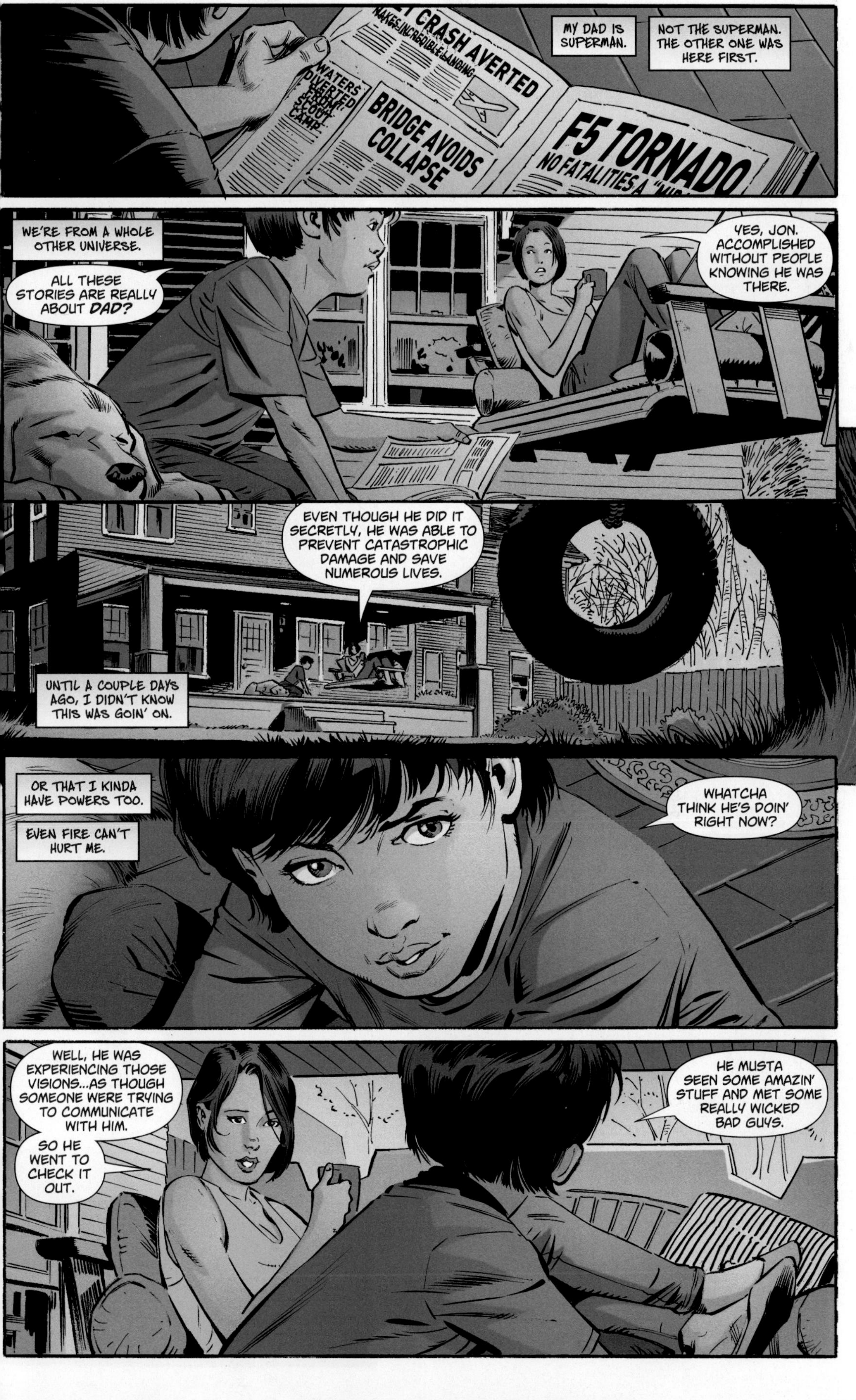
CRASH AVERTED
MAKES INCREDIBLE LANDING
WATERS DIVERTED FROM SCOUT CAMP
BRIDGE AVOIDS COLLAPSE
F5 TORNADO
MY DAD IS SUPERMAN.
NOT THE SUPERMAN. THE OTHER ONE WAS HERE FIRST.
WE'RE FROM A WHOLE OTHER UNIVERSE.
ALL THESE STORIES ARE REALLY ABOUT *DAD?*
YES, JON. ACCOMPLISHED WITHOUT PEOPLE KNOWING HE WAS THERE.
EVEN THOUGH HE DID IT SECRETLY, HE WAS ABLE TO PREVENT CATASTROPHIC DAMAGE AND SAVE NUMEROUS LIVES.
UNTIL A COUPLE DAYS AGO, I DIDN'T KNOW THIS WAS GOIN' ON.
OR THAT I KINDA HAVE POWERS TOO.
EVEN FIRE CAN'T HURT ME.
WHATCHA THINK HE'S DOIN' RIGHT NOW?
WELL, HE WAS EXPERIENCING THOSE VISIONS...AS THOUGH SOMEONE WERE TRYING TO COMMUNICATE WITH HIM.
SO HE WENT TO CHECK IT OUT.
HE MUSTA SEEN SOME AMAZIN' STUFF AND MET SOME REALLY WICKED BAD GUYS.

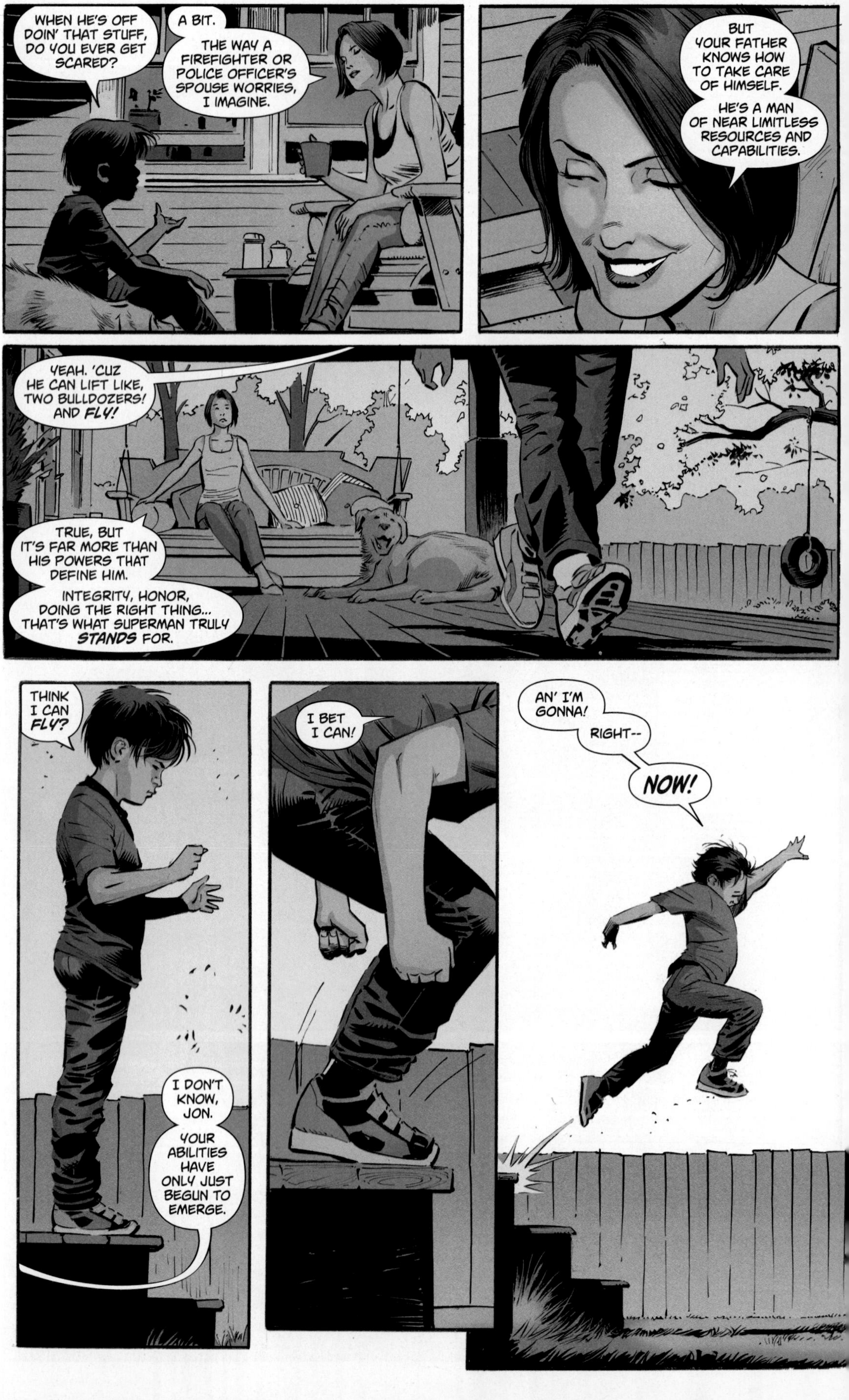

WHEN HE'S OFF DOIN' THAT STUFF, DO YOU EVER GET SCARED?
A BIT.
THE WAY A FIREFIGHTER OR POLICE OFFICER'S SPOUSE WORRIES, I IMAGINE.
BUT YOUR FATHER KNOWS HOW TO TAKE CARE OF HIMSELF.
HE'S A MAN OF NEAR LIMITLESS RESOURCES AND CAPABILITIES.
YEAH. 'CUZ HE CAN LIFT LIKE, TWO BULLDOZERS! AND FLY!
TRUE, BUT IT'S FAR MORE THAN HIS POWERS THAT DEFINE HIM.
INTEGRITY, HONOR, DOING THE RIGHT THING... THAT'S WHAT SUPERMAN TRULY STANDS FOR.
THINK I CAN FLY?
I DON'T KNOW, JON.
YOUR ABILITIES HAVE ONLY JUST BEGUN TO EMERGE.
I BET I CAN!
AN' I'M GONNA!
RIGHT--
NOW!

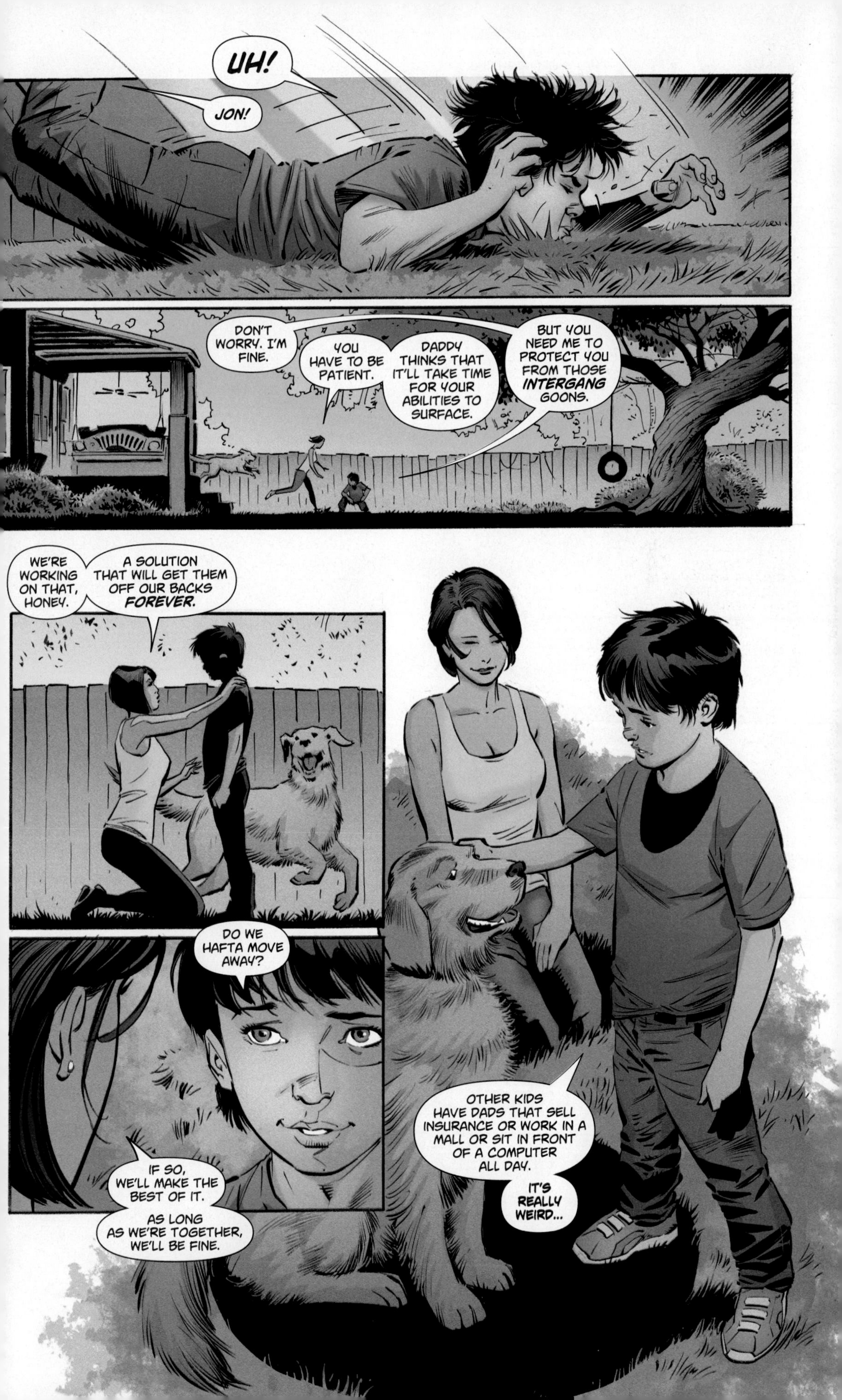
UH!
JON!
DON'T WORRY. I'M FINE.
YOU HAVE TO BE PATIENT.
DADDY THINKS THAT IT'LL TAKE TIME FOR YOUR ABILITIES TO SURFACE.
BUT YOU NEED ME TO PROTECT YOU FROM THOSE INTERGANG GOONS.
WE'RE WORKING ON THAT, HONEY.
A SOLUTION THAT WILL GET THEM OFF OUR BACKS FOREVER.
DO WE HAFTA MOVE AWAY?
IF SO, WE'LL MAKE THE BEST OF IT.
AS LONG AS WE'RE TOGETHER, WE'LL BE FINE.
OTHER KIDS HAVE DADS THAT SELL INSURANCE OR WORK IN A MALL OR SIT IN FRONT OF A COMPUTER ALL DAY.
IT'S REALLY WEIRD...

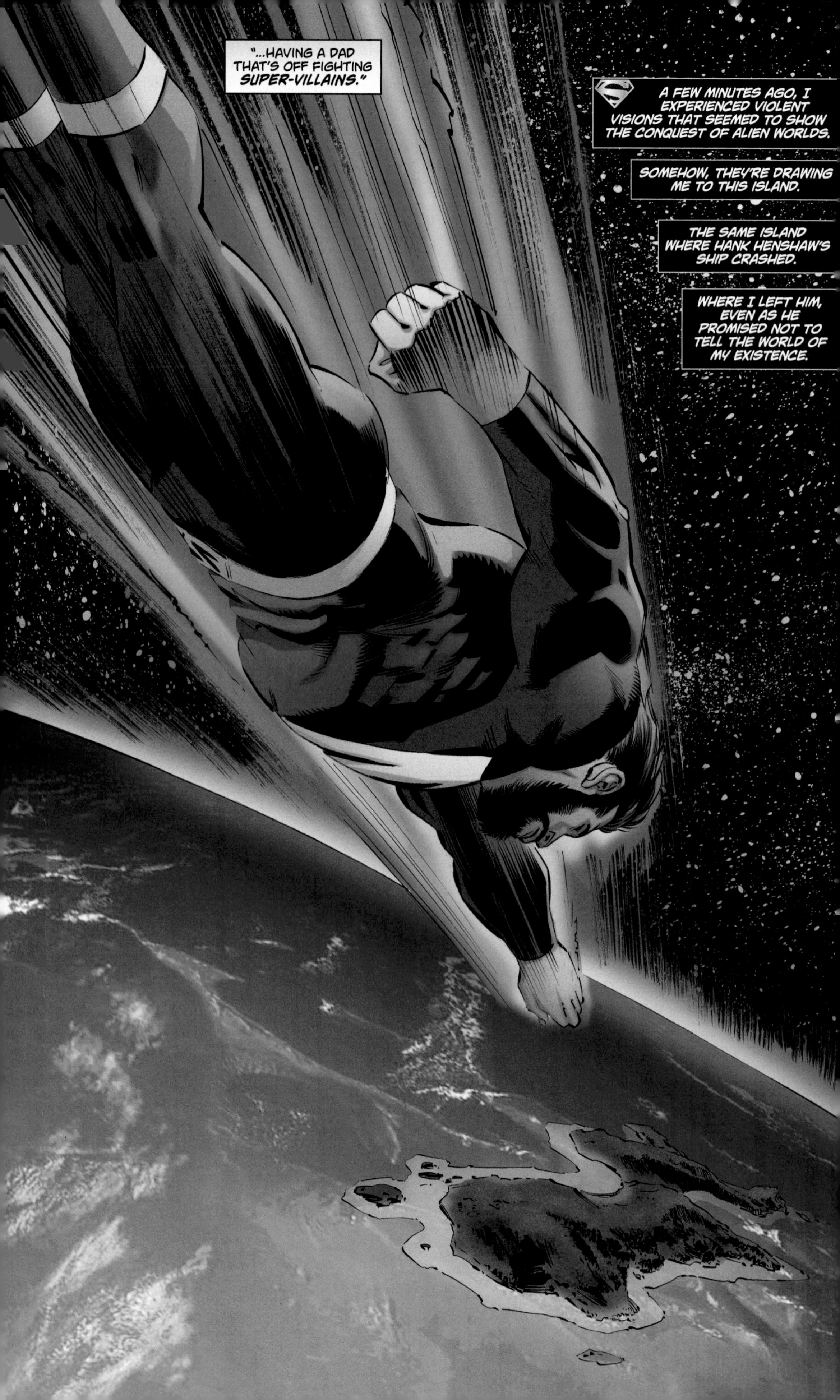
"...HAVING A DAD THAT'S OFF FIGHTING SUPER-VILLAINS."
A FEW MINUTES AGO, I EXPERIENCED VIOLENT VISIONS THAT SEEMED TO SHOW THE CONQUEST OF ALIEN WORLDS.
SOMEHOW, THEY'RE DRAWING ME TO THIS ISLAND.
THE SAME ISLAND WHERE HANK HENSHAW'S SHIP CRASHED.
WHERE I LEFT HIM, EVEN AS HE PROMISED NOT TO TELL THE WORLD OF MY EXISTENCE.

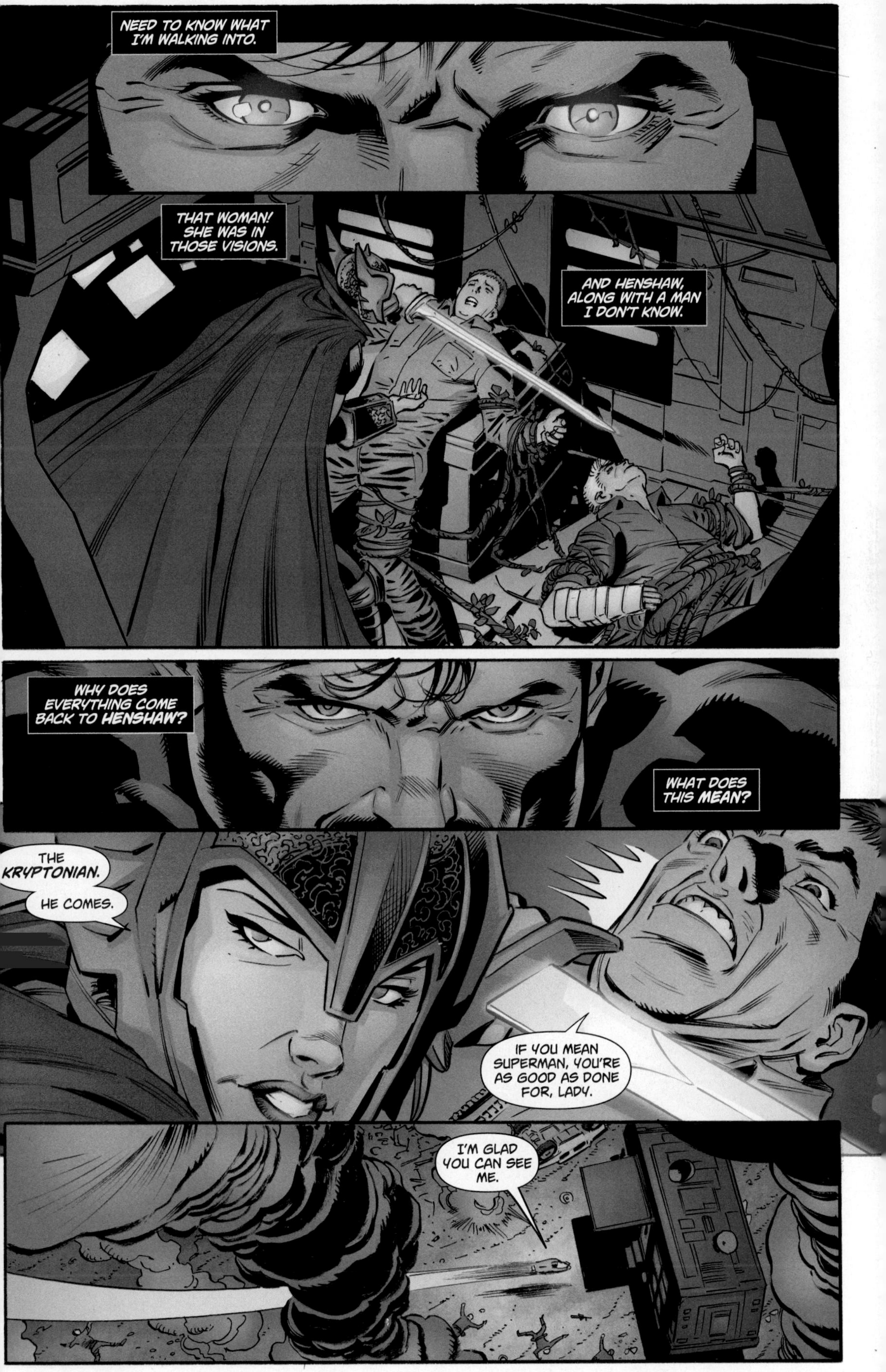
NEED TO KNOW WHAT I'M WALKING INTO.
THAT WOMAN! SHE WAS IN THOSE VISIONS.
AND HENSHAW, ALONG WITH A MAN I DON'T KNOW.
WHY DOES EVERYTHING COME BACK TO HENSHAW?
WHAT DOES THIS MEAN?
THE KRYPTONIAN.
HE COMES.
IF YOU MEAN SUPERMAN, YOU'RE AS GOOD AS DONE FOR, LADY.
I'M GLAD YOU CAN SEE ME.

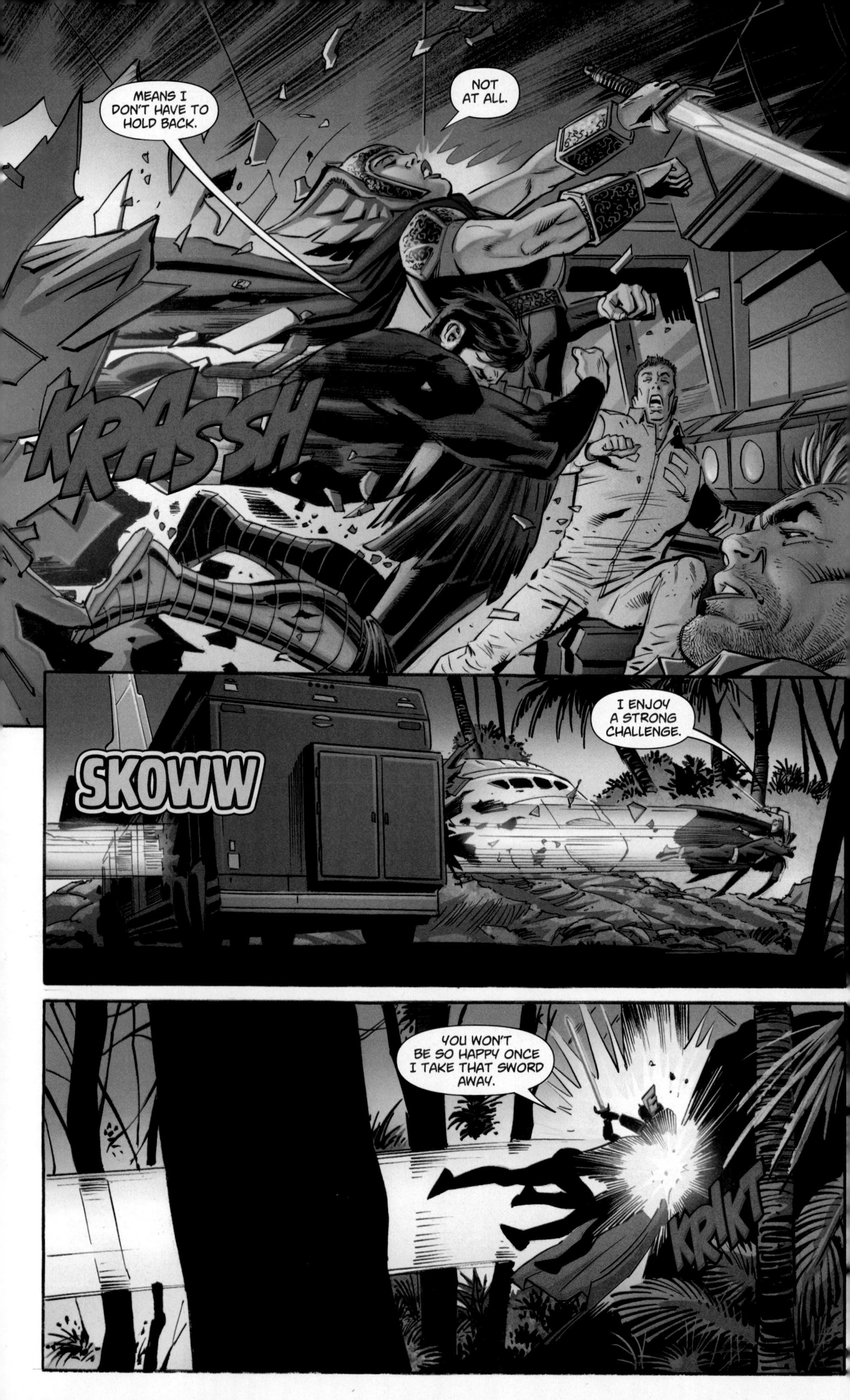
MEANS I DON'T HAVE TO HOLD BACK.
NOT AT ALL.
KRASSH
SKOWW
I ENJOY A STRONG CHALLENGE.
YOU WON'T BE SO HAPPY ONCE I TAKE THAT SWORD AWAY.
KRIKT

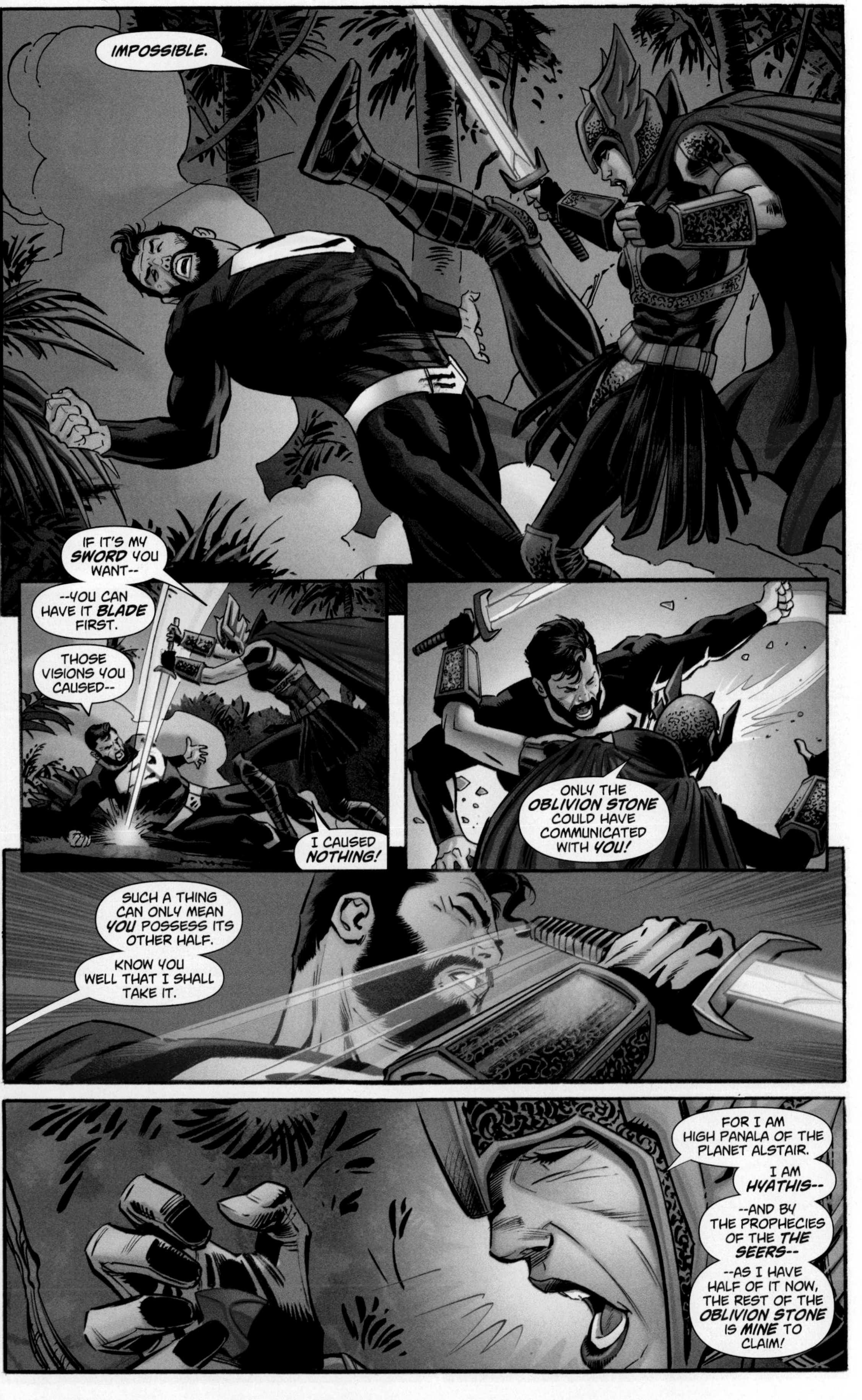
IMPOSSIBLE.
IF IT'S MY SWORD YOU WANT--
--YOU CAN HAVE IT BLADE FIRST.
THOSE VISIONS YOU CAUSED--
I CAUSED NOTHING!
ONLY THE OBLIVION STONE COULD HAVE COMMUNICATED WITH YOU!
SUCH A THING CAN ONLY MEAN YOU POSSESS ITS OTHER HALF.
KNOW YOU WELL THAT I SHALL TAKE IT.
FOR I AM HIGH PANALA OF THE PLANET ALSTAIR.
I AM HYATHIS--
--AND BY THE PROPHECIES OF THE THE SEERS--
--AS I HAVE HALF OF IT NOW, THE REST OF THE OBLIVION STONE IS MINE TO CLAIM!

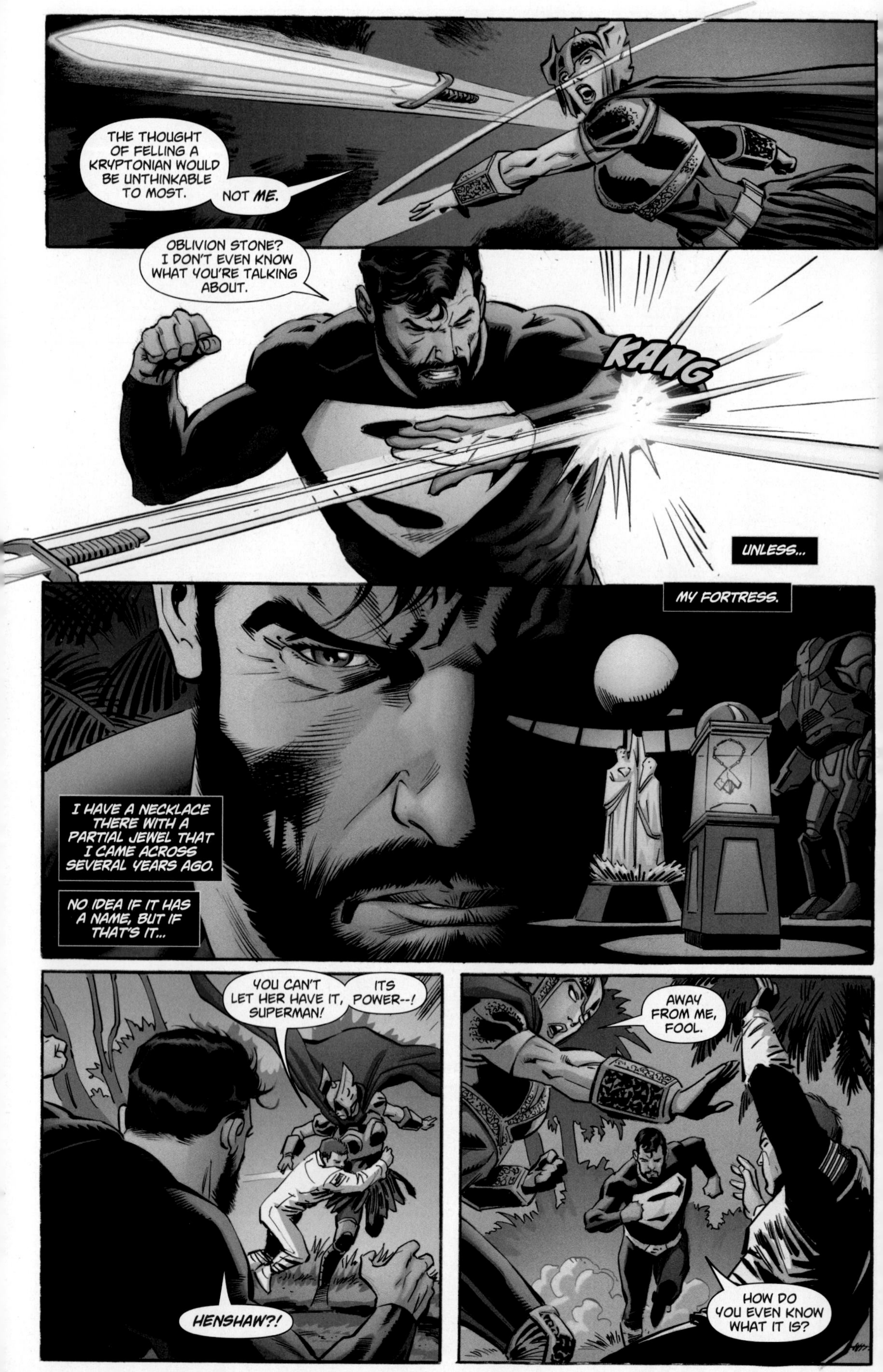
THE THOUGHT OF FELLING A KRYPTONIAN WOULD BE UNTHINKABLE TO MOST.
NOT ME.
OBLIVION STONE? I DON'T EVEN KNOW WHAT YOU'RE TALKING ABOUT.
KANG
UNLESS...
MY FORTRESS.
I HAVE A NECKLACE THERE WITH A PARTIAL JEWEL THAT I CAME ACROSS SEVERAL YEARS AGO.
NO IDEA IF IT HAS A NAME, BUT IF THAT'S IT...
YOU CAN'T LET HER HAVE IT, SUPERMAN!
ITS POWER--!
HENSHAW?!
AWAY FROM ME, FOOL.
HOW DO YOU EVEN KNOW WHAT IT IS?

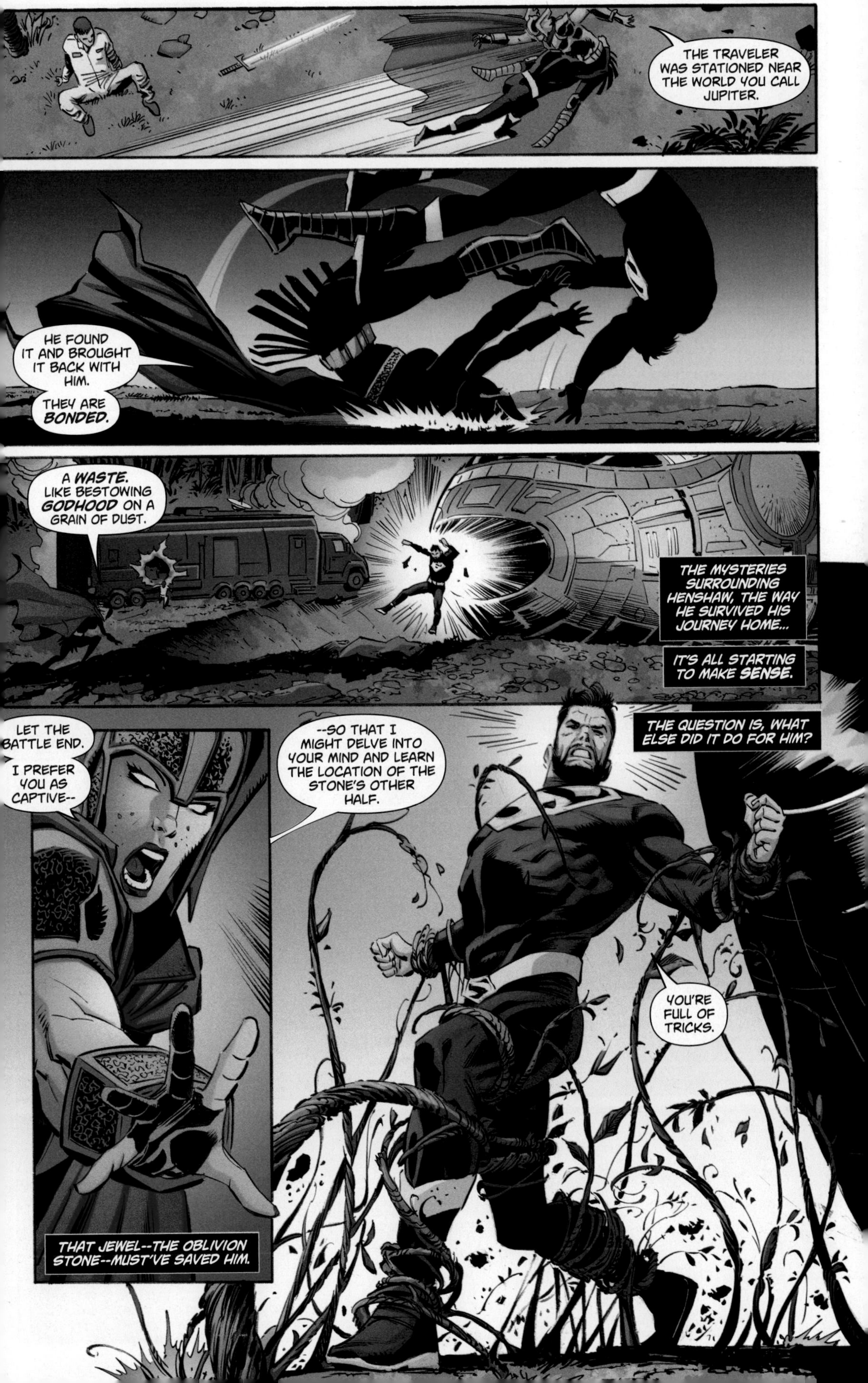

THE TRAVELER WAS STATIONED NEAR THE WORLD YOU CALL JUPITER.
HE FOUND IT AND BROUGHT IT BACK WITH HIM.
THEY ARE BONDED.
A WASTE. LIKE BESTOWING GODHOOD ON A GRAIN OF DUST.
THE MYSTERIES SURROUNDING HENSHAW, THE WAY HE SURVIVED HIS JOURNEY HOME...
IT'S ALL STARTING TO MAKE SENSE.
LET THE BATTLE END.
I PREFER YOU AS CAPTIVE--
--SO THAT I MIGHT DELVE INTO YOUR MIND AND LEARN THE LOCATION OF THE STONE'S OTHER HALF.
THAT JEWEL--THE OBLIVION STONE--MUST'VE SAVED HIM.
THE QUESTION IS, WHAT ELSE DID IT DO FOR HIM?
YOU'RE FULL OF TRICKS.

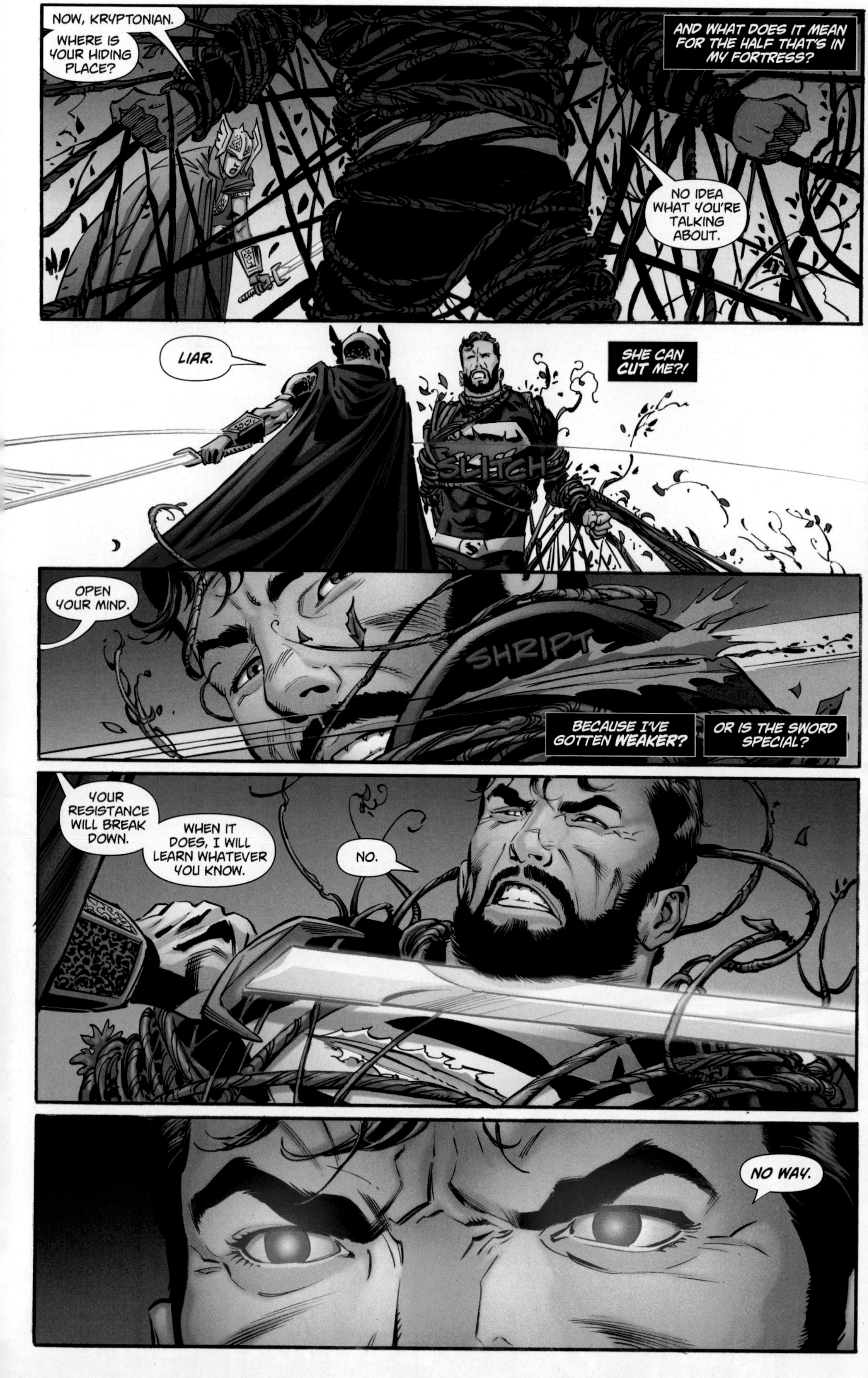

NOW, KRYPTONIAN.
WHERE IS YOUR HIDING PLACE?
AND WHAT DOES IT MEAN FOR THE HALF THAT'S IN MY FORTRESS?
NO IDEA WHAT YOU'RE TALKING ABOUT.
LIAR.
SHE CAN CUT ME?!
SLITCH
OPEN YOUR MIND.
SHRIPT
BECAUSE I'VE GOTTEN WEAKER?
OR IS THE SWORD SPECIAL?
YOUR RESISTANCE WILL BREAK DOWN.
WHEN IT DOES, I WILL LEARN WHATEVER YOU KNOW.
NO.
NO WAY.

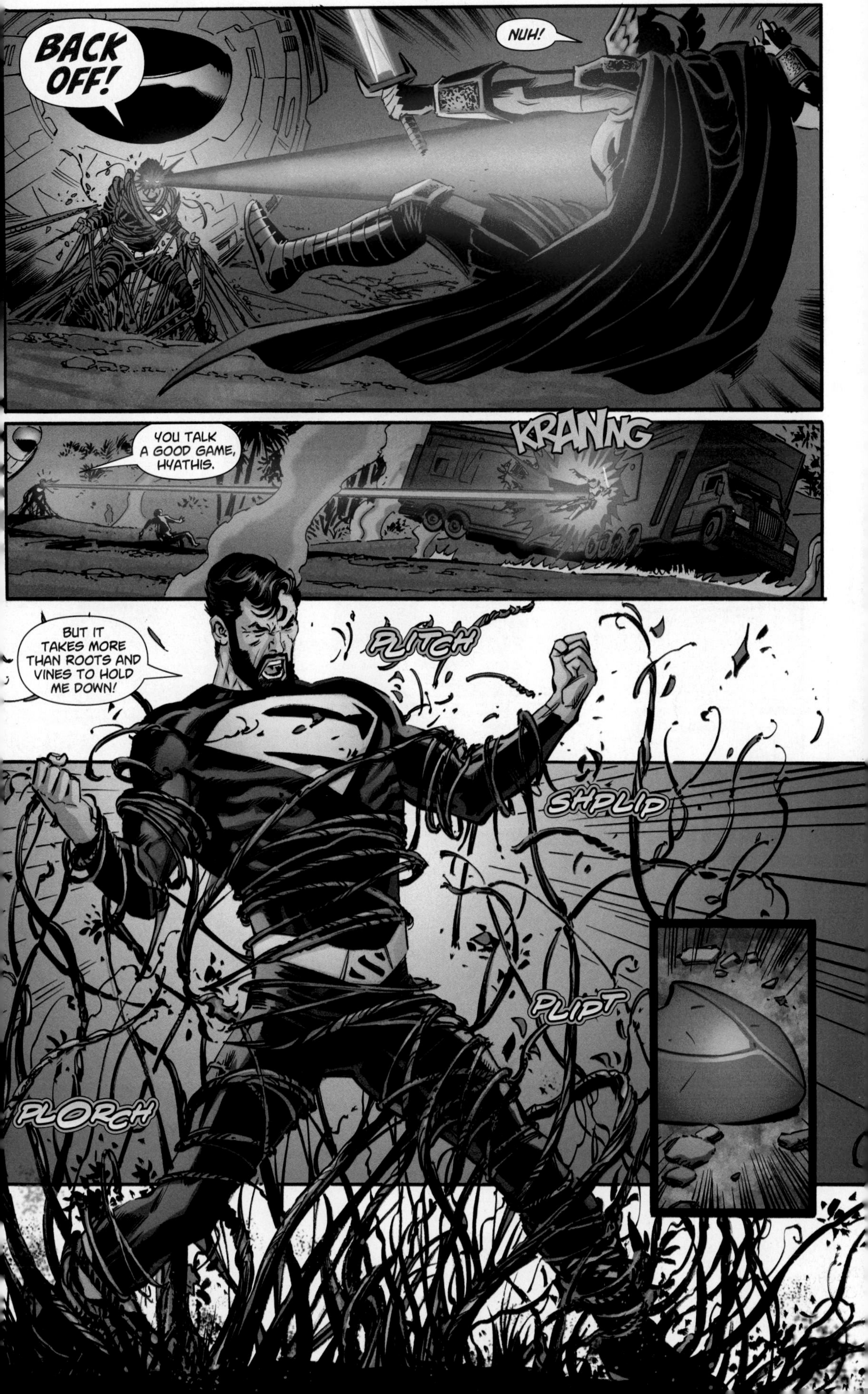
BACK OFF!
NUH!
YOU TALK A GOOD GAME, HYATHIS.
KRANNG
BUT IT TAKES MORE THAN ROOTS AND VINES TO HOLD ME DOWN!
PLITCH
SHPLIP
PLIPT
PLORCH

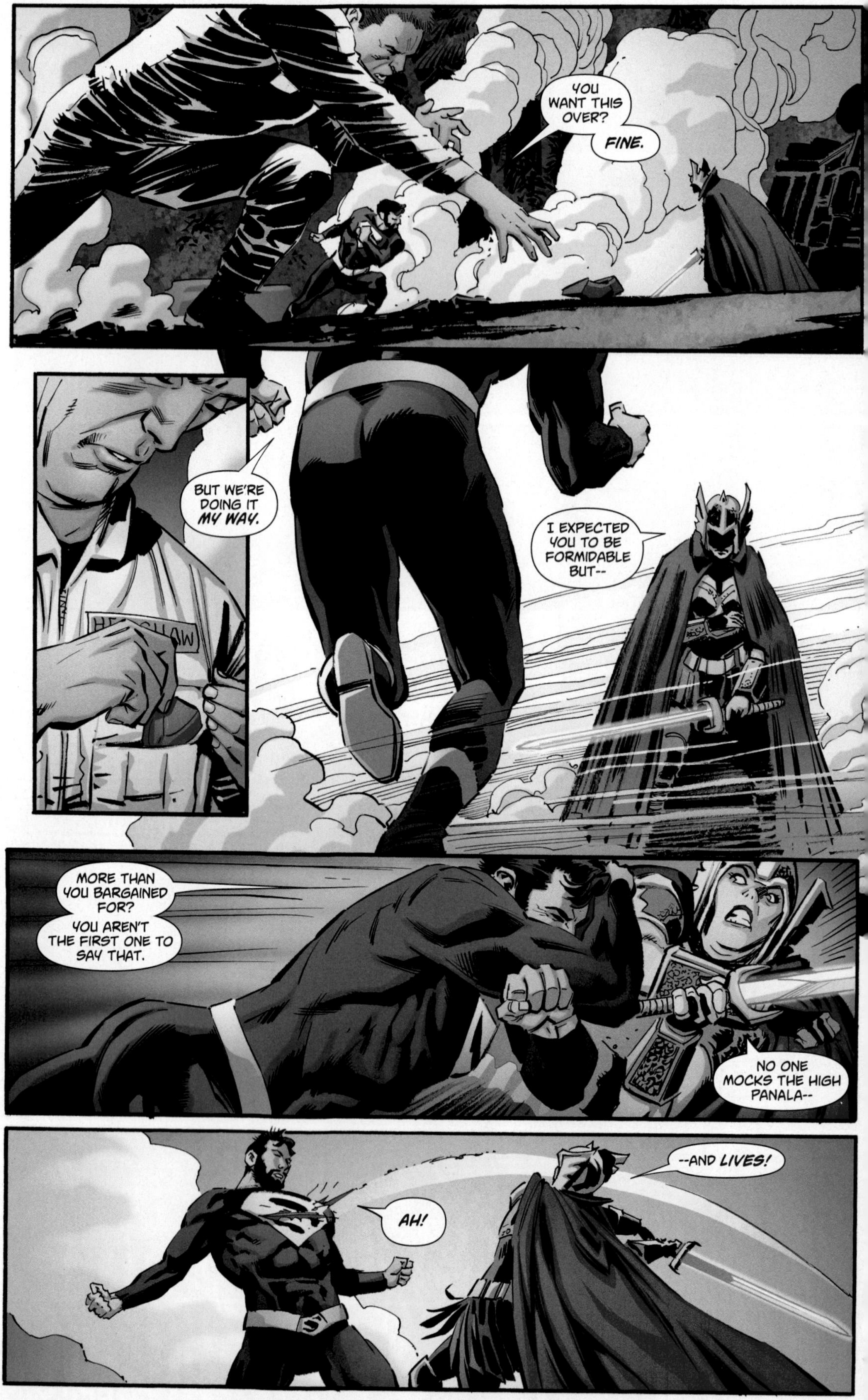

YOU WANT THIS OVER?
FINE.
BUT WE'RE DOING IT MY WAY.
I EXPECTED YOU TO BE FORMIDABLE BUT--
MORE THAN YOU BARGAINED FOR?
YOU AREN'T THE FIRST ONE TO SAY THAT.
NO ONE MOCKS THE HIGH PANALA--
--AND LIVES!
AH!

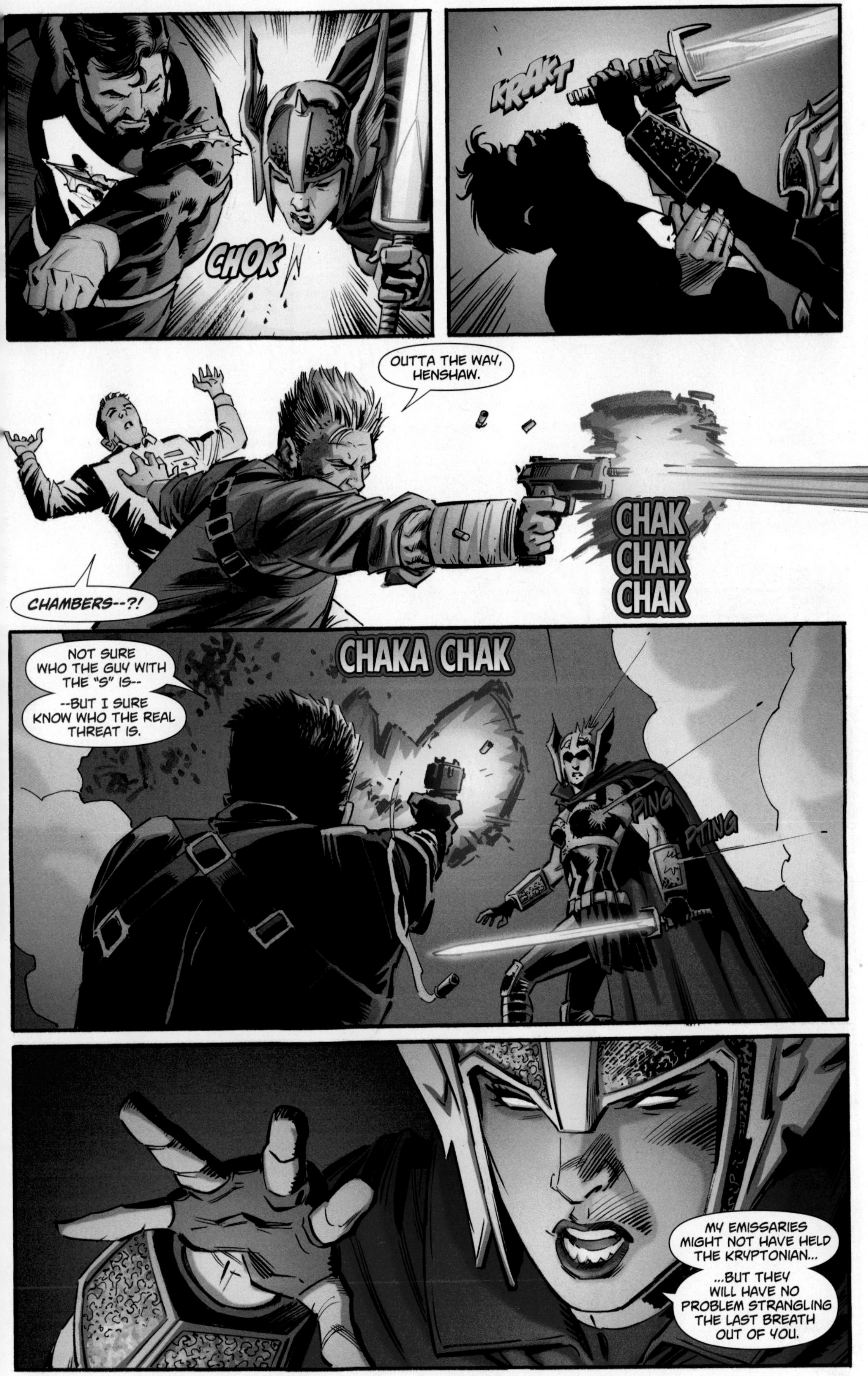
CHOK
KRAKT
OUTTA THE WAY, HENSHAW.
CHAMBERS--?!
CHAK CHAK CHAK
CHAKA CHAK
NOT SURE WHO THE GUY WITH THE "S" IS--
--BUT I SURE KNOW WHO THE REAL THREAT IS.
PING
PTING
MY EMISSARIES MIGHT NOT HAVE HELD THE KRYPTONIAN...
...BUT THEY WILL HAVE NO PROBLEM STRANGLING THE LAST BREATH OUT OF YOU.

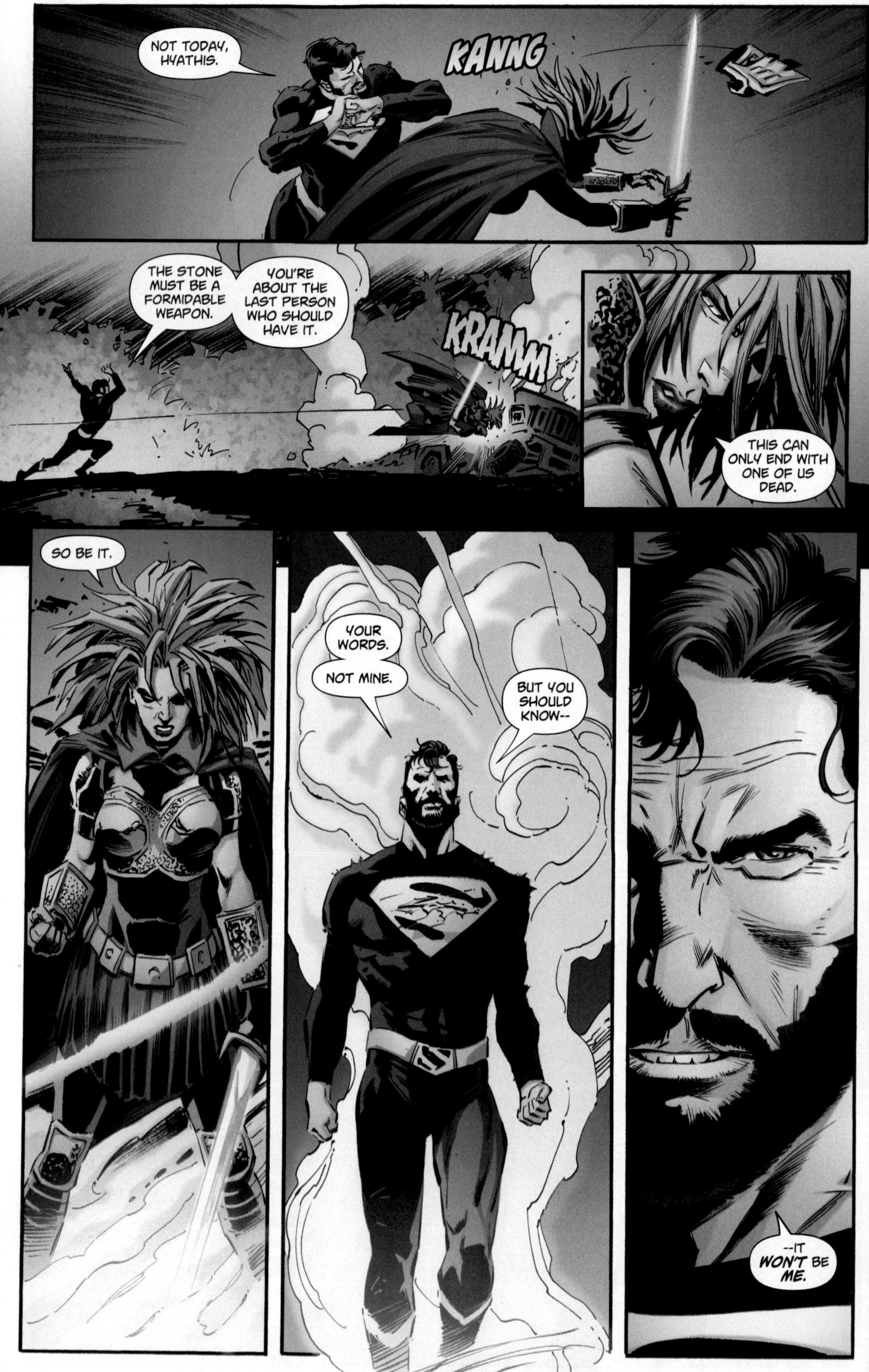
NOT TODAY, HYATHIS.
KANNG
THE STONE MUST BE A FORMIDABLE WEAPON.
YOU'RE ABOUT THE LAST PERSON WHO SHOULD HAVE IT.
KRAMM
THIS CAN ONLY END WITH ONE OF US DEAD.
SO BE IT.
YOUR WORDS.
NOT MINE.
BUT YOU SHOULD KNOW--
--IT WON'T BE ME.

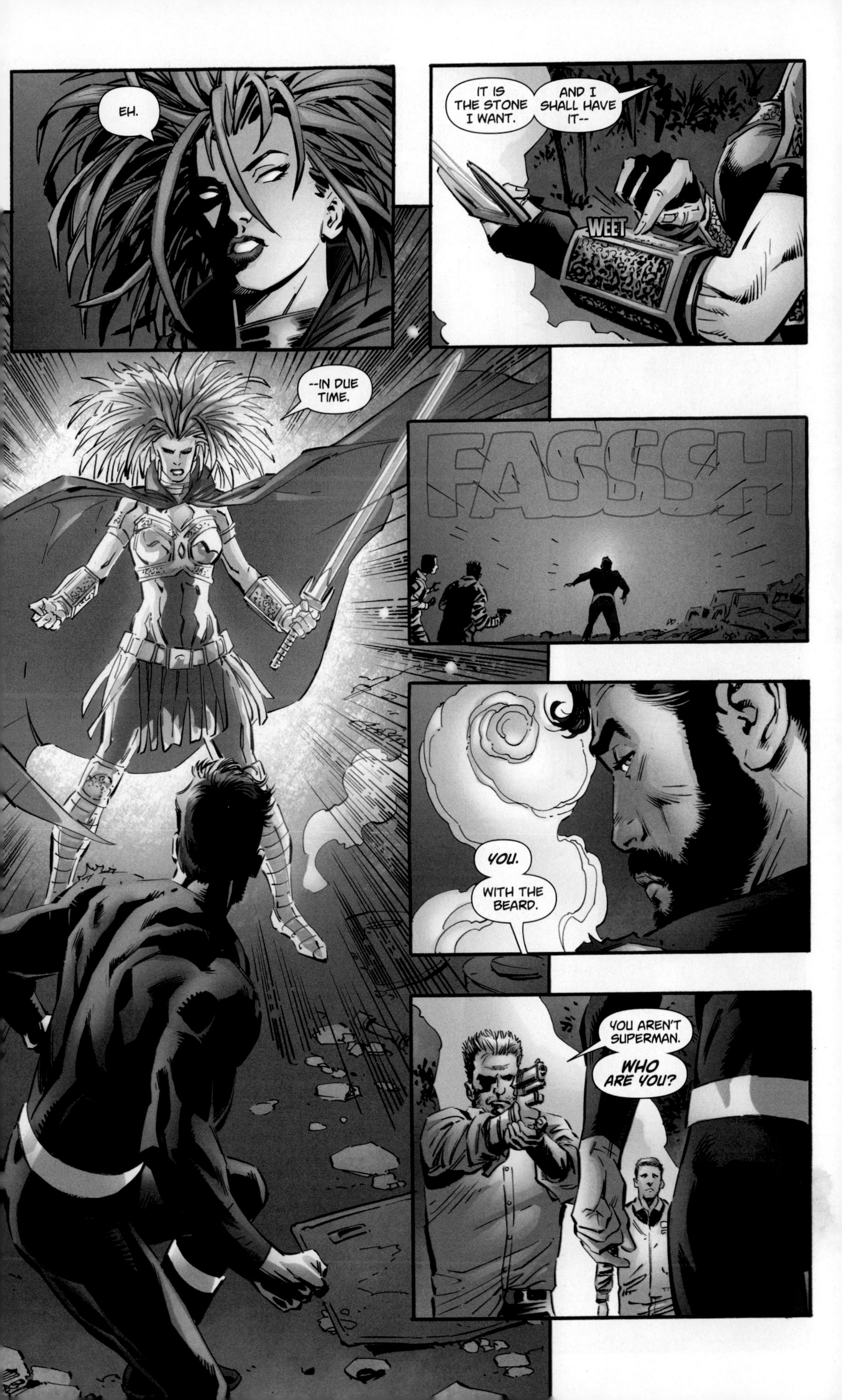
EH.
IT IS THE STONE I WANT.
AND I SHALL HAVE IT--
WEET
--IN DUE TIME.
FASSSH
YOU.
WITH THE BEARD.
YOU AREN'T SUPERMAN.
WHO ARE YOU?

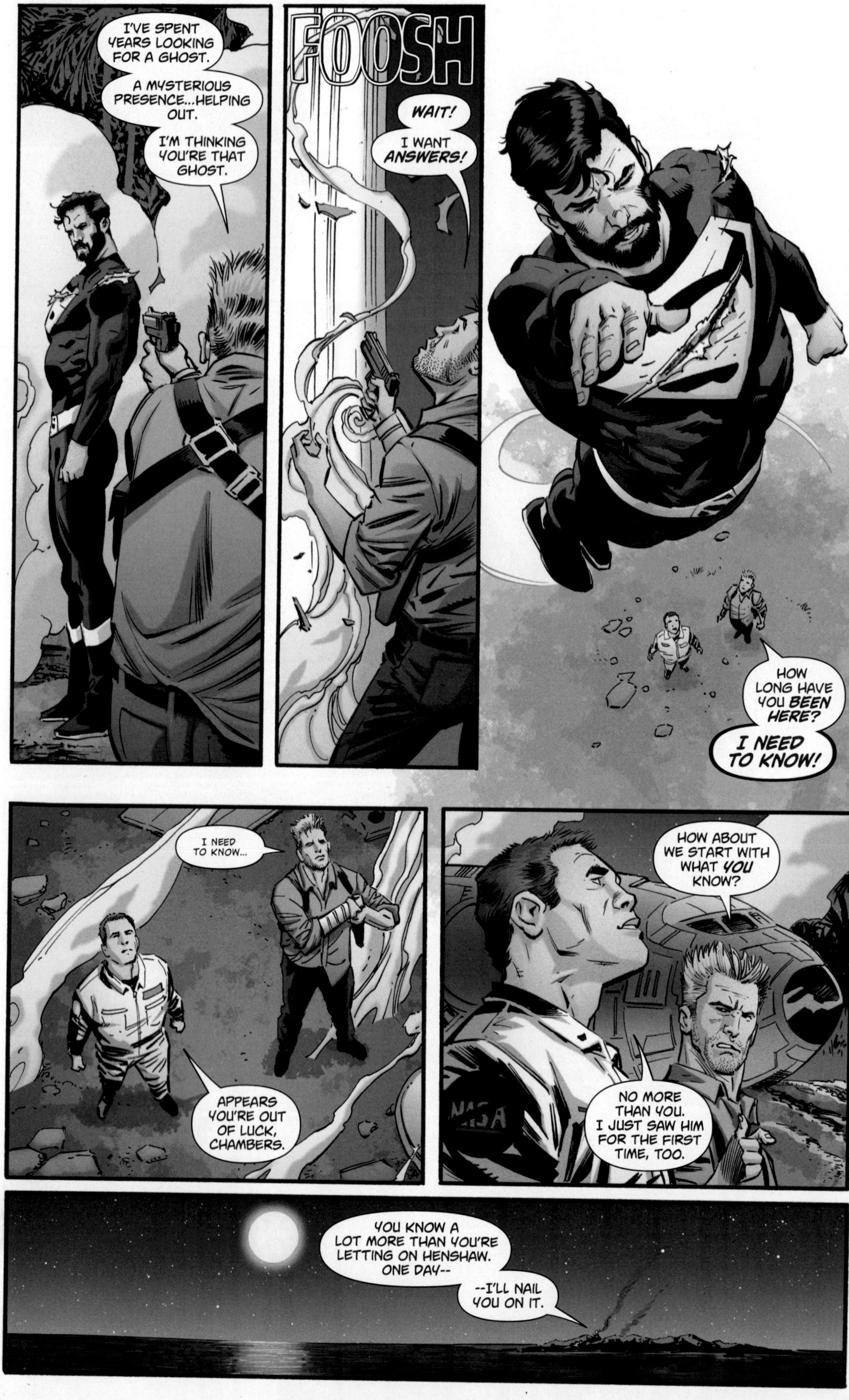
I'VE SPENT YEARS LOOKING FOR A GHOST.
A MYSTERIOUS PRESENCE...HELPING OUT.
I'M THINKING YOU'RE THAT GHOST.
FOOSH
WAIT! I WANT ANSWERS!
HOW LONG HAVE YOU BEEN HERE?
I NEED TO KNOW!
I NEED TO KNOW...
APPEARS YOU'RE OUT OF LUCK, CHAMBERS.
HOW ABOUT WE START WITH WHAT YOU KNOW?
NASA
NO MORE THAN YOU. I JUST SAW HIM FOR THE FIRST TIME, TOO.
YOU KNOW A LOT MORE THAN YOU'RE LETTING ON HENSHAW. ONE DAY--
--I'LL NAIL YOU ON IT.

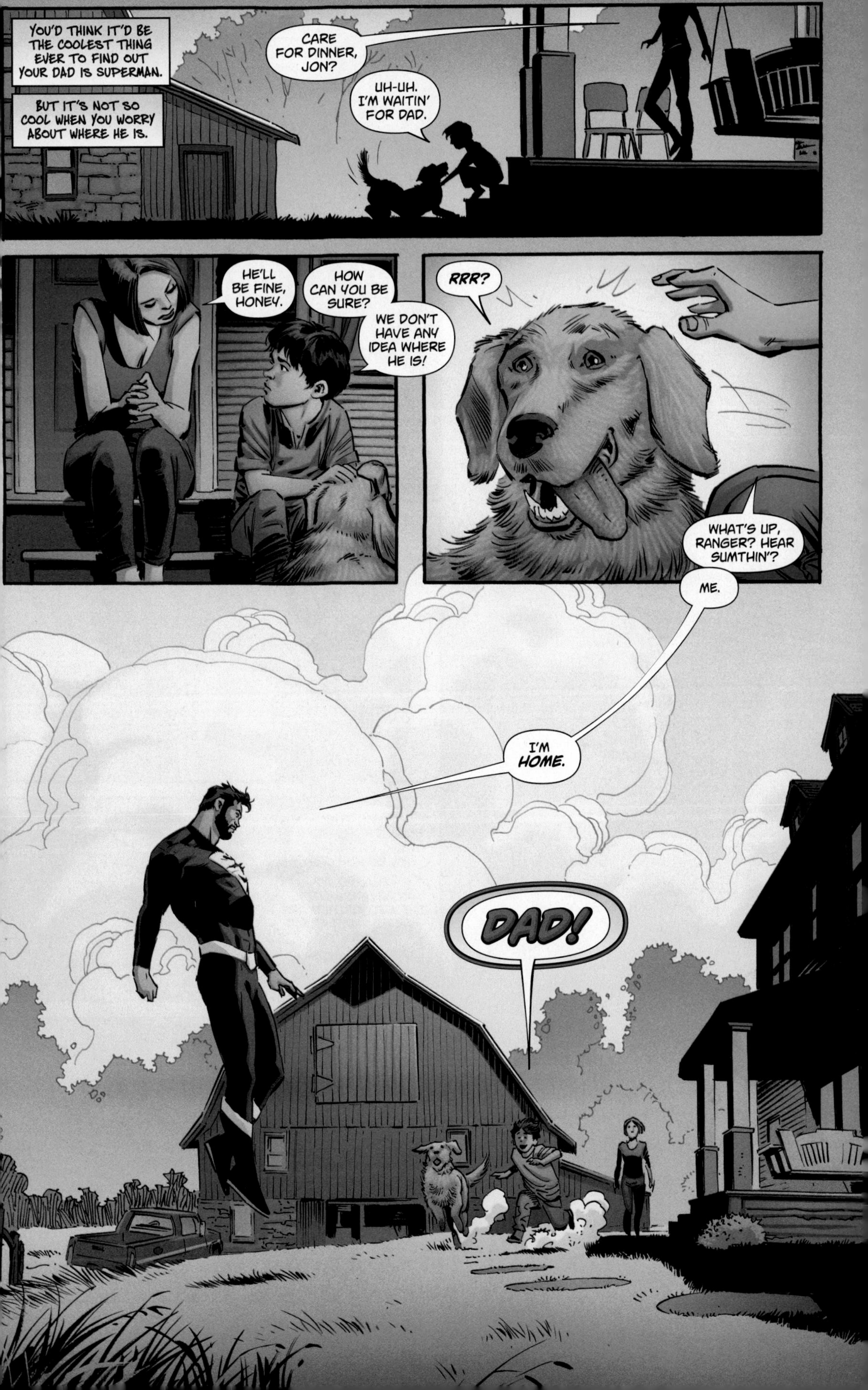
YOU'D THINK IT'D BE THE COOLEST THING EVER TO FIND OUT YOUR DAD IS SUPERMAN.
BUT IT'S NOT SO COOL WHEN YOU WORRY ABOUT WHERE HE IS.
CARE FOR DINNER, JON?
UH-UH. I'M WAITIN' FOR DAD.
HE'LL BE FINE, HONEY.
HOW CAN YOU BE SURE?
WE DON'T HAVE ANY IDEA WHERE HE IS!
RRR?
WHAT'S UP, RANGER? HEAR SUMTHIN'?
ME.
I'M HOME.
DAD!

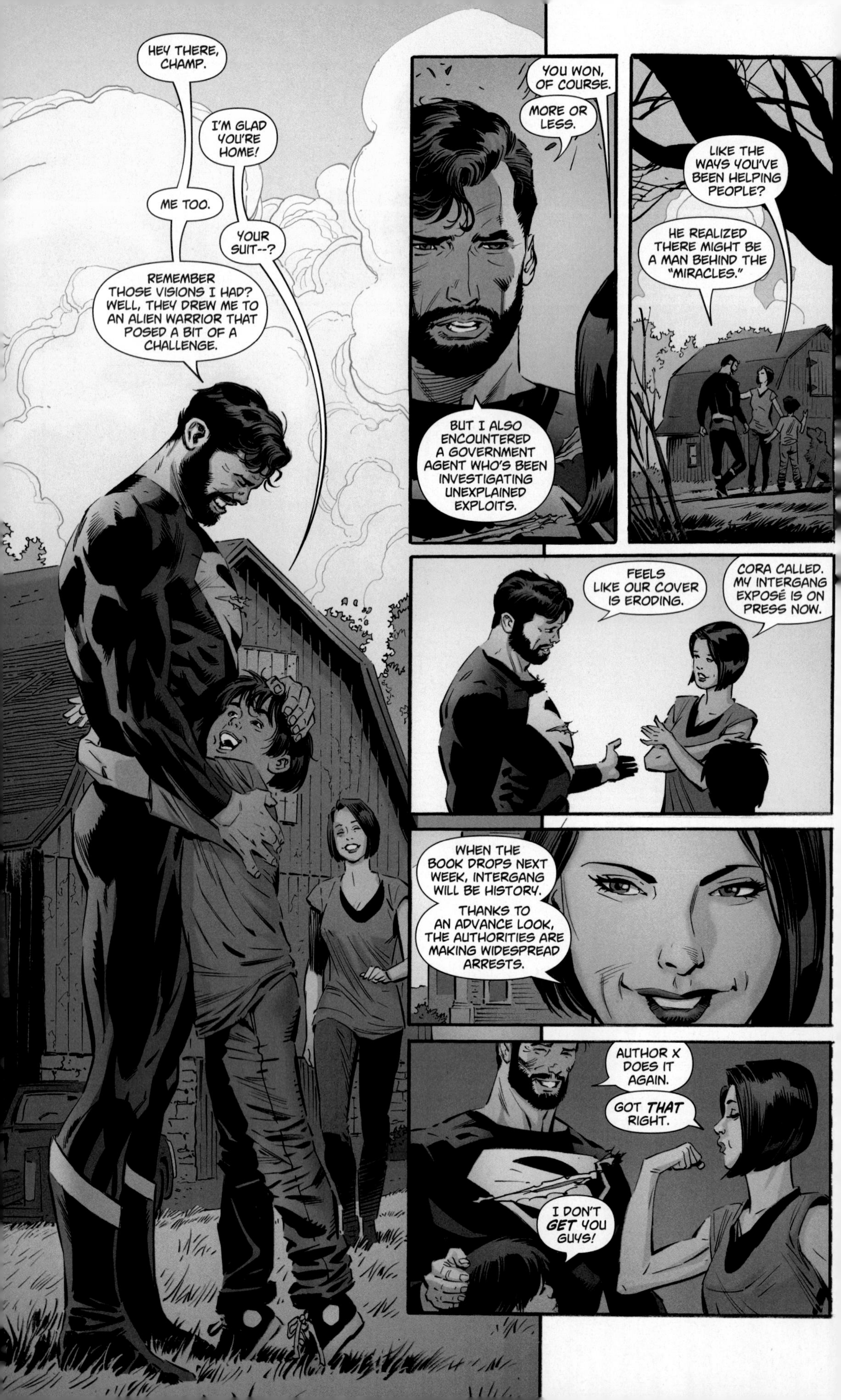
HEY THERE, CHAMP.
I'M GLAD YOU'RE HOME!
ME TOO.
YOUR SUIT--?
REMEMBER THOSE VISIONS I HAD? WELL, THEY DREW ME TO AN ALIEN WARRIOR THAT POSED A BIT OF A CHALLENGE.
YOU WON, OF COURSE.
MORE OR LESS.
BUT I ALSO ENCOUNTERED A GOVERNMENT AGENT WHO'S BEEN INVESTIGATING UNEXPLAINED EXPLOITS.
LIKE THE WAYS YOU'VE BEEN HELPING PEOPLE?
HE REALIZED THERE MIGHT BE A MAN BEHIND THE "MIRACLES."
FEELS LIKE OUR COVER IS ERODING.
CORA CALLED. MY INTERGANG EXPOSÉ IS ON PRESS NOW.
WHEN THE BOOK DROPS NEXT WEEK, INTERGANG WILL BE HISTORY.
THANKS TO AN ADVANCE LOOK, THE AUTHORITIES ARE MAKING WIDESPREAD ARRESTS.
AUTHOR X DOES IT AGAIN.
GOT THAT RIGHT.
I DON'T GET YOU GUYS!

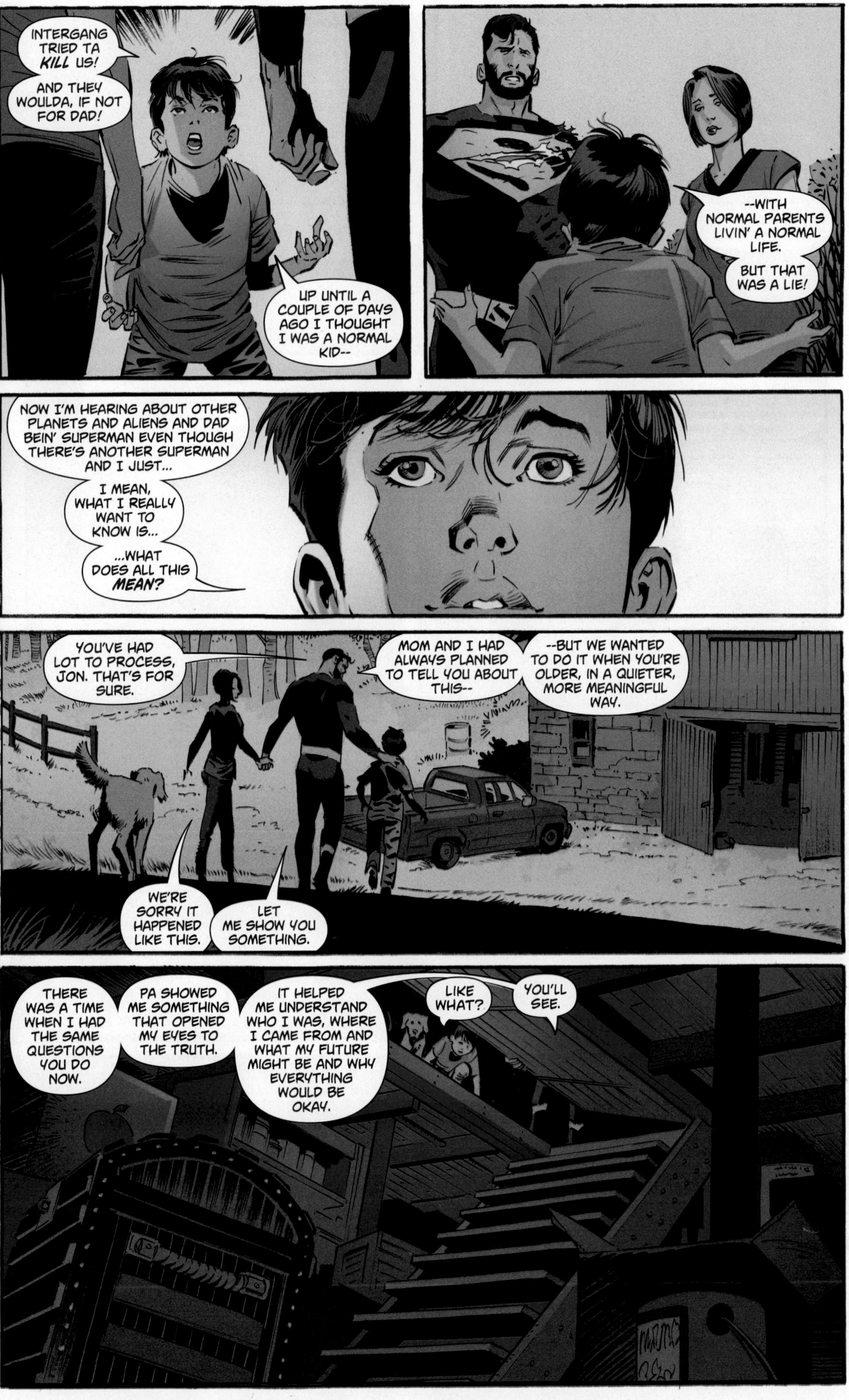
INTERGANG TRIED TA KILL US!
AND THEY WOULDA, IF NOT FOR DAD!
UP UNTIL A COUPLE OF DAYS AGO I THOUGHT I WAS A NORMAL KID--
--WITH NORMAL PARENTS LIVIN' A NORMAL LIFE.
BUT THAT WAS A LIE!
NOW I'M HEARING ABOUT OTHER PLANETS AND ALIENS AND DAD BEIN' SUPERMAN EVEN THOUGH THERE'S ANOTHER SUPERMAN AND I JUST...
I MEAN, WHAT I REALLY WANT TO KNOW IS...
...WHAT DOES ALL THIS MEAN?
YOU'VE HAD LOT TO PROCESS, JON. THAT'S FOR SURE.
MOM AND I HAD ALWAYS PLANNED TO TELL YOU ABOUT THIS--
--BUT WE WANTED TO DO IT WHEN YOU'RE OLDER, IN A QUIETER, MORE MEANINGFUL WAY.
WE'RE SORRY IT HAPPENED LIKE THIS.
LET ME SHOW YOU SOMETHING.
THERE WAS A TIME WHEN I HAD THE SAME QUESTIONS YOU DO NOW.
PA SHOWED ME SOMETHING THAT OPENED MY EYES TO THE TRUTH.
IT HELPED ME UNDERSTAND WHO I WAS, WHERE I CAME FROM AND WHAT MY FUTURE MIGHT BE AND WHY EVERYTHING WOULD BE OKAY.
LIKE WHAT?
YOU'LL SEE.

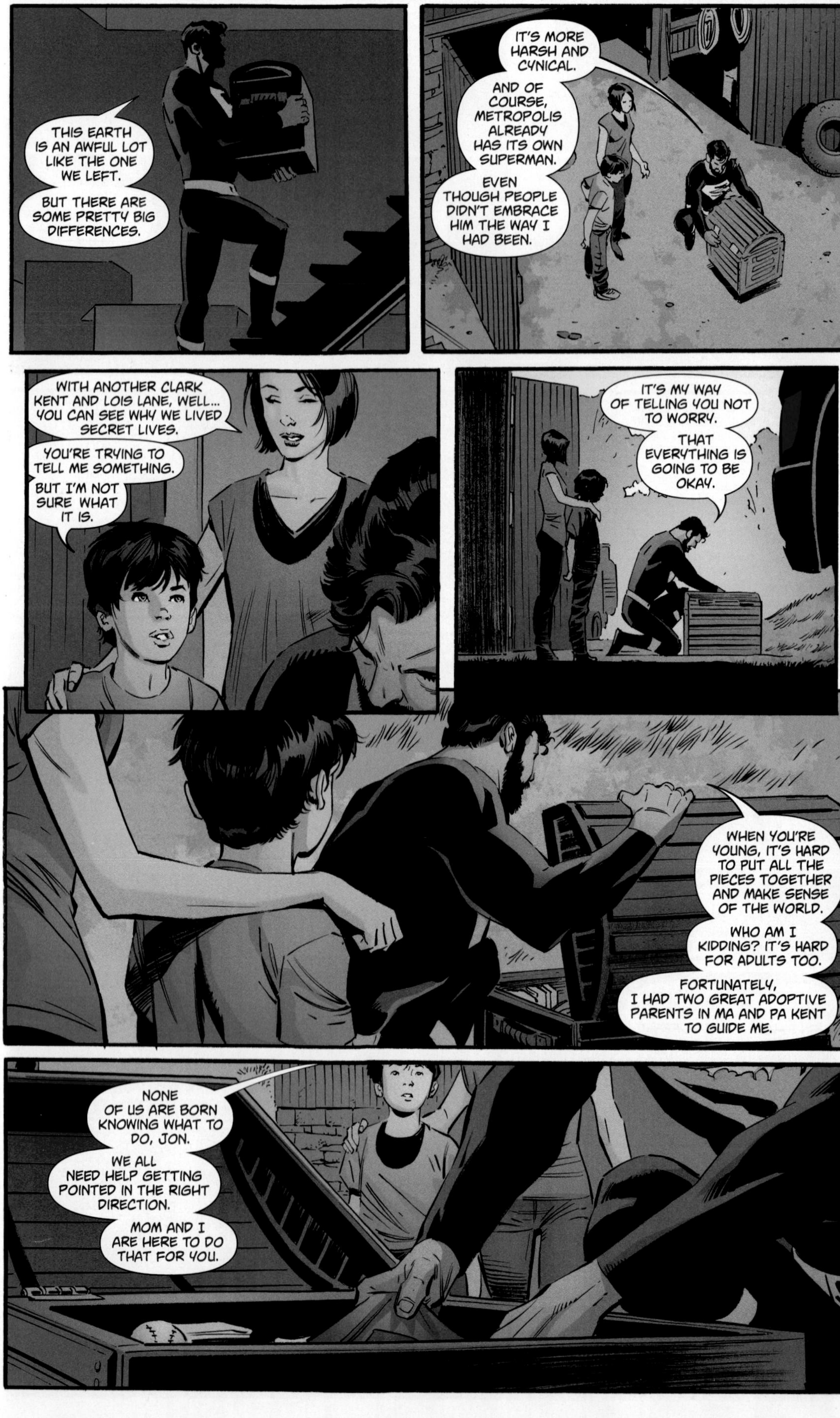
THIS EARTH IS AN AWFUL LOT LIKE THE ONE WE LEFT.
BUT THERE ARE SOME PRETTY BIG DIFFERENCES.
IT'S MORE HARSH AND CYNICAL.
AND OF COURSE, METROPOLIS ALREADY HAS ITS OWN SUPERMAN.
EVEN THOUGH PEOPLE DIDN'T EMBRACE HIM THE WAY I HAD BEEN.
WITH ANOTHER CLARK KENT AND LOIS LANE, WELL... YOU CAN SEE WHY WE LIVED SECRET LIVES.
YOU'RE TRYING TO TELL ME SOMETHING.
BUT I'M NOT SURE WHAT IT IS.
IT'S MY WAY OF TELLING YOU NOT TO WORRY.
THAT EVERYTHING IS GOING TO BE OKAY.
WHEN YOU'RE YOUNG, IT'S HARD TO PUT ALL THE PIECES TOGETHER AND MAKE SENSE OF THE WORLD.
WHO AM I KIDDING? IT'S HARD FOR ADULTS TOO.
FORTUNATELY, I HAD TWO GREAT ADOPTIVE PARENTS IN MA AND PA KENT TO GUIDE ME.
NONE OF US ARE BORN KNOWING WHAT TO DO, JON.
WE ALL NEED HELP GETTING POINTED IN THE RIGHT DIRECTION.
MOM AND I ARE HERE TO DO THAT FOR YOU.

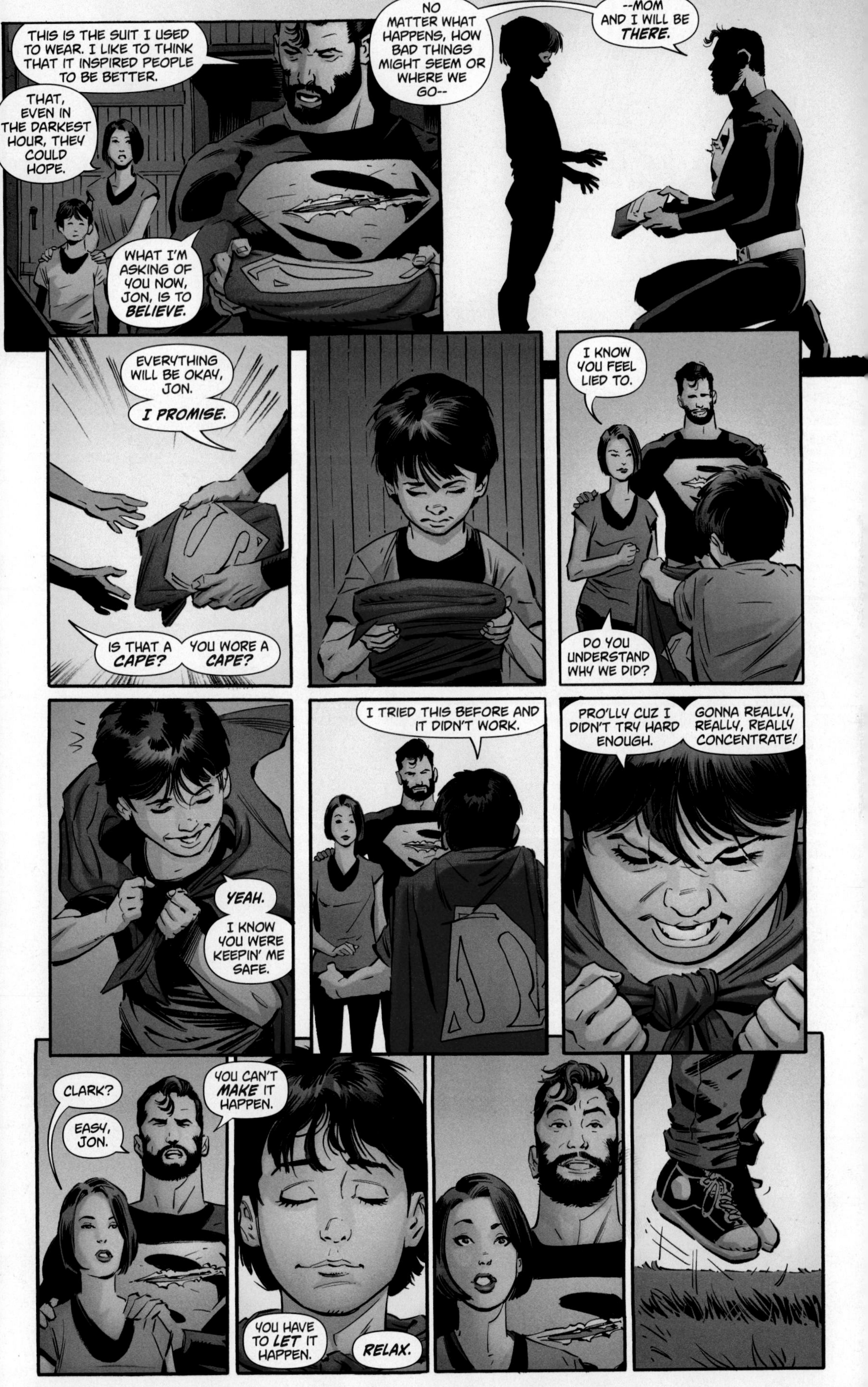
THIS IS THE SUIT I USED TO WEAR. I LIKE TO THINK THAT IT INSPIRED PEOPLE TO BE BETTER.
THAT, EVEN IN THE DARKEST HOUR, THEY COULD HOPE.
WHAT I'M ASKING OF YOU NOW, JON, IS TO BELIEVE.
NO MATTER WHAT HAPPENS, HOW BAD THINGS MIGHT SEEM OR WHERE WE GO--
--MOM AND I WILL BE THERE.
EVERYTHING WILL BE OKAY, JON.
I PROMISE.
IS THAT A CAPE?
YOU WORE A CAPE?
I KNOW YOU FEEL LIED TO.
DO YOU UNDERSTAND WHY WE DID?
YEAH.
I KNOW YOU WERE KEEPIN' ME SAFE.
I TRIED THIS BEFORE AND IT DIDN'T WORK.
PRO'LLY CUZ I DIDN'T TRY HARD ENOUGH.
GONNA REALLY, REALLY, REALLY CONCENTRATE!
CLARK?
EASY, JON.
YOU CAN'T MAKE IT HAPPEN.
YOU HAVE TO LET IT HAPPEN.
RELAX.

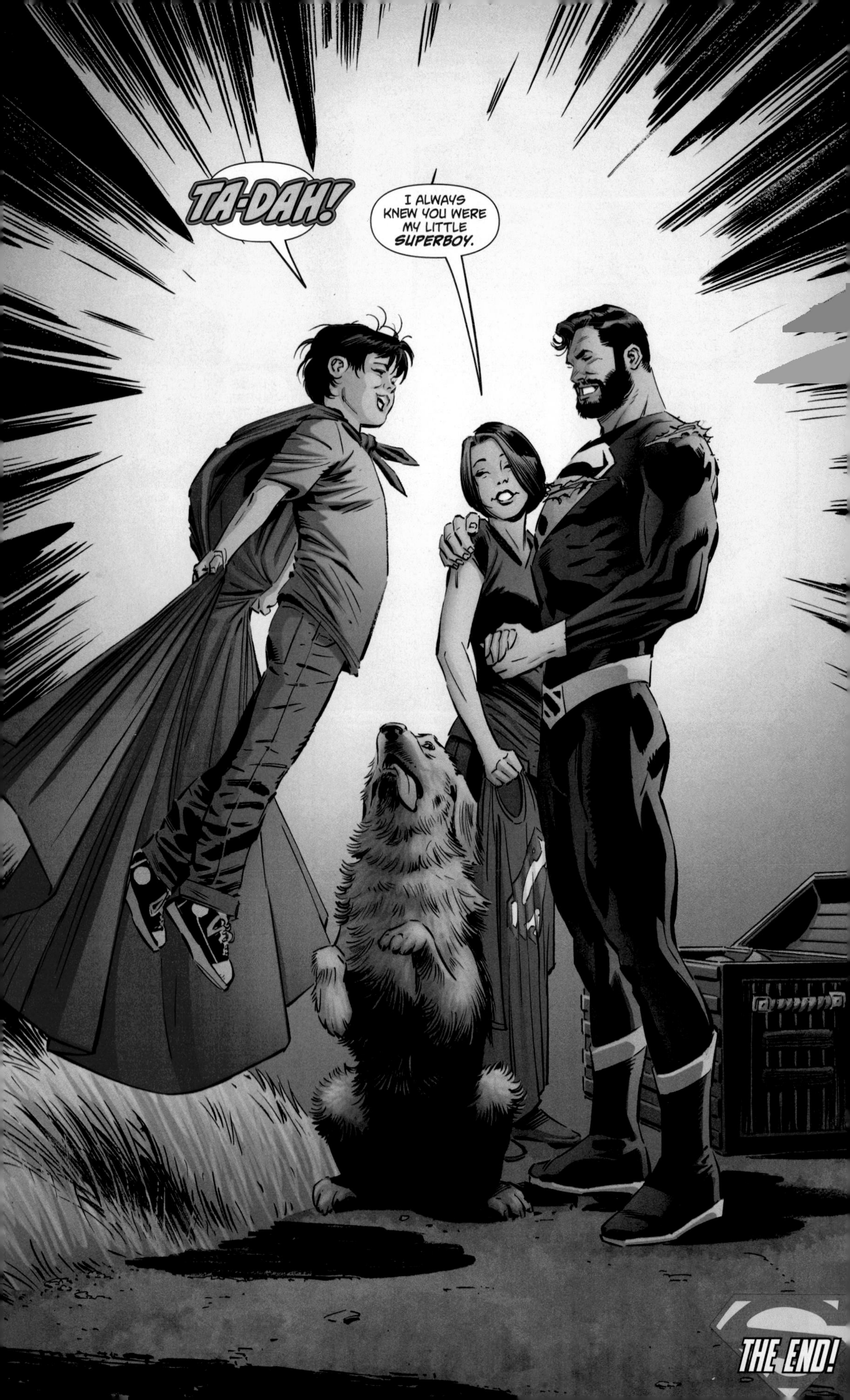
TA-DAH!
I ALWAYS KNEW YOU WERE MY LITTLE SUPERBOY.
THE END!

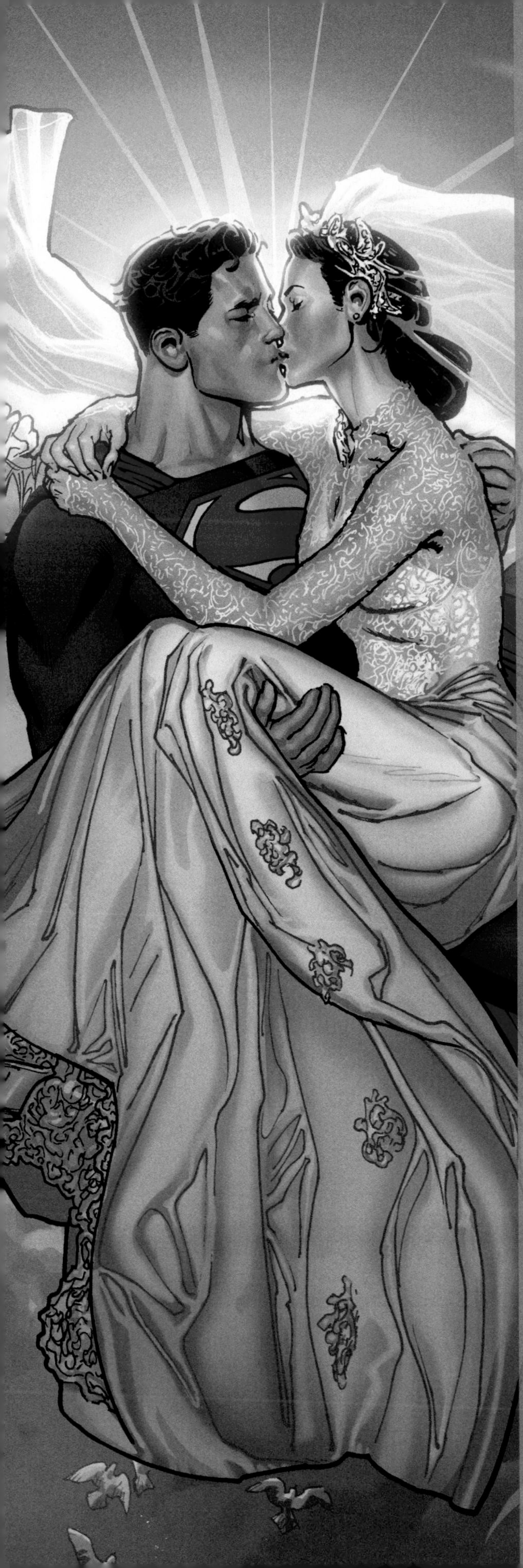

VARIANT COVER GALLERY

SUPERMAN: LOIS AND CLARK #1
VARIANT COVER BY
TONY S. DANIEL
& TOMEU MOREY

SUPERMAN: LOIS AND CLARK #4
VARIANT COVER BY
AARON LOPRESTI

SUPERMAN: LOIS AND CLARK #5
VARIANT COVER BY
NEAL ADAMS,
TERRY DODSON
& ALEX SINCLAIR

SUPERMAN: LOIS AND CLARK #7
VARIANT COVER BY
JOHN ROMITA JR., DANNY MIKI
& BRAD ANDERSON

DC COMICS PRESENTS SUPERMAN: LOIS AND CLARK
COVER BY RYAN SOOK

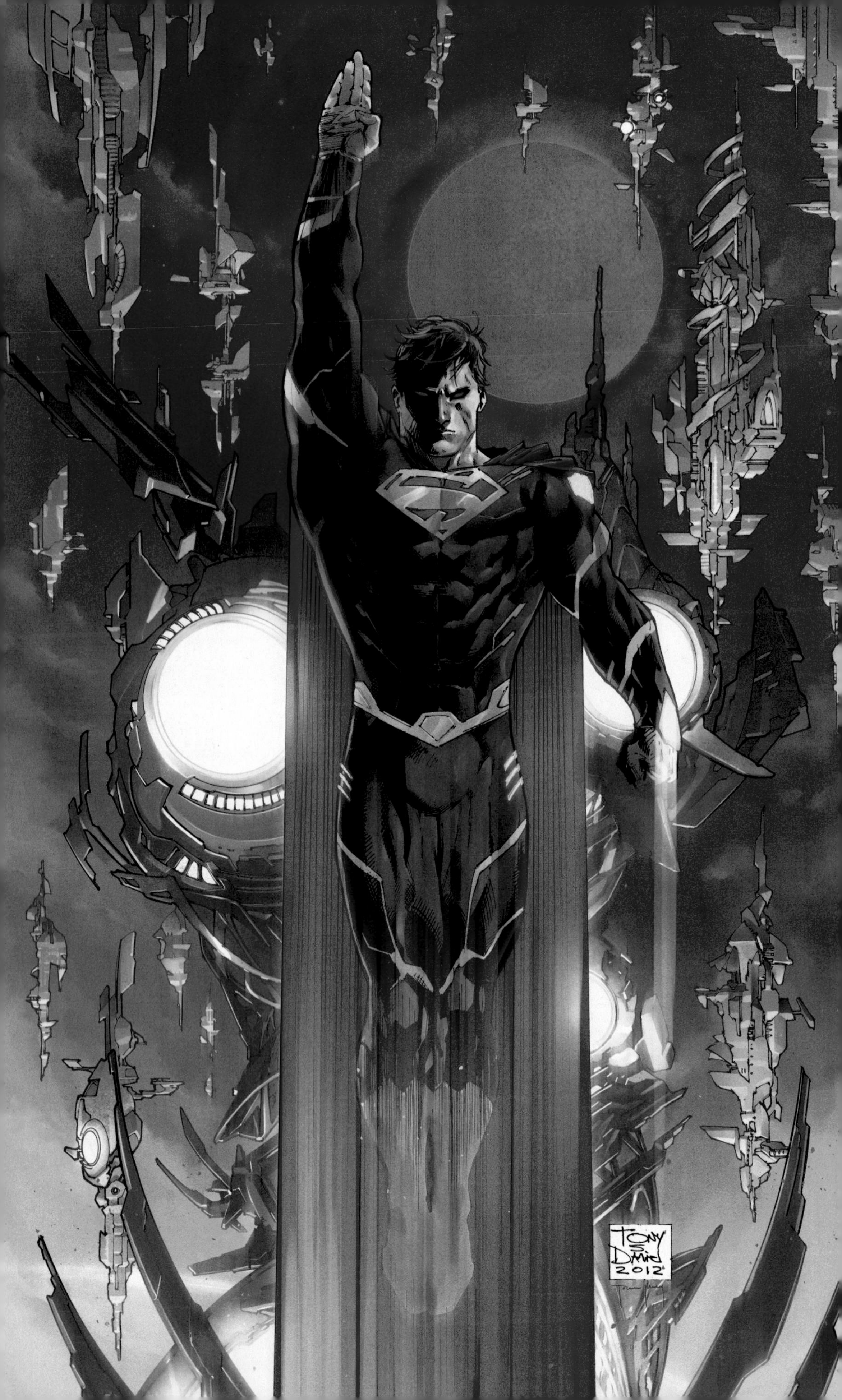
TONY S DANIEL 2012

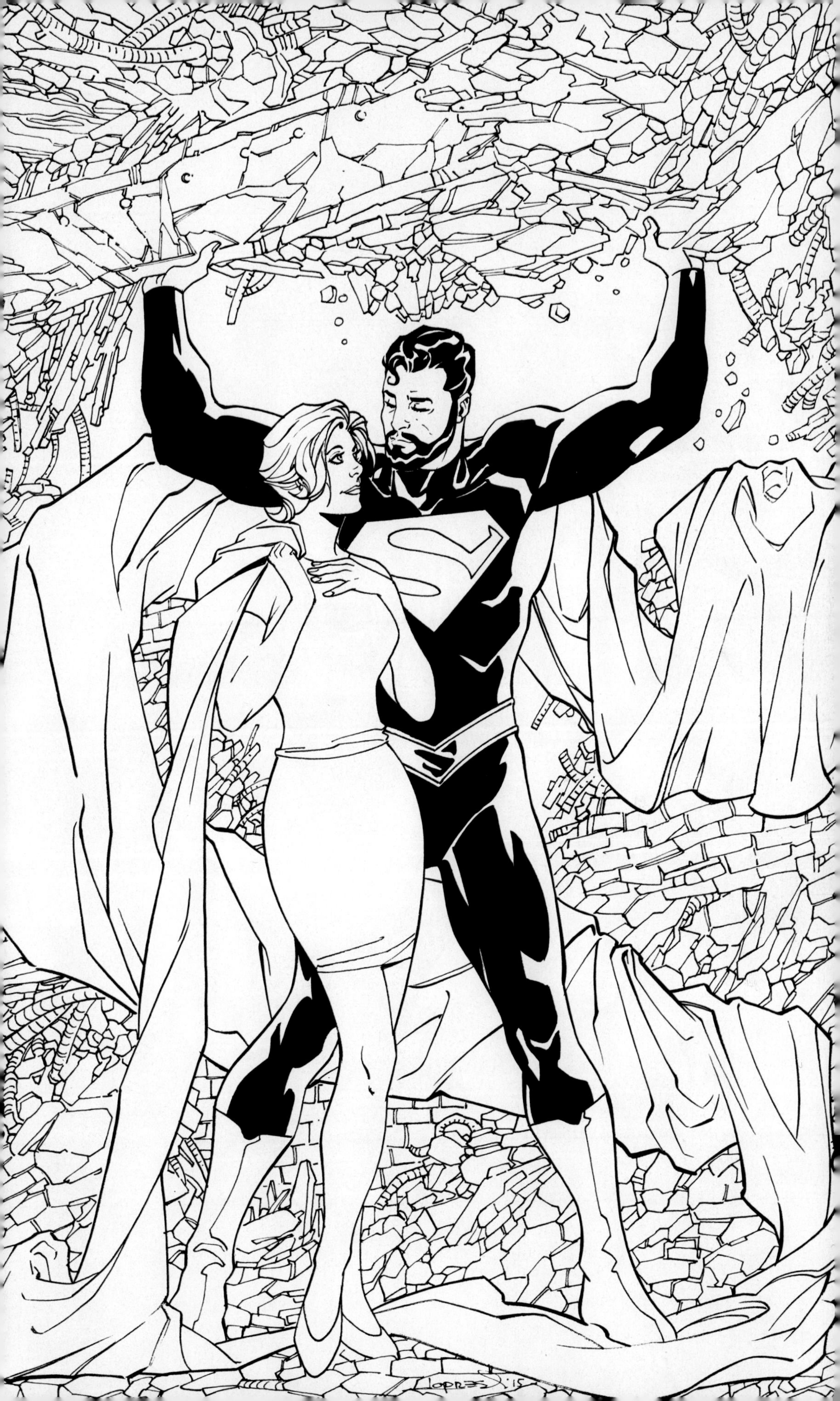

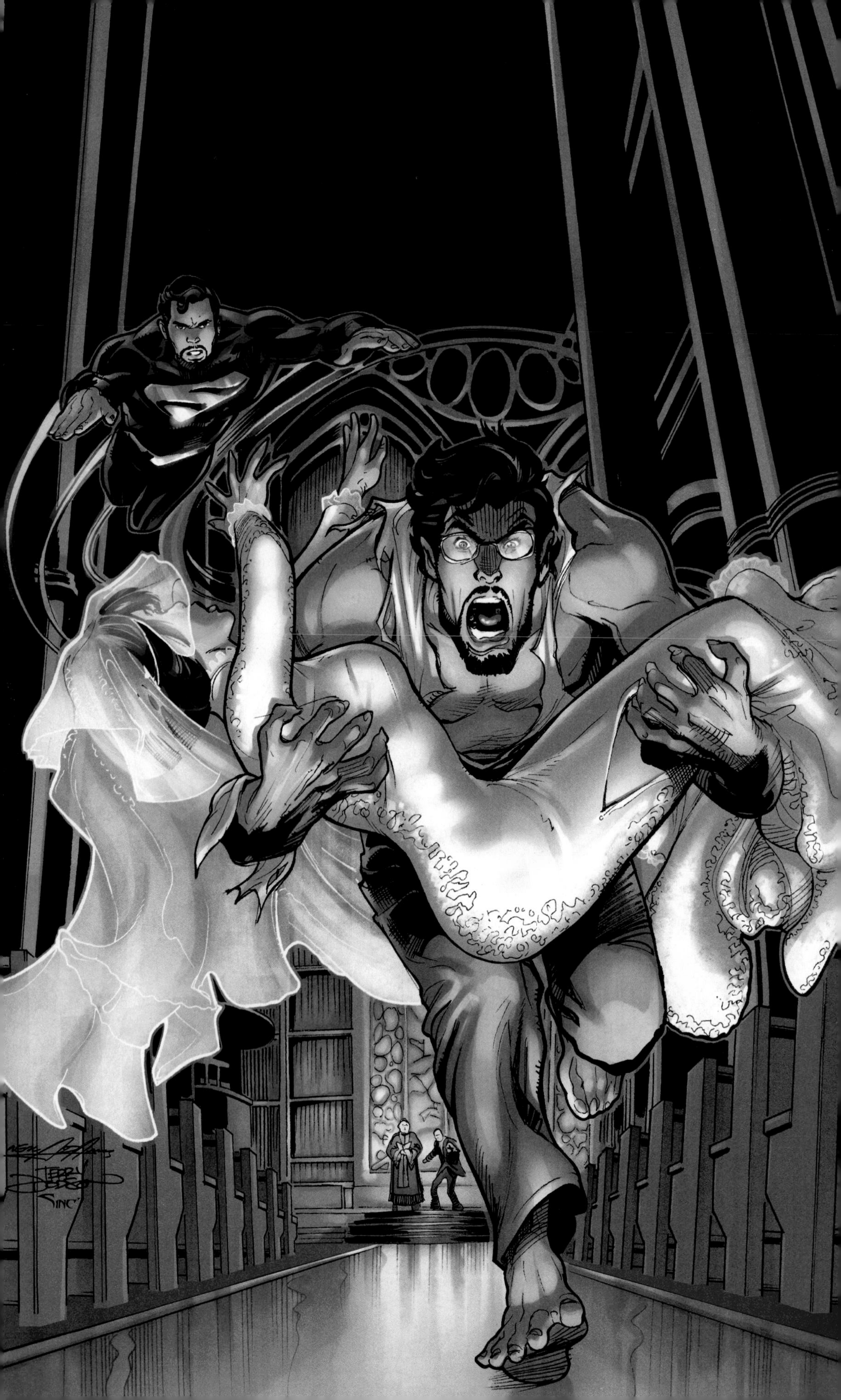

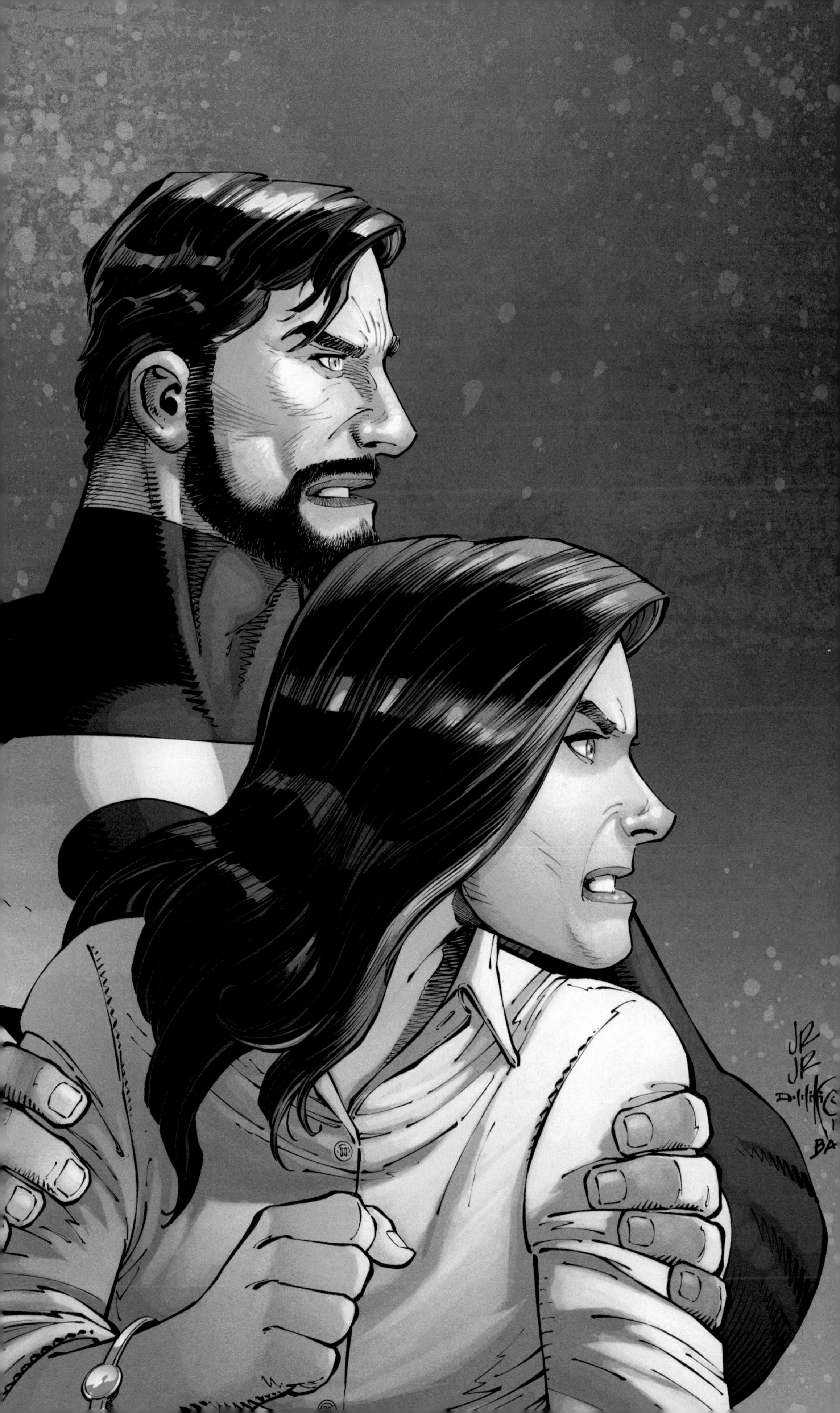

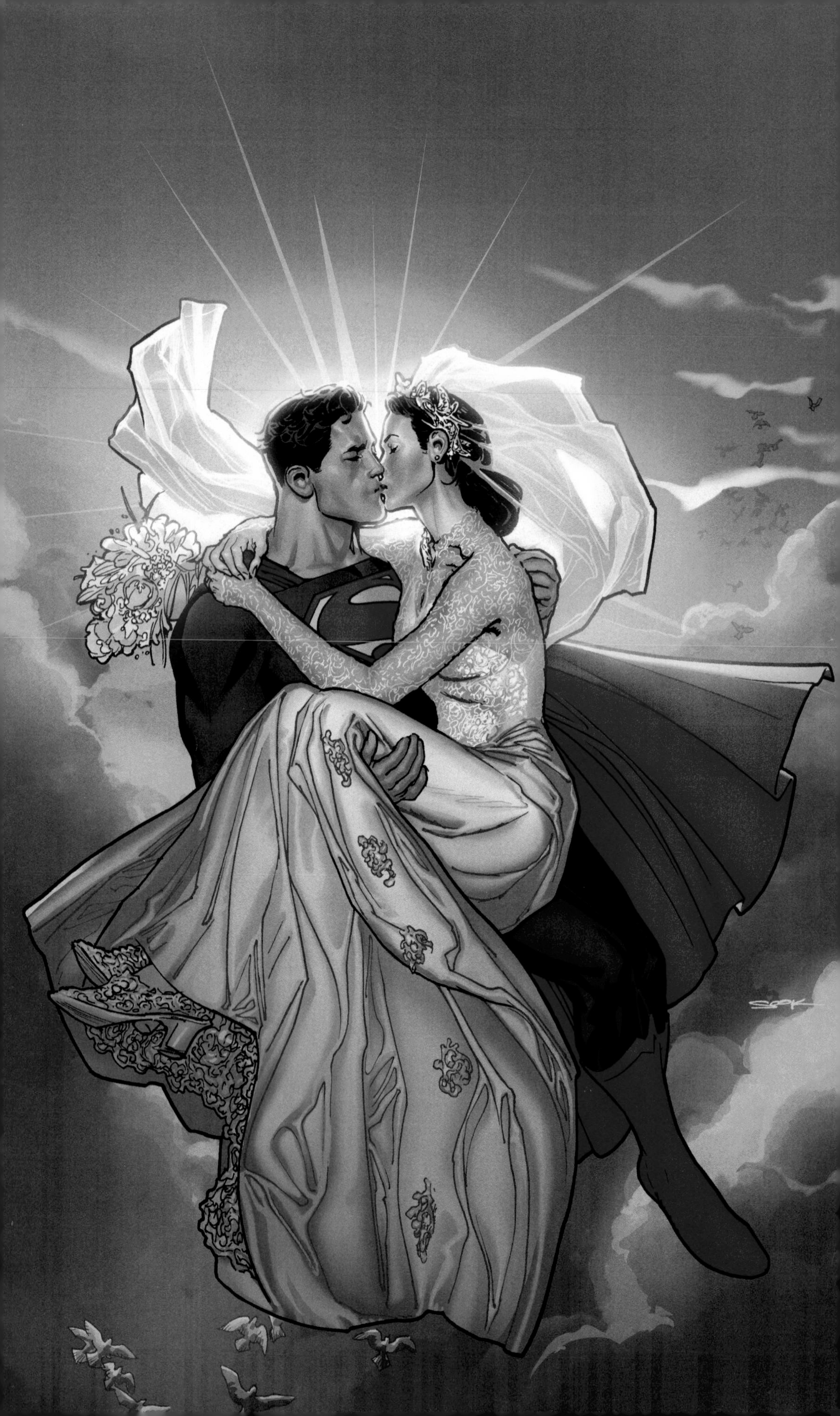

ISSUE #1 PENCILS BY LEE WEEKS

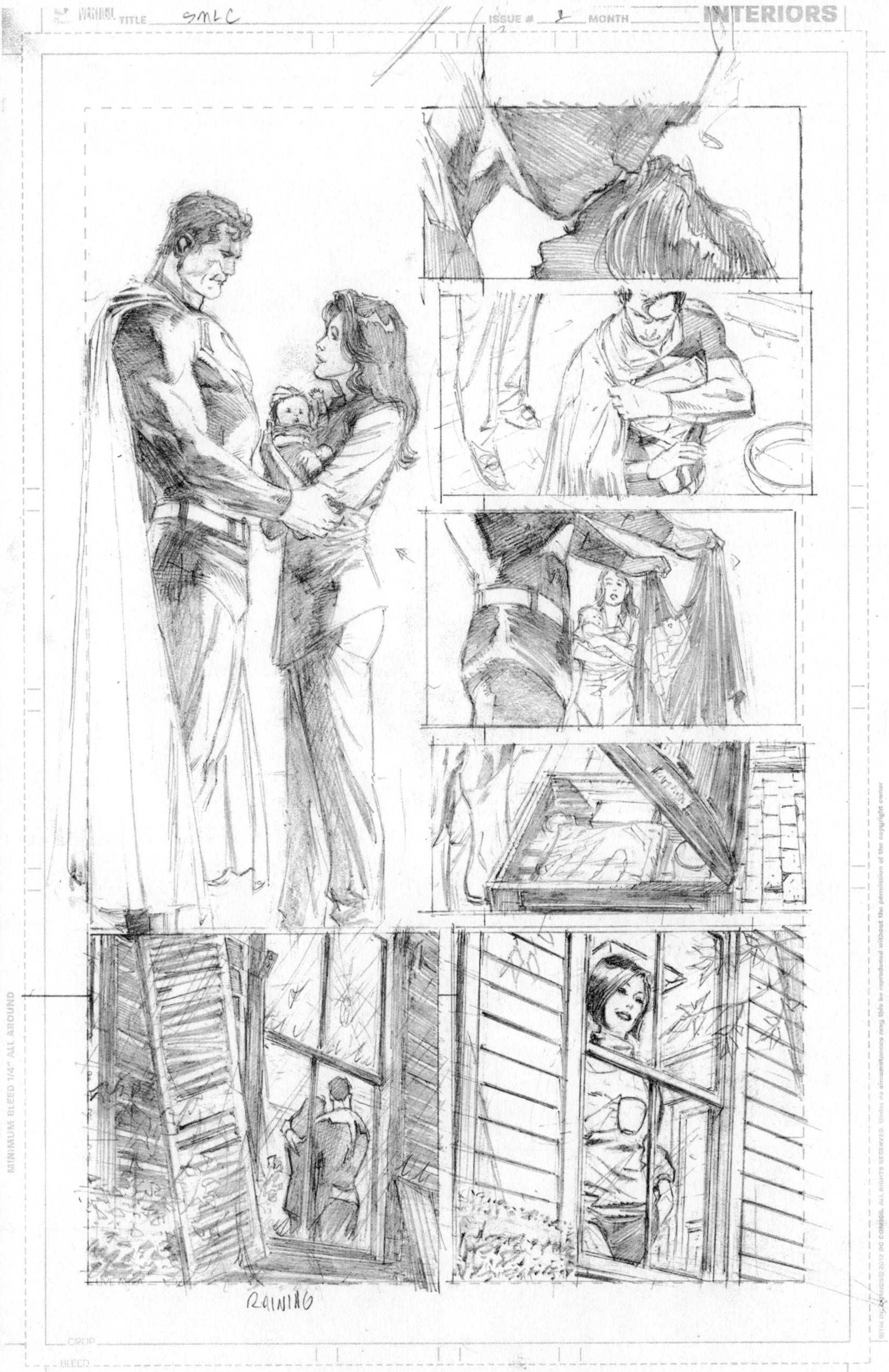

TITLE SMLC
ISSUE # 1
MONTH
INTERIORS
RAINING
CROP
BLEED
MINIMUM BLEED 1/4" ALL AROUND
CUT RIGHT-HAND PAGE AT THIS LINE
DOUBLE PAGE SPREAD: CUT AS SHOWN, ABUT PAGE EDGES, TAPE ON BACK, DO NOT OVERLAP
CUT LEFT HAND PAGE AT THIS LINE

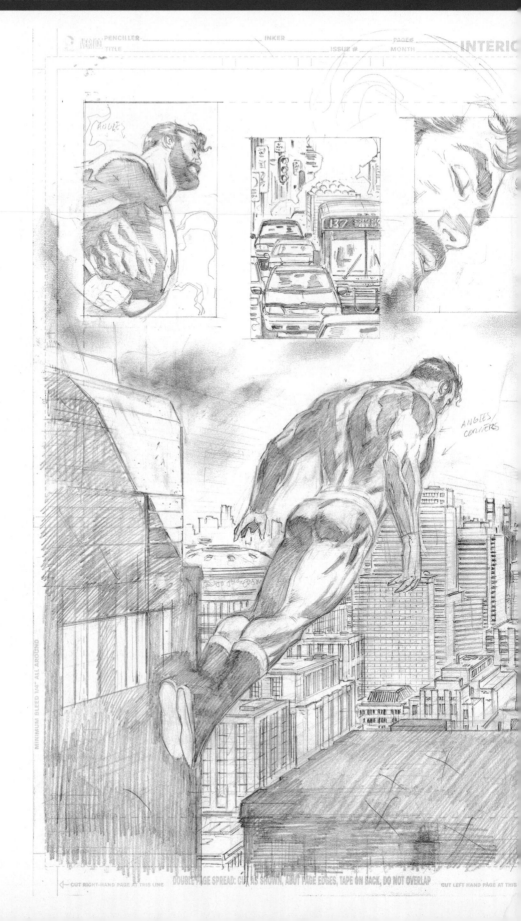

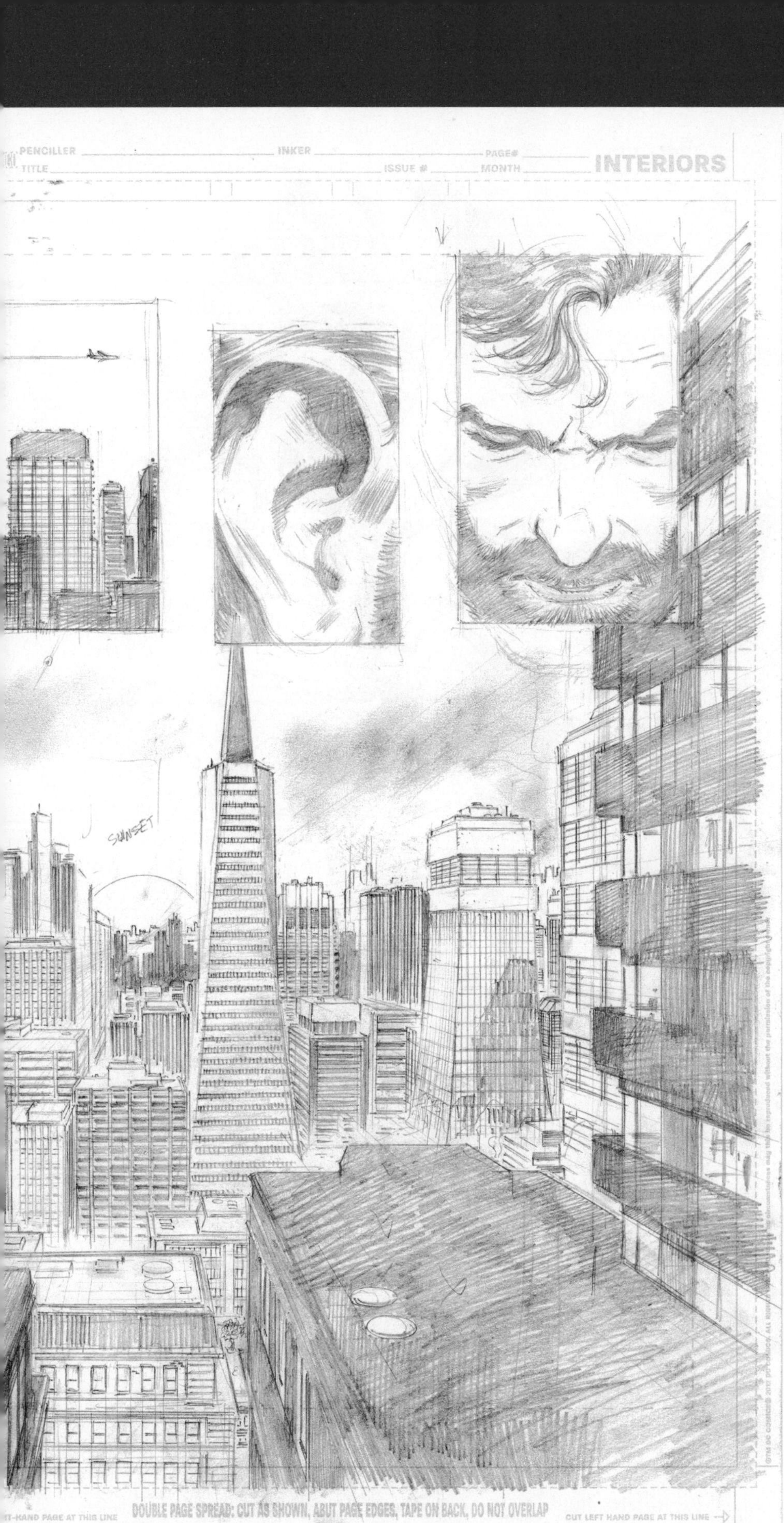

PENCILLER
INKER
PAGE#
TITLE
ISSUE #
MONTH
INTERIORS
SUNSET
DOUBLE PAGE SPREAD: CUT AS SHOWN, ABUT PAGE EDGES, TAPE ON BACK, DO NOT OVERLAP
CUT LEFT HAND PAGE AT THIS LINE

ISSUE #7 PENCILS BY STEPHEN SEGOVIA

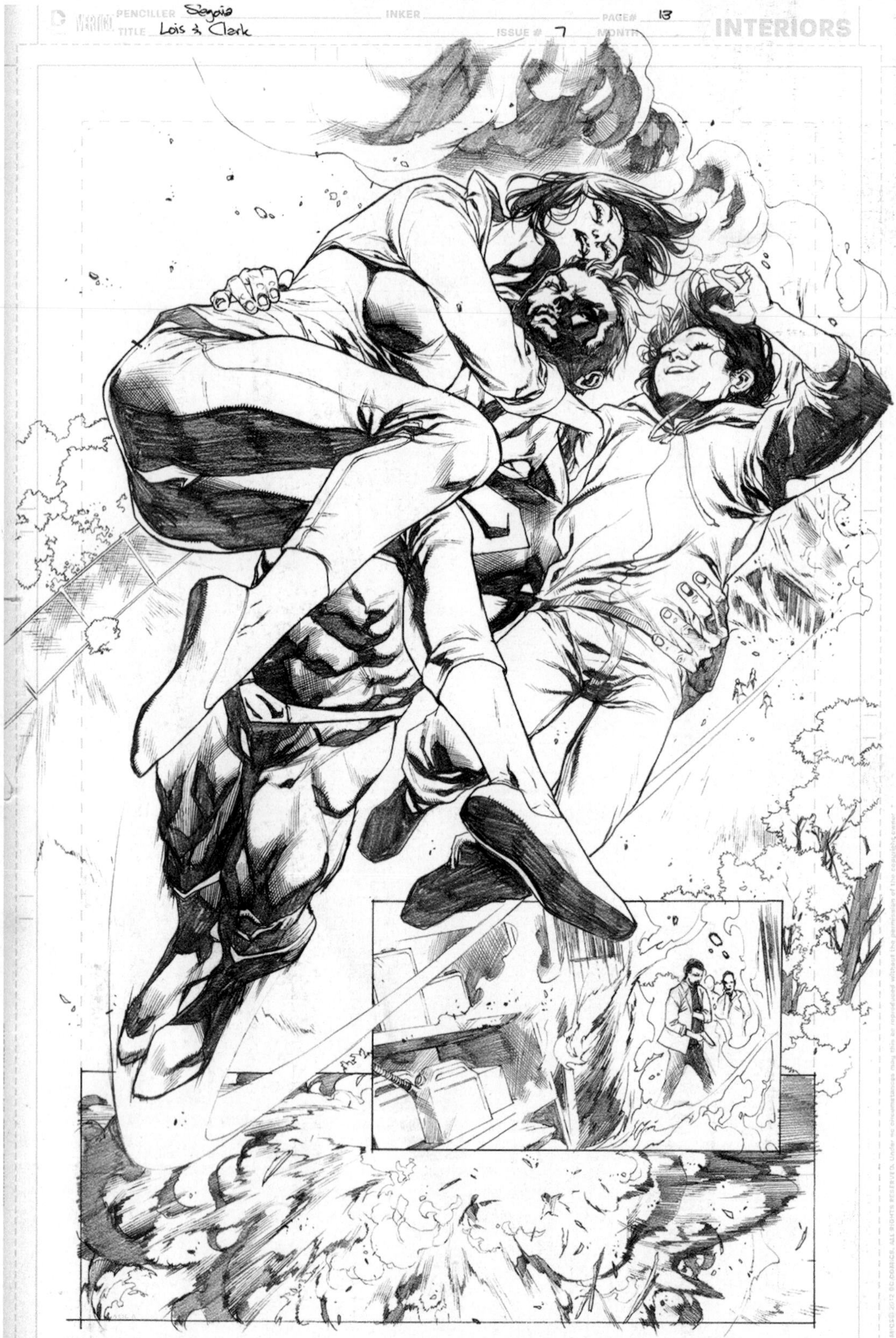
PENCILLER Segovia
INKER
PAGE# 13
TITLE Lois & Clerk
ISSUE # 7
MONTH
INTERIORS
CROP
BLEED
CUT RIGHT-HAND PAGE AT THIS LINE
DOUBLE PAGE SPREAD: CUT AS SHOWN, ABUT PAGE EDGES, TAPE ON BACK, DO NOT OVERLAP
CUT LEFT HAND PAGE AT THIS LINE